Learning from Practice

A Professional Development Text for Legal Externs

SECOND EDITION

J.P. Ogilvy ▪ Leah Wortham ▪ Lisa G. Lerman

and

Alexis Anderson ▪ Margaret Martin Barry ▪ Stacy L. Brustin ▪ Liz Ryan Cole

Mariana Hogan ▪ Arlene S. Kanter ▪ Linda Morton ▪ Avis L. Sanders

Alex Scherr ▪ Lucia Ann Silecchia ▪ Cindy Roman Slane ▪ Janet Weinstein

THOMSON

WEST

© West, a Thomson business, 1998
© 2007 Thomson/West
     610 Opperman Drive
     St. Paul, MN 55123
     1–800–313–9378

Printed in the United States of America

ISBN: 978–0–314–15284–8

 TEXT IS PRINTED ON 10% POST CONSUMER RECYCLED PAPER

Dedication

———

For Alex, Andrea and Margaret—with love
AA

*For Thomas and Kaitlin—in the hope they will have
many wonderful experiences upon which to build*
MMB

For Jeff, Benjamin and Julia
SLB

*For my family, who make it all possible—Jonas, Silas, Ethan,
Suzanne, Noah, Elizabeth and Chuck*
LRC

*For Jessica and Christopher who have taught me that experience is the
best teacher and to Bob for keeping me laughing through the experiences*
MH

For Steven, Rachel and Ari
ASK

For Philip, Sam and Sarah
LGL

To Lenny, my husband, and to Calen, my son, who are always there for me
LM

For Louise, Alec and Andrew—with love
JPO

For my wonderful family and circle of friends
ALS

*For Albert Scherr, whose care and judgment shaped me,
and for Candace Hawkes, whose love sustains me*
AS

For my family—with love
LAS

*For Mark, Kristin, Jeff and Kevin, and for Nana Brown, who always said I'd grow up to be
either a lawyer or a preacher, not realizing there might be a way for me to do both*
CRS

To RW for supporting me in everything I do
JW

For Eric, Alex, Liz and Anne
LW

Table of Contents

Preface—For Teachers

Genesis of the Book

The first edition of this book grew out of the authors' experiences in teaching and directing externship programs at Columbus School of Law of The Catholic University of America, Vermont Law School, and Washington College of Law of The American University.

The first edition was written collaboratively by seven people who had taught the externship seminar at The Catholic University of America titled *Becoming a Lawyer* and one person who, then and now, directs the externship program at Vermont Law School. Each contributor drafted one or more chapters for the book. J.P. (Sandy) Ogilvy, Leah Wortham, and Lisa Lerman edited the first edition and prepared it for publication.

In this edition, eight experienced externship clinicians have joined the original authors to expand material in the first edition on ethics and career planning and to add new chapters on creative problem solving, lawyer decision making, and judicial externships. These authors add expertise gained from work in externship programs at the American University, Boston College, California Western, University of Georgia, New York Law School, Syracuse University, and Quinnipiac University.

In production of the second edition, Sandy Ogilvy shouldered the major editorial load with assistance from Leah Wortham. Lisa Lerman took the lead in coordinating the revised ethics material, which now has been expanded from one to four chapters.

We recognize that externship programs vary in size, structure, and goals. Our objective remains to provide a menu of options among which a teacher may choose to provide materials and class activities that would best suit the goals of a particular externship course.

Structure of the Book

The textbook is divided into 20 chapters. Chapter 1 introduces the concept of experiential learning and establishes the recurrent themes for the chapters that follow. Chapter 2 explores the process of setting personal goals for the externship. Chapter 3 describes the supervisory relationship in externships and suggests strategies for the extern to maximize learning from supervision. Chapters 4 through 7 review ethical issues most likely to arise in externships. Chapter 4 introduces sources of relevant law, issues arising from the supervisor-extern relationship, the ethical duties of competence and diligence, truthfulness, and workplace abuses of power. Chapter 5 focuses on confidentiality. Chapter 6 applies conflicts of interest law to the externship situation. Chapter 7 reviews ethical issues that arise in litigation. Chapter 8 considers learning from the lawyering process, particularly through a focus on decision making. Chapter 9 centers on the concept of reflective lawyering, which is a cross-cutting theme of the book. Chapter 10 introduces students to creative problem solving for lawyers. Chapter 11 provides guidance for students who use journals to record and reflect on their externship experience. Chapter 12 focuses on how students can learn from observation of lawyering behavior during the externship. Chapter 13 is directed to students in judicial externships. Chapter 14 discusses use of externships to improve traditional lawyering skills, especially legal research and writing. Chapter 15 introduces another set of lawyering skills that are often neglected in the traditional law school curriculum: time management, planning, delegation, collaborative work, communication, and creativity. Chapter 16 considers issues of bias in the legal profession for reflection and discussion as part of an externship experience. Chapter 17 focuses on balancing a professional career and personal life. Chapter 18 discusses use of the externship in career planning. Chapter 19 guides students through the process of creating and delivering in-class presentations. Chapter 20, the final chapter, is designed to help the student reflect on the externship experience in order to consolidate and build on the lessons gained and to think ahead to close one cycle of learning and begin the next.

Both editions of the text were collaborative efforts. Chapter 5 includes confidentiality problems developed by Lisa Lerman, Cindy Slane, and Leah Wortham. Chapter 18 on externships and career planning incorporates some material written by Georgia Niedzielko for the first edition.

History and Importance of Externships

Most American lawyers were trained by *reading the law* in the offices of lawyers through the first few decades of the 19th century. Legal education involved years of apprentice-like training in a law office. Although the first American law school was founded in the 1780s, it was designed to provide apprenticeship experience to groups rather than to teach law to individuals in a university setting.

By 1830, university training of lawyers was beginning to push aside the apprenticeship model. In the university, legal training consisted of the study of treatises and lectures until the 1870s, when Dean Langdell at Harvard introduced the method of analyzing appellate case decisions. The case method of instruction quickly became and remains the dominant method of instruction in American law schools. It was not until the late 1960s and early 1970s that law schools began to create clinical legal education programs, which put practical training for law students back into the educational model. Spurred by grants from the Ford Foundation, law schools began to create legal aid and defender clinics and other in-house, live-client clinics to provide practical training to law students and service to indigent clients.[1]

One report on clinical legal education described the method of teaching this way:

> [S]tudents are confronted with problem situations of the sort that lawyers confront in practice; the students deal with the problem in role; the students are required to interact with others in attempts to identify and solve the problem; and . . . the student performance is subjected to intensive critical review. AALS Section on Clinical Legal Education, *Report of the Committee on the Future of the In-House Clinic*, 42 J. Legal Ed. 508, 511 (1992).

In live-client, in-house clinics, the "problem" may involve real situations rather than simulated ones and the supervision and review of the students' work is undertaken by clinical teachers rather than by practitioners outside the law school.

In-house, live-client clinics, to a greater or lesser degree, tend to pursue several teaching goals. These include the following: (1) developing modes of planning and analysis for dealing with unstructured situations, (2) providing professional skills instruction, (3) teaching means of learning from experience, (4) instructing students in professional responsibility, (5) exposing students to the demands and methods of acting in role, (6) providing opportunities for collaborative learning, (7) imparting the obligation for service to indigent clients, information about how to engage in such representation, and knowledge concerning the impact of the legal system on poor people, (8) providing the opportunity for examining the impact of legal doctrine in real life and providing a laboratory in which students and faculty study particular areas of law, and (9) critiquing the capacities and limitations of lawyers and the legal system.

As the student demand for relevant, practical legal training grew, additional resources were diverted from traditional legal education to in-house, live-client clinics. Because clinical teaching requires a higher teacher to student ratio, law school administrators felt the squeeze of responding to increased demand with limited resources.

---

[1] New teachers or teachers new to externship or clinical teaching may be interested in viewing *An Oral History of Clinical Legal Education—Part I: Seeds of Change*, available in most law school library collections or for loan from Professor Sandy Ogilvy at the Columbus School of Law, The Catholic University of America.

Externships too confront students with problem situations of the sort that lawyers face in practice and students may deal with some of these problems in role. Where student performance is subject to intensive critical review, the critique usually is provided by the fieldwork supervisor. The faculty supervisor, rather than acting as a coach on tasks performed at the externship, is more likely to guide the student through the process of reflecting on the fieldwork experience.

Externships share many of the teaching goals of in-house, live-client clinics. Some high credit-hour, closely supervised externships closely resemble in-house, live-client clinics. In most externship programs, however, students are given less responsibility for client representation than is available through an in-house clinic. On the other hand, externships may provide students with unparalleled opportunities to define and pursue individual learning goals, to explore career interests in a variety of legal jobs, and to build a professional network.

Through the externship program, the innovative teaching methodology of clinical education helps to reclaim the benefits of the apprenticeship programs of the last century and assists the student in learning how to apply the knowledge acquired in the classroom.

Introduction—For Students

How to Use the Book

This book is designed to be used by students and teachers as a menu from which to select material for learning through externships. In the preface, we described briefly what each of the chapters covers. In this introduction, we describe the premises that underlie the choices we made in selecting materials for the book. In addition, we identify the themes that recur throughout the book. Finally, we suggest some ways the book may be used to supplement fieldwork experiences.

Premises

In three or four years of formal graduate study, you cannot begin to learn all that you will need to know to practice law over the course of your career, which may extend forty years or longer after graduation. Lawyers today practice in specialties unknown only a few years ago. Lawyers are confronted with more and more statutes, regulations, and treaties every year. The globalization of law practice is a reality for many lawyers and will become so for many more in the coming years.

Because law school cannot teach you all you need to know to be a successful practitioner throughout your career, how are you to learn what is needed? You will learn from experience. As you practice your chosen career, whether in a law firm or in another setting, you will accumulate experiences. These experiences will be the "text" for your continuing education in law. How you use these experiences will determine how much, how quickly, and how well you learn from them. This book is an introductory study guide for the rest of your career.

Because learning from experience is so central to your professional development, you should devote a substantial amount of time during law school to *learning how to learn from experience*—learning how to maximize the learning that occurs from your work experience. This book does not seek primarily to transmit a body of information. Rather, the materials in this book encourage you to think about how you learn from experience, what can be learned from experience, how your learning strategies inhibit or facilitate learning, and how you might change your approaches to learning from experience to enhance what you gain from it.

Themes

Throughout this book, you will see certain themes repeated. One is a mantra-like method for reflective lawyering: Plan, Do, Reflect, Integrate. These themes are introduced in Chapter 1 and will reappear in nearly every chapter.

Another important theme is a focus on individual differences. People seek legal education for many different reasons and plan to use their education to pursue widely varying career plans. Many law school courses seek to convey the same information and skills to everyone in the class. In externship courses, different students can pursue dramatically different goals. Chapter 2 focuses on articulating each student's individual goals for the externship. Chapter 17 extends that concept to a focus on goals for your overall personal and professional life. Chapter 18 considers individual goals as they relate to career planning.

Developing critical awareness is an important component of learning from experience. Critical awareness begins with making sense of what is going on around you. Chapter 12 addresses the process of learning from observation. Most chapters offer lenses through which students may look critically at their externship and compare what they see to concepts discussed in the book, especially Chapters 4-7 on ethical awareness; Chapter 8 on lawyer decision making; Chapter 10 on creative problem solving; Chapter 13 addressing variation among judicial chambers; and Chapter 16 on bias in the legal profession.

A second aspect of critical awareness is self-awareness. Reflective writing, like that in journals, fosters both self-awareness and analysis of the workplace environment. Chapter 9 on reflective lawyering stresses looking within. Chapter 11 focuses on journal writing, and most chapters include suggestions of possible journal topics. Chapter 20 provides a framework for looking back at the externship and incorporating what was learned into one's future life.

A third aspect of critical awareness is to learn from the experiences of others. Each student only has a finite amount of time, but some externship programs allow students to learn from the experiences of other students, for example, through class presentations as discussed in Chapter 19.

The externship also, of course, offers the opportunity for skill development. Chapters 14 and 15 discuss skills important in many externships.

Author's Voice and Icons

This edition of the book is the work of fifteen authors. As such, it presents a variety of perspectives and voices. Whenever we use the first person plural, we intend to convey a shared perspective or experience of the authors. Whenever an author uses the first person singular, a chapter author is conveying his or her perspective.

Journal icon

Throughout the book you will notice icons in the margins of the pages. These icons assist the reader in finding similar materials in other parts of the book. For instance, Chapter 11 describes the use of journals as a tool for reflecting on experience. That chapter contains a number of suggested topics for journal entries, but other ideas for journal entries are identified throughout the book by the journal icon. Three other icons are used frequently. The reference icon will guide you to other parts of the book where the themes discussed in the text also are referenced or elaborated. The role play icon directs you to exercises that offer opportunities to learn through role plays and simulation. Finally, the thinker icon flags text where you are encouraged to stop and reflect. The text marked with the thinker icon also might suggest a journal entry or a topic for a class presentation. We have used wide margins in part to encourage you to record your ideas in the book as you read.

Reference icon

Role play icon

Thinker icon

Feedback to the Authors

We want to encourage both teachers and students who use this book to help us improve it. Please tell us what you liked about the book, what you did not like, and what you would like to see added, deleted, or changed in the next edition. To make communication with us easy, we have established an e-mail address just for users of the book, **csl-lextern@law.edu**. If you prefer ordinary mail, the address is

Professor J.P. Ogilvy
Columbus School of Law
The Catholic University of America
Cardinal Station
Washington, D.C. 20064

We look forward to hearing from you.

About the Authors

Alexis Anderson

Alexis Anderson is an Associate Clinical Professor at Boston College Law School. She currently serves as the Director of the Boston College Legal Assistance Bureau (LAB), the community law office that houses the law school's in-house civil litigation clinics. She joined Boston College Law School in 1983 and has taught a range of clinical courses. From 1983-89, she was a full-time faculty supervisor at LAB. Following that opportunity, she supervised BC Law's extern program and taught and coordinated a first-year lawyering skills and ethics course. Prior to coming to Boston College Law School, Professor Anderson was a litigator in a large, civil practice law firm in Philadelphia. She received her J.D. and a M.A. in legal history from the University of Virginia and a B.A. from Wake Forest University.

Margaret Martin Barry

Margaret Martin Barry is an Associate Professor of Law at The Catholic University of America. She teaches in the Families and the Law Clinic, a clinical program focusing on domestic relations and domestic violence litigation. Professor Barry also has taught the law school's externship seminar, Becoming a Lawyer, and has published articles on domestic relations law and clinical legal education. Professor Barry holds a J.D. from the University of Minnesota and a B.A. from Luther College.

Stacy L. Brustin

Stacy L. Brustin is an Associate Professor of Law and Associate Dean for Academic Affairs at The Catholic University of America. She teaches and supervises law students in the General Practice Clinic, a program of Columbus Community Legal Services at Catholic University. Professor Brustin has taught two externship courses, Becoming a Lawyer and Immigration/Human Rights Clinical Externship Course. She also has taught, conducted research, and written on the issues of professional responsibility, bias in the legal profession, and multicultural communication. She formerly worked as a staff attorney at Ayuda, Inc., a legal services agency representing immigrants and refugees in the Washington, D.C. metropolitan area. Professor Brustin holds a J.D. from Harvard Law School and a B.A. from Tufts University.

Liz Ryan Cole

Liz Ryan Cole, Professor and Director of the Semester in Practice/Environmental Semester in Washington, has taught at Vermont Law School for twenty-two years. The Sip/ESW is a full-time, semester-long clinic, which allows students to combine the best of the old-fashioned apprenticeship model of legal education with structured reflection and academic support provided by the law school. Before coming to Vermont Law School, she coordinated and oversaw the funding of training for legal services programs in Connecticut and for the Legal Services Corporation in New York, Puerto Rico, and the Virgin Islands. She also practiced law with Santa Clara County Legal Services and with Katz, Cole and Beam in San Jose, California. Professor Cole holds a J.D. from Boston University School of Law and a B.A. from Oberlin College.

Mariana Hogan

Mariana Hogan is a Professor of Law and Director of Externship Programs at New York Law School where she teaches Advocacy of Criminal Cases, Trial Advocacy, the Externship Seminar, and the Criminal Law Clinic. As Director of Externship Programs, Professor Hogan places students with judges and lawyers, oversees their experience, and develops the curriculum for the related seminars. Professor Hogan also teaches advocacy skills to law students and lawyers in programs at Pace University School of Law, St. John's Law School, and for the National Institute for Trial Advocacy. She serves on the Mayor's Advisory Committee on the Judiciary and the Indigent Defense Organization Oversight Committee in New York City. She is a member of the Board of Directors of New York County Lawyers' Association (NYCLA) and its Continuing Legal Education Oversight Committee. For the last six years she has co-chaired the Federal Criminal Practice Institute sponsored by NYCLA and the Federal Bar Council. Before becoming a law professor, she was a public defender in state and federal courts in New York City. She holds a J.D. from Georgetown University Law Center and an A.B. from Brown University.

Arlene S. Kanter

Arlene S. Kanter is a Professor at Syracuse University College of Law and former Director of Clinical Legal Education and of the Externship Program. She also developed and taught the Externship Program seminar focusing on lawyers' ethics. In 2005, she stepped down as clinic director and as externship director to direct the College of Law's Disability Law and Policy Program, which includes the first joint degree program in Law and Disability Studies, and to co-direct the SU Center on Human Policy, Law, and Disability Studies. She has written and lectured extensively on domestic, comparative, and international disability law, including her co-authored book, *Cases and Materials on International Human Rights and Comparative Mental Disability Law* (Carolina Press, 2006). She is founder and co-editor of the new SSRN *Journal on Disability Law*, and co-founder and immediate past chair of the new AALS Section on Disability Law, among other positions. Professor Kanter has served as the Associate Dean at the College of Law and holds a courtesy appointment in the SU School of Education. In 2005, Syracuse University named her the Laura J. and L. Douglas Meredith Professor for Teaching Excellence. She holds a LL.M. from Georgetown University Law Center, a J.D. from New York University, and a B.A. from Trinity College.

Lisa G. Lerman

Lisa G. Lerman is a Professor of Law at The Catholic University of America, Columbus School of Law, where she has taught since 1987. Professor Lerman serves as coordinator of clinical programs for the law school. She was director of CUA's Law and Public Policy Program from 1996 to 2007. Professor Lerman teaches contracts, professional responsibility, and externship and public policy seminars. Professor Lerman is a co-author of

Ethical Problems in the Practice of Law (Aspen Law and Business 2005). She has written many articles about lawyers, law firms, the legal profession and legal education. Professor Lerman is chair of the planning committee for the ABA National Conference on Professional Responsibility. She is a member of the National Advisory Committee for Equal Justice Works. She has served as chair of the Professional Responsibility Section of the Association of American Law Schools and as a member of the D.C. Bar Legal Ethics Committee. Professor Lerman received a B.A. with honors in history from Barnard College, Columbia University, in 1976. She received a J.D. in 1979 from New York University School of Law, where she was senior articles editor of the *N.Y.U. Review of Law and Social Change*. She received an LL.M. in Advocacy from Georgetown University Law Center in 1984 after a two-year clinical fellowship at the Center for Applied Legal Studies. Before joining the faculty at Catholic University, Lerman was a staff attorney at the Center for Women Policy Studies, a Clinical Fellow at Antioch and Georgetown law schools, a member of the law faculty at West Virginia University, and an associate in a law firm. She has taught at the law schools of American University and George Washington University.

Linda Morton

Linda Morton is a Professor of Law at California Western School of Law in San Diego. She has taught in the Internship Program since beginning at California Western in 1989. She also teaches clinical courses in the fields of Advanced Mediation and Problem Solving in Healthcare. Her research is in the fields of lawyering, problem solving, and legal education. She volunteers in the community as a mediator, mediation trainer, and facilitator. Prior to teaching at California Western, she taught in the Legal Drafting Program at the University of Florida College of Law. Before beginning her teaching career, she worked as a litigator in Boston for several years. Professor Morton holds a J.D. from Northeastern University School of Law and a B.A. from Princeton University.

J. P. "Sandy" Ogilvy

Sandy Ogilvy is a Professor of Law and the Director of the Office of Law & Social Justice Initiatives at Columbus School of Law, The Catholic University of America. He was the Coordinator of Clinical Programs at the Law School from 1991 until 2006. He directs an Innocence Project Clinic and teaches Civil Procedure and Torts. Professor Ogilvy has been chair of the AALS Section on Clinical Legal Education and was the chair for the planning committee for the 1996 AALS Conference on Clinical Legal Education. He was the recipient of the 2003 William Pincus Award. He has taught clinically since 1980, when he began teaching as a fellow in Georgetown University Law Center's Administrative Advocacy Clinic. He has taught in client-based clinics, externship programs, and simulation courses. Professor Ogilvy has published in the areas of clinical legal education, legal pedagogy, lawyering skills, and the courts. He is the Director of the National Archive of Clinical Legal Education and produced a documentary film on the early history of clinical legal education using materials from his Oral History Project on Clinical Legal Education. He is the owner or co-owner of two listservs for clinical and externship faculty and administrators. Professor Ogilvy holds an LL.M. from Georgetown University Law Center, a J.D. from Northwestern School of Law of Lewis and Clark College, and a B.A. from Portland State University.

Avis L. Sanders

Avis L. Sanders is the Director of the Externship Program at the American University Washington College of Law, where she teaches one of the externship seminars and oversees more than 25 externship seminars each year. She is the Co-Chair of the AALS Section on Clinical Legal Education. Prior to arriving at the Washington College of Law, Professor Sanders practiced employment discrimination law. From 1990 to 2002, she directed the EEO Intake Project at the Washington Lawyers' Committee for Civil Rights and Urban Affairs and worked as a staff attorney on a number of the Committee's individual and class action employment discrimination cases. Professor Sanders also was responsible for training and supervising hundreds of law students and attorneys who provided *pro bono* assistance to the Committee and developed EEO training programs for state human rights agencies. Professor Sanders holds a J.D. from the Benjamin Cardozo School of Law and a B.A. from American University. She also holds a second dan black belt in the Korean martial art of Tae Kwon Do.

Alex Scherr

Alex Scherr is Associate Professor and Director of Civil Clinics at the University of Georgia School of Law. Until 1996, he worked for Vermont Legal Aid as a staff attorney and managing attorney, with responsibility for training young attorneys in law practice. Since starting law teaching, he has overseen the creation or continuation of seven clinical and practicum programs. The first of these was the Civil Externship program, a course he designed and has taught every semester since 1996. He served as President of the Clinical Legal Education Association in 2005, as a member of the CLEA Board from 2000-2006, and as member of the Executive Committee of the AALS Section of Clinical Legal Education from 2000-2004. He also teaches Dispute Resolution, Public Interest Lawyering, and Evidence. He writes in the areas of evidence, dispute resolution, lawyering theory and practice, and mental health law. He holds a J.D. from the University of Michigan and a B.A. from Yale University.

Lucia Ann Silecchia

Lucia A. Silecchia is a Professor of Law at the Catholic University of America's Columbus School of Law. She received her B.A. degree *summa cum laude* from Queens College (C.U.N.Y.) in 1987 and her J.D. from Yale Law School in 1990. She then practiced law in the litigation department of Rogers & Wells (now Clifford, Chance) in New York City. Professor Silecchia joined the Columbus School of Law in 1991 as the Assistant Director of the Lawyering Skills Program. She has been on the faculty since then and served as the law school's Associate Dean for Academic Affairs in 2004 and 2005. She teaches or has taught Environmental Law, Property, Trusts and Estates, Corporations, Advanced Legal Research and Writing, Comparative Property, Environmental Crimes, Lawyering Skills, and Law Journal Writing. She has written in the areas of environmental law and enforcement, legal education, Catholic social thought, legal writing, law and literature, and social justice. Professor Silecchia has given presentations at national conferences for legal educators, law librarians, lawyers, religious groups, students, and environmental professionals. She also has advised the Pontifical Council on Justice and Peace and the Environmental Justice Project of the U.S. Catholic Conference, assisted the American Bar Association's CEELI Project in critiquing business association laws for Estonia, and taught in Catholic University's cooperative programs at Jagiellonian University in Cracow, Poland. She also has been a member of the teaching faculty for the international law students in the Washington D.C.-based Institute for United States Law.

Cindy Roman Slane

Cindy Roman Slane is an Assistant Clinical Professor of Law and Director of Field Placement Programs at Quinnipiac University School of Law. Before joining the Quinnipiac faculty, she was a trial department associate with Day, Berry & Howard (now Day Pitney) in its Stamford, Connecticut offices. Since 1994, she has been responsible for developing the law school's externship program, which now includes nine externship courses. She routinely teaches five of those courses: the Corporate Counsel, Criminal Justice, Judicial, and Public Interest Externships, and a second-semester externship sequel, Field Placement II. She is a three-term gubernatorial appointee to Connecticut's Permanent Commission on the Status of Women; has served as treasurer, vice-chair and chair of the Commission; and several times has represented PCSW before the Judiciary and Appropriations Committees of the Connecticut General Assembly. Since 1998, she also has served on the Connecticut Bar Association's Professional Ethics Committee. She has made numerous presentations on women's issues, legal ethics, and clinical law teaching before local, state, regional, and national audiences. She holds a J.D. from Yale University and a B.A. from Douglass College (Rutgers University).

Janet Weinstein

Janet Weinstein is a professor at California Western School of Law, where she is the Director of the Internship Program. She has been involved in clinical legal education since 1978, when she directed one of the first environmental law clinics in the country and has taught a variety of clinical courses including interviewing, counseling, and negotiation and mediation. She is involved in the creation of the new STEPPS program (Skills Training for Ethical Preventive Practice and Career Satisfaction) at California Western. In addition, she has been teaching interdisciplinary courses in the area of child welfare for many years and includes problem solving as an integral component of all her courses.

Leah Wortham

Leah Wortham created the Becoming a Lawyer extern course at The Catholic University of America where she is a Professor of Law. She was CUA's clinical coordinator from 1981-1990 and continues to teach in the extern program, as well as teaching Professional Responsibility and Criminal Law. She has been a member of numerous ABA/AALS accreditation site visit teams, chair of the Extern Committee of the AALS Clinical Section, and on the Board of Editors of the *Clinical Law Review*. Since 1996, she has worked with a number of law teachers and students abroad on introducing interactive teaching methods, establishing clinical programs, teaching legal ethics, and strategies for legal education reform. She has been Chair and Vice-Chair of both the Legal Ethics Committee and the Rules of Professional Conduct Review Committee of the D.C. Bar, the third largest bar in the U.S. with over 80,000 members. She also has served as a hearing committee member and chair for D.C. lawyer discipline cases. She served for five years as Associate Dean for External and Student Affairs at CUA. She holds a J.D. from Harvard University and a B.A. from Macalester College in St. Paul, Minnesota.

Acknowledgments

From concept to completion this book has been touched by many wonderful people. We are grateful to each of them for their contributions.

Carol Logie of Avatar Creative designed the cover and chapter headings and prepared the manuscript for publication. Steve Young, a research librarian at the Columbus School of Law, helped immensely with research, especially on Chapter 17. Georgia Niedzielko, Assistant Dean of Academic Affairs, was involved in developing the first edition and some of her work is retained in Chapter 18. Kathryn Bender, Associate General Counsel of The Catholic University of America, who has taught in the externship program as well, contributed to Chapter 19 and was involved in developing the concept of the book. Some of the suggestions on effective presentations incorporated into Chapter 19 were derived from the course materials prepared by Alayne R. Casteel and Dr. Gordon I. Zimmerman, of the University of Nevada at Las Vegas, for training continuing education faculty of the District of Columbia Bar.

Several students assisted the authors as research assistants. We are indebted to Scott Semple (Anderson), Jin Park (Barry), Kristin Gooray (Brustin), Jane Yoo (Hogan), Stanley Woodward (Lerman), Meadow Wirick (Sanders), and Jennifer Hill-Wilson (Wortham) for their invaluable assistance.

Excerpts from the following books, reports, articles, and materials appear with the kind permission of the copyright holders:

American Anthropological Association, Code of Ethics of the American Anthropological Association (Approved June 1998). Reprinted by permission of the American Anthropological Association. Not for further distribution.

American Bar Association, *Lawyers' Descriptions of Reactions to Stress*, The State of the Legal Profession, 73 (1990) © 1990 by the American Bar Association. Reprinted with permission.

American Bar Association, Section of Legal Education and Admissions to the Bar, Legal Education and Professional Development—an Educational Continuum (Report of the Task Force on Law Schools and the Profession: Narrowing the Gap, Overview of Skills and Values), pp. 138-141 (July 1992). ©1992 by American Bar Association. Reprinted with permission.

Anonymous, *Truth and Consequences: Journal of a Closeted Attorney*, 2002 SAN FRANCISCO ATTORNEY 44 (JUN./JUL. 2002). Reprinted with permission of San Francisco Attorney.

Barbara A. Curran and Clara N. Carson, The Lawyer Statistical Report: The U.S. Legal Profession in the 1990's, pp. 24-5, American Bar Foundation (1994). Reprinted with permission of the American Bar Foundation.

Dealing with Prejudice and Stereotypes on the Job, Managing Diversity (Mar. 1994). Reprinted by permission of Lee Gardenswartz and Anita Rowe, 12658 W. Washington Blvd., Suite 105, Los Angeles, CA 90066, 310-823-2466 and Managing Diversity, P.O. Box 819, Jamestown, NY 14702, 716-665-3654.

Dilbert Cartoon—DILBERT: © Scott Adams/Dist. By United Feature Syndicate, Inc. Used with permission.

Excerpt from Miles to Go: Progress of Minorities in the Legal Profession, 2005, published by the American Bar Association Commission on Racial and Ethnic Diversity in the Legal Profession. © 2005 by the American Bar Association. Reprinted with permission.

Michael Meltsner, James V. Rowan and Daniel J. Givelber, *The Bike Tour Leader's Dilemma: Talking About Supervision*, 13 Vermont Law Review 399 (1989). Reprinted with permission.

Vera Goodkin, The Consequences of Writing: Enhancing Learning in the Disciplines (Universal Microfilms International, 1986). Reprinted with permission.

Excerpt from Law, Life and the Pursuit of Balance (1996), published by the Maricopa County, Arizona Bar Association. Used with permission.

National MultiCultural Institute, *Exercise Two: First Memories of Difference and Reactions to Bias in a Legal* Setting, Reproduced from *Developing diversity Training for the Workplace: A Guide for Trainers*. Reprinted with permission from the National Multicultural Institute, 3000 Connecticut Avenue, NW, Suite 438, Washington, DC 20008. Tel: 202-483-0700.

Sheila Nielsen, The Balancing Act: Practical Suggestions for Part-Time Attorneys, 35 New York Law School Law Review 369 (1990). Reprinted with permission of the author and New York Law School Law Review.

Ann W. Parks, *Disability as a law firm diversity issue*, THE DAILY RECORD, May 19, 2006, at 1B. Reprinted with permission.

Relinking Life and Work: Toward a Better Future, Ford Foundation (1992). © 1996 Ford Foundation. Reprinted with permission.

Marta-Ann Schnabel, *Diversity in the Legal Profession: A Look at the Present and the Future . . . Are Women Still a Minority 53 LA Bar J. 114 (Aug./Sep. 2005)*. Reprinted from: Louisiana Bar Journal, Vol. 53, No. 2, copyright 2005, published by the Louisiana State Bar Association, 601 Charles Ave., New Orleans, LA 70130.

Excerpts from PARTICIPANT OBSERVATION 1st edition by SPRADLEY, 1980. Reprinted with permission of Wadsworth, a division of Thomson Learning: www.thomsonrights.com. Fax 800 730-2215.

The State of the Legal Profession: Career Satisfaction and Women in the Law. Copyright © American Bar Association, 1991. Reprinted by permission.

Unfinished Business: Overcoming the Sisyphus Factor, American Bar Association Commission on Women in the Profession (Dec. 1995). ©1995 American Bar Association, all rights reserved. Reprinted by permission.

Thomas S. Williamson, *Transcript of the Boston Bar Association Diversity Committee Conference: Recruiting, Hiring and Retaining Lawyers of Color, 44 Boston Bar Journal 8 (May/June 2000)*. Reprinted with permission of Boston Bar Journal.

Chapter 1

Learning From Experience

J.P. Ogilvy

Experience isn't what happens to you.
It's what you make out of what happens to you.
— Aldous Huxley

Why Are You Doing an Externship?

Before deciding to do an externship, you undoubtedly considered how you would benefit from a field placement experience. Your decision might have been based on little more than a desire to get out of the classroom and obtain some real world experience or your reasoning might have been multifaceted. Consider whether your motivation to do an externship includes any of the following.

- To pursue particular learning goals that *you* define. Up to this point in your legal education, you have been told what to study and how to study. You have been given a syllabus and assigned readings. You have been led through a discussion of materials and were tested on those materials. In an externship, you have much more say about what you learn and how you learn it.

- To apply classroom learning to the real world. Classroom courses are relatively good at providing instruction in *the law and legal reasoning*, but it is in the actual *practice* of law that one can really understand the application of law to real problems. An externship provides an opportunity to apply your classroom learning to the real world of practice.

- To pursue personal growth and development. An externship provides a place for you to learn professional skills and consider professional values. It offers an environment where you can improve the personal skills that contribute to professional competence and satisfaction. Through an externship you can improve problem-solving skills, and you can become more self-confident in work settings.

• To explore career interests. You might select an externship to try out a possible career path. You might discover that a path that seemed promising is not right for you. You might find a new career interest or confirm a choice you had made tentatively. An externship expands your opportunities for professional experience beyond summer and part-time employment.

• To provide service to others. You might choose a particular externship placement because it allows you to provide service to poor people, AIDS patients, people with disabilities, inmates, or another group of individuals with special needs.

• To increase your own awareness of community needs. An externship might provide opportunities to become aware of community needs and to work in a setting that seeks to address those needs. An externship in a local community development corporation, for example, might expose you directly to the unique needs of the homeless in your community.

• To work with persons different from you. If you stay in the classroom on campus, you might notice that you have little contact with elderly people, poor people, children, immigrants, or others whose life experience differs from yours.

• To improve your prospects for employment. Externships provide experience that employers will recognize. You often can produce writing samples that show how you think and communicate in a real work situation. A prospective employer then can judge you more on demonstrated abilities and less on the basis of your grades. An externship permits you to demonstrate other work-related competencies like perseverance, care, skill with others, creativity, and attention to detail.

• To build a professional network. Through an externship you can establish and build relationships with people in your own and other organizations. You can learn of potential job openings and develop contacts and references that will be useful when you are looking for a permanent job, a lead on an elusive research project, or someone with expertise in a particular area.

As you can see, externships offer many benefits, but the benefits are not a windfall. To reap the benefits from an externship experience, you must give careful thought to the selection of your placement, set goals for yourself, and reflect on your experience. You are no doubt prepared to *work* hard at the placement. You also should be prepared to *think* hard about the experience. In this chapter we examine some of the concepts of learning from experience. Your study of this material will help you to take full advantage of the learning opportunities provided by your externship and will help you to benefit from experiential learning throughout your legal career.

What Is Experiential Learning?

All learning is, to some extent, experiential. Everything we learn must be mediated through one of the senses from our experience with the world. This book focuses on a more specific understanding of the concept of experiential learning. It is learning grounded in a personal experience in an *authentic* setting. An authentic setting is one that is closely similar to the actual setting in which knowledge acquired later will be used.

Knowledge gained through experience is different both from "theoretical knowledge," which concerns the general or abstract principles connecting a body of material, and from "empirical knowledge," which is acquired through confirming and disconfirming evidence found in examination of data. Experiential knowledge rarely is sufficient to prepare for a job, especially a complicated one. Experiential learning usually requires the application of theoretical or empirical knowledge gained in other learning experiences. Many jobs, even simple ones, rely on written materials and classroom instruction to teach employees some of what they need to know to perform the job. In a law school clinic or at an externship placement, you will apply and test the theoretical and empirical knowledge that you have gained through reading in other law school courses or elsewhere. Experiential learning in law school offers an added dimension of personal experience with lawyers and lawyering.

Making the Most of Experience

Experiential learning should be distinguished from merely experiencing. It is what you do with experience that determines what and how much you will learn from it. Experiential learning comes from the active processing of experiences. The process of learning from experience is cyclical. As the model in Figure 1.1 illustrates, the field experience itself is only one part of a cycle of experiential learning. To maximize learning from experience, you need to plan for the experience, have the experience, reflect on what happened, and integrate or synthesize what has been learned with existing knowledge and other sources of learning. On both the macro and micro levels, you will gain the most from your externship experience through this process of planning, doing, reflecting, and integrating.

Figure 1.1 The Experiential Learning Cycle

While each of the elements of the experiential learning cycle is necessary for successful learning from experience, the most central elements are planning and reflection. Your externship will be most effective if you set goals and objectives for your externship. You should develop a plan for approaching each task with thorough preparation and active reflection. Before setting out on a long vacation, you may spend a significant amount of effort in thinking through how you want to spend your time by considering which experiences you want to have and which you want to avoid. Is your goal to learn something new or simply to pursue your favorite recreational activities? Similarly, to achieve your overall objectives for the externship, you must plan for the externship by clearly articulating to yourself goals and objectives that you will seek to achieve. Once you have begun your placement, you will undertake a large number of discrete tasks as you fulfill your assignments. Just as you will outline what you want to say before attempting a first draft of a brief, you must plan adequately before undertaking to accomplish each task and learning opportunity within the externship. Goal setting and planning are critical elements in learning from experience.

Reflection is an equally important element of experiential learning. It is the process that turns experience into learning. While you are preparing for the fieldwork experience, you reflect to explore what is required at the placement, what demands the setting will place on you, and what resources it has to facilitate your learning. Reflection during the externship is necessary to sort through your experience as it happens. Observations and actions might occur in rapid succession, leaving insufficient time to analyze and integrate your learning. Periodically, you should draw back from the experience to digest what is happening. After the externship ends, you will use reflection to make sense of the experience, to integrate your understandings into your knowledge base, and to prepare for new experiences.

Reflection can be a solitary or a communal activity. Much of your reflection will involve thinking quietly, turning events over in your mind, and trying to make sense of your experience. You might keep a journal to record some of these solitary reflections. Reflection also occurs communally in formal and informal class discussions. Your seminars might be devoted in part to reflective activities such as group discussions or presentations. Each of these will help you process the vast quantity of information that comes from your externship in order to enhance your learning from experience.

see Chapter 11 on *Journals*

see Chapter 19 on *Presentations*

Plan, Do, Reflect—The Big Picture

On a "macro" level, you should begin your externship experience by planning for it. This involves setting realistic goals and objectives for yourself. What do you wish to accomplish through the externship? What do you want to be able to do upon its completion that you now cannot do? What skills do you want to learn or improve? During your externship you should revisit your initial goals statement from time to time to reflect on and to evaluate your progress toward meeting your goals and objectives and to revise, as necessary, your goals and objectives in light of your experiences. At the end of your externship, you should take some time again to reflect on the total experience, to take stock of what you have learned and to integrate your new knowledge with your existing knowledge base as you prepare for your next set of experiences. You may find it useful to skim the final chapter of this book, *Looking Back Looking Forward* at this time and return to it at the end of your placement experience.

Plan, Do, Reflect—Specific Tasks

Let us examine how the model illustrated in Figure 1.1 might apply in a typical externship. In this example, we are focusing on the application of the idea of an experiential learning cycle in the "micro" sense. That is, instead of focusing on the entire externship experience, we want to focus on a specific experience within the externship.

Plan

Assume you are in a judicial externship and have been asked to draft an order for your judge to grant or deny a motion to vacate a default judgment. Before you begin drafting the order, you will want to think through some personal goals for the project. For instance, you might want to use the order as a writing sample. Will this be possible, since ultimately the order will be signed by the judge? You might want to use this task to get feedback on your legal research and writing skills. What specific skills do you want to improve? What type of critique and feedback do you want? You might discuss the task and review your learning goals with your faculty supervisor and seek the supervisor's input. After thinking about what you want to accomplish, you might devise a work *plan* that sets a timetable for accomplishing each research and writing task.

Do

Next, you execute your plan. You reread the motion, the opposition, and the supporting memoranda filed by the lawyers. You reread the applicable rules of civil procedure. You review the cases that seem closest to the facts of the case before you. Then you compose a draft and revise it several times before you present a polished draft order to the judge suggesting that she deny the motion to vacate.

The judge thanks you for your work. She suggests some changes in your writing style, such as, to use active rather than passive voice. More surprisingly, she says that she has decided to grant the motion even though your conclusion was appropriately supported by the cases that you cited. She explains that case law in the area gives judges considerable discretion in deciding whether to vacate a default. She believes that every defendant should have an opportunity to have a trial on the merits of the plaintiff's claim, barring extreme circumstances not present here. The preparation and drafting of your order and the judge's feedback is a concrete experience or *doing* in the model.

Reflect, Analyze, and Integrate

After meeting with the judge, you reflect on the experience. You could talk to the judge's clerk to get another perspective. You could write a journal entry about your experience. You could talk to other clerks or judicial externs or read articles about writing style or standards for reopening a default judgment. You could think about how to incorporate the judge's suggestions on your writing style in other writings you will do. On the standard for default judgment, you consciously or unconsciously will form theories, ideas, and concepts about the authority of judges, the uncertainty of the law, the discretion of judges, the process of judicial thinking, ways of presenting and opposing motions to vacate default judgments, and other matters. Although you might not think about all of these topics, and you might think of others, some *reflection* and *analysis* should lead you to *integrate* your learning from this experience with prior knowledge to create new, or to modify existing, knowledge.

Apply

The next time that you are asked to draft an order for the judge, you will use the ideas and impressions you developed in your earlier experience. By applying your new knowledge to another task, you begin a new cycle of learning. One application might relate to dealing with your fieldwork supervisor. You, for example, might have realized that you could work more efficiently if you had a model from which to work. When you get your next assignment, you might decide to ask the judge or the judge's clerk if there is a model that you could review. Or you might ask whether the judge is inclined to decide the matter one way or another. Some judges prefer that externs draft opinions without knowing the judge's inclination because the draft provides a fresh perspective for the judge, and the process gives the student a chance to work out the problem independently. Other judges are willing to give some guidance at the outset, based on their own reading of the papers or on the oral argument.

Further Reflection

Reflection is an element of the learning cycle that you can employ at every point in the cycle. You can reflect on your planning and on your performance of specific tasks during the externship. You also can reflect on the set of experiences such as we just described. This set of experiences might give you ideas about how you would approach a judge as an advocate seeking the judge's exercise of judicial discretion in your client's favor, that is, thoughts about what factors make an argument attractive. You might want to think about how willing you would be to vacate default judgments if you were the decision maker or what you see as the best policy. To what other kinds of reflections could this experience have led? What other ideas might you have developed? How might you use experiences like this to promote more self-directed learning in your externship or in your career as a lawyer?

This example illustrates how much more could be learned from this experience than, "Next time I am asked to draft a motion to vacate a default judgment, I will draft it to reopen unless certain conditions are met." You might not be asked to do this task again during the externship or during your work life. The learning value is greater if you are able to generalize more broadly from your experience. Then you can extrapolate from your experience to related, but not identical, situations.

Experiential Learning and Adult Learners

Experiential learning is especially suited to adult learners. For many years, educators at all levels saw themselves as transmitting knowledge to their students. Teaching was an active process. Learning was a passive one. Research into teaching and learning has cast doubt both on the efficacy of the transmission model and on the desirability of treating learners as passive recipients of knowledge. Fortunately, many law professors now use teaching techniques that permit students actively to construct knowledge. There is, however, a limit to how much active learning can occur in a large classroom. Clinical experiences, including externships, can enhance students' opportunities for active learning.

Most law students approach clinical experiences, such as externships, with excitement about moving into the real world to learn something about what real lawyers do. This enthusiasm is consistent with research observations about the educational preferences of adult learners. Most people prefer to be active participants in the learning process rather than passive recipients of knowledge. By the end of the first year of law school, most students are eager to get out of the classroom and begin working in actual legal settings. Students desire relevance and often learn better if they understand the relationship between the learning activity and some specific learning goal. In the traditional law school classroom, this desire for relevance is apparent in the frustration experienced by many first-year students before the end of the first semester. Their desire for relevance is reflected in their belief that they are in law school to learn the law, the black letter law. The desire for this particular relevance, admittedly misplaced, as first-year students eventually come to see, is frustrated by the professor's seeming unwillingness to teach what students think they want and need to know.

Adults seek authentic learning situations. Adults who want to acquire new knowledge or skills generally seek to learn what they want to know by engaging in the skill or activity in a setting where the skill or knowledge is used. In other words, adults tend to learn in settings other than classrooms. This attribute is perhaps best illustrated by the fact that after the first year, or even after the first semester, law students tend to seek legal employment or enroll in clinics because they prefer learning the law in the field to learning it in classrooms. Because they have had more experience than younger students, adults need acknowledgment of their past experiences and existing knowledge. They can draw upon their extensive knowledge and experience in subsequent learning activities. Our emphasis on adults is not intended to deny that children as learners often have similar approaches, needs, and preferences. Rather, our emphasis recognizes that the depth and breadth of experience brought to learning situations by adults differs substantially from the prior experience of children. This depth and breadth of experience deserves to be recognized in formal teaching and learning settings.

Adults bring to the learning situation their own learning style preferences. We do not all learn in the same way. You probably have noticed differences in learning styles between you and others. Assume that you want to learn how to compose and deliver an opening statement in a criminal case. Would you prefer to read about opening statements in textbooks, go to the courthouse to watch prosecutors and defense attorneys in actual trials, or deliver an opening statement and have it critiqued by an expert? Perhaps you would do all three. The starting points and types of activities you select say something about your preferred learning style. Your preference is not necessarily the best choice or the only reasonable choice among the available methods of learning, but it is your own personal choice.

Adults want to be autonomous and self-directed in developing learning goals. Adult learners accept that instructors and formal programs of instruction are not the only, or even the primary, way they will learn and are willing to take a greater share of responsibility for their own learning. In most classroom settings, the course syllabus is developed by the instructor and the learning goals and methods are dictated by the instructor. This is contrary to the learning preferences of most adults who prefer to establish their own learning goals. In an externship, the extern assumes primary responsibility for his own learning. The fieldwork supervisor and the faculty supervisor provide coaching, mentoring, support, and feedback, but the extern defines learning goals and takes primary responsibility for seeking tasks and feedback on performance of those tasks.

Summary

In this chapter we have described what research and education theory tells us about adult learning. We have introduced the idea of learning style differences among individuals. The concepts introduced in this chapter provide the foundation for the other chapters in this book. The experiential learning elements of *planning* and *reflection* are raised throughout the text in many different contexts because they are central to the successful completion of an externship.

The purpose of this book is to help you learn as much as possible from your externship about the skills and values you will need as a lawyer. The readings, exercises, journal questions, and other materials suggest methods to maximize experiential learning at your placement through the cycle of planning, doing, reflecting and integrating. We believe this book offers a menu of possibilities. Different readers will find some parts more useful than others. We encourage you to choose what seems most useful to you, but also to try new things. Most of all, we urge you to enjoy your field experience.

As you continue your lifetime of learning, much more of your learning will come in settings like your externship. After you graduate, you will rarely turn to formal classrooms and textbooks to learn what you need to practice law. Take the time to learn all that you can from your externship. Do not be satisfied with merely having experiences. Take advantage of this opportunity to improve your ability to learn from experience by planning and reflecting consciously and frequently. You will use these skills for the rest of your professional life.

Chapter 2

Setting Goals for the Externship

Leah Wortham

> If you don't know where you are going,
> you are likely to end up somewhere else.
>
> — Yogi Berra

Setting Goals and Developing a Learning Agenda

As Yogi Berra says, those who have an idea where they want to go are more likely to get there—or if not *there*, somewhere else they might like to go. Workers in all types of jobs like to have some control over what happens to them. Some of the lawyer dissatisfaction reported in recent studies can be attributed to lawyers' feelings of lack of control over their work lives. Conscious recognition of your goals for a work experience and forging your own path to achieve those goals may give you greater control over your professional life.

 Chapter 17 on *Work-Life Balance*

Law school externship courses differ with respect to how much choice a student is expected to exercise in placement selection. At some schools, students have broad latitude to choose among many placements depending upon their individual goals. At other schools, students are assigned to a particular fieldwork supervisor by the faculty member in charge with no prior input from the student. At others, the faculty supervisor places the student but takes into consideration interviews or written material from students and placements in making a match.

In programs with broad student choice, students usually are required to assess their learning goals for the externship at the outset. Discussion of these learning goals with the faculty supervisor may be an integral part of the course. In externship programs in which the faculty supervisor makes the placement assignment, there still are important reasons for students to consider their learning goals for the externship.

Even if your placement choice has been made for you, there will be many options for what your experience could be like on a day-to-day basis. In a classroom course, the teacher can assign every student to read the same material and answer the same questions. The real world is less predictable and controllable. Every day at your externship you will have choices about what opportunities to seek, and your fieldwork supervisor will have choices about which learning experiences to offer. Thinking about what you want from the experience and communicating those interests to your supervisor can enhance your learning significantly.

When students first express their goals for externships, their responses tend to fall into four categories:

- skill development;
- exploration of what type of job to seek after law school;
- desire to learn about a particular substantive area of law or legal institution, often combined with the desire to enhance credentials and make professional contacts;
- consideration of how to find satisfaction in work and balance with personal life.

Other chapters of this book provide background information that can help you turn vague instincts about what you may want to learn into more precise goal statements. Many students also are motivated in fieldwork by a wish to serve others, like people in economic need or those with a particular type of problem. For many students, this interest in service coexists with interest in what can be learned from the experience.

Exercise 2.1 Think about your goals for your externship. Write down all the things that come to mind. Do not self-censor. Do not worry about grammar and punctuation. Use whatever format comes most easily. This is a first step to get your creative juices flowing on a goals statement that you later will be willing to discuss with others.

see ▷ Chapters 14 & 15
on Skill Development and Chapter 18 on Career Planning

Exercise 2.2 If you are feeling stuck for ideas about goals through the deductive approach in Exercise 2.1, try an inductive one. Look at Chapters 14-15 and Chapter 18. Those chapters inventory some possible goals and provide assessment tools.

See if your program has descriptions of externships or descriptions/evaluations of experience by past externs that you can read. Talk to other students who have done externships about what they did and what they think were the greatest benefits. Ask lawyers about the most important things they learned in their first jobs. Make notes on what seems appealing and unappealing in what you read and hear. Try to figure out why you categorized things each way. For example, did experiences with more writing tasks seem more appealing or less appealing? Did the amount of client contact seem to make a difference? Were you interested by possibilities in a particular field of law?

Assume your first thoughts on goals are to

- develop my representation skills in criminal prosecution,
- improve my research and writing,
- consider whether I want to be a criminal prosecutor.

After you make your initial list of goals, try to refine your goals to clarify their meaning. Think about what kind of experiences would be attractive to you in pursuit of the goal. Consider the range of options within your first goal. Criminal prosecution can involve a broad array of skills, including fact investigation; interviewing; counseling; negotiation; statutory analysis; exercise of discretion in charging; and oral advocacy in openings, closings, direct and cross-examination. Consider which of these skills interest you most.

Understanding your goals can guide the fieldwork supervisor in choosing your assignments. The range of possible assignments in a prosecutor's office may vary widely. Refining your goals will enhance your ability to talk with your supervisor about what you would like to do.

Assignments in the misdemeanor division may provide experience in opening and closing statements, direct and cross-examinations, and responses to motions to suppress, but the issues arising in such cases may be repetitive and require little original research and writing. Assignments in the appellate division of the same office may provide opportunities to develop research skills and a thorough understanding of the substantive law. Appellate assignments, however, do not offer exposure to the pace, pressures, and demands of day-to-day prosecution in the trial courts where new prosecutors often begin their careers. In a smaller prosecutor's office, trial and appellate functions might be handled by the same lawyers rather than by different divisions, but the work in each area is likely to differ in the ways previously described. Doing both trial and appellate work may help you to think about whether or not you want to specialize in one or the other.

In addition to thinking about possible work assignments, consider what events you might like to observe or attend, for example, trials, status conferences, or in-office strategy meetings. You may not be informed about these or invited to attend unless you indicate interest. Your field supervisor may be able to arrange for you to attend in-service training. If supervisors know that career planning is an important goal for you, they may pass on articles or notices about speakers or information about a student division of a relevant professional organization.

A second way to refine goals is to review the pertinent experiences you already have had. This will prompt you to think about what you want to learn next and what existing knowledge you might want to apply or build on. If your goals are like the prosecution hypothetical above, pertinent questions might include the following: What experience did you have with the criminal justice system before coming to law school? Have you taken a simulated trial advocacy course? What relevant academic courses have you completed? This review also may remind you of background to add to your résumé or to mention to the fieldwork supervisor.

A third way to refine goals is to consider alternate meanings for terms in your draft goals statement. This will help you to avoid miscommunication with your supervisor about your interests. In using the term "legal research and writing," some students mean drafting of motions or other pleadings, while others are thinking of the in-depth legal analysis needed to write appellate briefs or research memos. Some students hope to produce a writing sample that could be offered to future employers. It is helpful for a supervisor to understand which of these ideas are expressed in the goal of improving legal research and writing.

While most externships offer chances to pursue multiple objectives, placements differ in what they offer and no placement serves every possible goal. The previous contrast of appellate and misdemeanor assignments in a prosecutor's office illustrates how placements may vary in their capacity to further different goals. You should consider not only the learning objectives that you have for an externship, but also the relative priority among those objectives: Which are the most important to you in this externship? In choosing and pursuing your externship, you should stay focused on your desire to meet your most important goals.

Exercise 2.3 Look at your initial ideas and goals. Refine them by generating a list of possible experiences that could further the goal, reviewing past experience pertinent to the goal, and considering possible multiple meanings for terms you used. Translate your early notes onto the Learning Agenda at Appendix 2.1 at the end of this chapter or write a Goals Memo as described in Appendix 2.2. Some externs and faculty supervisors prefer the graphic format of the agenda. Others prefer the narrative memo. Regardless of the format you choose, you should include statements of your goals that you have refined through the previously described devices and examples of experiences that you think would help you to progress toward your goals.

Exercise 2.4 Exchange the first draft of your Learning Agenda or Goals Memo with another student. Ask if your partner understands what you mean by the terms used and whether the statement would clearly and *tactfully* communicate your interests to a supervisor. Revise your first draft in light of the conversation with your partner.

The Etiquette of Accepting and Rejecting Externship Offers

Those of you who have a role in placement selection should be aware that there are some conventions similar to those used in considering and accepting employment offers. In general, you should not accept an externship and later withdraw because you have received a better offer. If you receive an offer from Externship A when you are still considering Externships B and C, ask Externship A for enough time to seek decisions from the other placement possibilities. You may wish to tell the first externship that you also are waiting to hear from another organization and would like to check with them before making a final decision. You then can contact Externships B and C, explain that you have received another offer, and ask them if they can give you an answer within a stated time frame. Before going through this exercise, analyze whether you prefer B and C to A. If you need additional information, gather it quickly so you can come to a final decision.

Chapter 13
on Judicial Externships

Most fieldwork supervisors will be understanding. Many lawyers have been in similar situations. Candidates for judicial clerkships in the federal courts, and a few state courts, generally follow a different and unique convention. When offered a federal judicial clerkship, applicants frequently are expected to accept on the spot rather than ask for time to think or check back on other options. Most judges do not expect an immediate answer for externships, but you should be aware of the convention on federal clerkships so you are not surprised if someone mentions it. If you apply for an externship and subsequently decide you are not interested, you should notify the potential placement promptly that you want to withdraw your application.

At Appendix 2.3 of this chapter, you will find my law school's detailed specifics on considering, accepting, and rejecting externships. If you have questions about their applicability in your law school, check with your faculty supervisor.

Exercise 2.5 Make a list of questions to ask a potential externship supervisor to determine whether an externship would help you to achieve the goals you have articulated and provide the experiences you seek. Identify other sources of information that you could use to get information about the externship and the likelihood your goals could be met in the placement.

Discussing Your Learning Agenda with Your Fieldwork Supervisor

Exercises 2.3 and 2.4 ask you to refine ideas about goals and experiences that would seem to further them. You should think about the goals and experiences that you desire before you go to interviews so you can explore how likely it is that your wishes and the placement's reality will mesh. You do not want to find out that the externship is not what you had in mind after you have accepted the position.

We refer to the Learning Agenda or Goals Memo as a draft throughout this discussion because it is an evolving document that is important for the processes that it guides and tracks. In a sense, it never becomes final. Chapter 20 suggests rereading your Goals Memo before a wrap-up discussion of your externship. It is fine if a goal has not been achieved or if you missed some experiences on your initial draft. Other goals and experiences may have taken the place of those first articulated.

The first purpose of formulating the agenda or memo is self-direction: to push you to think about what you want from the externship and what kind of experiences might lead you to those goals. A second purpose is communication with your field-work supervisor. The initial discussion of your draft communicates specific hopes and expectations.

This communication should stimulate the supervisor to think about learning possibilities at the externship and to create a mental tickler of your desired opportunities. Student goals vary widely. If the supervisor does not know your preferences, the supervisor may assume that you would like to do what she wanted to do as a student or what the previous extern preferred. The assignments based on those assumptions may not mesh with your wishes. I have seen students working with trial judges who were frustrated when they were given few research and writing assignments. I have seen other externs working with trial judges who were frustrated with research and writing assignments because these students felt this experience was available in law school. These students preferred taking in-court trial notes, organizing pleadings, talking with lawyers, and other experiences that seemed different from law school. Communicating preferences to your supervisor at the outset can avoid such mismatches.

Discussion of goals and experiences with a supervisor often stimulates the supervisor to suggest additions to the document. Your supervisor might suggest that your goals and preferences for experience are not realistic in the externship. It is well to identify anything that will be impossible early on to avoid later frustration and resentment. You can then discuss alternative work that might support your goals. Occasionally this discussion may reveal that the externship will not provide what the student desires, and other arrangements should be made.

Understanding your goals may prompt a supervisor to talk to you during the semester about topics in which she otherwise would not realize you had an interest. Think back to the hypothetical goal of "consider whether I want to be a criminal prosecutor." In the "experience" column, you might have written, "Talk with prosecutors about their likes and dislikes of the job." Many supervisors enjoy the mentoring role with a student and offer advice freely with little prompting. Others may be hesitant to make the time unless they know the student is interested.

In addition to its uses as a thinking and communication tool, the Learning Agenda or Goals Memo functions as a base or touchstone as you proceed through the experience. You should look at the draft periodically during the semester and think about your progress toward these goals. You also should review it with your supervisor at least once during the semester to see how the actual experience squares with your initial discussions. The agenda helps you to say to a supervisor, "I have been able to do A, B, and C. I haven't been able to be involved in any brief writing yet. Do you think there will be a chance to do that with the weeks left in the semester?"

Exercise 2.6 Mark your calendar at intervals that you select or that are assigned by your faculty supervisor. At these points, look at your agenda/goals and assess your experience thus far. Amend the original document if you have changed course. Appendix 2.4 to this chapter is a time sheet form that assists students to in assessing how their time is being spent. Even if your teacher does not require this form, you might keep this record to see if the way you are spending your time matches your goals for the externship. Look back at your journals to see if they also remind you of things you would like to raise about the way your experience has matched your goals. If there are items that still are of interest but have not been addressed, make notes about your concerns. Consider the best way to raise the concern with your supervisor. If you are not sure how to raise your concerns, talk with your faculty supervisor. These agenda reviews can provide fertile material for journal entries.

Identifying Learning Opportunities at Your Placement

When you write your initial goals statement, you may feel that you do not know enough about the externship, or legal work generally, to define everything that you would like to do. Even so, it is a useful starting point. No matter how much advance thinking you have done, there doubtless will be new opportunities and possibilities that you will discover once at the externship.

Keep your eyes and ears open. Talk with others in the externship. Lawyers, externs, and staff all can provide useful information. You can enrich your learning about skills, the profession, or the substantive law, and you may identify work at the externship in which you want to be involved. There may be docket sheets, annual reports, or staff meeting minutes that your fieldwork supervisor would be willing to share.

Ask whether you can work on projects that interest you. You must be ready to accept no for an answer, but volunteering for work suggests that you are interested and have initiative. Many supervisors do not have the time to consider all the alternative work in which you might be involved. Your communication about desired goals and experiences can expand the possibilities.

Measuring Whether You Are Achieving Your Goals

Up to now we have focused on formulating goals, identifying experiences that might further them, and sharing your draft ideas with your supervisor. This section challenges you to set "measurable objectives"—particular outcomes that demonstrate progress toward a goal. Many businesses, government, and non-profit organizations stress putting organizational goals into objectives that are demonstrable and can be measured. Strategic planning documents often are written this way. Employees may be required to write annual goals, and their review may be a part of the performance evaluation process.

Two ways of thinking about measurable objectives are presented in this section. The first is to develop benchmarks for the experiences you listed as desirable in your Learning Agenda. Benchmarks define how much of that experience you seek. Recall your hypothetical goal "develop my representation skills in criminal prosecution." Suppose your listing of experiences included "gain experience in interviewing witnesses." Developing a benchmark for this experience means considering how much of the experience you think will give you the competence level you seek from the externship. Do you mean two witnesses or twenty? Ideas about benchmarks and their review should help you to focus more clearly on your expectations and keep track of your progress.

Exercise 2.7 Look back at the goals and experiences described on your Learning Agenda or in your Goals Memo. Jot down some ideas about benchmarks for how many repetitions of each experience you contemplated. You may then tell your supervisor when you want more of an experience or that you are ready to move on to something else.

A second way of writing statements of measurable objectives toward meeting a goal focuses on how attainment of a goal would be defined, manifested, and measured. Objectives statements of this type should include

- standards for what would constitute achievement of the goal,
- active verbs that specify the behaviors that would be exhibited if the objective were met,
- results that can be objectively measured.

In some aspects of life, the standard defining success is unambiguous, for example, a single quantitative measure. A runner who wishes to set a record in the 100-meter sprint knows the standard defining success. Runners and trainers, however, might differ on optimum training objectives in such matters as strength, endurance, or concentration in pursuit of the ultimate goal of breaking the speed record.

Articulating standards by which to measure achievement can be one step toward achieving the goal. Consider the goal of "improve my research and writing." Careful thought about what makes a good legal researcher in itself may improve your research skills because of the review of research tools and strategies required. The runner's thoughtful review of what training regimen would improve her chances could provide analogous benefits.

If we asked a number of lawyers to define a good researcher, we likely would not find complete agreement, although we would expect themes to emerge in the answers. Consideration of questions to which there are not clear, single answers requires assessment of the weight to be given to different opinions. We likely would give greater weight to the opinion of lawyers with reputations for doing high quality research.

In formulating a standard for good legal research, you could review what you learned in first year legal research regarding standards. You could think of what others have said and ask others who you think are proficient, and so on. You might describe a good legal researcher as someone who

- knows how to use manual and automated research tools;
- understands how tools are organized in order to consider their strength and weakness for various research tasks;
- consistently finds sources efficiently, for example, with a minimum of expenditure of time and other resources;
- separates material found by degree of pertinence;
- produces answers that satisfy those who gave the assignment;
- is thorough enough that adversaries and colleagues do not often find relevant material that the researcher missed.

It may be useful to break down these statements further with respect to what needs to be learned to achieve the standard. For example, the first item might be broken down by enumerating the tools that a good legal researcher should be able to use. The number of available research tools is burgeoning so quickly that you may want to talk to lawyers in the externship about which tools they have found most effective for their legal work. You could ask the same questions of reference staff at your law library. Consider the range of tools that are available at your externship, for example, whether computerized research is an available option.

In addition to defining standards, consider how to measure their attainment. Measurement can be quantitative or qualitative. The runner may be able to set a quantitative measure for some training objectives, for example, pounds moved and repetitions on strength exercises, endurance goals in distances run. The runner's training objectives on technique or concentration may have to be judged by qualitative assessment by the runner and others who observe the runner. Few outcome objectives in externships will lend themselves easily to quantitative measures. More often, you will need to assess what you have done and consider the feedback of others.

A good researcher is someone who "produces answers that satisfy those who gave the assignment." If your supervisor knows you are interested in improving research skills, you may be given more feedback as you research.

Exercise 2.8 Look at the goals listed on your Learning Agenda/Goals Memo. What do you already know about standards to define accomplishments of your goals? What could you read or with whom could you talk in order to test your ideas on standards and get additional ideas to define accomplishment of the goal? Write some objectives statements for each goal that reflect standards for achievement. Include an active verb on how achievement would be demonstrated. Refer to a measurable outcome. Consider how and by whom the outcome would be measured. Recall the hypothetical's goal "develop my representation skills in criminal prosecution."

Suppose you wish to concentrate on the skill of fact investigation. How can you evaluate your progress on this skill? You might discipline yourself to look back at interviews and case preparation at later stages in a matter to ask yourself (and perhaps others as well) what you missed initially, consider why, and determine how to improve your efficiency in the future.

Differences Between Externs and Employees

You may have had an opportunity to observe a lawyer or other professional through a shadow program in which you follow someone around at work. You also may have read articles or books by authors who have been allowed to observe a work world, for example, to tag along on the pro-golf tour or observe the participants involved in designing and building a house. Such social scientists or journalists often only are observing, rather than being participant-observers who also are sharing in the work observed. Such observers may learn something about the skills performed by those observed, but a pure observer's role does not include the chance to do the work oneself and receive feedback on how well one did.

Chapter 12
on Observation

Observation can be a useful learning tool. The chance to see a skill modeled by an experienced lawyer can be very instructive. Observation may provide a model before you try a particular task. It may provide a basis for comparison with your own performance. Both observing the model and comparing it to your own work link the observation to a performance. Observation is most useful in skill development when it is combined with a chance to do some of the substantive work of the office and receive feedback on the performance.

Like externs, employees share in the work of an organization. How should an extern's experience differ from theirs? First, of course, the law school has educational goals when offering externships and has a responsibility to see that they are met. Generally, employees have a relationship with the employer without a third entity overseeing the relationship.

With a goal-setting employee and an *ideal* employer, the work assignment and feedback process may not look so different in the work situation versus the externship. Employees do their best work when employers take into account what workers seek from the experience and try to provide opportunities for workers to learn from the work. Even more so, in an externship the employer should undertake to provide learning tasks and opportunities for observation that will further particular educational goals. The fieldwork supervisor also should provide constructive feedback to the extern and insights on the placement's work to broaden the extern's understanding of the context of his or her work.

Chapter 3
on Getting Supervision

An externship supervisor should have sufficient knowledge and experience to teach skills or provide insights into practice and a commitment to take the time to do so. Even with the knowledge and commitment, however, novice learning from a practicing expert is not always simple. When performed by an expert, a complex task like lawyering appears seamless. Many experts are able to act instinctively on past learning without thinking step-by-step. In looking at potential externship supervisors, externship teachers and students need to consider the expert's level of expertise and how well the expert can introduce, explain, or coach the novice in beginning steps toward mastery. Chapter 3 provides suggestions on how the novice can cue the supervisor to break down the expert's performance into steps that can be understood and learned by the novice.

Feedback is an important component of learning from experience. Chapter 3 also explores what makes feedback useful and explains ways in which the supervisee can seek to enhance the value of the feedback received.

Although there are benefits in training employees, an employer can be justified in assigning employees to tasks the employer knows they can do well without further training. An externship, however, is undertaken to learn new skills. Thus, the supervisor should assign the extern tasks on which the supervisor expects performance to improve over time, not just tasks that the extern can do well on the first day.

Considering Permanent Employment at Your Placement

Some extern teachers and their faculty colleagues resist the notion that an objective of a student's externship can be getting a permanent job. This does not reflect lack of sympathy for the plight of job-searching students but expresses a concern that this goal will divert the student and program from a focus on education.

Perhaps there is no conflict between the objective of getting a permanent job and learning goals in the externship. Presumably, if you learn a great deal in your externship and you do a terrific job, you are more likely to get an offer than if you learned very little. For many employers, a self-starting and self-directed extern looks like the perfect employee.

On the other hand, there can be at least perceived conflicts between careerist and educational goals. Students who hope to get offers may be less willing to take risks. Such students may seek assignments that require only tasks they know they can perform well. Students may be reluctant to seek assignments that would offer opportunities to develop new skills and may avoid making waves. Students may take any assignment without protest, even if it involves excessive clerical work that is not appropriate for academic credit. They may not remind their supervisor of experiences that were promised but have not materialized or learning objectives that are not being addressed.

Consider the relation of externships to future job searches. If you would like to get a job at your externship, you may want to explore whether this is a realistic goal. The United States Attorney's office in Washington, D.C. has had a rule against hiring people directly from law school. When students told me they wanted to extern at the U.S. Attorney's office because they wanted a job there upon graduation, I told them about the policy. I also pointed out that some previous students had been hired by the U.S. Attorney after a judicial clerkship and that the experience had been valued in job interviews with other prosecutors and some firms. In other words, the experience might have indirect benefits, but it was unrealistic to assume a job after graduation would result.

It is a mistake to compromise learning goals based on perceptions about employability. The externship is a rare opportunity to seek what you want from legal experience rather than worrying about some of the complications that arise in permanent employment. You need to stretch yourself. You need to take some risks to learn. With most employers, these stretches and risks will not be a negative. Most supervisors will recognize the value of a student who says, "I haven't had much experience at X so I want to try it," but a few supervisors will seize on anything less than top performance to form a poor impression of a student's ability. It is useful to have a supervisor who will be willing to give a good reference, but it also is important to be able to pursue your learning goals without constantly looking over your shoulder to see what the supervisor thinks.

■ Appendix 2.1

Learning Agenda

Extern's Name	Supervisor's Name	Date of this Draft
Goals for the externship	*For each goal, list experience that you think would help in attaining that goal*	*Supervisor's comments on goals and experiences*
1.	1.a. b. c. d. e.	
2.	2.a. b. c. d. e.	
3.	3.a. b. c. d. e.	
4.	4.a. b. c. d. e.	

■ Appendix 2.2

Goals Memo

The Goals Memo is a statement of your goals in undertaking the externship and ideas on how to accomplish them. Your draft memo should be one or two typed pages and should be addressed to your placement supervisor and to your faculty supervisor.

The major purposes of the memo are to require you to consider what is most important to you in the experience, to encourage you to plot a tentative course to achieve those goals, and to provide you with a vehicle to communicate your thoughts to your supervisor. Your experience in the field will be shaped primarily by how carefully you formulate your goals. If you go into your fieldwork passively, thinking you will just see what happens and do what you are asked to do, your supervisor will determine your experience. On the other hand, if you have specific goals, they can lead you to the types of experience that you most desire.

Discussion of your goals with the placement supervisor should influence the assignments you are given. The articulation of goals encourages you to think of the field experience as an observation research project, to decide what you want to learn about, and to exercise control over how you spend your time.

Follow the directions in Chapter 2 on making the goals specific and challenging yourself to be sure your memo communicates clearly what you have in mind. Try a rough draft and then ask yourself

- Are these my real goals, or are they a means of accomplishing a more basic goal?
- Why am I really doing this?
- What do I expect to gain or learn?

Your faculty supervisor will provide deadlines for completion of the draft Goals Memo and explain the sequence for discussion with your placement supervisor and the faculty supervisor's review.

■ Appendix 2.3

Accepting and Declining Externships

Occasionally we receive irate phone calls or letters from attorneys at externship placements complaining that a CUA law student "accepted an externship with us, and has just called [or written] to tell us that s/he decided not to do the externship after all."

Such a call reflects poorly on the institution and on the individual student. Although such incidents are rare, they occur with enough frequency that we believe it may be useful to review some points of professional etiquette in accepting and declining externship opportunities.

1. You should approach each application for an externship as you approach employment applications.

2. Before accepting an externship, be certain that you fully understand the parameters of the externship.

3. Please communicate to any placement you are considering that your acceptance of the position for credit is always contingent on the approval of the placement by the Coordinator of Clinical Programs of the law school.

4. You may want to confirm an oral acceptance with an immediate written confirmation in which you sketch in some detail your understanding of your responsibilities and those of the placement site. You may wish to relate your understanding of the following topics:

   - start date,

   - department or division, if any,

   - supervisor,

   - days and times on site,

   - total number of hours to work during the semester,

   - last possible date of work (may be earlier, if hours are completed),

   - the nature of the tasks to be assigned,

   - opportunities for observation of the work of the placement site (for example, court observation if externing in judicial chambers, prosecutor's or public defender's office).

5. If you have made an application or serious inquiry with more than one potential placement, you should promptly notify any placement from which you hold out-

standing offers, or which may still be considering your application, of your decision to accept another offer.

6. When declining an offer, after thanking the organization for its interest in you, it is wise, but not necessary, to let the organization know where you plan to extern. This allows you to keep the lines of communication open for further contacts.

7. If you have accepted an offer of an externship from an organization, it is unprofessional behavior to decline to honor your commitment to that organization, if you later receive an offer from an organization for which you would rather work for pay or credit. If you have several applications pending, you may communicate that fact to each organization and request more time to consider an offer, but once you accept an offer, you should feel bound to honor your acceptance.

8. It sometimes happens that you are seeking both a paid position with one organization and an externship with another organization. You should fully disclose to both organizations your need for prompt action on your applications. However, if you accept the unpaid externship and then are offered the paid position, you should honor your commitment to the externship and accept the paid position only if you can capably manage both positions. You also should consult with your faculty supervisor about the conflicts of interest analysis to determine if simultaneous employment is permissible.

If you have any questions or problems, please contact the Coordinator of Clinical Programs.

■ Appendix 2.4

Timesheet

Student Name _____

Time Sheet #_____   due mm / dd / yy.

Reflection question to be turned in with time sheet. (Answer these questions on a separate sheet–preferably typed.)

1. Was there anything surprising or unexpected in your first days at the externship?

2. Do you have any reflections on how you spent your time at the externship thus far?

3. Note any problem, concerns, or any other point on which you would like feedback.

		HOW WAS TIME SPENT IN THE RECORDING PERIOD?									
DATE	TOTAL HOURS	LR	NLR	OBS	CC	W	DISC	ORG	CONV	CLER	OTHER	NOTES

The categories on the form are

Legal Research: This includes computerized or book research on cases, statutes, regulations, and so on.

Non-legal research: This includes things like checking out information on the world wide web, going to public records to collect information, making phone calls to gather information, and so on. Although the legal research and non-legal research categories may blur, I want a general ideal of how much time you spend on "traditional" legal research as opposed to looking to other sources or gathering other types of information.

Observation: This encompasses time for which you primarily are observing, rather than performing, a particular task, although time in this category might include taking some notes for your supervisor or being ready to hand over appropriate documents.

Client contact: This includes any time you are communicating with a client yourself orally, for example by interviewing, answering questions, or explaining things. If your supervisor is conducting the interview, put the time under observation, even if you ask a question or two. If it is really a joint interview in which you are playing an active role, put it under client contact. If you are drafting a letter to a client, list it as writing.

Writing: Record here time spent on any form of writing—legal memos, legal documents, client letters—at any stage in the process—initial draft, editing, revising, proofreading.

Discovery: This includes drafting of discovery requests, preparing responses to discovery, reviewing documents, preparing for depositions, and digesting depositions. Although drafting a discovery request is writing, put it in this category.

Organization in support of legal work: Record here time spent on things like reviewing and organizing client files or working on a system to retrieve sample pleadings—any type of organization that requires some legal knowledge and judgment, as opposed to a merely clerical task like photocopying.

Conversations/conferences with supervisor or co-workers: Include here all time spent talking with your supervisor or co-workers. If you want to differentiate between time spent on clarification of assignments and feedback versus other conversations, make a note in the final box.

Clerical: Include here things that do not require legal training or much exercise of professional judgment such as photocopying, answering phones, delivering pleadings to the court, and so on. If you occasionally pick up a call and take a message, you do not need to separate that out, but if you spend at least fifteen minutes on clerical/administrative duties of this sort, please record that time.

Other: If what you did does not fit in any of these categories, list the time here and note the activity.

The "Notes" section at the end provides space for you to give a little explanation on what you were doing on the particular day or to explain what "other" includes in this case. This, of course, can be expanded in the journal if you would like to comment further.

So to review the categories and abbreviations:

Legal Research/LR	Organization in support of legal work/ORG
Non-legal Research/NLR	Conversation/CONV
Observation/OBS	Clerical/CLER
Client Contact/CC	OTHER
Writing/W	NOTES—explanation or expansion
Discovery/DISC	

Chapter 3

Learning from Supervision

Liz Ryan Cole & Leah Wortham

Those having torches will pass them along to others.

— Plato

This entire book focuses on learning from practice—learning from real experience rather than in a classroom. Effective students set goals for their externship experience. They also do their best to apprentice with experienced and dedicated lawyers who also are good supervisors and teachers. What should a student do if those experienced and dedicated lawyers are not good supervisors and teachers? This chapter will help students maximize their ability to learn while being supervised in a legal practice setting.

Many fine lawyers are not good supervisors and teachers. Some people choose law as a profession under the mistaken assumption that because lawyers often work independently that means they work alone. They think they do not have and will not need to develop those skills necessary to supervise the work of others. By the time they discover the reality that lawyers spend much of their time supervising the work of others, they are already lawyers. Just because they must supervise, however, it does not automatically follow that they are good at supervision. The goal of this chapter is to teach you, the student, how to help your supervisor create an effective supervisory relationship. As a bonus, if you develop your skills as a supervisee, then you will very likely be a more effective supervisor when your turn comes.

If most lawyers' successes depend, at least in part, on using supervision to achieve the best quality results in the most efficient manner, one might question why

see *If you haven't yet set goals for your externship, go to* **Chapter 2** *first*

law schools spend so little time teaching about effective supervision. One reason may be that at least some of those who design the curriculum assume that good supervisors are "born, not made." We disagree. Many business and management schools devote considerable time to the subject. Some externship programs provide training for supervisors on many aspects of effective supervision. Some legal employers provide training for supervisors. We think this training can be very effective. Because you and your supervisors may not have had the advantage of learning about management and supervision in law school, we anticipate that the materials in this text and the experience of your externship will remedy this and provide you with a solid foundation.

Macro planning, micro planning, and feedback are all tools that will help to get the people around you—your supervisors in title or in fact—to make clear what they want you to do, what they think of your work, and how you can improve. In this context, macro planning is establishing long-term goals as one component of creating an effective supervisory relationship. When you macro plan you are setting and articulating goals for the semester and communicating these to the supervisor. Micro planning, or use of "assignment clarification" to establish the best approach and desired outcomes for each assignment, and "feedback," or communication between supervisor and supervisee, are the aspects of supervision we discuss in this chapter.

As an extern, you share the supervisor's goal of producing a quality product efficiently. You also want to impress your supervisor, experience minimum frustration, and avoid blind alleys. By learning when and how best to seek clarification of assignments, you should maximize the odds of producing the desired product the first time. Supervisors should give sufficient information about the task to allow externs to understand how to perform efficiently and what product is desired. Effective assignment of tasks reduces the odds that an extern will produce a useless product with the filing deadline three days closer than when the assignment was given. Despite this, many lawyer supervisors do not focus on what it takes to give a clear assignment. In order to maximize clarity in assignments you will use micro planning or "assignment clarification."

After you have submitted your work product you want to understand what you did well and what you need to do differently in the future. We call the aspect of communication used to get this information "effective feedback." When you learn how to elicit feedback, you will be more productive and efficient in the future.

Why is communication about work so difficult? When we ask students and supervisors to describe the characteristics of assignment clarification and effective feedback they almost always suggest many of the same components that education and management theorists identify as the essential characteristics for productive supervision. When, however, we ask students whether they have received helpful assignment clarification and feedback in legal jobs, their responses are discouraging. Students, whether in summer jobs or in other work settings, often get neither clear task assignments nor helpful feedback on their work. Why is there a gap between understanding and practice? We suspect the real difference comes out of the typical supervisor's belief that supervising is too hard emotionally and takes too much time from their "real" work. We know many lawyers in practice who believe that teaching law students is extremely time-consuming, involves "spoon-feeding," and interferes with their own efficient lawyering. One of your first jobs in your externship will be to address these preconceptions. By the time you complete this chapter, you will better understand the factors that sometimes prevent a supervisor from providing effective feedback and will learn how a supervisee might enhance the quality of the feedback received.

Becoming an effective supervisee is not easy. It is often said that the process of supervision falls into one of three categories: the good, the bad, and the ugly. The "good" relationship is one where the supervisor and supervisee are on the same wave length. The supervisor gives several staccato instructions. The supervisee nods intelligently, produces the work quickly and efficiently, and thanks the supervisor for permitting him to work with her. In a "bad" relationship, the supervisee creates a drain on the supervisor's time and requires handholding through each step of the process. The final work product is good, but the supervisor wonders if it would not have been faster and easier just to do it herself. All supervisors dread the "ugly" relationship. The supervisee does not "get it." The work product is late and has mistakes the supervisor can easily spot and probably some she cannot find without redoing the work. The supervisor cannot use the product and has to redo it or look for someone else to do it. It is a week closer to the deadline. She does not have time to redo the work *and* tell the extern his work is no good. In addition, she worries that the extern will be upset and might argue with her. She asks herself, who needs this?

Discussions of work problems can be unpleasant for the supervisee and the supervisor. The practical effect is that many lawyers avoid supervision as much as they can. What we and many experienced supervisors have learned, however, is that supervision, including conversations that are emotionally charged, does not have to be unpleasant. In fact, it may be extremely rewarding for both the supervisee and the supervisor. When supervision is working well—when a supervisee is part of an effective supervisory relationship—one sees a complex two-way relationship, which involves learning for both supervisor and supervisee. This type of supervision involves an exchange of ideas that go from student to lawyer and from lawyer to student. The process involves constant give and take. It may add some time in the beginning, but that investment can reduce the amount of work that must be redone and can promote efficiency in work on subsequent assignments. Lawyer, client, placement organization, and supervisee all can benefit. Some students and supervisors actually enjoy it.

Let us turn to the two aspects of supervision featured in this chapter: assignment clarification and effective feedback.

Assignment Clarification

Assume an extern receives this assignment at her placement.

Supervisor: I'd like to know what the requirements in Vermont are before a deeded septic easement can be deemed abandoned and if those requirements are different from those for abandoning other deeded easements.

What should the extern do?

> **Exercise 3.1** What are the things that the extern needs to know about the assignment in the example? What is the information that you generally need to know about an assignment to enhance the chances that you will produce what the supervisor wants? This and most other exercises in this chapter are appropriate for journal entries. Jot down some ideas before reading further.

Most fundamentally, the extern needs to know exactly what to do *and* what standards will be used to judge the work. In supervision theory, establishing what the extern should do and by what standards the extern will be judged can be accomplished in a step called an agreement conference. Sometimes, an agreement conference can be more successful if the supervisee simply asks follow-up questions.

In the easement assignment, the extern might respond to the supervisor's request by asking

- "When do you need this by?"

- "Are you interested in any law outside of Vermont? If so, where else do you want me to look?"

- "Do you want my conclusions only, or do you want a memo with cites? Do you want copies of the cases I've read? Or perhaps only the cases I thought were relevant?"

- "Who is my audience? Is there anyone other than you who will read what I give to you?"

- "What are the ways you will use this information? A letter to the client? A contract? A pleading?"

- "Do we already have any information here in the office about this client or problem?"

The supervisor may respond that the extern should begin his research with a particular legal encyclopedia and tell him to look in New Hampshire, Maine, Connecticut, Massachusetts, and New York as well as Vermont. She may want a memo with cites but tell the student not to copy the cases because she has WEST-LAW® on her desktop and easily can review any cases she wants. Finally, she may say that she wants this tomorrow to use over the weekend as she drafts a brief. This would lead the extern to remind the supervisor that he has classes all day tomorrow and to ask if submitting the work by Friday would be all right. The supervisor might respond that she is in court on Friday morning so 2:00 p.m. would be fine.

Simple? Yes, but just because it is simple and quick does not mean it is done. Imagine instead what could happen if there had been no clarification.

The scene is Thursday afternoon in the office: The supervisor *(S)* says, "Where is that student? I needed that memo today!" She asks her secretary to track the student down and rushes off to complete other tasks. She is frustrated.

On Friday morning, the extern *(E)* hurries to the office and discovers that *S* is in court. *E* now realizes that he did not have to work very late Thursday to get this memo done. He is frustrated. When *S* finally returns the following dialogue ensues.

S: "So, what did you find out about easements?"

E: "There are no cases in Vermont that distinguish septic easements from other easements."

S: "Well, that's not exactly what I asked. But tell me, where did you look? What cases did you find?"

E: "Oh, I didn't know you wanted the cases if the answer was that there were no differences."

S: To herself: "Expletive!! Now I know what I'll be doing this weekend!"

What a difference a few questions made!

Some possible answers to Exercise 3.1 include the following:

You may want to know *why* **S** wants to know. Often understanding how something will be used enables you to understand what to produce. Particularly in an externship, it also is useful for **S** to provide this information so a student can learn more about the "big picture" parts of learning, for example, how specific components fit into a strategy and how legal research and fact gathering relate to building a theory of the case.

The ideal supervisor would provide this context for its value in assignment clarification and enhancement of student learning, but the busy supervisor may skip this step. Consider how you could ask questions that acknowledge respect for the supervisor's choices about how much information to give and the constraints on her time but also provide you the needed information.

You may want to know *how* **S** likes answers to a question. Her response might provide a more precise understanding of how the product will be used and also might reveal matters of personal preference and work style. Think about the variations in ways that supervisors may want information returned and ways to ask about them. Perhaps it would be useful to ask if there is a model of other responses that **S** has liked? Would the supervisor find it helpful to have a log of your research trail to know what avenues you tried? Does she want copies of cases? Relevant pages? Does she like key phrases to be highlighted?

You, of course, want to know *when* **S** needs the product. It also likely will be helpful to understand how this deadline relates to the ultimate deadline—the previous *why* question. That will help you to understand more fully how nearly perfect your product is expected to be. If you have bad news for the supervisor on the feasibility of the deadline against your other responsibilities, it is better to make this information known now instead of at the time of a missed deadline.

You may want to know *if* there are any research tools that **S** recommends you use. The answer to this seemingly mechanical question also may draw out more information from **S** on what **S** already knows about the topic and on the desired product.

You may want to know *how much* effort **S** wants expended on the project. If you were a paid clerk in a law firm, a likely factor would be how much the lawyer believed the client was willing to spend on the project. Even if the circumstances of your externship mean this is not a factor, you likely have agreed to provide a finite number of hours in the externship, and **S** may wish to consider how **S** will "spend" those hours.

You may have other questions about the ultimate *what* of the assignment. Is it a draft of a brief that is desired or only a background memo? Is there a particular length that *S* has in mind? As described in the *how* question, does *S* want some of the raw research materials as well as the draft or memo?

These questions include some matters of *standards* for judgment, for example, the use to which the product will be put, the deadline, the form for submission. How else might you determine the standards expected? Can *S* give you an example of a similar product that *S* thought was very good?

Once you have this information we suggest you memorialize it. Once you have gotten as much clarification as you can, write down what you understand. It does not have to be long. Send or give it to the person who has given you the assignment. Summarize. It can be as simple as these four points:

"I have been asked to . . . ."

"I will begin the process by . . . (list books and other print and electronic resources if your assignment has a research component)."

"My audience for this assignment is . . . . It will ultimately be used for . . . ."

"The date you need this by is . . . ."

Even if you and your supervisor are in perfect agreement about all aspects of the task when you begin your work, your supervisor may continue to think about it, developing her thoughts over time. By the time you submit your assignment, your supervisor may have forgotten just what she asked you to do. It is good practice to be able to refer to your initial memo in the event there are differences of understanding. If it is sent by e-mail, it is easy for S to check a couple of days later and reply with a change in direction or an additional suggestion.

Exercise 3.2 Reread the previous paragraphs. Are they covering anything more than common sense questions anyone might need to know how to answer to assure that an assignment will provide what is needed? So why does a supervisor sometimes fail to give such guidance in the initial assignment? Jot down some of your ideas before reading further.

Here are some possibilities.

- *S* may forget how big the differences between a law student and an experienced attorney can be. The actual age difference in law students and their supervisors may be small, but the difference in law practice experience is likely to be significant. With practice, professional judgments become almost intuitive. It may require some thought for an experienced lawyer to break out the step-by-step process that a less experienced law student should pursue.

- As with a variety of day-to-day communication, we may come to know something well and forget that others do not have our level of knowledge. Have you ever worked so hard to research a paper that everything about the topic seemed "obvious" to you and then you were told by a reader that your points needed more explanation? How many times are we reminded that people cannot "read our minds"?

- *S* may be rushed and want to limit the time spent on explanation unless *S* sees, or you can help *S* see, that failure to give adequate explanation the first time can result in wasted time.

- *S* may not, in fact, have figured out exactly what *S* wants to know and why. In many collaborative relationships, the doer of the task ultimately may refine and develop what is to be done, but that is a high risk proposition for a new legal extern. If *S* does not know exactly what *S* wants, you need to think of a diplomatic strategy to clarify *S*'s thinking.

Thus far, we have given some examples of the kinds of questions that might be asked at the time of assignment to clarify the task. It is wise to have a pad and pen at hand during *every* meeting with a supervisor so you do not have to trust your memory on what was said.

What if more questions come up once you have started the project? It may be useful to ask at the outset where you can go for help if something comes up during the project. The response may be, "Come back and ask me," but the question also may elicit the information that *S* is going to be out of the office during the assignment period. *S* may suggest others who can help, but you may want to ask permission to frame the question as a hypothetical and get some help from the faculty supervisor at the law school, a professor in the field, or a classmate. Even if *S* is out of town or in court, *S* may suggest communication by e-mail, voice mail, or a note.

What if your supervisor seems impatient with questions? First, think back over your questions to the supervisor. Were they specific? Were they framed to communicate why you wanted to know and how the answer would be useful to *S*? It may be easier for *S* to respond to specific options like "Do you want copies of important cases that I find?" than a more general "In what form would you like my research?"

You also may consider whether there are other ways to get clarification. Are there others in the placement who often work with *S* and would have an idea about the particular assignment or at least about *S*'s general preferences? As mentioned earlier, can you ask *S* (or someone else knowledgeable) for a sample of similar products? Are there previous experiences with *S* from which you have learned about how *S* likes things to be done?

If you have been introduced to the Myers-Briggs Type Indicator® this would be a good time to think about your preferences and those your supervisor may have. Are you an Extrovert who is thinking out loud about a problem when your supervisor is an Introvert who gets cranky when interrupted while focusing on another task? Do you need to schedule a regular time to talk with your supervisor?

Finally, negative reactions to legitimate requests for clarification raise the question whether such a person is suited to be a supervisor in an externship program. Your experience should be discussed with the faculty supervisor. The faculty supervisor may have suggestions about other ways to approach the supervisor. The faculty supervisor also may need to take this information into account in preparing other students for the placement or in considering whether to continue the placement if *S* is not open to reasonable requests for clarification from an extern.

Exercise 3.3 Think of a recent assignment. Write out the answers to these questions.

- What was I told?

- What did I discover I needed to know but was not told?

- Which things should I have asked about? Were there things that came up that could not have been anticipated? How should I have handled the unanticipated questions?

- If questions came up later, how did I decide what to do? What else could I have done to resolve them?

- If I were going to take on this assignment again what would I do differently?

Effective Feedback

Receiving feedback on our work and incorporating what we have learned from that feedback is one of the most common ways we learn from experience. The term feedback comes from the electronics field and was incorporated later into the language of space science. A rocket going into space is guided by signals that bounce back to Earth where revised signals are generated to modify the rocket's course. This transmission, which leads to changes in trajectory, is called feedback. As with the rocket, helpful feedback guides a supervisee in charting a course toward producing the work desired and improving skills. It is in the supervisor's interest to give effective feedback that a supervisee can "hear" without becoming defensive so that the supervisee will provide what the supervisor wants. Nonetheless, just as supervisors sometimes fail to clarify an assignment adequately, they often fail to give feedback that will lead to performance improvement.

see Chapter 6 *on Conflicts*

Consider the following feedback memos. The extern has been assigned to write a brief in support of a motion for disqualification of John Taylor, who represents Allison Gordon. Ms. Gordon is suing the firm's client, Harry Jones. Taylor formerly represented Jones. The brief contends that Taylor should be disqualified from representation adverse to Jones in the current matter because the previous and present matters are substantially related, thus meeting the test for disqualification in this jurisdiction's version of Model Rule of Professional Conduct 1.9 and the related case law.

MEMORANDUM

To: Eric(a) Extern

From: Sam(antha) Supervisor

Re: Draft Brief in the Jones case

You seem to have done a great deal of research. Your writing needs work in several respects. I made a number of comments on the brief, and you can see the changes I made in reworking the final draft. This summarizes some language patterns that I think need work.

You dilute the power of what you have to say in several ways:

1. Strip out legalese expressions such as: above-mentioned, aforementioned, henceforward, thenceforth, to wit, and so on.

2. Avoid passive verbs and surplus words. For example, substitute "Jones said . . ." for "A statement was made by Jones to the effect that . . . ." "Bound" substitutes for "was binding upon." "When" can substitute for "at the time of." "Does not" is better than "does not operate to." I have marked a number of examples of passive voice and participles, infinitives, gerunds, and other noun or adjective forms denoting action when a finite verb would have done better.

3. A former professor of mine used to say, "Whenever you are tempted to say 'clearly' or 'obviously,' STOP. It must mean that your proposition is neither clear nor obvious." "Clearly" and "obviously" rarely strengthen an argument. Watch overuse of adverbs in general.

You need a clearer road map of your argument. Use a topic sentence at the beginning of an argument to forecast what a section will say. On page three, a topic sentence could make clear why you are reciting the facts. For example, "In Taylor's prior representation of Jones, confidences important to this litigation could have been divulged." Then identify the confidences that might have been shared in that representation. Sum up with a characterization favorable to our client's position. For example, "Effective representation in *Wadsworth v. Jones* required communication of information about Jones's solvency. That information would be useful in Gordon's current claim against Jones."

Arguments should be listed in order of their strength and the ease with which a judge could adopt them. Our jurisdiction's version of Model Rule 1.9 has not been construed by the courts. We are asking the court to adopt the majority definition of "substantial relationship" and to reject a contention that the Rule permits screening to cure imputed disqualification. That also is the majority view, and the view retained by the ABA. It is a much smaller leap to ask the judge to construe the rule in line with the majority view than to ask for a decision based on public policy.

Make the arguments in this order: 1. Rule explication—this is what the Rule says. 2. Follow the majority—this is how they have construed the Rule. 3. Explain the public policy reasons supporting this view. I dropped the legislative history argument. The Model Rules went through too many revisions, and there has been too much case law to make the Rules' drafters' 1981 comments and other legislative history in the ABA of much relevance.

Use key terms consistently. You refer to the initial meeting, the first interview, the first client conference, and the first talk that Jones had with Taylor. I gather you mean all to refer to the same event, the meeting on June 14, 2005. Pick a single descriptive phrase and stick with it.

After you have gotten on paper the arguments you wish to make, it may help to outline the points and reconsider their order. In Section II, you seem to make four or five subpoints in support of your argument. It is not clear where one starts and another ends.

I do not think our courts have found that general information providing "insight" about a client is relevant to a finding of substantial relationship. Review all the cases again and look at cases on this point from all over the United States. If you do not think your argument needs revision in light of that, photocopy for me all the cases on which you rely so I can read them.

MEMORANDUM

To: Eric(a) Extern

From: Sam(antha) Supervisor

Re: Draft Brief in the Jones case

Your draft brief reflected extensive and thorough research. I was amazed that you found the 1981 drafters' original research comments, but I decided not to use that part of the brief.

Your public policy argument on the construction of Model Rule 1.9 was nicely stated. I think it's better to start with the rules construction argument so I moved the policy argument to after the rules' construction argument.

Your writing could use tightening. Say things clearly and succinctly.

It is helpful to give the reader a little better sense of where you are going.

I dropped the point about "insight" into the client.

Thanks a lot for all your hard work. Your research was a big help to me in getting the brief done on time. Tightening your writing and doing more road mapping will help me to use more of your work as written, but this was a terrific first effort.

Exercise 3.4 What would you think and feel if you received each of the memos above? What do you think was helpful and not helpful about each? Jot down some reactions before reading further.

,

Some students say they would be upset by the tone of the first while others profess not to care and prefer its greater specificity and suggestions of particular alternatives proposed. Most acknowledge more useful content in the first while some complain that it focuses more on style than substance.

Exercise 3.5 What are the characteristics of feedback that are useful in helping the extern to be more likely to produce the product that the supervisor desires in the future? Make a list before reading further.

Webster's *New World Dictionary* gives one definition of feedback as "a process in which the factors that produce a result are themselves modified, corrected, strengthened, etc. by that result." One often hears people talk about positive and negative feedback. We prefer the terms affirming (what you may think of as a positive statement) and corrective (what you may think of as a negative statement). Affirming feedback affirms and reinforces behavior one would like to see repeated in the future. Corrective feedback suggests changes in behaviors that one does not want repeated in the future and offers constructive recommendations.

What Makes Feedback Effective?

Step One: Reflection

The first step is a *reflection* of the performance on which feedback is being given so the supervisee knows precisely that what the supervisor is commenting upon and "sees" it through the reflection of the supervisor. This usually involves an identification and a description of the point to be addressed. For example, the supervisor might comment, "On page 3, you began the argument about why screening in a law firm should not be allowed to cure an imputed disqualification with the public policy reasons."

An effective reflection is one in which behavior is *described* in a *nonjudgmental* manner with *examples* that are *specific*. To understand nonjudgmental, think of a factual description that a lay witness would be allowed to make. Contrast this to a conclusion that an expert would be permitted to make after a foundation was laid.

Consider the differences in these two lists of non-legal examples of pure description.

Descriptive, Specific, and Nonjudgmental

- The chair is made of maple. It has four legs. The back is made of six tubular wooden slats.

- My classmate is male, six-feet tall, and has black hair and freckles.

- At 10:25, 15 minutes after the class started, Kathy walked into the classroom. She sat down, dropped her books, and put her raincoat, which had drops of water on it, on the back of her chair. Jim and I looked at her.

Judgmental/opinion

- The chair is pretty, elegant, comfortable. . . .

- My classmate has a warm smile, is attractive, is strong . . . .

- Kathy came late to class. She looked frazzled. She disrupted the class by the way she came in and dropped her wet raincoat that then dripped all over everything.

When feedback begins with a conclusory opinion, it may trigger defensiveness in the hearer or fail to communicate the point.

Step Two: Reaction

After a nonjudgmental description with examples specific enough to identify the point, the person giving feedback reacts to it. In most instances, it is useful to begin by gaining an *understanding* of what the person receiving feedback was trying to do, for example, why particular methods were chosen.

Why did you decide to begin with the public policy reasons against screening to cure imputed disqualification?

Reactions are opinion. If they come from a supervisor, they are opinions that "count," but it is well to acknowledge they are opinions. When my students look at the Eric(a) Extern memos, some react to the first as "style" rather than "substance." I might counter that the style suggestions given are conventional ones that are accepted as indicia of good writing generally and powerful legal writing in particular. Even if (unlike these) they are not widely accepted, the supervisor's preferences set the standards for work done for that person. I once suggested to a student that he delete words like "aforementioned" and "heretofore." He responded that he once wrote in the simpler manner I advocated until he started working at a law firm where the lawyers all wrote that way. At the firm, he might venture that his teacher suggested deletion of such terms, but ultimately, on matters of style—as opposed to ethics—"when in Rome . . . ."

If you are in the position of giving feedback, remember that it may be easier to "take" if it is stated as a personal opinion. Use "I think . . . ," "In my opinion . . . ," "I prefer . . ." rather than making the statement absolute. When you receive feedback from a supervisor who does not follow this rule, you may want to mentally edit the comments you are hearing to remind yourself these are the opinions of the speaker. These opinions may be generally accepted and should be considered for adoption in one's future repertoire of performance. At the least, they reflect this supervisor's preferences to adopt in future work for this person.

Step Three: Prescriptive Feedback

Prescriptive feedback offers specifics on how things should be done in the future. It often is useful to give examples of alternatives that the person giving feedback thinks would have been better. As with the reflection step, it is easy to fail to communicate exactly what is meant. In Feedback Memo B, does the supervisor's direction to the extern to "tighten up" the extern's writing provide the extern with useful information for the future? Feedback Memo A provides some alternative language illustrating the changes the supervisor would like.

Once the point on which feedback is being given has been *reflected* (with description, examples, and specificity) and the supervisor has given a *reaction*, it should be clearer what the supervisor wanted and why the performance is thought to be insufficient. At this point, a good supervisor often asks what the extern thinks would have been a good alternative. It can be useful for the supervisor and extern to brainstorm alternatives that might have been more effective.

When my students discuss Feedback Memos A and B, they usually come up with the important elements of the model previously presented: specificity, examples, opinion recognized as such, affirmation of positive performance as well as things to be changed, examples of alternatives preferred. Students generally report not receiving this type of useful feedback in past work situations.

Exercise 3.6 Why do lawyers fail to give useful feedback to the people they supervise? Make notes of your answer before reading the following.

Here are some common responses.

- They do not want to take the time.

- They did not take the time to figure out what about the performance they did not like and the further time to suggest alternatives.

- They are afraid of hurting the supervisee's feelings and getting a defensive reaction.

- They find it easier to identify and focus on the negative than to reinforce the positive.

- They do not think about what it takes to motivate people.

What others were on your list?

Exercise 3.7 What can you as an extern do to enhance the possibility of getting effective feedback? When time is an obstacle, what are some ways to address the problem? Note some possibilities before reading further.

If the product was a draft to be finalized and sent out, the supervisor was required to make judgments about your work. The supervisor either left it as it was or changed it. If the supervisor did not return a copy of the marked-up draft, ask for it from the supervisor or the secretary. If the draft was edited on the computer, compare the changes. Are some conclusions obvious from the comparisons? If you are not sure about the reasons for some changes, prepare some questions for the supervisor. Of course, these questions should sound like an earnest extern seeking to improve his work not those of hostile opposing counsel.

Using examples from the feedback memos, one might make statements like

"I see that you moved the public policy arguments against screening to the end of the section." Then, if the supervisor does not leap in and start telling you why he moved them, you can say, "I am interested in knowing the reasons to learn for my next effort."

"I see that you took out words like 'aforementioned.' I thought lawyers wrote that way. Should such words never be used or just not in these circumstances?"

"Information memos," assignments that ask for background memos for the attorney or assignments to "find some cases" and provide copies or an oral briefing, present a challenging situation for the supervisee eliciting feedback. In these circumstances, there is no final copy against which you can compare your draft to glean patterns in the changes. When a supervisor decides to leave or revise a draft, the supervisor, at least implicitly, makes some judgments about what was preferred. In making the changes, the supervisor may not have articulated the reasons, but when you ask a question, the supervisor probably can articulate the reason for a change. In an information memo, on the other hand, the supervisor often makes a much more general judgment that something is "enough," "okay," or not. Of course, it also is difficult for the supervisor to know what you did not find if she does not already know the law on the point. (If she did, she probably would not have given you the assignment.) As a supervisee you might say, "I often have difficulty deciding when I have done enough research. How do you decide? And what do you look for in a memo of this sort, that gives you the confidence to rely on it?"

Part of the question on helpful feedback goes back to the Chapter 2 questions on your objectives for the externship. If one of your primary goals is improvement in research and writing, you may want to ask about whether you could receive some assignment that would involve a draft of a final product that must go out. You also might say this to your supervisor:

"I realize that there may not be any reason for you to critique my writing style and the logic of my arguments in a background memo, but I know that critique of my writing will be important in my clerkship next summer. Could you take one memo and tear it apart for me to tell me how you think it could be better written? That would really help me for the future."

The previous example also addresses another obstacle—fear of hurting another's feelings. In an externship, it is easy to see yourself as the "powerless" one who is there to please the supervisor. It may be harder for you to see that most supervisors want to be liked by their externs. Moreover, your supervisor may have had an unpleasant experience with an extern who became very defensive about suggestions for change. You can go a great deal of the way toward getting effective feedback on your work if you tell the supervisor that a critique is important to you. You can list the areas in which you particularly would like reaction. You can give thanks and other positive reinforcement for the critique, even if hearing it "hurts" a little more than you thought it would.

When supervisors are very busy, and most are, consider what seems to be the best time and place to approach them. If the supervisor is someone who likes to talk while driving, are there opportunities to ride with the supervisor and talk? Do things wind down at the end of the day such that the supervisor would be more relaxed and willing to talk after 5:00 p.m.? For most supervisors, it is also wise to schedule specific time on their calendars for feedback on projects and any questions that have come up in your work, rather than waylaying the supervisor in the hallway.

Summary

The **DESUSA** of Effective Feedback

DESCRIBE behavior in a nonjudgmental manner using

EXAMPLES that are

SPECIFIC. Ask questions to

UNDERSTAND what the supervisee was trying to accomplish and listen to why the choices were made. Characterize your reaction to the supervisee's choices in a

SUBJECTIVE manner. For example, "I think. . .," "In my opinion . . . ." If you are giving corrective rather than affirming feedback, describe the

ALTERNATIVES that you think would have been better with enough specificity to clarify your meaning. Ask the supervisee for suggestions of other alternatives now that discussion may have made the task and your thoughts clearer. Supervisor and supervisee may brainstorm together on alternative courses.

Use **DESCRIPTION, EXAMPLES, SPECIFICITY,** and **UNDERSTANDING** to identify items on which you are giving affirming feedback and those on which you are giving corrective feedback.

This summary is written from the supervisor's point of view, but there are a number of things that you, as the supervisee, can do to move an interaction closer to this model of effective feedback. If your supervisor's comments are not clear, ask for examples that illustrate general comments so you are clear about what is being said. If the supervisor's reaction seems to assume a premise different from the one you followed, explain what you were thinking. Remember that comments are the reactions of the individual supervisor. Weigh their validity. They may reflect generally accepted standards in the legal profession and may guide your future work. They may reflect a style choice of the individual attorney, but that is still relevant to work done for this attorney in the future. Even if your supervisor does not offer or invite suggestions of alternatives, look for opportunities to test your understanding of the feedback with the supervisor.

These principles also can provide guidance in giving feedback to your supervisor on things you might like to change in the externship. If you would like to change some aspect of your experience, you may wish to describe the situation to communicate your reactions, to explain why you would like things to be different, and propose the desired change. Here are some examples:

> You had a meeting with opposing counsel on the Jones case on Tuesday. It's really of interest to me to see what happens in informal exchanges among lawyers. Will there be other meetings with counsel or in chambers that will be coming up that I could attend?

> For the last three weeks, the secretary has asked me to cover the phones for two hours while I am here. That is a quarter of the time I am here each week. I'm happy to help out, but the law school expects me to be involved in the type of work that lawyers do.

The extern has described an event specifically but nonjudgmentally. As a reaction, the student might have only said how he or she thought or felt about this situation, but here the extern has chosen to cite the law school's requirements.

After this reflection and reaction, the student might propose a specific alternative or it might be effective to ask the lawyer for suggestions.

> I don't want to be unhelpful, but are there alternatives for covering the phones?

Exercise 3.8 Think of something you would like to change about your externship. Write a plan of how you could improve the situation. Consider whom to talk to, what to say, when to initiate the conversation, and what reaction you are likely to get.

I sometimes ask students to practice these principles in giving feedback on student presentations from others in the class. In reviewing these written feedback forms, I notice how much easier it seems for all of us to give corrective rather than affirming feedback. Affirming feedback is equally if not more important than corrective feedback. Part of the negative student reaction to Feedback Memo A is its corrective tone. Many people are able to hear and incorporate corrective feedback more effectively when it is combined with a sincere affirmation of things done right.

Affirming feedback is more than "good job." Effective affirmative feedback should describe with examples and specificity if you want it to be effective in encouraging good future performance. You cannot assume that people will repeat the things you liked about their performance if your positive reaction is not articulated. When your supervisor does something you like, for example, gives effective feedback on your performance, be sure that your response communicates your pleasure. Again, remember to describe with specificity what you liked so the point is clear.

> I found it very helpful when you gave examples by line editing those three paragraphs to show what you meant about more active voice and succinct writing. I understand better how you want things done in the future, and I appreciate the feedback on my writing.

Here the supervisor took the time to give examples and explanation. Unless the supervisor hears from the extern that it was useful, the supervisor may not be as motivated to take that time in the future.

Exercise 3.9 Suppose your supervisor asks for feedback on the supervisor's performance in clarifying assignments, providing feedback, etc. Script the comments that you would give based on your experience with your supervisor thus far. Use the principles of reflection, reaction, and prescriptive feedback in your comments.

Finally, remember that for feedback to be most effective it needs to be invited and be given in a timely fashion. Your supervisor probably will assume that you, by virtue of your appearance at a work site, are inviting feedback. Nonetheless, you should explicitly invite feedback and then reinforce the behaviors you want from your supervisor by using these same feedback techniques. Do you see how?

Exercise 3.10 Imagine your supervisor has just spent 30 minutes with you reviewing a significant written product. You are ready to revise your work and give her a finished product tomorrow. Not only did her questions help clarify the portion of the analysis that was somewhat confused, but her comments on your resources made you feel validated for the care you took with the research. How would you give feedback to your supervisor?

FURTHER READING

Alice Alexander and Jeffrey Smith, *A Practical Guide to Cooperative Supervision for Law Students and Legal Employers*, 29 LAW OFF. ECON. & MGMT. 207-26 (1988-89).

Jack Ende, MD, *Feedback in Clinical Medical Education*, 250 A.M.A. 777 (Aug. 12, 1983).

Steve Maher, *In Praise of Folly: A Defense of Practice Supervision in Clinical Legal Education*, 69 NEB. L. REV. 537 (1990).

Michael Meltsner, James Rowan, and Daniel Givelber, *The Bike Tour Leader's Dilemma: Talking About Supervision*, 13 VT. L. REV. 399 (1989).

Richard Neumann, *A Preliminary Inquiry into the Art of Critique*, 40 HASTINGS L. J. 725 (1989).

Donald A Schön, *Educating the Reflective Legal Practitioner*, 2 CLIN. L. REV. 231 (1995).

Chapter 4

Ethical Issues in Externships:
An Introduction

Lisa G. Lerman

A Regulated Profession

The state supreme courts have a primary role in the governance of the legal profession. The high courts decide who should be admitted to practice and adopt ethics codes to govern the conduct of lawyers. In most states, these rules are based in part on the American Bar Association's Model Rules of Professional Conduct, but there is substantial variation among the state rules.

In most states, the requirements for admission to the bar include graduation from an accredited law school, obtaining a passing score on the bar exam, and being found to possess the necessary "character and fitness" to practice law. Upon admission to the bar, each lawyer agrees to comply with the state rules of professional conduct. Violation of these rules can result in a disciplinary proceeding and can lead to disbarment, suspension, reprimand, or some other sanction.

Law students who work as externs in practice settings should read the applicable state ethics rules at the beginning of the field experience. Even though law students are not formally subject to discipline unless they are licensed under the student practice rule, study of the rules is an important part of orientation to professional life. Also, if a law student engages in conduct that violates the ethics code, the supervisor could be subject to discipline and the student's bar admission might be jeopardized.

Students licensed under student practice rules may appear in court on behalf of clients. Some states allow admission under the student practice rule only of law students enrolled in clinical courses taught by full-time instructors representing indigent clients. Other states allow some supervised externs to be admitted under the student practice rules.

Civil and Criminal Liability for Lawyer Misconduct

Lawyers, like other people, are bound by a whole array of statutory and regulatory law. Lawyers who commit crimes may be prosecuted under general criminal statutes; a surprising number of lawyers have gone to prison for crimes such as mail fraud, securities fraud, or nonpayment of taxes. Lawyers who injure others may be subject to civil liability. A lawyer who harms a client by conduct that is dishonest, incompetent, or otherwise violates accepted professional standards might have to pay civil damages or endure criminal penalties. A client who suffers harm as a result of the lawyer's conduct might sue his lawyer for legal malpractice, breach of fiduciary duty, or breach of contract. If the client prevails, the lawyer might be ordered to pay money damages. Most lawyers carry malpractice insurance, which offers indemnification for some civil liability.

In addition to the law that governs the general public, lawyers are bound by an array of more specific legal rules. Lawyers who litigate, for example, may be sanctioned for filing frivolous suits, for withholding documents in discovery, or for other violations of the rules of practice adopted by each court. Government lawyers are bound to comply with stringent conflict of interest statutes. Securities and banking lawyers must comply with various statutes and regulations that govern those industries.

Law students working as externs should be aware that the law that governs any given practice area may extend far beyond the rules of professional conduct. Reading the state ethics code is a good place to start, but there is much more to learn about the law that governs lawyers. Field experience provides opportunities to interact with and learn from experienced lawyers about this body of law. When you encounter a professional dilemma as an extern, the following sources may assist you in understanding the applicable law.

■ AMERICAN BAR ASSOCIATION, MODEL RULES OF PROFESSIONAL CONDUCT

The Model Rules of Professional Conduct were drafted and approved by the American Bar Association. After adoption by the ABA, the Model Rules are then reviewed by each state supreme court, which is free to adopt the recommended proposals or to vary from them. The Model Rules provide a good general reference, but when seeking guidance on particular practice issues, always refer to the applicable state ethics code rather than to the Model Rules. Both the Model Rules and the state codes are available through the website of the ABA Center for Professional Responsibility at http://www.abanet.org/cpr/home.html.

The American Bar Association maintains a copyright on its Model Rules and imposes stringent restrictions on their quotation in works published by anyone other than the ABA. For example, the ABA requires that any rule be quoted in its entirety and accompanied by all of the comments that follow the rule. The ethics codes as adopted by the states, however, are not copyrighted. Like other legal rules, they are in the public domain. The Delaware Rules of Professional Conduct are nearly identical to the Model Rules, so in this book, we quote from the Delaware Rules. If a quoted Delaware rule differs from the corresponding Model Rule, the difference is explained in a footnote.

■ AMERICAN LAW INSTITUTE, RESTATEMENT (THIRD) OF THE LAW GOVERNING LAWYERS

The American Law Institute produced this excellent synthesis of the body of law that governs lawyers. The Restatement includes information about ethics codes, rules of civil liability for legal malpractice and breach of fiduciary duty, bases for court sanctions against lawyers, rules on attorney-client privilege, protection of attorney work product, and other statutory, regulatory and case law.

■ ABA/BNA, LAWYERS' MANUAL ON PROFESSIONAL CONDUCT

This looseleaf service provides a comprehensive and up-to-date reference source on the whole range of lawyer law. Its scope is as broad as the Restatement, but its coverage is more detailed.

■ THE AMERICAN LEGAL ETHICS LIBRARY

This is a database that includes information on the state ethics codes and other sources of authority on regulation of lawyers. It is found at http://www.law.cornell.edu/ethics/.

■ ADVISORY ETHICS OPINIONS

The ABA and the state and local bar association ethics committees write advisory opinions for lawyers who seek guidance on ethical questions. These opinions are published in bar journals, on the Internet, and elsewhere. When you encounter an ethical dilemma, you might seek guidance in the advisory ethics opinions in your jurisdiction. Alternatively, you might call or write the bar ethics committee in your jurisdiction to seek guidance. Some ethics committees provide informal telephone guidance as well as formal or informal written advice on ethics issues.

Ethical Duties in the Workplace

This section concerns ethical duties related to the supervisory structure of the workplace itself, lawyers' duty to report serious professional misconduct of other lawyers, and restrictions on practice by law students.

Dilemmas that arise in the course of an externship can be awkward and intimidating, especially if they involve decisions or conduct of others in the workplace. The extern usually is a relatively inexperienced, temporary worker who may hope to make a good impression, make contacts, get a good recommendation, or even get a job at the placement after graduation. Depending on the nature of the problem, the extern may confront a conflict between these goals and a professional duty or moral obligation to turn down an assignment, question a supervisor's judgment, consult another lawyer (in or out of the office), blow the whistle, or resign. The following scenarios raise some examples of these difficult issues. While scenarios of this sort may be uncommon, it is worthwhile to consider these problems in hypothetical form, because they tend to arise in situations that are emotionally charged and that require a quick response with significant risk if the wrong decision is made. Being prepared by having thought through the issues in advance will reduce that risk.

Professional Standards for Workplace Issues

Supervisors, subordinate lawyers, and law students

Lawyers must abide by the state rules of professional conduct in the jurisdictions where they practice. Lawyers also must ensure that law clerks, secretaries, paralegals, and legal externs follow the rules. For example, employees in law firms should be trained to protect client confidences. Rules 5.1 and 5.3 explain that lawyers who have managerial authority should supervise, set policies, provide training, or take other measures to assure that all employees, both lawyers and non-lawyers, comply with the rules. If a subordinate employee (lawyer or non-lawyer) violates a rule, the supervising lawyer may be held responsible by the disciplinary authorities if the supervisor directed the conduct or knew about it and failed to intervene.

The rules require your supervisors to help you to understand the requirements and prohibitions of the ethics rules. For law students with little prior legal experience, this may sound reassuring. As a practical matter, however, you should assume responsibility for your own professional conduct by reviewing the relevant rules and seeking guidance when you need it. If you are authorized to practice under a student practice rule, you have an independent personal duty of compliance. Even if you are not admitted under a student practice rule, you will soon be admitted to practice and bound by the rules, so it is advisable to conform your work to the ethics code while you are in law school. Although you may not be subject to discipline for violating the code, your supervisor could be disciplined for your misconduct. Thus, your obligation to understand the governing rules is a serious one.

What if your supervisor directs you to do something that you know is improper? Consider an extreme example. Suppose that a supervisor directed an extern to forge the signature of the firm's managing partner on a check? Would the rules discussed above insulate the extern from the consequences of doing what the extern was told to do? They would not. First of all, forgery is a felony. Many people are prosecuted and punished for crimes they committed at the direction of another person. The rules of professional conduct apply in addition to, not in place of, other law. Also, forgery or other dishonest conduct would be a serious violation of Rule 8.4. While no one is subject to discipline prior to bar admission, the student could later be denied admission to the bar based on prior conduct like forging a signature on a check even if he was not criminally charged. The rules oblige your supervisors to guide you, but you must keep your moral compass by your side at all times and take responsibility for your own compliance with law.

What if your supervisor tells you to do something that seems wrong, but you are not sure? Do you follow the instruction or not? The rules provide guidance on this question. Rule 5.2 emphasizes that each lawyer is responsible for her own conduct, but if the lawyer "acts in accordance with a supervisory lawyer's reasonable resolution of an arguable question of professional duty," then the lawyer is not in violation of the rules and will not be subject to discipline. If you are asked to do something that might be unethical or unlawful, you should do some research and get professional advice from someone you trust. If there is a reasonable basis for thinking that the conduct is proper, you may defer to the judgment of your supervisor. If not, then you have a true workplace dilemma.

Duty to report misconduct

Every lawyer is considered to be "an officer of the court" and has a responsibility to protect our legal system. To some extent, the legal profession is "self-regulated." This means that lawyers are expected to have sufficient professional integrity to police their own profession. A central feature of this system of self-regulation is the duty imposed on lawyers in nearly every state by Rule 8.3(a), which requires states:

A lawyer who knows that another lawyer has committed a violation of the Rules of Professional Conduct that raises a substantial question as to that lawyer's honesty, trustworthiness or fitness as a lawyer in other respects, shall inform the appropriate professional authority.

The rule does not require that a lawyer report every violation of a rule. A lawyer who sees misconduct must assess whether the other lawyer's behavior is so serious as to raise a substantial question about her honesty, trustworthiness, or fitness. Reporting is required only if the lawyer "knows" that such a violation has occurred. Rule 1.0(f) explains that "knowledge" means "actual knowledge" that "may be inferred from circumstances." Also, Rule 8.3(c) explains that in reporting misconduct, a lawyer is not required to disclose client confidences. Does this exception excuse lawyers from reporting misconduct by lawyers in their own firms? Usually misconduct relating to another lawyer's work on a client matter can be disclosed without revealing client information, even if the reporting lawyer is employed by the same law firm.

Legal externs are not obliged to report unethical conduct to the bar counsel, but lawyers are. This onerous duty is worth some advance reflection. An extern who encounters what may be serious misconduct by a lawyer should be aware that other lawyers are bound by this rule. If you see a lawyer engaging in conduct that seems improper, you should consider consulting another lawyer in the office or one of your professors to better assess the situation. You might conclude that the facts are unclear, or that the propriety of the conduct is unclear, but you might encounter conduct that cannot go unreported to someone—at least to someone else in the law office.

Restrictions on law practice by students

Law students may not engage in the practice of law unless they are granted a limited admission under student practice rules. "Practice of law" is defined by state common law. While definitions vary, most states define the term to include representation of clients in court cases, administrative proceedings, or in transactions; drafting legal documents such as wills and contracts for clients; giving oral or written legal advice to clients; or any other work that calls for the professional judgment of a lawyer. "Giving legal advice" is commonly understood to involve explanation of how the law might apply to a particular set of facts. A non-lawyer may give information to others about the law (for example, explaining to a victim of domestic abuse how to get a civil protection order), but if a non-lawyer explains to another person how the law might apply to a particular set of facts, this advice might cross the line into unauthorized practice of law.

Most states have specific rules that allow law students to be authorized to appear in court, usually only if they are in law school clinical courses and if they represent indigent clients. Students who are not licensed under student practice rules may work on client matters under the supervision of lawyers, but they may not speak in court proceedings. Many administrative agencies (such as the Social Security Administration) allow both lawyers and non-lawyers to appear as advocates, so law students are allowed to handle some administrative hearings without being authorized under the student practice rules.

PROBLEM 4.1
A Chance to Try Cases

Fitz MacMillan is a second year law student. He hopes to become a prosecutor and eventually to go into politics. This semester, he is an extern with the county attorney's office. About a month into the semester, Fitz's supervisor, Sam Galway, told Fitz that he was impressed with his work and had decided to let him try some misdemeanor cases. Fitz was amazed and flattered. Also, he realized that this experience would be invaluable, and that if he did a good job, it might improve the odds of his being hired after graduation. Even so, he was a little uneasy.

Fitz mentioned to Sam that he was not admitted under the student practice rule, which he thought only applied to students supervised by professors. Sam said "Don't worry about it. I know you'll do a good job. When you stand up in court, just introduce yourself by name. This office is so big that the judges don't know all the lawyers. They'll just assume that you are new."

What should Fitz do?

Practical guidance on unauthorized practice

If your externship involves work on client matters or giving legal advice, read the rules on unauthorized practice in your state. If you are not admitted under a student practice rule, any legal work that you do, such as interviewing or advising lay people or drafting documents, must be supervised by a lawyer. Apart from the obvious utility of having the guidance of a more experienced person, your supervisor's oversight will protect you from crossing the line into unauthorized practice of law. As a general matter, you should avoid giving even the most casual legal advice to friends and family members until after you are admitted to the bar. Although your friends and family are unlikely to report you for unauthorized practice, there is a real risk that you might give advice that is incomplete or incorrect and that the person you are advising could suffer harm as a result.

Workplace Dilemmas

Competence and diligence

A lawyer who represents a client must provide representation that is both "competent" and "diligent." Competence, under Rule 1.1, "requires the knowledge, skill, thoroughness and preparation reasonably necessary for the representation." This rule requires that a lawyer who takes on a matter in a particular area of law must possess the necessary skills and knowledge before undertaking the matter, or the lawyer must obtain the relevant skills and knowledge through study or through affiliation with a lawyer who has experience in the type of work involved. Rule 1.3 explains that a lawyer also must be diligent in pursuing a matter on behalf of a client. The lawyer must devote the time and attention needed to learn the facts and to research the law and must then pursue the required analysis, drafting, negotiation, and advocacy in a prompt and professional manner. These broad standards are interpreted to require of each lawyer at least the level of competence and diligence that would be exercised by an ordinary member of the profession.

see⟩ **Appendix,** *pages 459-463*

What are the ingredients of competent and diligent representation? The ABA's MacCrate Report identified ten fundamental lawyering skills and four core lawyering values "with which a well-trained generalist should be familiar before assuming ultimate responsibility for a client." The listed skills include problem-solving, legal analysis and reasoning, legal research, factual investigation, oral and written communication, counseling, negotiation, litigation and alternative dispute resolution procedures, organization and management of legal work, and recognizing and resolving ethical dilemmas. One way to assess your own progress in professional training is to assess your own competency in each of these skill areas. Consider (if you know enough about your future professional path) which skills are likely to be important to your performance as a lawyer. You can use this process to identify "holes" in your legal education and then look for simulation or clinical courses that will help you to acquire the needed competencies.

An externship in a practice setting offers a law student the opportunity to observe practicing lawyers and to consider what is required to become a competent and diligent lawyer. Often the best way to understand competence and diligence is to see examples of law practice by lawyers whose work falls below these standards. Your placement supervisor probably will provide a positive professional model, so you may have to look elsewhere to understand why these standards are so important.

Exercise 4.1 Spend a few hours in your local courthouse. You may have opportunities to observe court proceedings as part of your externship. If not, take yourself on a field trip. Most court proceedings are open to the public. Often you can get information from one of the court clerks about what is happening in each courtroom and which proceedings may be observed. In general, you may simply walk into a courtroom and sit quietly in one of the seats behind the bar and watch whatever is going on. If you wind up in a courtroom where the proceedings are boring or too hard to understand, you can just slip out and try another courtroom. You may find it interesting to observe proceedings involving criminal, domestic relations, landlord-tenant, or small claims cases. In many jurisdictions, it is possible to observe lawyer disciplinary hearings. You can call your local bar counsel's office to ask whether you might sit in on a hearing.

Your primary task is to observe and evaluate the performance of the lawyers and the judges. Because you will not have read the pleadings, you may not fully understand the substance of the matters being heard. Even so, you can observe how the lawyers and judges do their work. Are they well-organized? Well-prepared? Is their conduct professional? If you were the client of each lawyer you observe, would you feel satisfied with the representation? Allow yourself to observe any and all aspects of the proceeding. You might get interested in the role of a law clerk or the reactions of people in the audience.

Note taking is permitted in some but not all courtrooms. If you are permitted to take notes, record your observations during the proceedings. Otherwise, take a break between observations, and find a place to sit and write down what you have seen and what you think about it. After your court observation is completed, write a journal entry about the most interesting things you saw and your reactions. Consider the implications of your observations for your own professional development.

Many law students who do court observation are very surprised that some of the lawyers they observe do not exhibit even minimal standards of competence or diligence. By recording your observations about the conduct that concerns you, you may gain perspective on law practice. For many students, this experience is a great confidence-builder. Whatever you may lack in knowledge and experience, you can make up for by careful preparation.

While most legal externs do not see professional conduct at their placements that falls below minimum standards of competence and diligence, there are some who do. Consider what you would do in the following situation.

PROBLEM 4.2
The Unreturned Phone Calls

Rebecca Bromberg accepted an externship with Mishkin & Cowle, a small firm that represents clients in criminal, domestic relations, and child abuse cases. Rebecca was to spend Tuesdays and Thursdays at the office, mainly working with Samantha Cowle.

When Rebecca came in to the office, Samantha often was not there but left assignments for Rebecca on her desk chair. The assignments tended to be cryptic, things like "Read the Gonzales file and write a complaint," or "Write a summary judgment motion for the Unger case." Rebecca tried to do as she was asked, but most of the time she felt like she had no idea what she was doing. She had no prior experience drafting legal documents.

When Samantha did come to the office, she tended to show up around eleven in the morning, rush around for a couple of hours trying to catch up, and then she would leave for lunch. Rebecca initially thought that Samantha was just terribly busy. She was frustrated because she could not get time to talk with Samantha about her assignments, and she got no feedback at all on the work that she turned in. Rebecca wondered if her own work was so bad that Samantha couldn't afford to take time to help her to do better.

After a few weeks, Rebecca began to realize that something was really wrong. She often heard Samantha's secretary, Ernie Kemp, on the phone with Samantha's clients, saying things like "No, I'm sorry, Mrs. ___, Ms. Cowle is not in today.... Yes, I gave her your messages.... Yes, I will be sure to let her know that you called again." One day when Samantha came back to the office after a long lunch, she smelled of alcohol and left again after an hour. The next week, when Rebecca opened a file drawer in Samantha's office looking for a client file, she found a large bottle of gin.

Once Rebecca was in the office and Ernie was out sick, so Rebecca was asked to answer the lines that Ernie usually covered. That day Rebecca talked to a number of Samantha's clients. All of them were angry and frustrated that they could not reach their lawyer. One was a woman who was facing possible termination of her parental rights. She said there was a hearing scheduled for the following day, and she had no idea if Samantha would appear. She said that she had not had any contact with Samantha since an initial interview two months before, when she had told Samantha her story and given her a check for $5,000.

If you were in Rebecca's shoes, what would you do?

Truthfulness

Under Rule 8.4(c), lawyers are obliged to avoid all "dishonesty, fraud, deceit or misrepresentation." While there are some circumstances in which a lawyer engaging in advocacy on behalf of a client might withhold information from an opposing counsel or might select what information to present (or not to present) in court, lawyers owe their primary loyalty to clients and are expected to be honest in dealings with their clients. Rule 1.4 mandates communication and consultation with clients. Rule 7.1 prohibits any "false or misleading communication about the lawyer or the lawyer's services." Despite the requirements of these rules, sometimes lawyers are not entirely candid with their clients. A lawyer who lies to or deceives a client or another person can sometimes present another workplace ethical dilemma.

PROBLEM 4.3
Some Questions about Billing Practices

Tim Connolly works as an extern at Goldberg & Lamont, a small general practice law firm. Tim spends about half his time on a *pro bono* case in which the firm is representing a group of patients in a public psychiatric hospital in a lawsuit demanding improved services and living conditions. The other half of his time, Tim works on various matters for paying clients. Tim's supervisor, Corey Lamont, asked Tim to keep careful records of all of his time, noting which matter he is working on and what he is doing. This is relevant even for the *pro bono* case, because the firm will file a fee petition if its clients prevail.

Several weeks into the placement, Elham Bolton, the firm's bookkeeper, comes to see Tim to go over his time records. She points out that Tim recorded 4.4 hours for the day he observed Corey taking a deposition in a child support matter. Elham said that Corey had recorded 7.6 hours for the same deposition. She wondered if he had made a mistake in recording his time.

"No mistake," Tim told her. "I'm new to this timekeeping business, so I'm extremely careful."

"Okay," said Elham, "but I already asked Corey, and he confirmed that the deposition went on for over seven hours."

"That's weird, because I was there the whole time," Tim replied. "We started just after nine and ended between 1:00 and 1:30."

"Perhaps he added some hours to compensate for some time he hadn't billed," Elham suggested. "In any event, I can't send the bill to the client listing you as 4.4 and Corey as 7.6, because it doesn't make sense. Maybe I'll just bill six hours for each of you."

"Wait," said Tim. "I didn't realize the firm was billing for my time. I didn't really do anything during the deposition except take notes and help locate a few exhibits."

"Oh, I didn't realize they hadn't told you. Your time is billed out at $85 per hour, just like the other law clerks," Elham explained.

"Gosh, I wish I had known that," Tim replied. "I would have tried to get things done more quickly. But I thought the firm wasn't billing for my time, because I'm getting credit instead of getting paid."

"Well, now you know," said Elham.

Tim is concerned about this news. He is upset that he was not told earlier that clients were being billed for his time. He suspects that the clients do not know that he is an unpaid extern rather than a paid law clerk. Also, he is concerned about Elham's apparent plan to add some of Corey's recorded hours to his time records.

Evaluate Tim's concerns and identify what he might do about them. What would you do if you were in Tim's situation?

Abuses of Power

Many students have placement supervisors who are wonderful professional role models and good mentors. Most supervisors, however, have various personal and professional strengths and weaknesses. Some lawyers' behavior toward their subordinates occasionally turns abusive or predatory. The following problem invites exploration of possible responses to such conduct.

PROBLEM 4.4

An Uncomfortable Workplace

Gwen Ormond was an extern in the United States Senate, working for Senator Boyd of Nebraska. She was having a mixed experience: some interesting work on a judicial confirmation, a couple of good research assignments, but too much time answering phones and responding to constituent letters. Usually, Gwen did not really mind pitching in with the administrative work; it seemed logical because she was the most junior person in the office. One day, however, she came to class feeling really upset by her experiences on the Hill. She explained what happened.

I feel like a baby for complaining about this, but Nancy Shaw, my supervisor, is just a b**** sometimes! She's always in a rush, and often she gives me assignments with virtually no explanation of what I'm supposed to do. I try to figure it out, and I do the best work I can, but today she came to my desk as soon as I arrived and started screaming at me because I'd distributed a "Dear Colleague" letter that had two typographical errors in it to all the other senators. This was my fault, because I had proofed the letter, printed it, run it through the autopen machine, and sent it out. But it was just two small typos! She yelled at me for about ten minutes in front of all the other staff. I don't think I've ever felt so humiliated in my life. I mean, I know that Nancy has a bad temper, but she called me a stupid cow! It was just so insulting.

After I came back from a good cry in the ladies' room, I settled down and made some progress on a research project. I was searching the web for ammunition that Senator Boyd could use to oppose a judicial nominee. About three that afternoon, John Chapman, the senior legislative assistant, called me into his office and said that "the Senator" wanted me to show up at this fundraiser tomorrow night. John said, "He asked me to give you this message personally—he really wants to see you there." Then, get this!, he said, "Just wear a silk dress or something—the senator likes silk."

Well, for one, I don't own a silk dress. For another, I don't want to go to this party. I told him I was busy. He said "Cancel your other engagement, whatever it is. This is important." He wouldn't take no for an answer!

What should Gwen do in response to her bad day? Should she say or do anything about Nancy's temper tantrum? Should she go to the party? In considering Gwen's dilemma, evaluate whether either Nancy or John, the lawyers on the senator's staff, have engaged in professional misconduct.

Conclusion

We hope that you will not encounter any issues as serious as those raised in the problems presented in this chapter, but you might. Those problems are based on true stories. Now and then law students are faced with very difficult dilemmas. This chapter and those that follow aspire to assist you in sorting through both minor and major ethical dilemmas.

FURTHER READING

AMERICAN BAR ASSOCIATION, SECTION ON LEGAL EDUCATION AND ADMISSION TO THE BAR, REPORT OF THE TASK FORCE ON LAW SCHOOLS AND THE PROFESSION: NARROWING THE GAP (Robert MacCrate ed., 1992).

Alexis Anderson, Arlene Kanter & Cindy Slane, *Ethics in Externships: Confidentiality, Conflicts, and Competence Issues in the Field and in the Classroom*, 10 CLIN. L. REV. 473 (2004).

Peter Joy & Robert Keuhn, *Conflicts and Competency Issues in Law Clinic Practice*, 9 CLIN. L. REV. 493 (2002).

Lisa G. Lerman, *Professional and Ethical Issues in Legal Externships: Fostering Commitment to Public Service*, 67 FORDHAM. L. REV. 2295 (1999).

LISA G. LERMAN & PHILIP G. SCHRAG, ETHICAL PROBLEMS IN THE PRACTICE OF LAW (2005).

DEBORAH RHODE & GEOFFREY HAZARD, JR. PROFESSIONAL RESPONSIBILITY AND REGULATION (2d ed., 2007).

Chapter 5

Ethical Issues in Externships:
Confidentiality

Alexis Anderson

The Scope of the Confidentiality Obligation

Confidentiality is one of the hallmarks of any lawyer-client relationship. Lawyers promise it; clients rely on it; state disciplinary boards demand it. If you become an extern in an organization that represents a client or clients, you become part of the legal team obligated to protect information related to the representation of clients. In addition, whether or not your workplace engages in direct client representation, you will become privy to other sensitive information that your employer will want you to protect. Confidentiality helps ensure client candor and trust, which are key to an effective lawyer-client relationship. Therefore, it will be incumbent on you, with guidance from your fieldwork supervisor and faculty instructor, to safeguard all confidential workplace information.

Protection of Confidential Information

Rule 1.6(a) establishes a broad and mandatory rule: "A lawyer shall not reveal information relating to the representation of a client" unless the lawyer is permitted to do so by one of the exceptions listed in Rule 1.6(b) or by another rule. This duty of confidentiality attaches when an individual consults a lawyer for legal advice, even if the lawyer does not accept that individual as a client. The duty protects communications between lawyer and client and all other information related to the representation, regardless of its source. A lawyer is obliged to protect as confidential information learned from witness interviews, research, discovery, and even information that is in the public domain.

Balancing the confidentiality duty to clients with other important public policies has been one of the most contentious issues in the adoption of the ABA Model Rules. This controversy often has been replicated in the states as they decide whether to adopt the Model Rules provisions on confidentiality or modify them. From their original enactment, the Model Rules gave lawyers discretion to reveal confidential client information if necessary to prevent a client from committing a crime that poses a threat of imminent death or substantial bodily harm. Efforts to broaden a lawyer's discretion to reveal confidences to prevent or remedy harm have led to endless debate. The ABA several times rejected proposals to add another exception for serious economic injury flowing from a client crime or fraud. In August 2003, after publicity surrounding Enron and other corporate scandals and in the face of Congressional action on the Sarbanes-Oxley Act, the ABA adopted recommendations from its Corporate Responsibility Task Force to include such an exception. By that time, more than forty states' rules allowed for disclosure of a crime or fraud that would result or had resulted in serious economic injury. Here is the current text of the Delaware Rule 1.6:

Rule 1.6 Confidentiality of Information

(a) A lawyer shall not reveal information relating to the representation of a client unless the client gives informed consent, the disclosure is impliedly authorized in order to carry out the representation, or the disclosure is permitted by paragraph (b).

(b) A lawyer may reveal information relating to the representation of a client to the extent the lawyer reasonably believes necessary:

(1) to prevent reasonably certain death or substantial bodily harm;

(2) to prevent the client from committing a crime or fraud that is reasonably certain to result in substantial injury to the financial interests or property of another and in furtherance of which the client has used or is using the lawyer's services;

(3) to prevent, mitigate, or rectify substantial injury to the financial interests or property of another that is reasonably certain to result or has resulted from the client's commission of a crime or fraud in furtherance of which the client has used the lawyer's services;

(4) to secure legal advice about the lawyer's compliance with these Rules;

(5) to establish a claim or defense on behalf of the lawyer in a controversy between the lawyer and the client, to establish a defense to a criminal charge or civil claim against the lawyer based upon conduct in which the client was involved, or to respond to allegations in any proceeding concerning the lawyer's representation of the client; or

(6) to comply with other law or a court order.

Other rules place further limits on a lawyer's duty to maintain confidences. For example, Rule 1.13 establishes another discretionary exception to Rule 1.6. A lawyer who represents an organization may disclose otherwise confidential information to prevent injury to the organization if the lawyer knows that a constituent of the organization has done something illegal or for which the entity may be held liable, if the action or omission will seriously damage the organization, and if the organization's highest authority refuses to act after the matter had been "reported up" to that authority.

Rule 3.3 specifies some additional exceptions to Rule 1.6, when disclosure of otherwise confidential information may be required because of an overriding duty of candor to a tribunal. (This is explained in Chapter 7 on Ethical Duties to Tribunals and Third Parties.) In some instances, a lawyer's duties to third parties likewise could require revelation. Rule 4.1(b) provides that a lawyer shall not knowingly "fail to disclose a material fact when disclosure is necessary to avoid assisting a criminal or fraudulent act by a client unless disclosure is prohibited by Rule 1.6." Because Rule 1.6 allows revelation to prevent, mitigate, or rectify a fraud, Rule 4.1(b) *requires* disclosure if silence would assist a fraud. Rule 1.6 does not explain that there are some situations in which a lawyer *must* disclose confidences, but a careful reading of the rules reveals this obligation.

In an externship in which a student is assisting a lawyer rather than acting as a lawyer, the fieldwork supervisor will decide whether a disclosure is permitted or required. Your own judgment will more often be concerned with honoring basic confidentiality duties. A careless comment or action by an extern could reveal information protected by Rule 1.6 and even could constitute a waiver of attorney-client privilege. Conversely, if a supervisor *fails* to make a disclosure required by the rules, an extern will be faced with the decision whether to challenge the supervisor's decision or to report the supervisor's conduct within the organization or to the disciplinary authorities.

In addition to ensuring the protection of client secrets, workplaces often have rules to safeguard other sensitive information. For example, a corporation may have procedures in place to protect proprietary information. Judges have internal rules designed to maintain the integrity of the judicial process and to protect confidential matters within their chambers. As you embark on your fieldwork, you should consult the ethical rules of your jurisdiction and ask your fieldwork supervisor about the confidentiality rules in your workplace. Then you must learn to conduct yourself in a manner that complies with these rules.

See Model Rules of Professional Conduct, Rule 1.13. While most references in chapters 4-7 are to the Delaware Rules of Professional Conduct, in this instance we refer to the Model Rules. Delaware has not adopted the "reporting out" provision of the Model Rules. The ABA adopted the "reporting out" language in August 2003 in response to the recommendations of the ABA Corporate Responsibility Task Force.

Relationship Between Confidential Information and Attorney-client Privilege

The lawyers ethical duty to protect confidences is related to, but distinct from, the rules of evidence that establish the attorney-client privilege and work-product doctrine. Confidential communications between a lawyer and a client relating to legal advice or legal services are protected by the attorney-client privilege. The Restatement of the Law Governing Lawyers (§§68-86) and Proposed Federal Rule of Evidence 503 provide useful summaries of the basic doctrine of attorney-client privilege, although state law varies on some points. To trigger the privilege, the communication, which can be oral, written, or electronic, must be made between privileged persons (which include the lawyer's staff) in private and for the purpose of seeking or providing legal advice or legal services.

The scope of the evidentiary privilege has been such a contentious issue that Congress did not include the proposals on the various privileges when it enacted the Federal Rules of Evidence. However, the proposed rule on attorney-client privilege has been adopted as law, on a district-by-district basis, by many federal districts. The proposed rule also has had considerable influence on state law. While Rule 1.6 concerns the ethical and fiduciary duty of lawyer to client, the privilege rule concerns whether matters within its scope are admissible in court. When the privilege applies, neither the lawyer nor the client can be compelled to testify regarding the protected information.

Information prepared for, or in anticipation of, litigation likewise may be protected from disclosure by work-product immunity. MR 1.6, Comment 3; Restatement §§87-93; FRCP 26(b)(3). Generally, the information shielded by either the attorney-client privilege or the attorney work-product doctrine is a subset of the larger category of information protected by the ethical rules on confidentiality.

Application of Confidentiality Rules to Externships

Given the broad sweep of the ethical rule requiring confidentiality and the professional duty to protect workplace secrets, is not the only safe course to keep completely mum about what you are doing at your externship? To adopt such a blanket prohibition, though, would undermine your ability to learn from practice and rob you of the opportunity to reflect on your externship experience. If you could not talk about your work at all, how could you complete journal entries, participate in seminar discussions with externs placed in other settings, or seek guidance on supervision matters and other ethical issues from fellow students or your faculty supervisor?

Would not a "gag rule" deprive you of an important opportunity to learn about when and how you may talk about your legal work without running afoul of confidentiality duties?

If you participate in an externship seminar, your discussions with your instructor and with other students, and your submission of journal entries connect you and your fieldwork supervisor (and, by extension, the clients, organization, or chambers you serve) to your law school community. This connection can be the source of ethical tension because neither your fellow students nor your faculty supervisor is part of the attorney-client relationship (or the legal staff) at your field placement. Hence the challenge: if you are to extract maximum learning from your externship experience by sharing those experiences with your faculty supervisor and seminar classmates while honoring your professional obligations as a lawyer in training, you will have to learn how to "talk shop" without disclosing confidential information.

To determine how best to navigate the confidentiality waters at your placement, you should seek guidance from your fieldwork and faculty supervisors before you discuss any aspect of your work with someone outside of your externship organization. The following exercise will help you learn and manage your confidentiality duties during your externship.

> **Exercise 5.1** Keeping in mind the material in this chapter, what questions do you have about your confidentiality obligations? Consider to whom you owe the duty of confidentiality. Does your placement provide direct service to clients? If not, are there any workplace secrets that nonetheless must be maintained? What is the source of those requirements?

If you wish to keep copies of your own work product from your externship, consult your fieldwork supervisor about workplace rules, and what, if any, information must be redacted. If you are interested in using redacted copies of your work product as writing samples for prospective employers, ask your fieldwork supervisor for permission. If your faculty supervisor requires that you turn in copies of your work product, be sure that your field supervisor understands this requirement and permits you to do so. Write a journal entry about what you may or may not discuss or reveal about your work. Learn what the ethical rules in your jurisdiction require and what workplace procedures also must be respected.

If your placement has given guidance on confidentiality, evaluate the relationship between the directions you received and the obligation imposed by the state confidentiality rules. Are the boundaries articulated by your supervisor more restrictive or less restrictive than the relevant rules? If there is a discrepancy between your supervisor's instructions and the state rules, what accounts for it? Which binds you?

One of the best ways to ensure that you understand the confidentiality mandate is to analyze the confidentiality rules in context. To that end, consider the scenarios presented below.

PROBLEM 5.1
"Talking Shop" Outside the Workplace

The evening after her first day at her externship, Meredith Blackburn went to dinner with her roommate and told the following story:

I just started my externship at Harmon, Guerney & Brown. When they offered me a chance to extern, I jumped at the chance. Even though it will be for credit not money, it will still be a great résumé builder. This is my big chance to see the inside of a big firm.

They told me not all the work would require major brainpower. I told them I was pleased to have the opportunity and would do any legal assignment.

Anyway, you wouldn't believe what I got for my first assignment! They asked me to proofread our client's new will. You won't believe who the client is! Mayor Virginia Wood! Okay, all I was doing at this point was reading stuff in her file, but it sure was interesting reading. Of course I can't tell you what is in her will, but I'll tell you one thing. There are going to be a lot of angry relatives when everyone finds out how she decided to dispose of her money!!

Questions about Problem 5.1

1. Did Meredith violate MR 1.6 in her conversation with her roommate? If so, which of her comments are improper? Do you have enough information to answer that question? What else do you need to know? If Meredith's client had not been a public figure, would your analysis change? Does the nature of the legal work (for example, juvenile case, highly publicized criminal prosecution, private business transaction) matter?

2. Apart from whether Meredith's conduct violates an ethical rule, what do you think about what she said? Can you articulate a principle from Meredith's conduct about what constraints lawyers or law students should impose on themselves in discussing client matters?

3. Assume that Meredith and her roommate are chatting over dinner later in the semester. Meredith recounts her experiences working on a different matter. Her second case assignment involves her work with a criminal defense lawyer at her firm on a matter that has received significant media attention. Meredith is careful not to use the client's actual name, but describes the new client as a suspected terrorist known as the "Shoe Bomber." Is that precaution sufficient to avoid violation of Rule 1.6?

4. Let us change the scenario again. Assume Meredith has just begun a placement at a local prosecutor's office and she has been assigned to assist with the prosecution of the "Shoe Bomber." Is she permitted to refer to her plum case assignment by that label during dinner conversation with her roommate? Who is the client of the prosecutor, and by extension, Meredith? If Meredith mentions that she is working on the prosecution of the "Shoe Bomber" case, what does she need to do to avoid violation of Rule 1.6?

5. Assume Meredith is externing with the local federal district court judge who has been assigned to preside in the "Shoe Bomber" case. Judges do not have "clients." To whom does Meredith owe her loyalty? What, if any, confidentiality concerns are involved here? May she mention to her dinner partner that she is working on the "Shoe Bomber" case?

During 2001, federal officials arrested an airline passenger who carried an explosive device on board the plane implanted in his shoe. Hence, he became known as the "Shoe Bomber." He was later tried and convicted of terrorism charges. See http://en.wikipedia.org/wiki/Richard_Reid_shoe_bomber (last visited March 16, 2007).

A good starting point in protecting client confidences is to refrain from mentioning the names of clients to anyone except your co-workers. More may be required to avoid revelation of client confidences. Context is very important. What might constitute appropriate safeguarding of client information in a big city may not be adequate in a small town setting (for example, one of many criminal prosecutions in a major city vs. the marquee trial in a rural community). Therefore, even if you do not use client identifiers, sharing details about your work in some situations may not satisfy your duty to protect client confidences.

See MR 1.6(a), Comment. 4; see also, MR 1.6(b)(4). Whether your faculty supervisor may render legal advice may be controlled by whether she is authorized to practice in your school's jurisdiction. Your instructor can point you to appropriate resources for an ethical consultation even if she cannot provide formal legal assistance.

Should you confront a situation in which you are unsure of your ethical duty, you should first consult your fieldwork supervisor, who is best positioned to instruct you in the proper handling of confidential information. In addition, consider consulting with your faculty supervisor. It is much easier to resolve confidentiality dilemmas before any disclosure has occurred. Do not wrestle with confidentiality issues alone.

PROBLEM 5.2
"What Merger?"

At the beginning of each meeting of an externship seminar for students working in corporate general counsel's offices, the faculty supervisor asks students for an update on placement activities. Georgia Anastas, who works in the in-house legal department of a large, publicly traded company, responds to the professor's inquiry in a despairing tone:

"Things have been pretty awful for the last two weeks."

"What's the problem?" the professor asks.

"It seems as though no one has any time for me," Georgia responds. "They're all too busy working on the merger."

"Is the merger public knowledge?" the professor asks with trepidation.

Georgia hesitates as she begins to grasp the significance of the question. "No, it isn't," she replies.

What, if any, ethical considerations are involved in this problem? Do the same restrictions apply if you are talking about your work with a roommate, a fellow extern, or your instructor? How might Georgia's disclosures impact her fellow students? Would your concerns be any different if Georgia had only written about her malaise in a journal rather than describing it in seminar?

How should Georgia proceed now that the proverbial cat is out of the bag?

PROBLEM 5.3
What You Can Take Away

Before law school, Rick Mendez was in a band that made some CDs. His placement this term is with the in-house legal department of a major record label. In his final journal reflecting on his externship experience, he wrote the following entry:

> *I now understand the fine points of negotiating a music deal— the issues on which artists have some flexibility to negotiate and the issues on which they do not. Those key points affect the label's decision to give a better deal. Now I can see the stupid things I did with my own band, and I can't wait to share this expertise with my friends to help them get the best deals possible. In fact, some of my music friends will be negotiating with the same label for whom I just externed. Won't that be a great extra plus from this experience!*

This problem also raises questions about whether Rick's loyalty to his client may be compromised by his self-interest. See Chapter 6 on Conflicts; see also Rule 1.8(b) regarding use of information relating to representation of a client to his disadvantage.

What, if any, ethical questions are raised by Rick's desire to use his on-the-site training for his and his friends' advantage? If Rick does not tell anyone the name of the record company for whom he externed, can he share the business tips he learned?

Suppose you want ethical guidance from your instructor or from the other students in your seminar. They are not part of the lawyering team at your workplace and therefore cannot become privy to workplace secrets. The most effective way to obtain advice without breaching confidentiality is to avoid disclosure of information that could identify the client and to pose your dilemma as a hypothetical. Comment 4 to Rule 1.6(a) encourages consultation to ensure compliance by condoning the use of hypotheticals "so long as there is no reasonable likelihood that the listener will be able to ascertain the identity of the client or the situation involved."

PROBLEM 5.4
The Attachment That Goes Astray

Carl Tanner, who is externing at a firm downtown, has just written the following journal entry for his faculty supervisor, but he is unsure whether he should send it.

During my externship, I received a copy of an e-mail which my field-work supervisor, Duane, had sent to a client. The e-mail referred to an attached memorandum offering advice on a particular legal issue I had researched. I opened the document with pride, assuming I would find a copy of the memo I had produced. I was shocked to discover that Duane had mistakenly attached the wrong document. In fact, the attached memo contained legal advice for another client. I brought the matter to Duane's attention. He was quick to express regret for the error. He asked me to send the correct attachment to the client. I questioned whether additional reme-dial steps needed to be taken. Should we request that the client destroy the erroneously forwarded document? Should we tell the client whose informa-tion had been leaked that the accident had happened? Duane basically rebuffed my questions and made clear that I should not press the matter further. This whole situation is still bothering me, though. I'm upset that we made this mistake and about my supervisor's response to it. I really think more needs to be done.

What, if anything, would you recommend that Carl do? Should he tell his faculty supervisor? If so, how? Can he seek advice from other stu-dents in the seminar or from other attorneys at his placement? If he were to seek guidance from others, what repercussions might result—to him, to Duane, to his instructor, or to the externship program? Would Carl's legal memo still be protected from disclosure if an adverse party were to demand its production?

PROBLEM 5.5
The Emotional Strain

Rosaline Watson, who is externing at a local Victim Rights' Center, submitted the following e-mail to her faculty supervisor:

My client, I'll call her Sue, is in a terrible situation. She is worried that the estranged father of her two children could become abusive. After hearing some of the threats he's made, I counseled her to go into court immediately and seek a restraining order (RO). But she said she was really scared to do that given how small her town is. She's worried that her hus-band's brothers will find out and come after her. She's also concerned about how the local families will react when they hear about the RO. Her kids are old enough that some of their peers might make life hard for them at school. I told her to think about her options and let me know if she'd like us to help her get a restraining order. Nearly a week went by and I was very concerned about her safety. Yesterday, she called back and said she did want our assistance in getting a RO. Evidently, her daughter's teacher had just called to advise that the school had filed a report of possible abuse by the father with the Department of Social Services. My supervisor and I got an ex parte *order that very day.*

Legally, it was a great result, but I'm still worried about Sue. My supervisor suggested I call the local police to warn them that Sue and her family might need their help. The duty officer said the department already knew the father all too well. I also reminded Sue to keep a cell phone with her at all times. But I can't help worrying about her safety. What if she or her daughter suffers because I didn't do enough?

Do you see any confidentiality issues in Rosaline's decision to share her emotionally draining case with her faculty instructor? Did she properly sanitize her description of her client's confidential information in her e-mail? Is there any difference between sharing the information with her instructor and sharing it with other students in the externship seminar? How might Rosaline get support and ethical guidance from her faculty supervisor?

Given the report to the government agency and the subsequent issuance of the restraining order, are Sue's revelations about the father's conduct still confidential? Are the professional duties that govern the teacher and the police officer different than those that govern lawyers?

Conclusion

Taken literally, Rule 1.6 bars lawyers from revealing any "information relating to representation of a client" absent exceptions or client consent. Workplace secrets, too, require protection. Now that you have had opportunities to study the confidentiality rules, to analyze the problems presented in this chapter, and to discuss the issues with your peers and faculty supervisor, you are ready to make the hard, but necessary, judgments that will allow you to "talk shop" respectfully, professionally, and consistent with all applicable confidentiality obligations.

Chapter 6

Ethical Issues in Externships:
Conflicts of Interest

Cindy Roman Slane & Arlene S. Kanter

Externs, even though they are not licensed lawyers, should avoid client representation that would involve conflicts of interest.[1] A potential or actual conflict of interest exists where a lawyer's ability to fulfill her professional responsibilities to one client may or will be impaired by the lawyer's responsibilities to another current or former client, the lawyer's duties to a third party, or the lawyer's own interests.

Concerns about lawyers' conflicts of interest have a long history. As early as 1280, a London ordinance forbade attorneys from engaging in a variety of activities that presented conflicts of interest, including representing parties on both sides of an action. Modern rules regarding conflicts of interest likewise are grounded in the lawyer's duty of undivided loyalty to each client he represents and the lawyer's obligation to safeguard confidential client information. Conflicts rules address the obvious conflict of interests that would arise if a lawyer represented opposing parties in the same matter. The rules also address other situations in which a lawyer's professional independence or the lawyer's ability to honor his duty of loyalty to an existing or former client may be compromised.

Many relationships and circumstances can give rise to actual or potential conflicts of interest. Conflicts may present directly, for example, as a result of a lawyer's representation of two present clients, a present client and a former client, a present client and a prospective client, or a prospective client and a former client. Conflicts may arise indirectly, too, when an individual lawyer's conflict is imputed to other

---

1 Although the term "conflicts of interest" has gained sway in the legal lexicon, the more accurate term is "conflicts of interests." In order for a conflict to arise, more than one interest or set of interests must be in play. Nevertheless, this chapter will refer to conflicts of *interest*, in deference to common usage in the legal ethics literature.

lawyers associated in practice with that lawyer. In other words, sometimes a conflict for one lawyer is a conflict for her partners as well. Finally, conflicts may arise between the interests of a client and personal or financial interests of the lawyer. As law firms have grown larger, as lawyers have become more mobile, and as liberalized joinder rules have produced more cases involving multiple litigants, the frequency of conflicts of interest has increased.

Some conflicts of interest can be resolved by obtaining the informed consent of the affected clients. "Informed consent" requires explanation of the risks posed by the conflict and the choices presented. Once fully advised, a client can waive the conflict. Other conflicts are so serious that they cannot be resolved by obtaining a waiver; these conflicts preclude representation of one or more clients.

Violation of conflicts rules can have serious repercussions for both lawyers and clients. In fact, conflicts of interest are among the most common grounds for disqualification motions and civil malpractice suits by clients against their attorneys. Therefore, lawyers and law students must master the conflicts rules and take care to recognize and avoid or resolve conflicts of interest. This chapter offers an overview of the legal ethics rules on conflicts and examines situations in which conflicts issues typically arise in externship practice. The chapter also includes a number of hypotheticals (each drawn from the experience of externs) designed to provide students with practice in recognizing and avoiding or resolving conflicts that might arise in externships. Finally, it offers guidance as to how externs can discharge their personal and professional responsibility to avoid representation that would result in conflicts of interest during their externship semester(s) and, later, during their legal careers.

The Rules Governing Conflicts of Interest

In evaluating conflicts between past and former clients, one looks to Rule 1.9 to assess a lawyer's obligations to a former client and to Rule 1.7 to assess the lawyer's obligation to the present or prospective client.

Rules 1.7 through 1.12, Rule 6.5, and parts of Rule 1.18 set forth the rules governing conflicts of interest. Rule 1.7 addresses concurrent representation conflicts, which are conflicts between two current clients or one current client and one prospective client. Rule 1.8 addresses conflicts that may arise in situations in which the lawyer's personal interests and a client's interests may differ, such as when a lawyer and a client become business partners. Conflicts between duties to current and former clients are addressed in Rule 1.9. Rule 1.10 prohibits lawyers from representing clients if other members of their firms have conflicts that are imputed to them. Rule 1.11 addresses conflicts that involve government lawyers. It offers guidance for lawyers who leave government practice to work in the private sector and vice versa.

Rule 1.12 prohibits lawyers who formerly served as judges, mediators, arbitrators, and judicial law clerks from representing clients who appeared before them, unless they receive informed consent from all parties involved. Rule 1.18 addresses conflicts arising from a lawyer's duty of confidentiality to prospective clients who do not subsequently become clients. Finally, Rule 6.5 establishes significantly relaxed conflicts-checking obligations and limits imputation of conflicts when lawyers participate in nonprofit or court-annexed limited legal services programs.

Nearly all state ethics codes follow the ABA Model Rules format, but most state rules vary to some degree from the Model Rules. The divergence among conflicts provisions is particularly notable. For example, a growing number of jurisdictions permit screening (without informed client consent) to cure conflicts that result when lawyers move between private firms, even though the Model Rules do not. Screening, in effect, "quarantines" a lawyer who has a conflict of interest, preventing her from communicating or receiving information about a conflicting matter in the same firm. Mastery of the Model Rules, therefore, is not enough: externs must become familiar with the particular conflicts rules in force in the jurisdictions in which their externship placements are located.

Concurrent Conflicts

Rule 1.7 outlines a number of circumstances that give rise to concurrent conflicts of interest and establishes the conditions upon which representation may continue notwithstanding the existence of such a conflict.

Rule 1.7 Conflicts of interest: Current clients

(a) Except as provided in paragraph (b), a lawyer shall not represent a client if the representation involves a concurrent conflict of interest. A concurrent conflict of interest exists if:

(1) the representation of one client will be directly adverse to another client; or

(2) there is a significant risk that the representation of one or more clients will be materially limited by the lawyer's responsibilities to another client, a former client or a third person or by a personal interest of the lawyer.

(b) Notwithstanding the existence of a concurrent conflict of interest under paragraph (a), a lawyer may represent a client if:

(1) the lawyer reasonably believes that the lawyer will be able to provide competent and diligent representation to each affected client;

(2) the representation is not prohibited by law;

(3) the representation does not involve the assertion of a claim by one client against another client represented by the lawyer in the same litigation or other proceeding before a tribunal; and

(4) each affected client gives informed consent, confirmed in writing.

Rule 1.8 expands upon Rule 1.7(a)(2)'s prohibition of representation where a lawyer's own interests will affect adversely the lawyer's ability to provide competent, diligent representation to a client. It governs, for example, where lawyers enter into business transactions with clients, and endeavors to ensure that a lawyer's superior knowledge and bargaining power will not give the lawyer an unfair advantage in such a transaction. It also identifies a number of other circumstances in which a transaction or relationship may compromise a lawyer's duty of loyalty and independent professional judgment. In some such cases, Rule 1.8 restricts the lawyer's conduct, for example, by requiring informed client consent,[2] recommending or requiring that the client secure independent representation in connection with the transaction,[3] or both. In others, it imposes an outright ban on such transactions or relationships.[4]

Rule 1.12(b) addresses a final set of circumstances in which a lawyer's personal interests may conflict with her professional obligations—the obligations a lawyer undertakes as a neutral. Absent informed consent from all parties, confirmed in writing, the rule prohibits a lawyer "serving as a judge or other adjudicative officer or as an arbitrator, mediator or other third-party neutral" from negotiating for employment with a party in a matter in which the lawyer, as neutral, is "participating personally and substantially." It does permit "[a] lawyer serving as a law clerk to a judge or other adjudicative officer [to] negotiate for employment with a party or lawyer involved in a matter in which the clerk is participating personally and substantially" without informed consent of the parties, "but only after the lawyer [serving as a law clerk] has notified the judge, or other adjudicative officer."

---

[2] Rule 1.8(b) (requiring informed client consent for use of information relating to the representation to the disadvantage of a client), (f) (requiring informed client consent where compensation for representing a client will come from one other than the client), and (g) (requiring informed consent from all affected clients prior to making an aggregate plea agreement or settlement of claims for two or more clients).

[3] Rule 1.8 (a) (governing business transactions with or acquisition of ownership, possessory, security or other pecuniary interests adverse to client) and (h) (governing agreement prospectively limiting lawyer's liability to client for malpractice or settling claim or potential claim for such liability).

[4] See, for example, Rule 1.8 (c) (banning the preparation of instruments conveying substantial gifts from clients to lawyers), (d) (banning negotiations and agreements for media or literary rights prior to the termination of representation), (e) (banning certain types of financial assistance to clients), (i) (banning acquisition of a proprietary interest in the cause of action or subject matter of the litigation), and (j) (banning initiation of sexual relations with clients).

Successive Representation Conflicts

Rule 1.9 addresses situations in which lawyers' responsibilities to former clients conflict or may conflict with their responsibilities to present or prospective clients. Rule 1.9 guides the analysis of such a conflict with respect to the *former client*. Rule 1.7 guides that analysis with respect to a *present or prospective* client. Rule 1.9 balances competing interests and duties: the lawyer's duty of loyalty to both former and current clients, the former client's interest in the ongoing protection of confidential information, the current client's interest in representation by counsel of his choosing, and the lawyer's interest in professional mobility.

Rule 1.7, which addresses concurrent conflicts, is "client based": it prohibits representation adverse to a current client—even in a wholly unrelated matter—without informed consent, confirmed in writing, from all affected clients. Rule 1.9, by contrast, is "matter-based": absent informed consent, confirmed in writing, from the affected former client, it prohibits representation adverse to that former client only in *matters* that are "the same as or substantially related to" a matter in which the lawyer represented the former client where the new client's interests are "materially adverse" to those of the former client.

Rule 1.9(b) limits the circumstances under which lawyers who leave a firm take the firm's conflicts with them to those in which departing lawyers themselves have acquired confidential information material to a matter that is the same as, or substantially related to, a matter in which the former firm provided representation to a client. It provides that

> [a] lawyer shall not knowingly represent a person in the same or a substantially related matter in which a firm with which the lawyer formerly was associated had previously represented a client
>
> (1) whose interests are materially adverse to that person; and
>
> (2) **about whom the lawyer had acquired information protected by Rules 1.6 and 1.9(c) that is material to the matter;**

unless the former client gives informed consent, confirmed in writing. [Emphasis added.]

Rule 1.9(c) requires all lawyers to protect the confidences of former clients. A lawyer may not use such information to the disadvantage of the former client or reveal such information unless permitted to do so by the rules.

Rule 1.12(a) also addresses successive conflicts, specifically prohibiting lawyers from undertaking client representation in "a matter in which the lawyer participated personally or substantially as a judge or other adjudicative officer or law clerk to such a person or as an arbitrator, mediator or other third-party neutral" without the informed consent of all parties, confirmed in writing.

Imputed Conflicts

Rule 1.10, the imputed conflicts rule, makes lawyers' conflicts "contagious" in some circumstances. Comment 2 explains that the rule flows from two related premises, "that a firm of lawyers is essentially one lawyer for purposes of the rules governing loyalty to the client" and "that each lawyer is vicariously bound by the obligation of loyalty owed by each lawyer with whom the lawyer is associated." The rule also assumes that lawyers who work together (for example, in a legal aid office, private law firm, or government law office) ordinarily have access to confidential information regarding every matter in which any lawyer associated with the office is involved. Whether they are "essentially one lawyer," or "vicariously bound" by their colleagues' obligations of loyalty to their clients, all lawyers associated with the office are obliged to safeguard that information. Rule 1.10(a), therefore, imputes the conflict of one lawyer to all of the other lawyers associated in the office, prohibiting all of them from

> knowingly represent[ing] a client when any one of them practicing alone would be prohibited from doing so by Rules 1.7 or 1.9, unless the prohibition is based on a personal interest of the prohibited lawyer and does not present a significant risk of materially limiting the representation of the client by the remaining lawyers in the firm.

Comment 4 following Rule 1.10 notes that paragraph (a) of the rule does not

> prohibit representation if the lawyer is prohibited from acting because of events before the person became a lawyer, for example, work that the person did while a law student. Such persons, however, ordinarily must be screened from any personal participation in the matter to avoid communication to others in the firm of confidential information that both the nonlawyers and the firm have a legal duty to protect.

This comment suggests that, in most instances, a lawyer may resolve conflicts acquired during an externship semester by screening.

Conflicts Rules for Current and Former Government Officers and Employees

Rule 1.11 addresses conflicts encountered by lawyers moving between private and government practice. Although it expressly binds former government lawyers to Rule 1.9(c) and current government lawyers to Rules 1.7 and 1.9, it is, in some respects, less restrictive than the rules that apply to lawyers who move between other practice settings.

In the absence of informed consent from the appropriate government agency, Rule 1.11(a) prohibits a former government lawyer from representing a client "in connection with a matter in which the lawyer participated personally and substantially as a public officer or employee." However, Rule 1.11(b) permits the former government lawyer's firm to undertake representation of such a party without consent of the government client, as long as

(1) the disqualified lawyer is timely screened from any participation in the matter and is apportioned no part of the fee therefrom; and

(2) written notice is promptly given to the appropriate government agency to enable it to ascertain compliance with the provisions of this rule.

Rule 1.11(c) bars a former government lawyer from representing a client if the lawyer, in the course of the representation, could make use of confidential information that the lawyer acquired about a person while in government service to the material disadvantage of that person. A former U.S. Attorney, for example, could not undertake representation in which she could make adverse use of information acquired during a criminal investigation. Rule 1.11(c), however, approves of screening to prevent the vicarious disqualification of other lawyers in a former government lawyer's firm.

Rule 1.11(d) prohibits a current government lawyer from "participating in a matter in which the lawyer participated personally and substantially while in private practice or nongovernmental employment . . . ." unless the relevant agency consents.

An extern who is engaged in federal or state government service (assigned to an executive, judicial, or legislative branch placement) or who hopes to work in a governmental practice setting after graduation should pay particular attention to the iteration of Rule 1.11 in force in the relevant jurisdiction.

Potential Conflicts

The rules that govern conflicts situations apply not only to actual conflicts of interest (conflicts that exist at present or will exist from the outset if a lawyer undertakes representation of a particular prospective client) but also to conflicts that may arise in the course of representing a prospective client. Whether a lawyer may undertake representation despite a potential conflict depends on the likelihood that a conflict will materialize in the future and on how adversely the conflict could affect the representation. A lawyer who faces a potential conflict and concludes that such representation is permissible may proceed with the representation, but only after receiving informed consent from all affected clients.

Positional Conflicts

Comment 24 after Rule 1.7 addresses a final category of conflict of interests: those that arise where

> there is a significant risk that a lawyer's action on behalf of one client will materially limit the lawyer's effectiveness in representing another client in a different case; for example, when a decision favoring one client will create a precedent likely to seriously weaken the position taken on behalf of the other client.

Such conflicts, referred to in ethical shorthand as "positional conflicts," can arise if a lawyer accepts representation that will require the lawyer to make an argument on behalf of one client to a particular tribunal and shortly thereafter make a contrary argument to the same tribunal on behalf of another client.

Very few situations in which lawyers propose to advocate in different settings on behalf of clients with conflicting interests give rise to authentic Rule 1.7 concerns. However, some clients may object to activities plainly permitted by the rule. Even if the representation is not prohibited, a lawyer should address such client concerns as a matter of good client relations. For example, a lawyer who represents a business client in its environmental matters before state and federal regulatory bodies would not be prohibited by Rule 1.7 from engaging in *pro bono* advocacy in a different forum on an issue unrelated to the client's environmental matters. However, if the *pro bono* activity involves an issue about which the client has strong, opposing views, and the client learns of the lawyer's involvement on the "other side" of the issue, the client could decide to take its legal business elsewhere, rendering any Rule 1.7 "blessing" irrelevant.

Conflicts of Interest in Externship Practice

We turn now to a discussion of the conflicts that students are likely to encounter through externship participation. Conflicts relating to an extern's prior, current, or future legal employment, or her personal views or activities, may arise early on during the application process. Suppose, for example, that a student is considering an externship with a judge who is presiding in a murder case in which the prosecutor is seeking the death penalty. Suppose the law student is a vehement opponent of the death penalty and a regular participant in demonstrations and vigils at the prison where the defendant is incarcerated during trial. This law reform work might affect the extern's ability to work on the matter or might create an appearance of impropriety for the prospective supervising judge.

Conflicts could arise during the externship semester, as well as after the semester ends. For example, a conflict might present in connection with an extern's legal work at the placement or during discussions in a seminar or in journal entries submitted for faculty review or when a former extern seeks employment or pursues *pro bono* activities.

Conflicts of Interest in the Externship Placement Process

The avoidance or resolution of conflicts of interest identified during the externship placement process will govern whether a student will be able to work in a particular placement. As Comment 3 after Rule 1.7 explains, "[a] conflict of interest may exist before representation is undertaken, in which event the representation must be declined, unless the lawyer obtains the informed consent of each client under [certain] conditions." Some conflicts may be fairly obvious. For example, it is unlikely that a law student employed part-time as a social worker for the Department of Children and Families could extern at a legal services organization that has filed a lawsuit against the Department. Other conflicts are harder to detect. For example, even a careful conflicts inventory may not disclose that a client on whose family matter a student worked extensively and personally as a summer law intern at a legal services office will be a witness against a client represented by a prospective externship supervisor in an eviction proceeding. Identifying and avoiding or resolving all such conflicts, though, is imperative.

Externship programs vary considerably in their application requirements and placement procedures. Some programs encourage or require eligible students to find their own placements. Others place students at established placements in law offices or judges' chambers. Still others arrange interviews for students at pre-approved placements, with faculty supervisors assigning selected students to placements based on the outcome of those interviews.

Where students arrange their own placements, the responsibility for identifying and avoiding and resolving conflicts falls primarily on fieldwork supervisors and externs. If the faculty supervisor makes placement decisions, she plays a significant conflicts-checking role. In every circumstance, identifying and avoiding or resolving existing and potential conflicts is essential. Doing so protects clients and spares all of the externship players the time, distress, and embarrassment of dealing with later-discovered conflicts that could have been detected and addressed before the semester began.

Exercise 6.1 In preparation for participation in your law school's externship program, conduct a conflicts inventory of your own. (A form for this purpose is provided as Appendix 6.1 to this chapter.) List your previous employers, legal and non-legal, paid and volunteer positions, as well as all of the business and legal matters, whether litigation-related or transactional, in which you have had substantial personal involvement at each of your previous jobs. Suppose, for example, that you worked part-time last year at a law firm. You should include on your list any matters on which you did enough work that you learned some client confidences.

For each matter that you list, include the names of the parties involved. For example, if you worked at a small company before beginning law school, and that company merged with another company— whether before you left or after, include in your inventory your employer, the company with which it merged, and the new entity. Remember ordinary business transactions sometimes evolve—or devolve—into legal disputes. For example, creditors in a bankruptcy proceeding often mount retrospective "fraudulent transfer" challenges to the sale of business assets, even though the transactions at issue may have raised no red flags at all prior to the bankruptcy filing.

Include in your inventory all of your organizational memberships, for example, in the Sierra Club, the National Rifle Association, the Boy Scouts, Students for Choice. List, too, any other responsibilities, associations, activities, and/or strong personal views that could give rise to conflicts: "I work weekends as a *per diem* registered nurse, so I am a mandated reporter of child abuse and neglect;" "My wife is a lawyer who appears in federal court in this jurisdiction;" "I own three national sandwich-shop franchises in my home state;" "I could never be a zealous advocate on behalf of a defendant if I believed she intentionally harmed a child."

Discuss your completed inventory with your faculty and prospective fieldwork supervisors during the externship placement process. Update it as your externship semester progresses. Make careful notes on the matters in which you are involved at your placement. Keep your inventory handy, though not accessible to others, for it almost certainly will contain confidential client information. You will need to refer to it and update it as you search for post-externship legal employment!

An extern's responsibility to identify and avoid or resolve conflicts of interest does not end when her placement is confirmed. Students must take care to update their conflicts inventories throughout the semester and bring to their fieldwork and faculty supervisors' attention any new activities or developments—for example, job offers, *pro bono* activities, and other volunteer work—that give rise to conflicts.

Concurrent Representation Conflicts

Among the many conflicts that persons involved in externships must identify and avoid or resolve are concurrent representation conflicts. For example, because the state (the "client" of every extern in a prosecutorial placement) is an adverse party to every defendant facing criminal charges in the applicable jurisdiction, a student who works in a part-time job at a local criminal defense firm during his externship semester almost certainly will be barred from working as an extern at the local office of the district attorney.

The extern cannot accept the prosecution placement unless he can avoid or resolve the actual or imputed conflicts that would result from his contemporaneous law firm employment during the externship semester. Although subsections (a)(2) and (b)(2) of Rule 1.7 establish client consent as a means for resolving concurrent conflicts, consent is unlikely to be available here. The student's desire to work for the prosecutor probably would make the clients of the criminal defense firm worry about the student's loyalties. Those doubts would undermine the clients' trust in the student and therefore materially—and thus impermissibly—limit the student's ability to provide them with competent representation.

In this instance, the extern can avoid the concurrent conflicts by declining the prosecution externship placement or by giving up his part-time job at the law office. Even if the student elects to avoid the concurrent conflicts by giving up his part-time job, he and his fieldwork supervisor will have to be alert to any successive representation conflicts the student may bring to the prosecution placement by virtue of his previous employment.

Exercise 6.2 Steven has applied for an externship at the District Attorney's Office. He has been working for the past year at a family law firm in the jurisdiction and plans to continue his part-time job at the firm while he is participating in the externship. He does not believe that this plan presents any conflicts issues because his firm does not represent clients in criminal matters. Is Steven correct? Explain your conclusion.

Consider another example of a possible concurrent conflict. Suppose a law student working at the public defender's office has applied for a contemporaneous externship with a judge who hears criminal cases in the public defender's jurisdiction. Although the extern would not be representing clients with conflicting interests (because, as a judicial extern, the student would not be representing clients), her duties to the supervising judge could conflict with her duties to clients represented by the public defender. Suppose, though, that this extern is screened at both practice settings from involvement in public defender cases assigned to her supervising judge. Would screening resolve the conflicts? Perhaps not, because the student's *ex parte* access to a judge who presides over cases litigated by the public defender's office might give rise to an appearance of impropriety of the sort banned by the Code of Judicial Conduct. *See* Model Code of Judicial Conduct, Canon 2. In view of the student's conflict, the prosecutor's office might even request that the judge recuse herself from all cases in which the public defender's office has a role.

Suppose another extern seeks placement with a judge who currently is presiding over a case in which the student's spouse, partner, or other close family member is representing one of the parties, or with a judge who will preside over a case presented by lawyers at the student's current or future employer. Although screening might resolve some such conflicts, these conflicts generally will not be apparent from a student's résumé. Consequently, the student must bring them to the attention of her faculty and fieldwork supervisors.

Externship participants also must identify and avoid or resolve a final subset of concurrent conflicts—positional conflicts—during the externship placement process. Consider the dilemma presented in the scenario that follows.

Exercise 6.3 Adrienne, a 3L enrolled in a fall-term externship program, has been volunteering for almost a year at a not-for-profit advocacy organization devoted to abolishing discrimination on the basis of sexual orientation. Over her second-year summer, Adrienne worked extensively on an amicus brief that the organization since has filed in the state appellate court. The brief supports an equal protection challenge to the state's refusal to issue marriage licenses to same-sex couples. Adrienne's supervisor credited her as "law student intern on the brief," in acknowledgment of her significant contribution to the final product. Adrienne has committed to continue volunteering at the organization, at least until she graduates from law school in the spring.

Because she is interested in working in the government after graduation, Adrienne has applied for an externship placement at the state Attorney General's Office. She receives a phone call inviting her to interview for a position in the unit that represents the state's Youth Services Division. Adrienne does not disclose her association with the advocacy organization during her interview with her prospective externship supervisor. She sees her pro bono work as purely a personal matter, unrelated to the work she will do as an extern at the AG's Office. Adrienne's interview goes well; her placement is confirmed.

When the externship semester begins, the same-sex-marriage case is still pending before the appellate court, with oral argument scheduled for mid-December. In late September, Adrienne's field placement supervisor calls her into his office to give her a new assignment. He tells her that he would like her to begin work on a brief in response to an equal protection challenge to a Division policy that does not allow same-sex couples to adopt. The case, he says, is pending in the state appellate court.

Reread Rule 1.7 and Rule 1.10 and their respective comments. Identify the provisions that are relevant in this scenario. List all of the actual or potential conflicts of interest that Adrienne's concurrent activities present. How might these conflicts cause problems for Adrienne, for the advocacy organization and its lawyers, for the Division of Youth Services and its lawyers, for the externship program, and for Adrienne's faculty supervisor? Would the situation be any different if Adrienne had contributed research and drafting assistance on the same-sex marriage brief but her supervisor at the advocacy organization had not acknowledged her as "on the brief"? if the appellate court already had heard oral argument and taken supplemental briefs on the case? if it already had ruled on the case?

What steps could Adrienne, her fieldwork supervisor, or both, have taken to identify and avoid or resolve Adrienne's conflicts during the placement process? What policies and procedures should the faculty supervisor of an externship program implement to help avoid the kind of dilemma in which the parties in the problem find themselves?

Finally, what would you advise Adrienne to do now?

Successive Representation Conflicts

Actual or potential successive representation conflicts often come to light during the externship placement process because many externs come to an externship with at least one summer's legal work experience. Because a lawyer's duty of loyalty runs both to current clients and to former clients, an extern's prior legal experience may give rise to a conflict with respect to the clients of the extern's prospective externship placement.

Rule 1.9 allows resolution of some successive conflicts by obtaining informed consent from the former client. However, even without the consent of the former client, a law student whose previous legal employment includes a summer at a local law firm may accept an externship placement at a non-profit organization that represents a client who is adverse to a client of the law firm in a matter that is the same as or substantially related to a matter in which the student was involved during her summer at the firm. She may do so, however, only if the advocacy organization timely screens her from any involvement in the matter and both she and the advocacy organization are careful to safeguard confidential information she acquired during her former employment. See Rule 1.10, Comment 4.

Likewise, because externs are law students, where an extern *previously* has worked in a general practice firm and *subsequently* applies for an externship placement in an in-house legal department at a corporation the firm opposes in litigation, any resulting conflicts may be resolved by screening. However, if an extern whose placement is in the in-house legal offices of a corporate client works *con-*

currently at a general practice law firm, both the student and the lawyers at each office may be barred by Rules 1.7 and 1.10 from undertaking representation adverse to the clients of either practice without the informed consent of all affected clients.

Exercise 6.4 Pamela has applied for an externship at the U.S. Attorney's Office. Last summer she worked as a summer associate at a law firm, and she has accepted an offer to return to the firm following graduation. Pamela became interested in the position at the U.S. Attorney's Office after she observed an attorney from that office argue a motion in a case on which she was working for the firm. She is not sure if the case is still pending.

May Pamela work as an extern at the U.S. Attorney's Office? Explain your conclusion.

Conflicts of Interest that Present During the Externship Semester

Even if a careful, pre-placement, conflicts check discloses no actual or potential conflicts, a conflict may arise after the student begins working at the externship site. These late-blooming conflicts might spring from an extern's activities at the placement, or they might involve the extern's participation in the academic component of the externship program.

Conflicts that Arise from Placement Activities

Perhaps the most frequent conflicts that confront law students involve those who work in two legal practice settings during a single semester. A student might have a paid job with one office and an externship at another. A careful pre-placement conflicts check may identify some such conflicts, but a lawyer who supervises an extern who holds another legal position also must conduct *ongoing* cross-checks to identify conflicts that arise from the student's duties to clients of either office.

If a student works only on a single matter or a discrete set of matters at the law office and has no access to confidential information about other matters, both the externship host and the legal employer may be willing to assume this ongoing responsibility. If, however, a student proposes contemporaneous *association* with two law offices, checking for conflicts could be quite burdensome.

A student who works in only one practice setting during the externship semester also must be alert to conflicts. An extern placed at a prosecutor's office, for example, may be surprised to see the name of a classmate, relative, friend, or even law school faculty member, on the court docket at his placement. Worse still, the extern may receive an evening phone call from a friend or family member scheduled for a court appearance the next morning. If the caller knows that the extern is working in the prosecutor's office, he may be hoping that the student can use his influence to secure a reduction in a fine or a dismissal of a charge. In such a situation, the extern's perceived or actual responsibilities to the caller, or the friendship or family loyalty involved, is in conflict with the extern's duty as a member of the legal team at the prosecutor's office. The student must explain to the caller that it would be inappropriate for him to be involved and should consider reporting the contact to the placement supervisor.

In all such interactions, of course, the student must be mindful of the provisions of Rule 4.3 (lawyers' dealings with unrepresented persons) and Rule 3.8 (special responsibilities of prosecutors) and be alert to the dilemma that would result if, during the conversation, the caller discloses inculpatory information.

Another type of conflict could arise because of a mid-semester job search or an offer of part-time, summer, or post-graduation employment. As Rule 1.7, Comment 10 notes, "when a lawyer has discussions concerning possible employment with an opponent of the lawyer's client, or with a law firm representing the opponent, such discussions could materially limit the lawyer's representation of the client."

Rule 1.12(b), in contrast, expressly authorizes lawyers serving as law clerks to judges or other adjudicative officers to "negotiate for employment with a party or lawyer involved in a matter in which the clerk is participating personally and substantially, but only after the lawyer has notified the judge or other adjudicative officer." Students externing in other practice settings also should advise their fieldwork supervisors of the particulars of ongoing job searches and of any job offers so that the supervisors can identify and remedy any potential conflicts.

Conflicts that Arise from Seminar Participation and Journaling

Participation in an externship seminar may give rise to conflicts as externs working in diverse practice settings share observations about their placement experiences in seminar meetings, tutorials, or journal entries. These academic activities are among the defining features of externship practice, setting for-credit externships apart from most other "real world" legal experiences available to aspiring lawyers. Although students learn much from conversations with seminar colleagues and exchanges with faculty supervisors, they must approach these activities with some caution to avoid discussion that would reveal confidences or create conflicts of interest.

The extent to which students in an externship seminar may discuss client matters in class depends on the structure of the particular externship program.

In hybrid programs, all seminar participants work in the same off-campus placement under the direct supervision of a supervisor who also teaches the externship seminar. In such a program all seminar participants are members of the same firm, and therefore can speak freely in class about confidential client matters.

In other programs, the students in an externship seminar work at a diverse array of placements. Two externs in such a seminar may work with lawyers who represent clients who are adversaries in litigation. Similarly, two students may be placed at organizations that have opposing positions in a public policy debate. May externs assigned to the local district attorney's office report on placement activities in a seminar attended by externs working in the public defender's office in the same courthouse? May an extern assigned to a national anti-death penalty advocacy organization participate in an externship seminar with students from a local district attorney's office if that office seeks the death penalty in selected cases? May an extern for a local federal judge participate in a seminar with students externing at the local Office of the United States Attorney? With some careful attention, externship programs can manage these problems. Students can benefit greatly from exposure to the ideas and experiences of students working on "the other side."

see Chapter 5 *on Confidentiality*

The general conflicts of interest rules prohibit a lawyer from representing a client if such representation will be directly adverse to another client and impute conflicts among lawyers practicing together. *If* the common seminar were a law firm and *if* the students in the class were "practicing together," the resulting conflicts might be insurmountable. But an externship seminar is not a law firm, so the participants in a common seminar do not, by virtue of that participation, become part of the lawyering teams at one another's placements. Rather, as long as seminar participants take appropriate measures to safeguard confidential client and chambers information in discussions with faculty supervisors and classmates, they can avoid any potential ethical problems.

Most externship programs—even those with no seminar components— require students to submit journal entries about their field experience. These narratives may both reveal and give rise to conflicts of interest. For example, suppose a student is concerned about what he believes to be a serious violation of a rule of professional conduct by a placement supervisor and discusses that conduct in a journal entry submitted for faculty review. If the student asks for guidance as to his own ethical obligations in the situation, his journal entry may be protected as a confidential lawyer-client communication.[5] Suppose, though, that the student does not ask for advice but makes this disclosure in reliance on his faculty supervisor's general assurance that she does not share student journal entries with others without student consent.

If the ethical breach is as serious as the student thinks it is, the conflict in this situation is apparent. The student's self-interest in completing the externship and securing a favorable reference from his fieldwork supervisor conflicts with the duty to report lawyer misconduct set out in Rule 8.3.[6] Even if he may not be formally bound to comply with the rules, the student, soon to be admitted to practice, should grapple with this obligation. In addition, if the student's faculty supervisor is admitted to practice, the student's disclosure would give rise to a conflict between her promissory obligation to keep student journal entries confidential and her own professional reporting obligation under Rule 8.3.

Disclosures in journal entries may give rise to conflicts and confidentiality concerns too, when faculty supervisors unexpectedly find themselves in possession of information about the strategies of parties opposed to one another in litigation. A student assigned to a busy, urban, prosecution placement, for instance, while taking care not to disclose what she believes might be identifying details about a case, may discuss in a journal entry her discomfort with her supervisor's decision to pursue very serious charges against a young, female defendant who has raised a battered-wife-syndrome defense. A student working in the public defender's office in the same jurisdiction may submit a journal entry recounting his discomfort with the "pushing the envelope" tactic his supervisor used midway through an initial interview to suggest what the student fears may be a baseless battered-wife-syndrome defense to a young, female client who had made no mention of spousal abuse. ("I can't say yet what the prosecutor is thinking about this case, but I can tell you one thing: jurors don't like to convict a young woman like you of murdering her husband if we can convince them that the husband had it coming—that she didn't see any other way to get out of an abusive relationship.")

In this situation, even though both students have been careful not to disclose the defendant's name or anything more than broad characterizations of the case, the faculty supervisor may deduce that both students are working on the same matter. If the faculty member is not admitted to practice in the jurisdiction, of course, she may

---

5 *See* Rule 1.6(e), authorizing the disclosure of otherwise-confidential information "to secure legal advice about the lawyer's compliance with these Rules."

6 Rule 8.3(a) requires a lawyer who has knowledge of another lawyer's violation of the Rules of Professional Conduct giving rise to doubts about the other lawyer's "honesty, trustworthiness, or fitness as a lawyer in other respects" to report the misconduct to "the appropriate professional authority."

not offer legal advice to either student without engaging in the unauthorized practice of law. If she is locally admitted, though, the question becomes whether she may assist either of her students as they struggle with the ethical issues presented by their case-in-common or whether, in doing so, she herself would be engaging in activity prohibited by Rule 1.7.

There are no easy answers in such challenging situations, but externs and their faculty supervisors should notice and discuss these problems. They can work together to develop appropriate guidelines to ensure protection of placement information, both in the classroom and in journal entries.

Exercise 6.5 Tony and Sonja are enrolled in the same externship seminar. At the beginning of the semester, neither has selected a placement. Both interview for externships during the first week of classes. Tony accepts a position with the local Social Security Administration office. Sonja accepts a position in a disability rights advocacy organization, which handles appeals for individuals with disabilities who are challenging the Social Security Administration's decisions denying their applications for disability benefits. Tony's and Sonja's law school requires that all externs participate in the externship seminar. This semester, there is only one section of the seminar. During seminar meetings, the externs discuss various aspects of their experiences. Each student also is required to make a presentation about the student's placement and to turn in journals detailing placement activities and reflections on the externship experience.

What ethical issues are presented by the students' placement in offices that routinely are adversaries in litigation? Should their faculty supervisor restrict Tony and Sonja's discussion of their placement activities in the seminar? In their journal entries? Are any other special precautions in order given their placements? If so, what precautions would you recommend, and why?

What if Tony is assigned to assist in the defense of a case in which Sonja is involved on behalf of the petitioner? How should they and their instructor handle this situation?

Externship Conflicts and the Post-Externship Job Search

Conflicts of interest issues related to externship participation may arise weeks, months, and even years after both the application process and the academic component of an externship program are over. The duty to protect the confidences of former clients is not extinguished when an externship ends, but continues, following externs into all subsequent job searches. Whenever a former extern proposes to accept a new legal job, she must check for possible conflicts with previous legal employment, including externships. This task will be infinitely easier if each student keeps a careful list of the names of all client matters in which she was involved.

Exercise 6.6 Michael is a summer extern at the city law department. Michael's fieldwork supervisor includes him in a series of meetings at which city lawyers discuss strategy for an ongoing case. His supervisor tells him that the litigation has been extraordinarily contentious and that the outcome is very important to the city government. In fact, the city views this lawsuit as the most significant problem that the city has faced in the last decade. When the externship ends, Michael begins a job search and lists his externship experience on his résumé. He participates in an on-campus interview with the law firm that represents the plaintiffs in the litigation involving his former placement, receives a job offer from the firm, and begins working part-time at the firm during the spring term of his third year. Michael does not disclose his new job to his former externship supervisor. The supervisor learns of Michael's new position at the firm when, several months later, Michael calls her to ask for a bar affidavit.

The supervisor is concerned. Michael says that because the firm did not ask him about his "employment" in the city law department during his interviews, he "did not think it created any ethical problems."

Is Michael's analysis of the conflicts issues correct? Explain your conclusion.

Program Protocols for Identifying and Avoiding or Resolving Conflicts

Identifying Actual and Potential Conflicts

The best way for an externship program to avoid conflicts is to develop an effective conflicts checking process, one that will gather as much information about the extern's work and personal history as early in the application process as possible, and thereby facilitate the identification of both actual and potential conflicts that might require client consent or that might preclude representation of one or more clients.

The crucial first step in such a process is a requirement that each prospective externship student conduct a detailed "conflicts inventory." Some externship programs use forms like that provided at the end of this chapter for this purpose. Although some potential or actual conflicts will be apparent from a prospective extern's résumé, a résumé ordinarily will not list the individual matters in which a student has been involved in the course of her prior legal employment, nor will it itemize every organization to which the student belongs (for example, membership in People for the Ethical Treatment of Animals, which could preclude a placement at a company that does animal research), nor catalogue the student's strongly-held personal beliefs (for example, strong opposition to abortion or the death penalty). Therefore, identifying all actual and potential conflicts will require that students share both their résumés *and* the results of their conflicts inventories with their faculty and fieldwork supervisors. Because responsibilities to non-legal employers also may present prohibited Rule 1.7 conflicts, careful conflicts checking will require that students disclose all contemporaneous non-legal employment as well.

Given the mandate of Rule 1.6 that lawyers keep confidential all information related to the representation of clients, the prospective extern is presented with a dilemma: how much information about prior or contemporaneous client representation may a student disclose in the course of a conflicts-checking protocol? Although the rules are silent on this issue—even the circumstances under which a client's name may be protected as confidential remains an open question under the rules—most commentators agree that lawyers may disclose the names of clients in order to check for conflicts. In successive representation situations, they also may identify the matters in which they provided representation to those clients.

At least one state bar ethics committee has issued a formal opinion regarding the amount and type of information an attorney may reveal for the purpose of checking for conflicts. Applying the relevant sections of the Code of Professional Responsibility, the New York Committee on Professional Ethics has opined that law firms must obtain the names of clients previously represented by each newly hired lawyer and, in some cases, by all other lawyers in the newly hired lawyer's former firm.[7]

As to requests for personal information from the extern, the rules likewise offer little guidance. It is advisable, therefore, for students who are applying for externships to discuss this issue with their faculty supervisor and to provide at least enough information to allow the faculty supervisor to determine if further investigation regarding any actual or potential conflict is warranted.

Exercise 6.7 Imagine that you and two classmates have decided to form your own law firm after your law school graduation. How would you go about setting up a conflicts-checking system for the new firm? Where would you turn for guidance as to how to design and implement such a system? What information would you have to gather with respect to your work history as law students? What information would you have to gather from prospective clients in order to identify all actual and potential conflicts that might arise from their representation? Ask a member of your law school's clinical faculty or a lawyer in a law office in which you have worked about the conflicts-checking systems employed in that practice setting. Compare that system with the recommendations of at least one legal ethics or law practice management resource (for example, an article in a law review or bar journal, materials published by the Practicing Law Institute of New York, or an opinion by the ethics advisory committee in your jurisdiction).

Avoiding or Resolving Conflicts

If a student's careful, pre-placement review of her conflicts inventory, with either the faculty supervisor or a prospective fieldwork supervisor or both, discloses

---

7 See N.Y. St. Bar Ass'n Comm. on Prof'l Ethics, Op 720 (1999), which refers to the 1996 amendment to the New York Code that requires all New York law firms to institute formal systems to identify conflicts of interests. The Opinion concludes that when a lawyer moves to a new law firm, the new firm must seek the names of clients represented by the lawyer. Depending on the size of the firm, the lawyer may have to reveal the names of all clients of the former firm, within a reasonable period of time -in the past, unless the client's name is protected as a client confidence or secret. See New York Code of Prof'l Responsibility DR 5-105(E) (2002).

an actual or potential conflict of interest, or if a job search or an offer of contemporaneous or future employment gives rise to such a conflict, both the student and the supervisors must take appropriate steps to avoid or resolve the conflict.

Avoiding Conflicts: Declining Representation

Avoiding a conflict that is certain to arise in a particular placement generally requires either that a student accept an alternate placement or relinquish plans for the contemporaneous employment or activity that gives rise to the conflict. While such "conflict avoidance" is appealing in its simplicity, its consequences may be harsh for a student who is committed to completing an externship at a particular placement and who is equally committed to maintaining other employment or continuing particular categories of volunteer work during the period of the externship. Unfortunately, in many cases, these activities will be mutually exclusive.

Resolving Conflicts: Informed Client Consent

In other cases, informed consent from all affected clients, confirmed in writing (*i.e.*, consent provided after disclosure of the conflict and consultation with respect to its possible impact on the representation), may resolve, or "cure," a conflict. However, if even one affected client withholds consent, or if the conflict will limit the student's ability to provide competent and diligent representation to an affected client, the student will not be able to work as a law student extern at the prospective placement.

Resolving Conflicts: Screening

In some situations, screening may be available to address conflicts of interest that students bring with them to their externship placements, or that develop during an externship semester. Rule 1.11, for example, permits notice to affected clients and screening to cure imputed conflicts even without client consent when lawyers move between government and private employment. Rule 1.12 allows similar measures to cure imputed conflicts arising from prior employment as a judge, arbitrator, mediator, or other third-party neutral. Rule 1.18 likewise permits notice to a prospective client and screening to cure imputed conflicts where, during a discussion with a prospective client, a lawyer receives information that would otherwise disqualify the lawyer and his associates from representation of a client with interests materially adverse to those of the prospective client in the same or a substantially related matter, as long as the lawyer "took reasonable measures to avoid exposure to more disqualifying information than was reasonably necessary to determine whether to represent the prospective client."

The Rule 1.10 commentary, which also provides for screening to avoid the imputation of conflicts in some circumstances, offers particular comfort to students concerned about the extended impact of the potential successive representation conflicts they are accumulating through externship participation. While affirming that a lawyer may be individually disqualified from representing a client because of work the lawyer did while in law school, the commentary notes that the general rule of imputed disqualification "does not prohibit representation [by others in the law firm] if the lawyer is prohibited from acting because of . . . work that the person did while a law student." It cautions, though, that the disqualified lawyer "ordinarily must be screened from any personal participation in the matter to avoid communication to others in the firm of confidential information that both the nonlawyers and the firm have a legal duty to protect."

Where representation giving rise to a conflict of interests may proceed only with informed client consent, that consent frequently is conditioned on a promise that the conflicted lawyer will be screened from any involvement with the matter that gives rise to the conflict. Screening, however, is not available in all jurisdictions. In 2002, the ABA House of Delegates specifically rejected a proposal to amend the Model Rules to provide screening as a method of curing imputed conflicts when lawyers move from one law firm to another.

Externship faculty supervisors, for their part, often are reluctant to approve placements conditioned on screening. Although screening may be a desirable means of resolving at least some of the conflicts of interest faced by lawyers, it is less appropriate when the individual to be screened is a law student extern. Because a primary goal of most, if not all, externship programs is to expose students to as broad a range of lawyering styles and professional experiences as possible, faculty supervisors encourage externs to develop professional relationships with as many members of the legal team at their placements as possible and to work on as diverse an assortment of matters as possible. They urge them to talk with their placement colleagues about other matters on which the students will not work directly and to seek guidance from them with respect to the extern's own developing legal skills and career aspirations. To screen a student from involvement in a particular matter, or from contact with one or more members of the legal team at the placement, is necessarily to limit the extern's exposure to some subset of the lawyering experience available at the placement site, cutting the student off from potentially rich learning opportunities.

Avoiding Conflicts: Withdrawal from Representation

Where a non-consentable conflict arises during an externship semester or a consentable conflict arises after the semester is under way and an affected client withholds consent to the representation, the conflicted student may be required to discontinue work at the externship placement. In that case, the student's options may be limited to forfeiting some or all of the fieldwork credit the extern would have earned or scrambling to make arrangements to complete the requisite fieldwork at another placement site.

Conclusion

One of the advantages of externship participation is the opportunity it offers students to "practice" practicing law while they are still in law school, under the guidance of capable mentors and supervisors. With the privilege of practicing law as a law student comes the responsibility to become aware of and to conform one's conduct to the applicable rules of professional conduct in the placement jurisdiction.

Among the most important of the rules that govern the conduct of lawyers and the legal externs who work under their supervision are those addressing conflicts of interest. Violation of the conflicts rules can carry serious consequences for law students and their faculty and fieldwork supervisors, and, by extension, for the externship program itself. We hope that this Chapter has helped you to become familiar with the rules that govern conflicts situations and to recognize and respond appropriately to the conflicts issues you will encounter as a law student extern and as a practicing lawyer.

■ Appendix 6.1

EXTERNSHIP PROGRAM CONFLICTS OF INTERESTS INVENTORY

Name: _____

Externship: _____ Course: _____

Prospective Placement(s): _____

The information you provide here will help you and your faculty and field supervisors to identify any actual or potential conflicts of interests that would jeopardize the confidentiality and loyalty you owe to your prospective externship placement. Please take your time to answer these questions thoughtfully and completely. (Attach additional sheets if necessary). NOTE: *You have an obligation to update this form to reflect any change in circumstances prior to your beginning work at your externship placement and/or during the semester(s) in which you are enrolled in the Externship Program.*

1. Are you now working or volunteering, or have you worked or volunteered for a law firm, legal services office, corporation legal department, governmental agency, judge, hearing examiner, or in the securities industry (legal or non-legal) prior to enrolling in the Externship Program?

    Yes [ ]   No [ ]

    If yes, where are you working/have you worked? [List **all**, starting with most recent and providing dates and locations.]

    On what type(s) of cases did you work at each location?

2. Are you planning on being employed or volunteering at any office in any of the categories listed in question #1 during your externship semester?

    Yes [ ]   No [ ]

    If yes, where will you be employed or volunteering?

    On what type of cases are you (will you be) working?

3. Are you planning on maintaining any other non-legal employment, board affiliation, or volunteer activity during your externship semester?

    Yes [ ]   No [ ]

    If yes, where will you be employed, serving as a board member, or volunteering?

    What type of work will you be doing?

4. Please list any entities to which you have applied for future employment, including law firms, legal services offices, corporation legal departments, governmental agencies, judges, hearing examiners, or employers in the securities industry (legal or non-legal). You need not include a prospective employer from whom you have received either a "no-thank-you" letter or an offer of employment which you have declined. If, between now and the completion of your externship, you contact any other prospective employer not listed on this form to explore a potential employment relationship, or if any prospective employer contacts you for that purpose, you must update this form to include that prospective employer.

5. Are there any other personal, financial, or family interests that could present conflicts of interests for you at your proposed placement(s)? If so, please identify them here.

6. Have you been enrolled in the Law School's Externship Program or in an In-house Clinic before?

    Yes [ ]   No [ ]

    If yes, please indicate the semester(s) in which you were enrolled (including summer sessions) and identify your clinic and/or externship program and placement below.

    Please Note: You have an obligation to update this Conflicts of Interests Inventory if any of the information you have provided changes between the date you submit this form and the end of the semester in which you are enrolled in the Externship Program.

Chapter 7

Ethical Issues in Externships:
Duties to Tribunals and Third Parties

Lisa G. Lerman

Some legal externs work in law offices that represent clients in litigation. Ethical questions arise in all arenas of law practice, but litigators can scarcely walk across a room without stumbling over an ethical question. Some litigation ethics issues involve duties to clients, of course, but many dilemmas that arise in litigation involve conflicts between a lawyer's duty toward a client and the lawyer's duty toward a judge, an adversary, or a witness.

The pace of a busy litigation practice may not allow much time for explicit discussion of ethical issues. Legal externs may find their best opportunity to discuss questions and concerns in a fieldwork seminar or in reflective writing. In this chapter, we introduce some of the ethics rules that govern lawyers in litigation settings and present some problems for your consideration.

Duties to Tribunals

Lawyers admitted to practice are considered to be "officers of the court" even if they are in private law practice. Every lawyer has a duty to protect the integrity of the system of justice by showing respect for law and the legal system and by maintaining high standards of professional conduct. As officers of the court, lawyers have a duty to be truthful in presenting evidence and arguments to tribunals. For the court system to produce fair and accurate decisions, judges must receive accurate information about the facts of each case and the applicable law. American judges rely on lawyers to present facts. Generally, judges do not go out and find witnesses or documents. They simply review what is presented to them. Therefore, lawyers are not allowed to present false information about facts or law to finders of fact. In some situations, lawyers have an affirmative duty to disclose information to judges; this even may require disclosure of otherwise confidential information.

Consider the following example to understand how the integrity of the justice system depends on the truthfulness of lawyers. Suppose a lawyer is representing a police officer who has been incident of assaulting a suspect. The client denies that he participated in the assault, but the lawyer has interviewed four other officers, all of whom were present when the incident occurred. All four state that the lawyer's client pushed the suspect to the ground, sat on his chest, and punched him in the head repeatedly. The suspect suffered a fractured skull. The officer's knuckles are bruised. After the lawyer completes his fact investigation, the lawyer is certain that his client did, in fact, assault the suspect.

Suppose the case goes to trial. The client wants to testify under oath that he was not present during the assault and did not participate. The client wants his lawyer to call his girlfriend to testify that she was with him at his apartment when the assault took place. The client wants the lawyer to argue vigorously that the client has been falsely accused by coworkers trying to frame him. Should the lawyer follow his client's instructions?

While there are many who argue that the lawyer representing a criminal defendant should follow his client's instructions, the ethics codes in nearly every state prohibit lawyers from knowingly presenting false testimony. If lawyers were allowed to present false facts and argue from them, the finder of fact might believe the witness and reach an unjust result based on an incorrect understanding of the facts.

Rule 3.3 summarizes a lawyer's duty of candor toward a tribunal. Read the language below and compare it to the corresponding rule in your state to see if there are differences.

Rule 3.3. Candor Toward the Tribunal

(a) A lawyer shall not knowingly:

(1) make a false statement of fact or law to a tribunal or fail to correct a false statement of material fact or law previously made to the tribunal by the lawyer;

(2) fail to disclose to the tribunal legal authority in the controlling jurisdiction known to the lawyer to be directly adverse to the position of the client and not disclosed by opposing counsel; or

(3) offer evidence that the lawyer knows to be false. If a lawyer, the lawyer's client, or a witness called by the lawyer, has offered mate-

rial evidence and the lawyer comes to know of its falsity, the lawyer shall take reasonable remedial measures, including, if necessary, disclosure to the tribunal. A lawyer may refuse to offer evidence, other than the testimony of a defendant in a criminal matter, that the lawyer reasonably believes is false.

(b) A lawyer who represents a client in an adjudicative proceeding and who knows that a person intends to engage, is engaging or has engaged in criminal or fraudulent conduct related to the proceeding shall take reasonable remedial measures, including, if necessary, disclosure to the tribunal.

(c) The duties stated in paragraphs (a) and (b) continue to the conclusion of the proceeding, and apply even if compliance requires disclosure of information otherwise protected by Rule 1.6.

(d) In an ex parte proceeding, a lawyer shall inform the tribunal of all material facts known to the lawyer that will enable the tribunal to make an informed decision, whether or not the facts are adverse.

The application of this rule raises many questions. For example, what is a false statement? Does this category include statements that are literally true but incomplete or misleading? How do you distinguish a material fact from a non-material one? How sure about "falsity" must a lawyer be to "know" that she has offered false evidence? You can find guidance on these and other questions in the comments that follow Rule 3.3 in your state ethics code and in court opinions and advisory ethics opinions that interpret or apply the rule. We offer a brief explanation of two key issues in this arena.

If a lawyer has offered false evidence or knows that someone else has engaged in criminal or fraudulent conduct related to the proceeding, the lawyer must take remedial action. What must she do? When is disclosure necessary?

"Remedial action" means that the lawyer must take steps to ensure that the finder of fact is not misled. The rules encourage lawyers to carry out this duty without disclosing client confidences, if possible, and if a disclosure is necessary, to disclose as little as possible. See Comment 11. If a client has made a false statement in court or in a deposition, a lawyer first should try to persuade the client to make a statement correcting his own testimony. If the client refuses to correct his testimony, the lawyer might seek to withdraw from representing the client and explain to the court that the lawyer is withdrawing because continuing to represent the client would require the lawyer to engage in unethical conduct. This is known as a "noisy withdrawal." Such a statement often is sufficient to alert the judge to a problem in the evidence that has been presented. If withdrawal is not possible or would not put the court on adequate notice of the problem, the lawyer may need to make a direct disclosure to the judge.

None of this is easy or fun, of course, but the rules in most states are clear that a lawyer may not sit by and watch her own client or a witness present false information in court. The integrity of the judicial process is so important that, in some cases, it takes precedence over a lawyer's duty to a client.

What is a "tribunal"? At first glance, Rule 3.3 appears to apply only to lawyers presenting information in courts. In fact, the rule applies whenever a lawyer is presenting information to any finder of fact, whether the proceeding is in a court, an administrative agency, a legislative hearing, or an arbitration proceeding. See Rule 1.0(m). Rule 3.9 explains that except for ex parte proceedings, the duties articulated in Rule 3.3 apply even if the lawyer is representing a client in a non-adjudicative proceeding before a legislative or administrative agency. This means the duty of candor toward "tribunals" would apply, for example, to a lawyer submitting comments on behalf of a client in an agency rulemaking proceeding and to a lawyer representing a client in testimony on proposed legislation.

PROBLEM 7.1
False Testimony

Isaiah Goodwin told the following story in his externship seminar:

I'm working at the prosecutor's office, mainly working for this one guy named Steven Charney. Yesterday I went with him to court to watch him try a case in which the defendant, a twenty-four-year-old man, was charged with possession of cocaine. It was a pretty straightforward felony case, except for one thing.

The arresting officer got on the stand and testified that when he searched the suspect, he found a large bag of white powder, which turned out to be cocaine, in the suspect's right jacket pocket. The bag of powder was introduced into evidence. The defendant did not testify. He was convicted, of course. A sentencing hearing was scheduled. The defendant had one prior drug conviction, so he probably will go to prison for a long time.

After this case was concluded, Steve stayed in the courtroom to prosecute another case, but I left to go back to the office to work on a research memo. I stopped at the water fountain in the hallway outside the courtroom. I noticed that the officer who had testified was chatting with another policeman a few feet away. So I took a long drink and listened.

The arresting officer was boasting to his friend about how this guy was going away for years, for sure, and that it was about time, because everyone knew he was a dealer. "Of course I didn't really find anything when I searched him, but no one will ever know that now. It's about time that guy got taken off the street."

I felt like I had just stumbled onto the set of *Law and Order*. I couldn't believe it. When Steve got back to the office, I went in to see him and told him what I had heard. He said, "Well, Isaiah, welcome to the real world. These things happen all the time. It's just part of law enforcement." I tried to argue with him, but he became incredibly patronizing. He said something like, "Last time I checked, I was the one with nine years' experience as a prosecutor, and you were the law student volunteer. I suggest you try to learn a few things instead of telling me how to do my job."

To be honest, I'm pretty freaked out. For one, my boss now thinks I'm a total idiot and the rest of my semester is probably shot, not to mention my chance of getting a decent reference. For another, I was planning to become a prosecutor, but now I'm wondering whether this sort of attitude is typical. Maybe I should be a defense lawyer instead. And one other thing. What about this guy who is about to get sent to prison based on false testimony? My boss seems unconcerned. Maybe I should tell someone else, maybe even the judge. To sit silent seems so dishonest!

What are Steve's and Isaiah's obligations under Rule 3.3? What do you think Isaiah should do in this situation? What are the risks presented by each possible course of action? Also, consider whether it was proper for Isaiah to eavesdrop and then tell this story in class.

PROBLEM 7.2
Adverse Authority

Annette Sanderson was an extern at the Employment Law Center. She worked for Micah Portman, who handled employment discrimination cases. Micah had received a motion to dismiss one of his cases. The motion argued that the statute of limitations had run. Micah drafted a response to the motion, citing the relevant statute of limitations and a case that supported an interpretation of it favorable to the Center's client. He asked Annette to take his draft response and check whether any other authorities should be cited.

Annette's first step in her research was to look for cases that cited the opinion Micah had cited. Immediately she found a just-published opinion by the intermediate state appellate court that overturned the decision Micah relied on and interpreted the statute of limitations the same way as the lawyer who filed the motion to dismiss. This decision was on appeal to the state supreme court.

Annette checked the defendant's motion to dismiss to see if this new case was cited. It was not. Annette reported to Micah on her research. Micah said, "I'm glad you found this case, but I don't think I'm obliged to cite it. We'll let the defendant's lawyer do his own research."

Is Micah correct? How should Annette respond to his analysis?

Duties Toward Opposing Counsel, Witnesses, and Others

As you have seen, lawyers' have an array of ethical obligations toward their clients and toward the justice system. In addition, lawyers are required to be truthful and to conduct themselves in a professional manner in their dealings with opposing counsel, witnesses, and others.

Truthfulness

The ethics rules are organized into sets of duties lawyers owe to clients, tribunals, and others. As you read in the previous section, Rule 3.3 addresses the duty of truthfulness toward tribunals. Other rules (including 1.4 on advice and 7.1 on communication about legal services) address the lawyer's duty of candor to clients. Rule 8.4(c) prohibits any and all "dishonesty, fraud, deceit or misrepresentation." Rule 4.1 articulates a lawyer's duty of candor toward adversaries and third parties.

Rule 4.1. Truthfulness in Statement to Others

In the course of representing a client a lawyer shall not knowingly:

(a) make a false statement of material fact or law to a third person; or

(b) fail to disclose a material fact to a third person when disclosure is necessary to avoid assisting a criminal or fraudulent act by a client, unless disclosure is prohibited by Rule 1.6.

In dealings with opposing counsel or other third persons, lawyers are not permitted to make false statements, but they have no affirmative duty of disclosure under Rule 4.1 unless by withholding information the lawyer would be "assisting" a "criminal" or "fraudulent" act by a client. In that case, a lawyer is required to share the information unless revelation is not permitted under Rule 1.6. Like the other standards we have mentioned, this one raises more questions than it answers, especially because facts do not come with labels saying "true," "false," "material," or "fraudulent." Consider the following problem.

PROBLEM 7.3
Child Support

Maritza Karski was an extern in a domestic relations firm. Sam Guzman, her supervisor, invited Maritza to come to a meeting to negotiate a child support and visitation agreement for Catherine Carvino, a client of the firm. Maritza had been working on this case, calling the client to obtain various documents and information that Sam needed. The meeting was to be held at the law office of Travis Johnston, who was representing Alan Carvino, Catherine's soon-to-be-ex-husband.

The case was simple enough. Catherine had stayed home for three years raising Jaden and Nicholas, the couple's two sons, and then had started working part-time in a daycare center. Alan worked as an air traffic controller, so most of the family income was from his earnings. The couple had separated after Alan confessed to Catherine that he had had a four-month relationship with a woman he had met on the Internet.

Catherine has accepted the inevitability of divorce, but she is anxious about her ability to manage as a single parent unless she gets a substantial child support settlement. Two weeks before the meeting, Maritza had called Catherine to get a copy of one missing tax return. During their conversation, Catherine mentioned that her great-aunt Dana had just passed away after a long illness. Catherine said she would drop off a copy of the missing tax return that afternoon on her way to Dana's funeral. Catherine mentioned that Dana, who had no children of her own, had promised to leave her 24-acre estate to Catherine.

"This could make all the difference in our lives," Catherine said. "There's a four-bedroom house, and a barn, and a pond . . . the boys would be so happy there."

"Are you sure she's leaving the estate to you?" Maritza asked.

"I haven't actually read the will," said Catherine, "but Aunt Dana and I have talked many times about this. We had one conversation about it three days before she passed away. I promised to take good care of the house and to try to keep it in the family."

"I'm sorry for your loss, but that's really good news about the estate." said Maritza. "When you get a copy of Dana's will, perhaps Sam can look it over for you."

"Yes, that would be great," said Catherine. "I'll ask the executor for a copy."

Maritza meant to tell Sam about what Catherine had said, but Sam was in court the afternoon that she talked with Catherine, and it slipped her mind. Maritza's spring break started the next day, and she spent eight wonderful days at the beach. The next time Maritza saw Sam was the week after spring break, when they met in the elevator on the way to the settlement meeting. Alan and Travis, Alan's lawyer, also were on the elevator, so there was no chance to talk.

During the meeting, Catherine sat between Sam and Maritza on one side of the table. Alan and Travis sat on the other side. Sam and Travis reviewed the financial statement listing the earnings, assets and debts of both clients, and began to discuss how much Alan should pay in child support.

Maritza sat in the meeting looking at her own copies of the documents. She noticed that there was nothing on the financial statement for Catherine about great-aunt Dana's house. Then Travis asked Sam and Catherine:

"Do you anticipate any changes in Catherine's financial situation that would change this picture in any way?"

Sam looked at his client for an answer. Catherine said "Not unless I win the lottery."

If Sam knew about the bequest, what would be his ethical obligations in this situation? Does his ignorance excuse him from any possible duty of disclosure? What should Maritza do?

Communication

Lawyers owe duties of candor and professional courtesy to other lawyers and to unrepresented persons with whom they deal. As with other ethical duties, a lawyer may not ask an employee to do something that the lawyer may not herself do. Many legal externs interview witnesses, deliver papers, make phone calls, and do other delegated tasks that involve dealing with opposing counsel, witnesses, and others, so externs need to be familiar with these boundaries.

Communication with represented persons

Rule 4.2. Communication with Person Represented by Counsel

> In representing a client, a lawyer shall not communicate about the subject of the representation with a person the lawyer knows to be represented by another lawyer in the matter, unless the lawyer has the consent of the other lawyer or is authorized to do so by law or a court order.

This means that a lawyer or someone working for the lawyer may not call or visit an adverse party in a case or someone else who is represented in the matter by another lawyer unless the other lawyer has given permission for the contact. Even an informal conversation with a represented adverse party could lead to disciplinary action or to disqualification of the lawyer whose employee (or extern) had the prohibited contact. If you are uncertain about whether the person you are contacting is represented, the first question to ask when you contact that person is "Do you have a lawyer?" If the answer is yes, simply get the name and number of the lawyer and consult with your supervisor about next steps.

This rule seems simple enough, but there are some wrinkles. If the opposing party is a government agency, the rule may not apply, because citizens have constitutional and legal rights to communicate with government officials. If the opposing party is an organization that is represented by counsel, a lawyer (or a legal extern) may communicate directly with some employees of the organization but not others. Comment 7 after Rule 4.2 provides in part:

> In the case of a represented organization, this Rule prohibits communications with a constituent of the organization who supervises, directs or regularly consults with the organization's lawyer concerning the matter or has authority to obligate the organization with respect to the matter or whose act or omission in connection with the matter may be imputed to the organization for purposes of civil or criminal liability. Consent of the organization's lawyer is not required for communication with a former constituent.

If you are asked to interview employees of an adverse party that is an institution, first study your jurisdiction's version of Rule 4.2 and its comments, and then consult with your supervisor about which employees you may interview.

Communication with unrepresented persons

If the opposing party in a case is not represented, a lawyer may communicate directly with that person. In this situation, however, a lawyer must take care not to mislead the other person or to give legal advice to the other person.

Rule 4.3. Dealing with Unrepresented Person

> In dealing on behalf of a client with a person who is not represented by counsel, a lawyer shall not state or imply that the lawyer is disinterested. When the lawyer knows or reasonably should know that the unrepresented person misunderstands the lawyer's role in the matter, the lawyer shall make reasonable efforts to correct the misunderstanding. The lawyer shall not give legal advice to an unrepresented person, other than the advice to secure counsel, if the lawyer knows or reasonably should know that the interests of such a person are or have a reasonable possibility of being in conflict with the interests of the client.

These constraints are intended to prevent lawyers from taking advantage of others whose understanding of law and the legal system may be limited. A lawyer who misleads an unrepresented person also may be found to have violated Rule 8.4(c), which prohibits all "dishonesty, fraud, deceit or misrepresentation."

PROBLEM 7.4
A Fender Bender

Julie Maynard is a legal extern at the state Department of Consumer Affairs (DCA). She assists with investigations of complaints of unfair and deceptive trade practices by local merchants. The agency has recently received several complaints about the Mitch Dawson's Auto Body Shop. State law requires all merchants who perform car repairs to give customers itemized written estimates of the cost of repairs before doing any work. The law also prohibits charging customers more than the amount stated on the estimate. Mitch Dawson apparently tends to provide no estimate or only a "ball-park" oral estimate before doing work on a car.

Leo Gonzales is Julie's supervisor at DCA. He's preparing to file suit against Dawson. One morning, Julie's car gets rear-ended on the way in to the office. The back fender is crumpled. Julie is late to work and comes in frazzled, explaining apologetically about the accident.

"It wasn't my fault," Julie tells Leo, "but I had to stay until the police had completed their report."

Leo's eyes twinkle. "Tell you what," he says. "Why don't you take your car in to Mitch Dawson. Put this tape recorder in your jacket pocket, and turn it on before you get there. Just act like a normal customer. Tell him you want him to fix your fender and ask how much it will cost. Regardless of whether he gives you an estimate, leave your car for him to repair. If he follows the law, no problem, you get your car fixed. If not, you can be a plaintiff in the case and be my star witness. If we win, you may get a refund of the cost of the repair and possibly additional damages. Okay?"

How should Julie respond to Leo's request? Are there any ethical problems with this plan? If so, is there a way that Julie could undertake this investigation without violating the rules?

Conclusion

In this chapter, we have examined only a few of the ethical rules that constrain the conduct of lawyers in litigation. There are many other relevant rules and an enormous variety of situations that might present ethical quandaries for legal externs. For example, what if you are preparing documents to respond to a discovery request and your supervisor instructs you not to produce a particular document that you believe is covered by the request? What if you believe that a client or a lawyer has altered a document that is to be produced?

One of the goals of this chapter and the preceding ones on legal ethics issues is to provide you with some practice in attending to your own moral radar. Even if you work as an extern or as a lawyer with experienced lawyers who have high standards of professional conduct, you need to exercise independent ethical judgment. Law students should become familiar with the ethics rules and the other law that governs lawyers, but they also should hone their ethical sensitivity—their ability to recognize ethical dilemmas.

Fieldwork can provide rich opportunities to notice and think about ethical issues. There may be some issues that you do not want to ask your supervisor about. Some may seem trivial; others might raise questions about the conduct of your supervisor or another lawyer in the office. It is worthwhile to notice and evaluate the questions that occur to you even if you do not bring them up at work.

Here is a simple protocol for increasing your ability to recognize and evaluate ethical dilemmas: Pay attention whenever you see or do something that makes you feel a bit uneasy. Once you notice a question, do a little research. Is there an ethics rule or some other law that addresses the question? Discuss the question with your faculty supervisor or with a friend or family member—if you can do so without revealing client confidences. Exploring the questions about ethical issues that you encounter in early practice experiences will give you the skills you need to address larger issues in the future.

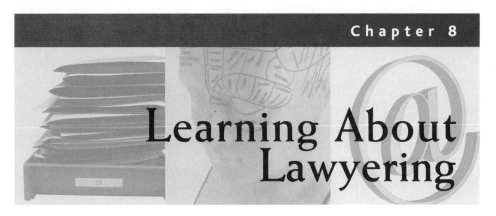

Chapter 8

Learning About Lawyering

Alex Scherr

Whatever your reasons for taking an externship course, your fieldwork gives you the chance to find out what lawyers do. Even if you do not start with that focus, you will soon draw conclusions about legal work, its challenges and intricacies, its subcultures, and its extraordinary effect on the lives of the people and causes for whom lawyers work. You will find yourself deciding what is good and bad—not just political or ethical appraisals but also assessments of good and bad practice. Your externship offers the chance to walk alongside lawyers as they work, to watch what they do, to assess to how they think, and to gauge their effectiveness in helping their clients.

You, however, might find it difficult to get a comprehensive, or even a coherent, sense of the lawyering going on around you. Your workplace may assign you relatively discrete tasks, covering only a part of the office's overall practice. Your schedule may not allow you to see key phases of your office's work. The legal problems in your office may take longer than one semester to resolve. Key decision makers may not work in your office or department. Your supervisors may not share much of their work or their thought processes with you. You may not get to see key events or be included in critical meetings. New lawyers too often encounter these limitations in the years right after law school. This book offers advice on how to compensate for them by creating learning agendas, dealing with supervisors, and reflecting on your experience.

This chapter will help you to understand the lawyering that goes on at your work place by putting it in context. It focuses on the exercise of good judgment by lawyers in making and implementing decisions. It offers an overview of the lawyering process and a roadmap to the different kinds of law practice. It identifies ways to gain deeper insight into the lawyering at your placement and to start developing your own standards of quality. Finally, the chapter identifies ways to bring your learning about lawyering into the context of your own development as a lawyer.

Lawyering, Decisions, and Practical Judgment

Lawyers and Decisions

Consider the following question: if plumbers work with pipe, and carpenters with wood, with what do lawyers work? Reasonable answers to this question might include words, or people, or laws, or values, or money. A more general answer suggests that lawyers work with problems. Lawyers are problem solvers. The term "problem" may imply that lawyers work only where conflict or difficulty exists. While lawyers do handle these situations, problem solving also includes the work that lawyers do in structuring deals, realizing opportunities, and reducing the risks of future problems. Lawyers respond to requests for help *both* to resolve current disputes *and* to accomplish future goals.

Decision making forms the heart of problem solving. In a more specific sense, lawyers work with decisions. Lawyers help to assess, make, and implement choices between alternate stories from disputing parties, between alternate agreements, and between different ways to structure behavior in the future. For clients and their lawyers, the experience of problem solving is thus the experience of decision making. Early on in your externship, you should try to understand the impact your work has on decision making at your placement, so as to grasp how all parts of the practice work together to solve problems.

Lawyers do not hold a monopoly on helping people make decisions; the helping professions generally advise people struggling with important choices. Indeed, your placement may rely on these other professionals as part of its practice, including expert witnesses, investigators, special masters, and the like. Lawyers, however, do have a monopoly on advice for certain kinds of decisions: those affected by legal rules and those that require access to legal process. The essence of legal work involves assessing how the law affects particular problems and how legal process can advance particular goals. Lawyers mediate the influences of the law on client decision making.

Lawyers do not consider *only* the law. Most legal problems respond to a variety of influences, and lawyers must be as adept in working with these influences as in analyzing the law. These diverse influences include the situation's history and momentum; its affective and intellectual aspects; the web of relationships involved; the relative power of the participants; the intensity of the stakes; and practical limits on solutions, in terms of money, time, and other realities. Legal problem solving asks lawyers to apply the law in a context shaped by all of these influences, and more besides. You may notice how much more "real" legal issues feel at your placement. The sensation results from the immediacy of the human context in which legal problems occur.

Exercise 8.1 Select a case on which you are working or a case that you have observed. Do a standard law school assessment: identify the legal issues and ask how they apply to the facts as you understand them.

Then step back and ask other questions: Who are the parties? What relationship have they had? What else do you know about the case history? What do you know about the parties' interests? What kind of power did they have to pursue their concerns? What needs will your legal work satisfy? What resources can each party bring to bear? How will the parties react to the legal outcome? How will that outcome affect their future dealings?

Now bring the legal issue back into focus. How does this issue relate to the context you have identified? The legal issue should now appear as one thread in a complex weave of influences, with a strong, and perhaps even decisive, influence on the case outcome.

Decisions made by lawyers and their clients become the law of the client's problem. In effect, what lawyers do about their cases becomes the law itself. It is thus no stretch to say that, as an extern, you are helping your supervisors to make law. Lawyering produces law whenever a lawyer helps to resolve a problem. This law is often transient and local, may bind no one other than the client, and may have limited impact even there. The practice habits and analytical assumptions of lawyers, however, become the templates for future handling of the same or similar problems. More generally, the practice habits of lawyers help to structure the norms of both disputes and deals. These norms shape both routine and unusual client action and have a distinct impact on the evolution of particular concerns into common law and legislative decision making. You have an ideal opportunity at your placement to observe how the norms of your placement both embody what the law says and affect what the law may become.

Decision Making and Practical Judgment

Decision making requires the capacity to choose among several available courses of action, commonly referred to as "judgment." Judgment is a basic life skill. It is the ability to make choices both small and large. We exercise judgment daily. The verb indicates its active, organic quality. Despite its prevalence, identifying and discussing good legal judgment is difficult, especially for new lawyers. Law schools tend to fractionalize lawyering behaviors, singling out intellectual competencies (such as legal analysis or legal research) or performance competencies (such as trial advocacy or legal drafting) for specialized focus. This typically leaves discussions of judgment, especially overall judgment about case handling, to active experience in law practice, including your experience in a clinic or externship.

Part of the problem lies in describing exactly what constitutes "good" judgment. You should not have to reflect for more than a minute to recall a good decision and perhaps even less to recall a bad one! But even if you listed all these decisions, you still would find it hard to define a process for exercising good judgment in every situation, or even in a given situation. Good judgment is local, problem specific, subject to unique facts, involving diverse people with distinct interests and preferences, and presenting variable risks and opportunities. Similarly, good legal judgment requires more than good legal analysis. A lawyer has to account *both* for legal rules and processes *and* for the non-legal influences that affect the decision. Decision making by lawyers in their cases is deeply pragmatic. This chapter encourages you to consider how your supervisors exercise practical judgment in the handling of their cases.

Some believe that you cannot learn good judgment, that like talent or cool, you either have it or you do not. People do vary in their abilities to make decisions. The consistency with which some people make good (or bad) ones supports the idea that judgment grows out of innate traits. We believe, however, that through practice and reflection, you can *develop* your ability for practical judgment. Your placement should give you many examples (good and bad) from which to start developing that competency. Do not expect to acquire it in a day, a semester, or even a year. Practical judgment requires you to understand a decision in different dimensions, not just the conceptual framework of the law, but also the human realities from which the decision emerges and which the decision will affect. Practical judgment matters the most when exercised over time and in the real world, on real problems, and for real clients. You may not understand all of the reasons your supervising attorneys make certain decisions, but you can learn a lot by watching how they choose to proceed, asking them why, and evaluating their answers against your own sense of what to do.

Exercise 8.2 Consider which lawyers at your placement have good reputations and which do not. For example, if you work in a large office, you may notice that many lawyers go to a particular colleague for insight and advice about a case. If you work in a judge's chambers, you may notice that the judge listens more carefully to some lawyers than others. Try to determine what accounts for that special reliance and deference. Is it specialized knowledge? Greater candor? An engaging personality? An open office door close to the elevator? While all of these may play a role, these lawyers have most likely earned their reputations through the exercise of good judgment about the cases that they handle—and for giving good advice when asked for help on others' cases.

Practical Judgment and the Lawyering Process

Talking about judgment means talking about the inner experience of lawyering: finding and analyzing law, absorbing and assessing influences, structuring and evaluating decisions. Legal judgment occurs in real time and in the real world, in active relationship to other people, tasks, and deadlines. This section talks about lawyering not as a decision but as a process, that is, a series of behaviors through which lawyers encounter, make, and implement their decisions. The discussion offers you a roadmap of the core competencies of lawyering. It does not go in depth into any of these competencies because to do so would take far longer than this chapter, or even this whole book. A roadmap can suggest how one behavior affects others and encourage you to focus on different phases of your placement's law practice. It also can help you compare your placement with other law practices. Finally, it should help you to assess your own development as a lawyer and to develop a plan for improving your own competencies as a lawyer.

Legal problem solving has a work flow similar to other problem solving. It includes identifying the problem and assessing its dimensions, formulating and making decisions, and implementing choices through planned action. This work flow is goal oriented and moves generally from initial contact to final resolution; however, the phases of problem solving do not separate easily. Lawyers often move back and forth among phases of assessment, decision making, and action as they move towards their goal. The cyclical nature of the lawyering process makes it hard to see it whole. In a given case, you may do or see only a narrow portion of the problem-solving activity. For example, doing legal research, organizing documents, or drafting a single clause in an agreement are discrete activities that contribute to

Legal problem solving does differ from other problem solving.

1) Lawyers use legal principles and processes as the dominant conceptual framework.

2) Lawyers have a monopoly on certain activities, including legal advice, courtroom advocacy, and certain kinds of opinions.

3) Lawyers have special lines of accountability: for practitioners, to clients or client interests; for judges, to parties and appellate courts; and for all lawyers, to rules of law and ethics.

Other professions share some of these aspects of professional life, but a lawyer's specialized relationship to the law and legal processes sets the legal profession apart. How does this specialty affect the way lawyers, compared to other professionals, think about problems?

the outcome but form only part of the overall case handling. Observation of case events also may limit your vision of problem solving. You may see only a single hearing in a judicial placement, an isolated deposition in a litigation placement, or the closing in a transactions placement. These isolated tasks and events represent stages in the overall handling of the matter by your office. You should start to ask about the broader context of problem solving within which these events occur.

Assessment

Good lawyering depends on accurate assessment of cases. A lawyer's appraisal constructs both the client's choices and the lawyer's actions. Appraisal and reappraisal occur throughout the lawyer's work. The lawyer must respond to new information, new theories, and new pressures from other parties. Thus, acquiring good habits of case appraisal represents a key phase in the development of your abilities as a lawyer. Your placement should give you many chances to observe and evaluate different methods of preparing and assessing cases. You should look to assess how your placement acquires its cases, how it develops the relevant facts and law, and how it assesses the likely outcomes of its work.

All lawyering starts with an ***initial encounter***, which might take the form of a phone call, a client interview, a police referral, or the assignment of a file by a docketing clerk. During this encounter, the lawyer develops some first impressions and charts out the next steps in case development. These first impressions, and the choices they prompt, not only influence the lawyer's or judge's next steps, but also influence how the lawyer understands and addresses the problem itself. Try to find out who handles this initial contact at your placement and how your office assures prompt, uniform, and otherwise professional responses to those initial contacts.

> **Exercise 8.3** Most law practices depend on forms and files, both paper and electronic. Your first hours—perhaps even days—will be occupied in learning your placement's approach to files and the associated paperwork. This work can be tedious and picayune, but it is worth your time to consider how it relates to your placement's problem solving. Common forms include intake forms and opening memos, case information sheets (including docketing sheets in judicial chambers), and phone and contact logs. Most offices use a uniform format for memos, case notes, and even the sequencing of paper in the file. Ask how these help the practice. Do they help to manage case tasks? Do they make it easier to pick up a long-dormant case? Do they promote the sharing of files among attorneys? Do they assure compliance with rules of ethics and malpractice?

Your office also must develop the factual information and legal concepts necessary for its assessment through the phases of *investigation* and *legal research*. Externs typically participate actively in this phase of the case, handling investigation or research tasks on assignment from a supervisor. You will find differing degrees of certainty in these assignments and differing levels of clarity for both fact and law. You may receive research assignments that have minimal factual context or assignments that require you to assess how different scenarios would affect possible legal outcomes. Similarly, you may have to interview witnesses and review documents in support of a particular legal claim or to see how many legal claims a given set of facts might support. Lawyers' understanding of the facts affects the legal issues that they identify and assess, and legal research typically highlights additional facts that the lawyer must explore. In effect, investigation and research converge, each informing and shaping the other.

Exercise 8.4 Lawyers often express their developing understanding of a given problem with a simplified story that captures its essential elements: a theory of the case. A theory of the case is a brief, persuasive description that merges both legal and factual knowledge into a short statement of goals and justifications. In litigation, a theory of the case might well consist of a few sentences, even a catchphrase, that shapes opening and closing arguments. In transactions, case theory represents a brief statement of the deal that expresses its key agreements and assumptions. Negotiating lawyers use theory of the case both to persuade other parties and to manage opportunities for settlement. Judges may develop a "theory of the decision," in response to the competing case theories of the parties.

As you reflect on your work, choose a case on which you have worked and try to articulate your office's theory of that case. Does that theory account for what you know? Does it tell you anything about the underlying decisions? Does it work?

The focus of that convergence is the task of *merit assessment*. This task requires the lawyer to assess law and fact together. For example, litigators must predict the likely outcome of litigation in order to assist client decision making, to plan for trial, and to assess negotiations. Similarly, transactional lawyers must determine the extent to which the law will regulate a proposed deal. In either case, the lawyer must integrate an appropriately thorough legal analysis into a reasonably thorough version of the facts, so as to appraise the likelihood that legal rules will permit the client's desired result. This conclusion has a direct effect on the office's handling of a case. Even as an extern, you may be asked your recommendation on what to do in light of the known facts and law. When that happens, you will feel the weight of responsibility that attaches to these judgments.

As important as legal merit assessment is, however, it forms only a part of legal problem solving. The lawyer still must integrate that assessment into other practical realities. For example, a litigator must assess not only the likelihood of success in court but also the client's tolerance for risk, need for a remedy, and aversion to trial. Similarly, a lawyer helping to form a business must determine not only what ways of organizing a business are available, but also help the client assess how those organizational forms help or hinder the client's ability to achieve personal and financial goals. You also will find judges influenced by pragmatic considerations, balancing the strictly correct legal result with the practical demands of docket management and the interest in achieving a durable solution to the particular dispute.

The lawyer's assessment task thus weaves purely legal assessments together with other practical dimensions, so as to see the problem in depth and to generate effective solutions. At your placement, keep track of what happens to the legal analyses that you perform. How do your assigning attorneys use them? What effect do they have on decisions in the overall cases? What other factors seem to influence the way that decisions take shape and strategy forms? Answering questions like these should deepen your grasp on the lawyering at your placement.

Decision making

It pays to distinguish between a final decision and the decisions that lead to it. While all lawyering seeks a final decision (a verdict, a binding agreement, an agency ruling), finality emerges from a series of smaller, connected decisions shaped by the lawyer's appraisal and handling of the case. Moreover, legal decision making occurs from a particular point of view. Both advocates and planners seek to advance particular goals and interests. In the paragraphs that follow, we will talk about two aspects of decision making that you can assess at your placement—the development of choices and strategies and the process of deciding itself.

Preparing for a decision means identifying choices and developing strategies to accomplish each choice. The identification of choices starts early, during the assessment phase. As the lawyer gathers information and analyzes legal rules, she will gain a better sense of the possible outcomes that the problem allows, the *options* for decision. At the same time, she will start to identify what it will take to achieve those outcomes, the collection of actions and events, or *strategies*, that may accomplish each outcome. In so doing, the lawyer must be both creative, able to imagine the goals and means relevant to the problem at hand, and realistic, able to assess how plausible each outcome and strategy is within the restrictions of time, energy, and resources. This ability to assess legal and practical realities and to create a reliable picture of available choices and strategies lies at the heart of "thinking like a lawyer."

Here are some examples as illustrations:

• In a litigation placement, a tenant has asked the lawyer for help with a notice of eviction for nonpayment of rent. After investigating and researching potential defenses, the lawyer concludes that the client has plausible but not airtight affirmative defenses, based on the landlord's failure to make repairs, which if lost at trial might form the basis for a successful appeal. The client's fundamental options include staying in the apartment, with or without necessary repairs, or moving, either now or in the future. Strategies include litigation through trial to appeal; litigating, but seeking a settlement that allows the client either the ability to stay or the time to move; or vacating the premises without litigation. The lawyer faces the task of advising the client on which of these best meets the client's goals and interests.

• In a transactional placement, a community group wants to encourage local economic development. After interviewing the group's participants and researching relevant possibilities, the lawyer concludes that a variety of different organizational forms might fit the group's goals. The client's fundamental options include continuing as a loose association or organizing as a legal entity and continuing as a volunteer effort or seeking some form of funding. Strategies include continuing without further legal organization or entering into a corporate form, with a subsidiary choice on for-profit or non-profit status. The lawyer faces the task of helping the client assess which option best meets the group's collection of goals and interests.

• In a judicial placement, a judge has been assigned a complex tort lawsuit involving multiple plaintiffs and a large corporate defendant. Upon reviewing the pleadings and pending motions, the judge and the judge's clerk conclude that the issues of causation and damages might be triable separately and that causation involves contested facts that require expert testimony. The judge will have choices about bifurcating the trial, about the admissibility of expert testimony, and about the use of special masters. The judge has different possible strategies for choosing: waiting to respond to motions from the parties or using pretrial conferences to encourage the parties to reach agreement on what to do. The judge faces the task of working with the parties and attorneys on a trial process that leads to an accurate and final resolution of the relevant claims.

When you are assigned a case at your placement, take the time to ask how your assignment relates to the ultimate outcome of that case. When you observe a hearing or a negotiation, try to discern how each lawyer's actions both express and advance particular goals. The more you understand the choices and strategies underlying the work that you do or see, the more you can learn about how lawyers identify and pursue the solutions they achieve.

We have left until now the question of how to decide about choices and strategies. Legal problem solving does not stop with thorough assessment and careful construction of strategy. Choices must be made about which goal to pursue and in which way. The process through which this decision occurs traditionally is called **counseling** and, in the most traditional sense, it involves a conversation between a lawyer and a client. This traditional model has the lawyer presenting her assessment of the case, identifying options and associated strategies, and evaluating how those options will accommodate the client's various goals and concerns. The client chooses what to do, and the lawyer proceeds to implement the client's choice.

While this traditional model is still in place for many lawyers, it is very possible that you will never see it at your placement. First, your particular placement may have set up your involvement so that you do not have exposure to the client. If this is true, consider asking to sit in on a counseling session as an observer. Second, your placement may not have a "client," at least in the traditional sense. Consider a prosecutor's office, a federal enforcement agency, corporate counsel, or a county attorney. Each of these pursue distinct interests and concerns, but none has a single individual as the client. At best, a particular individual has representative authority to make decisions. In some cases, such as for a prosecutor, the decision maker may be the attorney herself. Finally, the traditional model breaks down completely when applied to judging. Judges are subject to a range of different influences, including the parties to a case, appellate courts, and the legal system itself, but do not have a client.

Try to determine early in your placement exactly who the client is and what your placement's governing concerns are. In asking the question, consider not just which individual or group appears to have final say over cases, but also what goals or interests your office seeks to pursue. When representing an individual, a lawyer pursues that client's goals. When representing an agency, a lawyer makes decisions under an overarching statutory mandate to enforce certain laws and policies. Prosecutors must make their case decisions "in the public interest," a moving target that consists of legal, pragmatic, and political influences. Finally, as already noted, judicial decision making occurs under a range of influences, from the competing claims of the parties, to the judge's pragmatic sense of durable outcomes, to the risk of reversal on appeal.

The process by which decisions are made may match the traditional conversational model, but other processes exist as well. For example, in agencies, the process may involve internal office hierarchy or stated office priorities. An assistant prosecutor may have to seek approval from the elected prosecutor to pursue a controversial case. Decision making may involve multiple people or groups of people. For example, a consumer fraud lawyer may have to seek approval from an agency panel to pursue a new class of commercial offenders. As you explore this decision-making process, consider the role and relative influence of each person in the process. As you do so, pay particular attention to the lawyer's role. By gathering the facts and articulating legal theories, the lawyers exert a distinct influence on the decision, through both their assessments and the options they develop for decision.

Action

Through television and film, we have become accustomed to the image of lawyers as litigators, typically in the criminal justice system, focused on the demands of advocacy. This image severely understates the wide variety of activities lawyers actually do. From politics to private transactions, from litigation to arbitration to mediation, from judging to legislating to deal making, lawyers as problem solvers occupy a huge field of action. Lawyers focus their practices in particular subject areas (for example, criminal law, commercial contracts, estate planning), around particular skill sets (for example, brief writing, case management, interviewing), and in particular venues (for example, courtroom, legislature, regulatory agency). Indeed, larger firms usually divide their practice into groups that focus on particular kinds of legal action, even within the same subject area. For example, a commercial contracts group may be separated from a commercial litigation group. We will cover some of the distinctions between types of law practices a bit later. This section focuses on the core activities of lawyering and on how they relate to the other phases of the lawyering process.

Three activities form the basic structure of lawyering: advocacy, planning, and negotiation.

- Advocates take on the task of persuading the decision maker to rule for the advocate's client. Advocates typically work on disputes arising from past events and use preset procedures to force (or to resist) a particular outcome to those disputes. Advocacy practices typically involve litigation, but increasingly entail arbitration, administrative hearings, and similar processes. Advocacy is fundamentally adversarial in nature. The advocate acts in opposition to another advocate. Final decision making rests with a neutral actor—judge, jury, hearing officer, or arbitrator.

Lawyers also perform one other fundamental law job, the task of making binding decisions. *Judging* is quintessentially lawyer's work (even though lay judges still serve in many states). The task differs from other lawyering. Unlike advocates, planners, or negotiators, judges make final decisions, ones that can be enforced against the loser by the state's authority. This creates a demanding and highly personal sense of responsibility; each judge has distinct habits and processes for handling that weight. If you work for a judge, try to discern how your judge goes about reaching decisions, particularly hard ones. How does she handle the gravity of the judicial role? On what resources does she draw? What role does her past experience seem to play?

- Planners take on the task of structuring future behavior, relying on the parties' consent as binding authority. A planner's work anticipates and assesses future risks and opportunities, usually from a perspective that stresses the durability of her plan against future change. These practices cover a diverse range of plans: for individuals (for example, estate planning), for two parties (for example, contracts, real estate transactions), for groups (for example, business formation, construction contracts), and for communities (for example, zoning, legislation.) The heart of planning lies in the anticipation and management of risk. The planner seeks to create a transaction that satisfies the client's goals into the foreseeable future. Decision-making authority rests with the parties rather than with neutral non-parties. The plan's success or failure is not known until the future. The deal becomes final when the parties have completed performance or (as with business forms or public rules) as long as the form or rule remains in place.

- Negotiators take on the task of reaching a solution by consent. Advocates use negotiation to expedite their disputes and to settle claims. Planners rely on negotiation to achieve binding consent to a longer-term transaction. Like advocates, negotiators engage in persuasion; unlike advocates, negotiators also must be open to persuasion if a settlement is to be reached. Like planners, negotiators seek a result through agreement.

One way to see the difference between advocacy and planning practices is by looking at the written work that each requires. Litigation practices require skill at persuasive writing, presenting a position so as to move a decision maker to favorable action. By contrast, planners must draft legal documents that will elicit the consent of all parties and that serve as a private constitution for future behavior. Planners must take pains to use very precise language so as to avoid the disputes that arise out of ambiguity. Litigators are like novelists, telling stories about the past so as to move their audiences to sympathetic action. By contrast, planners are like playwrights, creating scripts that other actors will perform. The measure of a planner's success is the extent to which those actors stick to the script, avoiding improvisation.

You should find your supervisors engaged in some measure of all three activities. Both litigators and planners use negotiation as a central part of their practice. If at all possible, try to observe those negotiations, and ask yourself why the attorneys chose to negotiate then, on those issues, and with what goal. Less obviously, both advocates and planners usually must acquire some ability with the other's skill set. Litigators must decide what remedy will satisfy their client's goals in the dispute;

these choices affect the parties' lives after the dispute in important ways. Similarly, planners regularly assess whether a future dispute will arise from the proposed plan. Indeed, the written memorialization of a deal often includes a dispute resolution clause that structures how future disputes will be handled. You can track this overlap at your placement. For each case you work on, and each event you observe, try to sort out the long-term consequences of advocacy or the disputes that might arise out of a planned transaction.

This overview of the phases of lawyering process should help you to deepen your grasp on your placement's approach to problem solving. Each practice organizes these activities in different ways. The next section describes and distinguishes several major types of law practices. Remember that neither the process nor its competencies are goals. Instead, they are the means through which lawyers exercise practical judgment to address the underlying problem. The craft and challenge of lawyering focuses the lawyer's ability to manage the relevant process so as to apply good judgment to the demands of each project.

Law Practices

By now in your law school career, you will have noticed the wide variety of work for graduates of law school. To list each and every one of these jobs would take more space than we have. It is ambitious even to map out the major distinctions in the type of problems on which lawyers work. Having said that, we think that it helps for you to have a point of comparison between your placement and what other lawyers do in other types of practices. In reading what follows, consider where your placement's practice fits and how your placement's problem solving matches or contrasts with the problem solving of other lawyers.

We already have introduced one major distinction between types of law practice, the distinction between transactional and dispute resolving practices. While this is a major distinction, other important distinctions in practice type also exist as a series of paired contrasts.

- Criminal/civil: Lawyers working in the criminal justice system include both prosecution and defense lawyers. Civil lawyers work on legal problems outside the criminal justice system, including those between private parties and between private parties and governments. Note that a category of quasi-criminal practices exist, including work on child delinquency cases or mental health commitments.

- Commercial/personal: Commercial lawyers work on disputes and transactions between businesses, both implementing deals and resolv-

Advocacy, planning, and negotiating are elemental law jobs that regularly combine to produce distinctive kinds of legal work. Consider other roles that lawyers play. Lawyers serve as legislators (or lobbyists); as community organizers; as mediators, diplomats, or other conciliators; as fiduciaries; as court-appointed monitors; and in many other roles. If your placement does not offer clear-cut examples of "litigators," "planners," or "negotiators" that means that you have encountered something distinctive. Try to assess what actions the lawyers take to advance their clients' interests and how these actions relate to the elemental law jobs.

see Chapter 18
on Career Planning

Just as the layman's image of lawyers is dominated by courtroom litigation, the law student's image of law jobs is dominated by jobs in large private law firms. If this chapter and your experience in your placement do anything, they should open up your perspective to other kinds of practices and other ways of living as a lawyer. This chapter suggests different aspects of the craft of being a lawyer. These have a distinct effect on what it feels like to work as a lawyer and offer choices that might suit your personality and temperament in distinctive ways. Use your experience as a point of comparison with the job offerings you see on the interview schedule. Talk with your supervisors and with other students about the career paths they have pursued.

ing disputes. Lawyers working on disputes between non-commercial parties may focus on property or money issues or focus exclusively on relational or decision-making issues between individuals, such as family, divorce, child custody, or guardianship cases. Many lawyers work on disputes that mix personal and commercial issues, including tort litigation against businesses, consumer disputes, or the management of family businesses.

- Government/private: Government lawyers represent federal, state, and local interests on a wide range of disputes. By contrast, private lawyers represent individuals or businesses. Key distinctions between these practices lie in the nature of the client interests protected (as noted above) and in methods of payment for the legal work.

- Public interest/private: Public interest lawyers typically work in firms, organizations, or agencies that have a particular set of issues or concerns as a dominant focus of the practice, even if the practice represents individuals within that overall focus. These practices include government lawyers, prosecution and criminal defense lawyers, and lawyers working for private, non-profit law organizations. By contrast, private lawyers represent interests or concerns of a particular client, whether a business or an individual.

- Representative/policymaking: Representative lawyers serve the needs of identified clients or client interests in deals and transactions. This model applies throughout government, public interest, and private spheres of lawyering. Some lawyers, however, instead of representing clients, engage in policy-making practices, developing policy that can affect large segments of society. For example, policy-making lawyers work on the promulgation of regulations for government agencies, on developing position papers for non-profit "think tanks," and on strategic plans for corporations.

Most law practices fit into one or more of the categories identified above. As you consider where your placement fits, remember that these practice types often overlap. You can find civil law practices that combine many of the features of different types of lawyering. Large private firms, governments, and large corporate legal departments often seek to cover all of these areas, even though individual lawyers within those practices are specialized. A civil poverty law practice may have lawyers working on litigation, administrative hearings, health care planning, wills drafting, policy advocacy, community education, and testifying before legislative bodies.

The distinctions above focus on the lawyer's role, the type of client, and the subject matter of the problem. We also can distinguish between types of lawyering based on the way the lawyer's work is organized and managed.

- Billing/non-billing practices: In billing practices, lawyers charge clients a fee for services, based on an hourly rate, a flat rate, by service, or as a percentage of the recovery. The lawyer must maintain the infrastructure necessary for timekeeping and accounting and must develop work habits that permit the work to be accomplished in an amount of time that is worth it to the client. Billing lawyers must justify fees to clients and face the market pressure of competing with other lawyers. By contrast, many lawyers work in practices in which no fee is charged. For example, public defenders and criminal prosecutors or non-profit poverty lawyers and government attorneys usually do not bill for their services. (Note, however, that many non-profit firms may need to track time for cases in which they request attorney's fees or in response to the requirements of grants.) Ask yourself what impact these arrangements have on how your supervisors handle their cases.

- Fee-paid/salaried practices: In fee-paid practices, especially in smaller firms, the lawyers' income relates directly to the fees they collect. The lawyers take the risk that their work will produce sufficient fees and sufficiently reliable payment from clients to cover their costs and also provide a reasonable return. The solo practitioner presents a classic example of a fee-paid lawyer, but larger firms face most of the same pressures, at least at the partnership level; staff and lawyer employees get paid first and the partners share whatever is left over. By contrast, salaried practices buffer lawyers from this risk, to a greater or lesser extent. Government lawyers provide a good example of salaried practice, as do private non-profit lawyers and corporate counsel. Salaried lawyers, however, are not necessarily free from the need to seek funding or justify costs. Corporate counsel may face demands from management to justify salaries, management of a non-profit may spend more time seeking grants and gifts than on law practice, and government lawyers may have to fight for their department's share of the agency's budget. Consider how your supervisors are paid and how these arrangements affect their legal problem solving.

- Solo/partnership/hierarchical practices: The financial realities of practice relate to the way practices organize themselves. Solo practitioners provide the simplest organizational model. Decision-making authority over cases, financial risks, and ethical responsibility all rest in the individual lawyer. Partnership practices diversify these risks and responsibilities. The partners must determine how to decide on cases, to distribute gains and losses, and to absorb the practice's costs. Partners must negotiate with each other over these choices, adding a separate layer of organizational process. Hierarchical practices cover a broad range of legal work. Government lawyers working in a civil service model, public interest lawyers working in private non-profit corporations under an executive director, and associates working for management in a commercial law partnership usually are organized in hierarchy. These hierarchies create tensions around the individual lawyer's case handling within the organization's overall priorities and policies. These practices may have a tight or a loose hierarchy. Lawyers in one practice may have strict oversight from management, seeking formal approval of major and minor case decisions, while lawyers in other practices may enjoy autonomy in case decisions. You can learn a lot at your placement by tracking the autonomy that supervisors have in handling their cases and their accountability to others in their office for their work.

• Case volume and selectivity: The ability to control the volume of one's caseload represents a key determinant of the work life of a lawyer. The number of cases flowing through the practice affects each lawyer's individual caseload, as well as the demands of managing the overall practice and the resources required to sustain it. Case selection affects case volume. Being able to say no to cases and to select among them has a huge impact on the lawyer's load. In some practices, there is no selectivity. A public defender's office must represent all clients who qualify for their service. Other practices maintain strict control over their caseload and refuse to accept cases that would stretch them beyond their resources. A private non-profit seeking to advance a particular mission through specific means, for example, the ACLU, has the freedom to refuse all cases outside of its mission or means and to accept only cases that best serve its goals. Most practices fall in between these extremes, routinely accepting cases for some portion of their practices and exercising discretion over the rest. In-house counsel for a corporation, for example, usually handle most legal problems of the corporation, but may refer some matters to outside counsel both to control case volume and to ensure competent representation.

Exercise 8.5 Caseload and case selection directly affect the quantity and quality of time the lawyer spends at work. You should expect to work hard as a lawyer. In fact, you already may know that your future practice will require a certain number of "billable hours" per year. At your placement, you should be able to assess how the lawyers balance their different life commitments, including their commitment to work. What do you think of that balance as a template for your own life? If the attorneys limit their work hours, and leave evenings and weekends free, what effect does that choice have on problem solving at your placement? If your attorneys work long hours, what leads them to do so? Are they required to bill a certain number of hours each month or do the cries of the unrepresented call them back to office? Questions like these can lead you to reflect both on their motives for lawyering and on yours.

Case selection bears a direct relationship to the working conditions at your office. Not coincidentally, it reflects a key phase of the lawyering process. The case assessment task has as its goal accurate and clear appraisal so that an informed decision can be made to accept or refuse the case. If your placement does have the power to select its cases, try to track both the standards by which it makes those choices and the process through which selection occurs. Are decisions made by individual lawyers, by staff as a whole, or by a lawyer or committee higher up in the office's hierarchy?

• Specialization/generalization: Another significant aspect of law practice lies in the degree to which the lawyer develops expertise in a particular case type or legal issue. In other words, what is the degree of specialization within the practice? Lawyers usually specialize in particular areas of law, on particular types of lawyering, even on particular processes or skills. Specialization has distinct advantages. It makes it more likely that a lawyer will make the correct decision, more efficiently, with less time needed to get up to speed. Specialization also can offer the marketing advantage of exposure to a concentrated pool of clients. How does the organization of your placement capitalize on the advantages of specialization? A public defender's office may encourage its lawyers to specialize in certain types of cases (felonies, misdemeanors, or delinquency), in certain types of offenses (violence against persons, drugs, gangs, or embezzlement), or particular courts and judges. At your placement, consider whether and how its lawyers specialize and the effect that its choices have on its ability to manage its practice.

Law practices differ in many ways: in the problems they address, in the legal skills and legal processes they use, in the role of the lawyer, in the nature of the client, and in a wide variety of practice realities. Each of these aspects can help you to focus your reflection on your placement and help you assess your own personal and professional goals. The next section offers a way to bring them all together into a more comprehensive picture of problem solving at your placement.

Bringing It Together: A Lawyering Audit

This chapter has discussed three main aspects of lawyering: decision making and practical judgment, lawyering process, and various types of law practice. It is now time to bring all these threads together, by doing an "audit" of the lawyering at your placement. This audit consists of a series of questions that integrate the various concerns above. As we ask each question, to make things more concrete, we offer answers that might apply to three distinct practice types: a non-profit providing representation to individuals; a government enforcement agency; and a judge's chambers. (Judicial clerks also might try to apply the questions below to the practices of attorneys that appear before their judge.)

General Questions

- What type of **legal problem** does your placement handle? For the non-profit, identify both the overall goals of the practice and the more specific case acceptance criteria. For the agency, identify the statutory mandate, as well as current policy about which cases to pursue within that mandate. For the judge, consider the court's subject matter jurisdiction and ask how many of each type of case the court handles during your placement.

- What **client** group or interests does your placement represent? For the non-profit, list the specific client demographics or problem types accepted. Agencies have the public and the public interest as their client, but they might also have a specified segment of the population (individuals with disabilities) to protect. Judges do not represent clients in the traditional sense, but you might assess your judge's sense of accountability. What obligations does the judge feel to the parties? their attorneys? the docket? the appellate courts?

- What **role** does a lawyer at your placement play? For example, judges act as decision makers, but also as administrators, office supervisors, and even time managers for the lawyers on each case. Agency attorneys frequently assume specialized roles, but these can vary. Some are primarily litigators, while others handle promulgation of regulations or the development of policy. Non-profit attorneys may be litigators, planners, or negotiators. Try to assess where on the continuum between generalization and specialization a given attorney falls.

- What size *caseload* do attorneys at your office carry? Assess not only the number of cases but also the rate of turnover, the average time elapsed between opening and closing, and the number of tasks involved for each case. From this, consider what role time pressure plays in case handling. How does the attorney assure adequate attention to each problem within the overall time demand of the practice?

- What *organization* does your office have? Judicial chambers usually work hierarchically, with the judge at the apex, but you might examine the working relationships between the judge and the law clerks, between judges within the forum, or between judges and the clerk's office. Government agencies too usually are hierarchical, with a regional chief overseeing the local office. Some agencies give more autonomy to regional offices and to individual attorneys within offices. Try to map the lines of authority within your office. The intensity of oversight and management varies considerably within non-profits. Your office may make many decisions in staff meetings in a more or less collaborative format.

Assessment Questions

- How do cases *start* at your office? Non-profits often handle intake in stages, with phone calls going to an initial screener and live contact reserved for a later interview with an attorney. Some agencies may select cases from among citizen complaints, while others may seek out particular types of behavior to target. Judicial chambers will have highly regularized intake, with filed cases assigned to individual judges through a routine case assignment mechanism.

- Who investigates *facts* at your placement? Both agencies and non-profits may have a separate pool of investigators or paralegals who investigate claims, but lawyers may handle this task as well. How does the office divide up case investigation responsibilities? Are lawyers integrated from the start or do they review summaries prepared by others? Of course, judges do not normally investigate cases, but judges do help parties sort out contested from uncontested facts through case conferences or rulings on motions, so as to assure a focused and efficient trial. In all cases, ask yourself the impact that investigation and factual development has on the ultimate handling of the underlying problem.

- Who performs the **legal analysis** of the problem? Most offices properly allocate the task of legal research and analysis to lawyers. For agency and non-profit practices, this task usually goes to the attorney assigned the case, but that attorney may delegate some or all of the task to clerks (including you) and also may bring especially thorny questions to other attorneys or a staff meeting for fuller discussion. By contrast, and in theory, judges wait for the attorneys to present legal arguments, then assess and select between those positions. In practice, however, judges often do substantial research in preparation for cases and may discuss legal issues with the attorneys both informally in conferences and formally in hearings as they develop their opinions.

- How does **case acceptance** occur at your placement? Both agencies and non-profits will have some way to decide which cases to pursue and which to reject. Some may be screened out at the point of initial contact, while others might require some further development before the office makes a decision to accept or reject. Try to find out what happens to the rejected cases. Does the office offer no services or some form of opinion, quick advice, or referral? Judges, of course, usually cannot refuse cases placed on their docket, but may recuse themselves under certain circumstances.

- Who assesses the **merit** of cases in your office? In both non-profits and agencies, merit assessment often will occur in two phases. An individual attorney (or investigator, or even extern) will assess a legal problem as worthy of pursuit. Then, that assessment will receive one or more layers of review and approval before the office formally accepts the case. For judges, the rules of procedure typically give distinctive powers of "merit assessment." Motions for dismissal, summary judgment, and directed verdict give judges the authority to declare that a case lacks sufficient factual or legal merit to proceed to a jury for final disposition.

Decision-making Questions

- What **options and strategies** does your placement typically consider? Each legal problem is unique and, in theory, the choices available for handling one problem will not suit any other. In practice, however, lawyers typically consider a regular range of choices in deciding how to proceed on their legal problems. A non-profit focused on helping clients get public benefits typically might consider negotiating with a case worker, filing for administrative review, or advising the client to abandon the claim. An agency enforcing a particular law might choose to refuse a particular claim, send a warning letter, file an individual case, or pursue a whole class of offenders. Try to identify what choices the office routinely considers, recognizing that the range of choices will vary from problem to problem. In theory, judges respond to options for decision presented to them by the parties and only rule on motions initiated by the parties. In practice, however, many judges act more assertively to prod parties towards particular methods of case handling through conferences, motions, pre-trial memos, and the like. Moreover, judges often face decisions that are very similar from case to case. Does the judge maintain a data-bank of language that can be used and reused in these cases? If so, what effect does this practice have on the judge's thinking about the underlying problem?

- Who bears long-term responsibility for *case management*? As a practical matter, most law practices designate a particular attorney as lead counsel to make and implement decisions in consultation with the client. Consider who has this role at your placement. Both agencies and non-profits will assign single attorneys to cases, but also may assign teams of attorneys, especially on larger deals and disputes. Judges usually retain ultimate case handling responsibility for cases on their docket, but may delegate some portion of the responsibility for a disposition to magistrates or special masters. When and how does the judge use these devices?

- How does your placement set up *client relationships*? This question makes the most sense for the lawyer who represents individual clients. Here, the lawyer has a range of approaches to decision making with clients. The lawyer can present options together with their strengths and weaknesses, leaving the decision to the client. Or, a lawyer may strongly recommend particular options, seeking to persuade the client of particular choices. The lawyer must draw a line between those decisions the client must make and that pool of practice decisions reserved for lawyers. In the absence of an identified client, neither judges nor agency attorneys face the same set of choices. Agencies however may have some process to explain their decisions to complainants, and judges have some obligation to explain their reasoning to the parties in their opinions. What effect does the prospect of explanation have on their handling of the problem?

- When and how does *decision making* on cases occur at your placement? This question is not as easy as it looks. In some practices, a lawyer may meet with the decision maker in a *counseling* session on a single occasion, presenting options and prompting a decision. Similarly, in judicial placements, the process of decision making by judges is relatively clear-cut: the parties present motions and the judge deliberates and rules, either orally or in writing. Many times, however, decision making does not occur in one meeting or through one opinion but develops over time. A litigator may file pleadings and conduct discovery only to reconsider her approach in response to a dis-

Lawyering theory has identified different models for the lawyer's influence over the client. A "client-centered" lawyer seeks to maximize the client's autonomy. This lawyer presents the client with all options and evaluates them in light of the client's interests, but does not seek to persuade the client towards a particular choice. By contrast, a different lawyer might present the client only those choices the lawyer feels are appropriate and might seek to sell the client on a particular choice. Still others engage in an open-ended negotiation over how to handle the problem, with both lawyer and client influencing the decision. No one model applies to all practices or even to all situations in a particular practice. How lawyers relate to their clients varies widely between practices. Public defenders may deal with clients differently than private civil attorneys. As you watch your supervisors deal with clients (and as you do so yourself), see if you can work out what kind of influence the lawyer has on the client, and how the lawyer exercises that influence.

closure, a judicial ruling, or a settlement offer. A transactional lawyer may formulate an initial proposal for a transaction, only to adjust its parameters in response to new events and to the shifting interests of the various participants. A judge may hear argument pre-trial, but reserve final decision on a particular motion until trial itself. Try to get a sense of the patterns of decision making over the whole course of legal problem solving. What effect do early decisions have on later ones? What seem to be the key points of decision? How does your office prepare for and handle those moments?

Action Questions

- Which *legal processes* does your placement routinely use and for what purposes? By definition, litigation practices use the formal mechanism of government-sponsored dispute resolution to address legal problems. The purposes of that litigation vary. A non-profit lawyer may use litigation either to achieve a remedy for an individual client or to establish a precedent helping a group of clients. An agency may file suit to rectify a single harm or to deter a group of potential offenders. If your placement handles litigation, try to understand both the short- and long-term goals of the litigation. By contrast, in transactional practices, the legal process depends much more on the routine practices of that type of deal to structure its activities. For example, an agency responsible for guaranteeing loans for the construction of housing projects may have a many layered process for reviewing and approving potential deals. For another, a municipal attorney may face a maze-like series of committees and boards in drafting and implementing a zoning ordinance. Whenever possible, try to get a sense of the nature of the processes that structure your placement's activity and assess how the process serves the underlying goals of the parties to the deal.

- How does your placement assure *strategic action* in its handling of cases? All lawyering benefits from careful planning and thoughtful implementation of decisions, but the pressure of deadlines, limited resources, and active caseload often forces attorneys to react rather than act. Consider how your attorneys and your practice assure that case handling remains tied to client goals and overall strategy. This assurance may rest on individual case handling habits. For example, well-structured files with careful notation of events, with deadlines clearly noted, and a case plan in place will help. Some devices may be office wide: restrictions on new cases in response to high caseload, reassignment of cases for attorneys working on major projects, or hiring of additional staff to help to process an overload in a judicial docket.

- What role does *negotiation* play in your placement's problem solving? Consider how much time your supervisors spend in negotiation, on what kinds of issues, for what purpose, and at what point. For example, a private non-profit lawyer may suggest an early resolution of an eviction proceeding that satisfies the client's goals, rather than pursuing a legally questionable defense. An agency attorney may seek an early agreement with a minor offender in an enforcement action in an effort to obtain information vital to pursuing others. Judges may use their scheduling authority to push the attorneys on the case to focus on settlement in an effort to reduce the court's overall docket and free up judicial time for other trials. Attorneys and offices use negotiation in different ways and for different purposes. Try to track both the content and the style of negotiations you observe at your placement.

- How does your office define *success*? In theory, this question should be easy. For representatives, success lies in the satisfaction of underlying goals or interests. For judges, it lies in fair and final resolution of the litigation. In practice, defining success offers a much richer and more nuance set of appraisals. For example, in a private non-profit practice, limitations on client resources may make full achievement of a client's goals impossible. Consider how lawyers work with their clients in these cases to achieve some degree of closure for the client with nothing but bad choices. Similarly, an agency attorney may face a variety of different measures of success that apply to its work: successfully deterring a particular behavior, obtaining public exposure of a particular fraud, or satisfying a quota for a particular case type. Judges too have differing measures of success. One judge may focus on a low reversal rate, another on efficient management of the docket, and a third on a resolution that keeps parties from returning to court. Ask your supervisors how they define satisfactory handling of cases and listen carefully for the assumptions and values on which they base their answers.

Conclusion: Practice Quality and Professional Development

Before closing, we would like to focus on two aspects of your experience: your sense of what constitutes "good lawyering" and your planning for the development of your own abilities as a lawyer.

If you read carefully, you noted that the practice audit above assumes two basic criteria for "good lawyering": lawyering that accomplishes client or other specified goals and lawyering that achieves those goals efficiently and with a minimum investment of time and resources. As a general rule, these standards apply to most lawyering. You also should consider the range of lawyering that you have observed, both by your supervisors and by other lawyers that you have encountered. With luck, you will see nothing but the best lawyering: cogent and persuasive argument; clear, well-written briefs; unambiguous contracts, wills, and other documents; and careful, well-balanced judicial opinions. In practice, however, you may encounter what you can only describe as bad lawyering (by other attorneys, we hope, and not by your supervisors!). Each encounter with bad lawyering offers a learning opportunity. Ask yourself why you are reacting as you are and what makes that lawyer's performance sub-par. Consult with your supervisor and ask his opinion. As you consider these answers, try to articulate both what led the lawyer to act in that way and what you would have done differently if you had handled the case. This kind of reflection can be vital. As you assess "bad lawyering," you start to develop your standards for good lawyering.

You also should try to assess how your placement as a whole assures the quality of its work. The task of assuring a consistent quality of practice, under intense case pressure and time demand, constitutes one of the most difficult tasks of law practice management. A key part of this task focuses on the avoidance of ethical violations and legal malpractice: consistent documentation of case handling in files, effective use of calendars and other deadline management systems, and clear accounting for time and for client contact.

Avoiding ethical complaints and malpractice actions is necessary, but not sufficient. Your office also should have in place systems that assure the best possible practice consistent with available resources. Common approaches include careful screening and hiring, the training of new attorneys; mentoring of younger attorneys, regular performance reviews, reporting and critical assessments of caseload, rigorously applied case selection processes, and other similar devices. Frequently, quality control relies on office culture, a combination of mutual expectation, respect, and pride in the work that can reinforce the more mechanical devices. In assessing your experience, leave room to assess how well your office accomplishes quality control.

see⟩ Chapter 18
on Career Planning

This chapter began by proposing that you chose an externship to find out what lawyers do. We hope that this chapter expanded your notion of what that means. It also should help you to assess your own professional development and to ask and answer questions about what kind of lawyer you want to become. These questions have a number of dimensions. Initially, you may focus only on skill sets. Do you want to be a litigator, or do you prefer the quite different complexities of transactional practice? Your externship also can lead to other assessments. Do you want to work as a private lawyer in a for-profit enterprise or does some other lawyering context appeal to you? Would you prefer to work for clients on personal issues, for businesses, or for the government? Are you comfortable with a high intensity, high volume practice, or would you rather have a slower, more measured pace? Do you want to learn slowly over an extended apprenticeship, or would you prefer to jump feet first into a practice that gives you autonomy (and responsibility) early?

Finally, consider what role you want to play in the handling of legal decisions and how you want to use and develop your own good judgment as a lawyer. Your experience this semester should give you ample opportunity to consider how other lawyers make decisions and what their practices tell you about your own ability as a problem solver. You should begin to see the paths that you might take to improving your judgment. The progress of professional development for most lawyers runs from an apprenticeship, through increased decision-making authority, to relatively broad autonomy in the handling of their cases and their practice. Your placement should expose you to the weight of responsibility that rests on attorneys who work on client problems. We hope that you come to enjoy that weight and to recognize the personal and professional satisfaction that comes from meeting its challenges.

FURTHER READING

ROBERT M. BASTRESS & JOSEPH D. HARBAUGH, INTERVIEWING, COUNSELING AND NEGOTIATING (1990).

GARY BELLOW & BEA MOULTON, THE LAWYERING PROCESS: MATERIALS FOR CLINICAL INSTRUCTION IN ADVOCACY (1978).

DAVID A. BINDER, PAUL BERGMAN, SUSAN C. PRICE & PAUL R. TREMBLAY, LAWYERS AS COUNSELORS: A CLIENT-CENTERED APPROACH (2D ED. 2004).

JOHN S. BRADWAY, HOW TO PRACTICE LAW EFFECTIVELY (1958).

ROBERT F. COCHRAN, JR., JOHN M.A. DIPIPPA & MARTHA M. PETERS, THE COUNSELOR-AT-LAW: A COLLABORATIVE APPROACH TO CLIENT INTERVIEWING AND COUNSELING (1999).

STEFAN H. KRIEGER & RICHARD K. NEUMAN, JR., ESSENTIAL LAWYERING SKILLS (2D ED. 2003).

Chapter 9

Reflective Lawyering

Margaret Martin Barry

The life of law is not logic, it's experience.

—Oliver Wendell Holmes

You may wonder why, with a demanding externship and other obligations, you must spend valuable time in the classroom dissecting the field experience. You are finally at the point in your legal education when you get to *do* lawyering. Yet, you are dragged back into the classroom to discuss the opportunity to death— to *reflect*.

It is precisely because you assume a professional role at your externship that it is important that you evaluate your performance in that role. There is an adage that you can have twenty years of experience or a year of experience twenty times. The point of reflective lawyering is to maximize your chances of getting your full twenty years' worth of experience. The point of this chapter is to provide some tools for engaging in the process of effective assessment of your professional experiences.

This chapter is divided into two sections and explains, first, the reflective process and its relevance to lawyers, and, second, its use in specific lawyering contexts. The first section focuses more generally on what reflection means for professionals, why it is important and, specifically, why it is important for law students and lawyers. The second section uses contexts unique to the practice of law to demonstrate reflective tools.

The Reflective Process and Lawyers

Reflection happens constantly, but the reflective process does not. You may sit next to a friend at a party and chat about work, other friends, or politics without ever considering your motivations and the results of your actions. Your professional growth requires awareness. The reflective process provides tools to enhance your advocacy skills, address problems in particular cases, and predict outcomes for future analogous situations.

What is the Reflective Process?

Reflection in this context means thinking in a disciplined manner about what you do as a lawyer. You articulate observations about action taken to comprehend and integrate new knowledge so that it can become a basis for future actions.

The concept of reflective practice is described by Donald A. Schön in his book *Educating the Reflective Practitioner: Toward a New Design for Teaching and Learning in the Professions* (1987). Schön studied professionals in many disciplines to figure out how they used professional knowledge to achieve professional artistry. Professional knowledge, according to Schön, is a composite of "knowing-in-action," "reflection-in-action," and "reflection" *on* reflection-in-action. As the terms suggest, professional knowledge is derived from experience, and such knowledge is the result of a disciplined thought process.

"Knowing-in-action" is reflexive. It is based on knowledge obtained, but not consciously applied, like riding a bicycle or taking notes in class. Schön compares knowing-in-action to the philosopher Michael Polanyi's term "tacit knowing." Tacit knowing is knowing more than we can say—the kind of knowing that is exhibited by what we do. The experienced bike rider or note taker may find it difficult to explain what analysis triggers the actions taken. How do you decide which things to write down during class? These actions are hard to describe because they are reflexive. Attempts to explain them often fail unless the explanation can incorporate a demonstration. The bike rider straddles the bike and can then respond to questions about how to avoid a fall; the note taker can identify what is important to record by sitting in a lecture.

What might a note taker whose tacit skill was developed in lecture settings do when the teacher introduces a different format, such as a role play? What might a seasoned trial attorney do during a trial when a witness gives a completely unexpected answer? According to Schön, a student or an attorney might respond to such a surprise by "reflection-in-action." Either might decide what to do next by thinking about the gap between what was expected and what actually is happening. The actor might pause to consider the next step or might adjust instantly. A trial attorney, for example, might alter her line of questions based on the witness's unexpected answer, the judge's sigh, or the jury's inattention. As with knowledge-in-action, reflection-in-action is an intuitive and often unarticulated process.

Reflection is not just desirable or useful. Reflection is essential to learning from experience. As the French philosopher, Denis Diderot, articulated in *On the Interpretation of Nature*, no. 15 (1753), "[t]here are three principal means of acquiring knowledge available to us: observation of nature, reflection, and experimentation. Observation collects facts; reflection combines them; experimentation verifies the result of that combination. Our observation of nature must be diligent, our reflection profound, and our experiments exact. We rarely see these three means combined; and for this reason, creative geniuses are not common." Not common, but not unattainable.

Schön describes the acquiring of expertise as a process of adjustments. He points out that once an adjustment is made in response to surprise, the actor reflects upon reflection-in-action. In other words, the professional thinks back on what was done. How did the response to the witness's unexpected answer work? What new information did the attorney learn from the adjustment made? The depth of such reflection can mark the difference between the practitioner who has achieved a measure of professional artistry and the one who fumbles at the unusual turn. A novice who sees lawyering as a series of tasks that benefit from careful reflection can advance more rapidly to become a seasoned practitioner than the novice whose reflective skills are ill formed or underutilized. It is not easy—the seasoned practitioner just makes it look easy.

DILBERT: © Scott Adams / Dist. by United Features Syndicate, Inc.

Why Reflection?

Since the reflective process involves knowing-in-action, reflection-in-action, and reflecting on those two, you might assume you need a lot of experience with the process. You might conclude that this is rather attenuated for someone who has little or no body of experience that could form the basis of knowing-in-action and who is concerned about fumbling at the usual, much less the unusual, turn of events. But *usual* is a relative term, and your basis for knowledge-in-action is expanding continually.

For example, assume that on your first day at your externship your supervisor asks you to draft a complaint in a personal injury case for a client who slipped on a banana peel in a grocery store. What knowledge-in-action can you draw upon? You have some basic knowledge of tort law (what are the elements of a cause of action for negligence?) and civil procedure (what information needs to be included in a complaint?) from your first year in law school. You also have some knowledge about how to do legal research from your first-year research and writing assignments (how do I find the local application of the law and the rules for this court?). You have considerable non-legal experience, such as your understanding of how grocery stores operate (when was the floor cleaned last?) and your sense of community tolerance or lack of tolerance for certain activities (did anyone complain about the peel before your client's fall?).

These starting points can become the basis for brainstorming a list of things to do and questions to explore. Each step you take *builds on* your experience and *builds* your experience. You will take from this project a complaint that you can use as a starting point the next time you are asked to do such a task. If you also obtain a copy of the complaint as filed, after your supervisor has revised it, you can study what changes were made and learn from them. For the next project, you will be able to generate a better product in less time. By reflecting on your experience, you will gain transferable skills, even if the next project is to draft a complaint for breach of contract or to conduct a deposition in a personal injury case.

Why the Emphasis on Reflection During Externships?

Reflective observation, like any other skill, takes practice. Externships and other clinical experiences during law school offer excellent opportunities for developing the skills and habits of reflective lawyering. They provide legal experiences in the context of an academic environment where your learning is an explicit goal of the experience. Here is an excerpt from a law review article written by Professors Michael Meltsner, James Rowan, and Daniel Givelber about the opportunities for reflection during a law school clinical experience. Do you recognize yourself or any of your classmates in their description of a former student?

While individual conversations are lost to memory, the teacher remembered best one student he called the Achiever, not because he was more driven to succeed than his peers, but because his clinic semester had been characterized by an intense and unremitting rejection of explicit inquiry into how lawyers learned and how they felt about their work. As a student intern, the Achiever demanded clients, not discussion, reflection, or supervision; clients with cases he could deal with himself, free of interference from professors and fellow students. He came to the clinic with an excellent academic record. He had easily made the law review and thought he was quite capable, thank you, of doing what had to be done to advance his clients' interests. He was right. His record in representing low income consumers and public housing tenants was admirable, the envy of his peers. His instructors sought without much success to warn him that in their view he was missing something of importance about how he learned; some lessons about lawyering that might be of importance to his future. Their ideas and suggestions of larger purposes must have seemed incredibly fuzzy at the time, for the message of clinic supervisors was mixed. Their position, that taking on the lawyer's role self consciously "can shape not only what you do, but what and who you become," was combined with a belief in the individuality of student learning styles. In any event, the Achiever was in too much of a hurry trying out the lawyer's role to hear his instructors. They generally let him be, pleased at least that he did such a good job for the client at hand, if not for himself.

The Achiever loved learning by doing, because he found stimulation and reward striving for his clients' objectives. The work enhanced his self confidence and convinced him that he was growing. For him, the teachers served as little more than quick, convenient research tools because they knew names, phone numbers, and statutory citations. The actions that he took flowed instinctively from his analysis and the results proved the accuracy of his perceptions. However, the entirety of his clinical experience consisted of a series of undigested experiences. Without reflection, no transferable theory of how to act in similar situations emerged; nor was there any occasion for him to plan to alter his behavior in the future.

When encountered on the subway platform [after he had graduated and was working for a law firm], the Achiever looked deflated. He did not refer to his clinic experience, but his statement of the basic gripe made plain that, despite the views he held as a student, he had absorbed something of the clinic ideology. "I feel like a machine," he lamented, and explained: "For the first time in my life, I'm in over my head. And I'm not getting the help I need. I may not even know how to ask for it. In my firm, you're considered stupid if you ask too many questions."

—Michael Meltsner, James V. Rowan & Daniel J. Givelber, *The Bike Tour Leader's Dilemma: Talking About Supervision,* 13 Vt. L. Rev. 399, 400-402 (1989) (footnotes omitted).

Perhaps the Achiever was struggling because he was in a difficult setting and had not acquired the necessary tools to work his way through his problems. In his law school clinical experience, he had rejected the opportunity to plan and reflect on his experiences in a setting where his learning was of primary importance. Because the Achiever had devoted his considerable aptitude to moving forward as fast as he could without stopping to reflect, he lacked the tools needed to continue to build his skills in practice. One tool that may have been helpful to him is evaluating essential aspects of the work he was doing and determining what specific input was needed from what sources. This would help build insight into and confidence in what he knew and what it was reasonable to seek help in understanding.

Exercise 9.1 Do you think the partners at Achiever's law firm really thought that associates who asked questions were stupid? Perhaps the Achiever was having difficulty because his questions were not well thought out, or perhaps he was asking the wrong people for help. Think about your externship. How do you know when to ask for help and when to try to figure it out for yourself? When are you bothering your supervisor and when are you wasting valuable time by not asking questions? Developing judgment in this area is part of what you will begin doing in your fieldwork setting, but only if you allocate time and effort to that development. You must make it one of your priorities.

---

see > Chapter 3
*on Getting
Supervision*

We talk more in Chapter 3 about how to motivate your supervisor to provide the guided feedback that will help you, but keep in mind that your very lack of experience can be a benefit. Newcomers to a field of practice often overlook the special insights they bring to the profession. The seemingly naive question or off-the-wall approach can provide a solution to a problem that did not occur to the person who has worked in the field for a long time. Michael Hutchinson identified this "novice effect" in his book *Megabrain: New Tools and Techniques for Brain Growth and Mind Expansion* (Ballantine 1996). According to Hutchinson, initial exposure to a new field causes changes in brain chemistry that make the novice more receptive to new ideas. Thus, supervisors can learn from your questions and observations, just as you hope to learn from theirs.

A Lifetime of Reflection

In an increasingly complex world, the responsibility
for taking charge of one's ongoing learning needs
to rest with the individual lawyer over the term of
his or her professional life.

—Bill Lindberg, President of the Ash Grove Group

Every semester of law school, you create outlines and demonstrate your comprehension of substantive material through examination. In addition, you may have had the opportunity to apply your knowledge to hypothetical problems or to simulations. Externships present a new arena where the problems are real, not simulated, and where the focus is client service, not your education.

Reflection on your externship experience should help you begin the process of assessing what type of practice you will pursue and refining the moral and ethical standards you will bring to that practice. You may begin with an ill-defined idea of your professional interests. Alternatively, you may have a clear vocation in mind that may change or evolve as you continue your professional development.

The extent to which you achieve satisfaction from your work will depend on your ability to integrate your values into your professional choices. Regular reflection offers insight into work style, preferences, dissatisfaction, and other influences at the intersection of your values and your work. For example, you may think that you want to do criminal defense work because you believe that society has a duty to guarantee fairness to those accused of crimes. As you gain experience in the practice of criminal law, you may feel frustrated by the players and the process. This perspective may lead to changes in your professional goals. You may conclude that you want to work on policy or legislative changes in the criminal justice system rather than represent individual clients. Reflective observation will help you to capture your reactions to and thoughts about your professional aspirations.

Externships provide an excellent opportunity to observe and test complex professional thinking. Chapter 3, on supervision, discusses how to get effective feedback on your work from field supervisors. In addition to direct feedback, you can learn by observing an expert practitioner as she goes through a reflective process, as discussed in Chapter 12. The expert may seem to be making decisions intuitively, but in fact she may be thinking about decisions in a quite structured way. If you probe, she may realize that you are interested in her thinking process and share it with you. Not all experts are conscious of engaging in structured reflection; to some, the process seems automatic. Even so, your inquiries as to why she chose a certain course of action may trigger more conscious reflection and enable her to articulate the process used.

Awareness of the process used is key to improving professional practice. For example, litigators routinely draw upon their knowledge about individuals, society, politics, and the law to formulate an approach to resolving a particular plan of action on behalf of the client. This is called developing a "theory of the case." Theory of the case is an ordering system that allows the lawyer to focus on information relevant to a particular goal. It is the hypothesis that, if the facts exist as alleged, the client is legally entitled to the relief sought. There are, then, two components: factual and legal. A case theory is strongest if it can withstand three types of attack: factual sufficiency (it must state a claim for relief); persuasive sufficiency (it must meet its burden as to all of the elements of the applicable legal standard); and affirmative defenses. The legal component is based on statutes, case law, rules, or regulations. A good legal theory may draw on established law or may include an argument for a novel or expansive interpretation of the law. In evaluating a possible case theory, an attorney must use the reflective process to consider whether the theory is emotionally appealing, comprehensive, consistent with the client's short- and long-term goals, supported by the facts, legally and ethically sound, persuasive, and credible.

Once a theory of the case is identified, it does not remain fixed in place. The theory must be revised as the attorney learns more about the facts, the law, the judge, courtroom dynamics, local procedure, the opposing parties and counsel, and the client's goals and expectations. As the attorney proceeds through negotiation and other pretrial activities, she constantly refines her theory of the case by consciously reflecting on effective strategies and mistakes, making adjustments as she proceeds.

Thus, theory of the case is a systematic process of analysis and reflection. If applied with care, it not only informs the handling of a specific case but provides a framework for evaluating performance. The lawyer can consider how effective the theory was, whether his actions were consistent with the theory and what influenced deviations. The process avoids repeating mistakes, deepens analysis, and enhances expertise.

What to Look for in Your Externship Placement

The examples below are selected to encourage you to observe and reflect upon legal practice from the perspective available through your externship placement. Attempt to connect each topic to your own experiences. Be critical. Challenge assumptions. Analogize. Every externship is unique, but certain constants apply. How will you approach the following: (1) the relationship with clients, (2) the relationships with other lawyers, (3) interaction with the judicial system, (4) alternative dispute resolution, (5) use of legislative advocacy, (6) the relationships with or your role as a government lawyer, and (7) the relationship between your practice and values?

Reflecting on Relationships with Clients

While lawyers are bound to communal goals of justice and fairness, the fundamental relationship is with the client. Central to the success of that relationship is effective communication. What are some of the barriers to effective client communication?

Lucie White, who was a legal aid lawyer in North Carolina, tells the story of her representation of Mrs. G, a welfare recipient, who had been notified by the welfare agency that she had to pay back about $600 in welfare benefits because she had received a $600 lump sum payment from an insurance company for injuries she and her daughter had received in an automobile accident. Although Mrs. G had reported the income to her case supervisor and been told she could spend it on whatever she wanted, the authority now claimed that her welfare payment should have been reduced dollar for dollar because of the insurance payment. Lucie White's legal research had revealed that this personal injury payment would reduce the welfare benefits unless it had been spent on "necessities." In a meeting with Mrs. G to prepare for a hearing to challenge the agency's claim, the attorney worked with her client to identify how the money had been spent. Among the purchases identified were shoes that Mrs. G bought for her daughters. She told the attorney she had bought the shoes because the children's old shoes were "torn so bad that the other kids would make fun of them at school."

At the hearing, the attorney asked Mrs. G why she had spent the insurance proceeds on new shoes. Mrs. G said the children needed "Sunday" shoes for church. Ms. White and Mrs. G had gone over the testimony in advance. Mrs. G knew the list of purchases needed to consist of "necessities" if she was to win her appeal. Why had the client suddenly balked at answering the question as they had discussed in her attorney's office? In a law review article chronicling the incident, Ms. White speculates that by classifying the shoes as "Sunday" shoes, Mrs. G was conveying her sense of what should be a necessity. At the hearing, she was able to describe her purchases in light of her values rather than what the others present, including her attorney, thought her values should be. Perhaps the breakdown in communication between attorney and client occurred because the client acquiesced in, but did not agree with, the theory of the case her attorney had proposed. This story conveys some of the potential complexity of the relationship of lawyer and client and the extreme subjectivity of the process of interpretation. Lucie E. White, *Subordination, Rhetorical Survival Skills, and Sunday Shoes: Notes on the Hearing of Mrs. G.*, 38 Buff. L. Rev. 1 (1990)].

Inhibitors of Communication

In David A. Binder, Paul Bergman, Susan C. Price & Paul R. Tremblay, *Lawyers as Counselors: A Client-Centered Approach* 19-26 (2nd ed. 2004), the authors point out that effective client-centered lawyering begins with gaining a full understanding of the issues raised by the client. The first step is to conduct an interview that allows the client to disclose all the facts relevant to the case and the client's concerns. During the interview, an attorney must pay attention to inhibitors and motivators of communication. The authors identify several inhibitors to open communication.

1. A client might withhold information that threatens self-esteem. A client who has been beaten by her husband, for example, might not disclose that fact to her attorney because she believes the attorney would judge her negatively.

2. A client might withhold information that the client thinks would be harmful to the case.

3. A client might believe that revealing certain information would cause the attorney to doubt her and to lose interest in her case.

4. A client might not volunteer information because the client expects the lawyer to set the agenda.

5. A client might believe that the lawyer is in a position of authority and knows which subjects deserve inquiry and which do not.

6. A client may avoid relating facts that the client believes will shock, embarrass, or cause discomfort to the attorney, be reluctant to talk in detail about a traumatic experience that evokes unpleasant feelings, or respond half-heartedly to questions the client views as irrelevant.

7. A client may simply have a greater need to talk about a subject that is not relevant to the issue the lawyer is trying to address.

In one of my first cases, my client had told me that she wanted custody of her infant daughter and son. My client was only about 19 years old, and she suffered from a minor mental handicap. The children were allowed to remain in their maternal grandmother's custody pending trial, and the grandmother was quite disparaging of her daughter's wishes to have contact with the children. My client was allowed to see her children, but only under their grandmother's supervision. We discussed why my client thought it was a good idea for the children to be with her. We took pictures of her apartment; we discussed how she would care for the children on a daily basis. I investigated her medical history, and I spoke with friends and family. Prior to trial, I went over her testimony with my client. All seemed set to put on the best case possible. However, when I asked this client at trial the questions we had prepared, what unfolded, in the wonderful way things do at trial, was her understanding that custody meant she could spend time alone with her children. She wanted them to visit her, but she had no expectation of full custody. She had equated visitation with custody, and I had failed to decode my own language sufficiently to understand her goals.

As I reflected on this incident, several of the Binder, Bergman inhibitors seemed to apply. This client deferred to me, expected me to set the agenda, and avoided her own doubts about her capacity to care for her children. I can trace the error back to our first interview. We spoke at cross purposes. She told me she was seeking custody of her children, and I framed all information in response to my understanding of the term. Building on that experience has made me particularly alert to raising the dimensions of parent goals with regards to raising their children. While most parents mean sole physical and legal custody when they say they want custody, it is rare that the range of possibilities for balancing this goal against the wishes of the other parent, or one in *loco parentis*, have been considered.

Facilitators of Communication

Binder, Bergman list five facilitators of communication: empathy, fulfilling expectations, recognition, altruistic appeals, and extrinsic reward. *Id.* at 27-31. Fundamental to empathy is self-awareness. The lawyer needs to do the hard work of identifying personal barriers to appreciating what the client has conveyed. Those barriers include class, race, gender, ethnicity, education, personal experience, and the lawyer's predilection to jump in and fix things. There are many degrees of difference that separate us from each other; the lawyer must consciously explore those differences in order to hear and understand what clients have to say. Professor Susan Bryant discusses methods for crossing these barriers in *The Five Habits: Building Cross-Cultural Competence in Lawyers*, 8 Clin. L. Rev. 33 (2001). A simplified version of one of the exercises that she and Professor Jean Koh Peters devised follows in the exercise below.

> **Exercise 9.2** Take 10 minutes to interview a student in your class whom you do not know very well. Your objective is to learn as much as possible about what motivates the person to want to be a lawyer. What in the student's family and personal experiences; racial, ethnic and economic background; and so on influenced him or her? That student or another student then will have 10 minutes to interview you. At the end of the interviews, each of you should draw two columns on separate pieces of paper, labeling the first column "similarities" and the second "differ-

similarities + differences in motivations

ences." Do not critique or censor your list, but list as many similarities and differences that come to mind based on what was said, what you saw, and what you felt during your interview of the other student. You need not share all on your list with the class, but try to be as thorough as possible in generating your list.

The goal of this exercise is to gain a quick baseline for understanding similarities and differences. Similarities and differences create filters that can skew what you hear. The more conscious you are of these filters, the more able you are to recognize the barriers they create and develop methods for breaking through them in order to effectively serve your clients.

Client Decision Making

The ultimate decision whether to proceed with, settle, or forgo litigation belongs to the client. Binder, Bergman reminds us that the attorney's role is to give advice and the client's is to make decisions in light of that advice. If a client asks the lawyer's opinion as to what the client should do, the lawyer should state the reason for the opinion given and decline to assume decision making responsibility.

Exercise 9.3 Consider the following scenario. You are preparing to counsel your client about her options in a landlord-tenant suit in which the landlord is suing to evict her for failure to pay rent. She has not paid rent for eight months. She emigrated from Slovenia five years ago with her husband, who has since returned. She has two children, both of whom were born in this country. She works six days a week at a minimum wage job and relies on a neighbor to provide childcare. She says that she simply cannot afford to pay the rent. You have identified several housing code violations (water damage, a broken pipe, no railing on the back porch, poor heating) that can be raised in defense of the eviction action. When you spoke with her on the phone, your client had a hard time seeing these defects with her apartment as significant to her case. Consider what cultural differences may affect your communication with your client. Taking into account the Binder, Bergman analysis of inhibitors to full communication, what strategies would you use to counsel your client about her options?

Reflecting on Relationships with Lawyers

Relationships within the Same Enterprise

You can learn a lot about lawyering by interacting with and observing other lawyers. Much of your training has emphasized the value of individual work, and indeed that is important. Lawyers, however, increasingly are working together in large organizations, on joint projects, or reaching out for support in areas beyond their current expertise. Your challenge is to understand how to collaborate with other lawyers. Professor Susan Bryant in *Collaboration in Law Practice: A Satisfying and Productive Process for a Diverse Profession*, 17 Vt. L. Rev. 459 (1993), identifies three different models of organizing joint work: the collaboration model, the input model, and the parallel work model.

In the collaboration model, shared decision making is predominant with each lawyer having meaningful control over the direction of the task or case. In the input model, one person makes decisions after consulting with other group members. The success of this model depends on all co-workers making a genuine contribution and commitment to an enterprise for which someone else has control. In the parallel model, there is no sharing or consultation. Professor Bryant discusses the benefits of working under the collaborative model as reducing stress, increasing clarity through firsthand knowledge of the enterprise, and increasing the quality of the product through the benefit of multiple perspectives. She encourages taking the time to understand work styles and identify strengths as a premise to approaching tasks. Whether or not you enjoy the prospect of collaboration, you will find that employers increasingly expect it, and circumstances often thrust it upon the most independent of us.

> **Exercise 9.4** You and another student have been asked to list all available facts and legal arguments supporting your client's claim that she is entitled to damages as a result of the seller's failure to disclose certain ground contamination to her prior to the purchase of her home. What factors will determine how you will divide this task?

Relationships with Opposing Counsel

During a negotiation, you may have an excellent opportunity to observe the extent to which the way opposing counsel relate to each other can control the success of conflict resolution. According to Robert M. Bastress and Joseph D. Harbaugh in *Interviewing, Counseling, and Negotiating: Skills for Effective*

Representation (Aspen 1990), legal negotiators, like negotiators in other disciplines, exhibit two negotiating styles: competitive or cooperative. Likewise, they exhibit two negotiating strategies, adversarial or problem-solving. Effective *competitive* negotiators may be dominating, forceful, attacking, aggressive, ambitious, clever, honest, perceptive, analytical, convincing, and self-controlled. Effective *cooperative* negotiators tend to be trustworthy, fair, honest, courteous, personable, tactful, sincere, perceptive, reasonable, convincing, and self-controlled. An "adversarial strategy" supports zero-sum negotiation, in which the gains of one party equal the losses of the other. A "problem-solving strategy" involves identifying the client's needs, anticipating the needs of the other party, and looking for solutions that accommodate both. Choices of style and strategy are influenced by factual circumstances, client needs, the personal style of the lawyer, and the style and strategy of her opponent. Furthermore, these behaviors generally surface on a continuum, with some of each style and strategy exhibited by one attorney in the same negotiation.

Lawyers exhibiting these styles and engaging in these strategies must conduct themselves within the boundaries of acceptable professional behavior. Even the most aggressive advocate should be respectful of an opponent. Even the most cooperative advocate must not concede too much. Lawyers have become concerned about a certain lack of civility in the behavior of some attorneys. Many jurisdictions have adopted professional codes that encourage lawyers to conduct themselves with respect towards clients, opposing parties, opposing counsel, courts, and the public. For example, a civility code might require attorneys to treat other counsel in a courteous and civil manner, honor express promises and agreements, confer early on with opposing counsel to assess settlement possibilities, make good-faith efforts to resolve by agreement objections to matters contained in pleadings and discovery requests, respond reasonably to document requests, and make a good-faith effort to avoid scheduling conflicts. *See, for example, Final Report of the Committee on Civility of the Seventh Federal Judicial Circuit*, 143 F.R.D. 441 (Dec. 1992).

see▷ **Chapter 16**
on Bias

Some comments directed at opposing counsel have resulted in sanctions against lawyers. *See, for example, Principe v. Assay Partners*, 154 Misc.2d 702, 586 N.Y.S.2d 182 (N.Y.Misc. 1992) ("I don't have to talk to you, little lady"; "Tell that little mouse over there to pipe down"; "What do you know, young girl"; "Be quiet, little girl"; "Go away, little girl." The court fined the offending attorney $1,000 and referred the matter to a disciplinary committee for imposition of possible additional sanctions); *In re Petition for Disciplinary Action against James Malcolm Williams*, 414 N.W.2d 394 (Minn. 1987) ("sheeny Hebrew tricks"; Williams received a reprimand and was suspended from practice for six months); *People v. Sharpe*, 781 P.2d 659 (Colo. 1989) (prosecutor received a public censure for referring to Latino defendants as "chili-eating bastards"); and *In re Farmer*, 442 S.E.2d 251 (Ga. 1994) (plaintiff's attorney in case alleging racial discrimination was found to be in contempt of court when he referred to opposing counsel as Judas and, after being admonished by the court, referred to him as "a person who is betraying the cause and constitutional quest of racial equality"). For a full discussion of bias and lack of civility, *see* Chapter 16.

Exercise 9.5 When you came to law school, what kind of negotiating style did you think you had or would use? What kind of style is generally attributed to lawyers? How does this stereotype affect legal practice? Which negotiating style and strategy would you be most comfortable using now? Identify one or two examples of incidents in your past when you have negotiated a dispute with your parents or someone else (for example, "I am old enough to get my ears pierced"). Write an account of the negotiation. Can you identify your style and strategy? How should civility standards be enforced? Through the courts? Through bar proceedings? Can you think of a circumstance in which incivility may be appropriate?

Reflecting on the Judicial System

Attorneys need to be vigilant in assessing the judicial system and in challenging inappropriate behavior, both as advocates protecting their clients' interests and as officers of the court. Critics have accused courts of perpetuating racial, ethnic, and gender stereotypes. For example, in Maryland, a committee composed of judges, lawyers, and law professors heard testimony from parties and practitioners concerning gender issues in the Maryland state courts. The most compelling testimony (*see* Maryland Special Joint Committee, *Report of the Maryland Special Joint Committee on Gender Bias in the Courts*, May 1989, at 5) concerned cases involving allegations of domestic violence. One assistant state's attorney testified that "the prevalent judicial attitude" is that criminal cases involving domestic violence are a "waste of time," "not serious," and "do not belong in the criminal justice system."

Among the incidents reported by the committee was one in which the husband was charged with kidnapping his wife, hitting her with a stun gun, and threatening her with death by gasoline fire. While he was out on bond, he followed and harassed his victim. Revocation of bond was denied because the judge said the defendant was permitted to follow the victim in order to gather evidence for the divorce. Furthermore, the judge thought the victim was "being a fretful woman for worrying about that sort of thing" because it was obvious the defendant would not hurt her.

A recent example of just how dangerous judicial indifference can be is seen in the case of Yvette Cade. In 2005, her then-husband attacked her in the store where she worked and set her on fire. "My flesh was dripping off me," she said. She suffered third-degree burns on 60 percent of her body, and her right foot was broken in five places where her husband had stomped on it A few weeks prior to this incident, the judge had dismissed her protective order despite her claims that her husband was intimidating her. Allison Klein, *After Fiery Attack, Md. Woman Finds Meaning in Taking Bold Steps*, Wash. Post, Jun. 21, 2006, at A1.

A walk through just about any courthouse will confirm that class plays a central role in the delivery of justice. University of Maryland Professor Barbara Bezdek and her students studied the "rent court" in Baltimore, Maryland, to determine why the right of landlords to be paid seemed always to take precedence over the right of tenants to housing that met the city's housing code. She observed that the tenants frequently were silent in court and rarely raised the claims and defenses available to them. The judges presiding in rent court expect tenants to be able to use the court as the law provides, that is, to state and prove their claims and defenses involving rent and property conditions in the same manner as the landlords' agents do. Neither side is necessarily represented by attorneys and the hearings are informal so that it will be easier for non-lawyers to represent themselves. However, the landlord's agents often are educated and skilled. The judges appear to be satisfied with the process, even as they bemoan tenants' ineffective participation in it. Thus, while the laws are designed to assure decent housing, tenants are unable to assert their statutory rights in a system that overlooks the fact that it is inaccessible to them. Professor Bezdek observes that

> One cannot meaningfully study institutions without attending to the human expressions and effects of their operations. A study of an institution necessarily draws meat and meaning from the behaviors of people operating within it . . . . In its dysfunction, the court fails one class of people and privileges another.

Barbara Bezdek, *Silence in the Court: Participation and Subordination of Poor Tenants' Voices in Legal Process*, 20 Hofstra L. Rev. 533, 537 and 600 (1992).

Professor Bezdek offers several examples of judicial dysfunction in the Baltimore rent court. The hearings are conducted in a building not served well by public transportation. This makes it difficult for the mostly low income tenants to get there. The tenants enter under a sign that says "Silence—Court in Session." The agents for the landlords sit in a separate area below a sign that says "Authorized Personnel Only." The docket clerk accommodates the landlords' agents by clumping together their cases and calling them earlier or later than listed. No such schedule accommodations are made for the tenants. If a tenant's case is called while she has stepped out of the courtroom to go to the restroom or to quiet a child—almost all are women accompanied by small children—the court will enter judgment against her. Professor Bezdek concludes that the tenants are "functionally voiceless" because the court system is so intimidating and so difficult to use.

Exercise 9.6 If you think the system described by Professor Bezdek is unfair, what do you think would be the best way to change it? Would you be more comfortable serving as a tenant advocate in the court to assist individual tenants; working for legislation to change the procedures; working to change court rules; teaching workshops to train courtroom personnel to be more sensitive to the needs of tenants; teaching workshops to train tenants and lay advocates to navigate the system; or conducting a study similar to Professor Bezdek's and contributing to the literature in this area? What other possibilities come to mind?

Reflecting on Alternative Dispute Resolution

Although popular culture portrays lawyers at work in courtrooms, most disputes are not resolved by litigation. Resolving disputes through mechanisms other than litigation is generally referred to as alternative dispute resolution (ADR). Pressures inside and outside of the court system have led to experiments in case management and other techniques to reduce the burden of litigation on litigants and on the courts. Mediation is a popular ADR technique. In the 1970s, it was primarily a private method of resolving disputes and as such had benefited from the conviction of parties that sought it out. Today, with many courts requiring participation in mediation, it has become another step in the process of resolution. Proponents of mediation argue that it avoids anguish, preserves autonomy, and saves money. Opponents argue that procedural safeguards are undermined in this informal process and that this tips the balance against less powerful parties even further.

Below are examples of three forms of ADR used in domestic relations cases: early judicial intervention, arbitration, and mediation.

Judge Donald B. King of Superior Court for San Francisco, California, initiated a case management system to encourage the settlement of cases. Instead of the practice of assigning cases to a particular judge at the time of trial, Judge King offered "to act as case manager and provide judicial oversight with a focus on early settlement." Cases were assigned to Judge King shortly after a response to the initial complaint had been filed and only after parties consented to his intervention. Judge King asked the parties to direct their attorneys to cooperate to reduce "the pressure on counsel to posture for the client." Discovery was done informally, with conflict resolved through direct access to the Judge. Judge King describes the process as "less expensive, quicker, and leav[ing] the parties feeling better about themselves." This procedure has now been codified in California by a provision of the Family Code that permits lawyers to design the divorce process for their cases. *Judicious Intervention: What One California Judge Has Done to Expedite Settlement*, 19 Fam. Advoc. 22 (1997).

Arbitration also may be used in divorce proceedings, although it is far more common as a contractual requirement for resolving business disputes. Arbitration allows parties to choose a time and place to resolve issues that have arisen relating to property settlement and support. It frees them from the congested calendars and public nature of judicial proceedings. Some jurisdictions also permit resolution of child custody and visitation issues through binding arbitration, even though courts traditionally made these decisions under the doctrine of *parens patriae*, through which courts have assumed a special responsibility to protect the interests of minors.

Mediators assist parties in arriving at their own settlement. Once an agreement is reached, it is reduced to writing and signed by both parties and their attorneys. This agreement then may form the basis of a court order. Approaches to the mediation process vary. Some mediators prefer to keep the parties together throughout the mediation process. Others prefer to shuttle back and forth between the parties, encouraging disclosure and compromise. Attorney participation varies according to the wishes of all involved. Where mediation is mandatory, some jurisdictions allow parties to bring their attorneys to mediation; others discourage it. While some mediators may view attorneys as intrusive, the advice provided by attorneys can protect the parties' interests. For example, in domestic relations cases, facilitative mediators may refuse to provide information about the law to unrepresented parties on the ground that it undermines the autonomy of the parties. Thus, while a mediator may be aware of provisions in domestic relations law that encourage joint custody awards, the mediator may not be familiar with or fail to reveal exceptions that discourage it where there has been a history of domestic violence. The court, applying local domestic relations law, may reject a settlement that is clearly insupportable. In many cases, however, the lack of legal guidance is not evident, and the court may not be able to protect the parties from the results that are contrary to their legal interests.

Some mediators recognize the difficulty mediation poses for disadvantaged parties. For example, where domestic violence has been alleged, some mediators advise against keeping such parties together during mediation. Some have urged that mediation should never be used where domestic violence has been alleged. Some believe that, depending upon the circumstances of the violent relationship, parties can and should mediate.

Courts have been criticized for using mediation in a way that denies access to traditional procedures, with unrepresented parties often making uninformed and disadvantageous decisions. Professor Trina Grillo discusses the negative impact of mandatory mediation on poor people, racial minorities, and women. Professor Grillo describes mandatory mediation as "more, not less, disempowering than the adversary system—for it is . . . a process in which people are told they are being empowered, but in fact [they] are being forced to acquiesce in their own oppression." *The Mediation Alternative: Process Dangers for Women*, 100 Yale L.J. 1545, 1610 (1991). According to Professor Grillo, mediators are not always impartial and prejudice thrives in private settings. Some parties to mediation lie with impunity because there is no mechanism for testing the accuracy of their statements. Anger is delegitimized in mediation, so anger that needs to be expressed in order to facilitate clarity and build strength is stifled. Laura Nader goes a step further, condemning ADR generally as "an often coercive mechanism of pacification" that neutralizes attempts to vindicate protected rights. *Controlling Processes in the Practice of Law: Hierarchy and Pacification in the Movement to Re-Form Dispute Ideology*, 9 Ohio St. J. on Disp. Resol. 1 (1993).

Exercise 9.7 The purchaser of a new home signed a sales contract that includes a clause requiring that all claims against the builder be resolved through binding arbitration as specified in a later clause that indicates that the arbitrator will be chosen from a list provided by the Association of Homebuilders. Is such a clause fair to the buyer? What if there were no such clause, but upon filing a claim against the builder the court automatically referred the case for either mediation or arbitration? Does requiring the parties to submit to some form of alternative dispute resolution deny them access to the courts? Should parties be encouraged to waive procedural and other safeguards in exchange for a more expedited, less antagonistic process? What might be sacrificed to gain efficiency and privacy?

Reflecting on Legislative Advocacy

In their primer for the legislative advocate, *Lobbying Congress: How the System Works* (Congressional Quarterly 1996), Bruce Wolpe and Bertram Levine outline the basic principles for success in the profession. The lobbyist should be accurate and honest; never promise more than can be delivered; listen carefully to the expressions used by the legislators because the messages often are conveyed through carefully chosen phrases; work with staff, do not try to go around them; and spring no surprises on legislators. Thus, assuming adequate access, the challenge for a lobbyist is not simply to tell the truth but to provide full disclosure about how the issue plays out within the political environment. Members and staff need to know the source and degree of opposition and support for any bill and the risks of pursuing a given course of action.

Federalist Paper No. 10 is a letter written by James Madison on November 22, 1787, to the people of the State of New York. In the letter, Madison responded to criticism that state governments were "too unstable, that the public good was disregarded in the conflicts of rival parties, and that measures were too often decided, not according to the rules of justice and the rights of the minor party, but by the superior force of an interested and overbearing majority." In supporting his vision of representative government, Madison described the checks and balances of our government as providing "a chosen body of citizens, whose wisdom may best discern the true interest of their country, and whose patriotism and love of justice, will be least likely to sacrifice it to temporary or partial considerations." The influence of factional interests as represented by campaign contributions and influential lobbyists imperil the protections contemplated by Madison and his colleagues. Nevertheless, the legislative process fosters a rich dialogue informed by, for better or worse, and reliant upon the expertise of the lobbyist.

Exercise 9.8 *Lobbyists* are linked to the *special interests* they represent, and both terms are generally used as pejoratives. Yet it is clear that the process relies on the information and analysis that legislative advocates provide. Consider the debate about global warming. While the scientific consensus on global climate change is hard to contest, policy is still influenced by those that consider the issue inconclusive and the reports of climate change alarmist. What is the role of the legislative advocate in advancing this debate? Is it reasonable to expect the advocate as well as the legislator to be guided by Madison's vision of legislating in the "true interest" of the country? Is the appropriate role for the advocate to present her arguments to legislators much like the litigator who advocates for his client and leaves the decision making to the trier of fact?

Reflecting on the Role of Government Lawyers

Jack B. Weinstein, former Chief Judge for the United States District Court for the Eastern District of New York, offers some observations on how an attorney working for a governmental agency should deal with conflicts between the client agency's position or conduct and her own view of the issues. Government attorneys represent not only the government entity, but the public as well. The statutes and rules governing the ethical obligations of government attorneys support independent ethical decision making. Judge Weinstein concludes that

> Certainly it is easier for a government attorney to take an unreflective view and to obey mechanically the wishes of the government agency client. Nor do I discount the danger for abuse in an approach that advocates independent thinking—and action—on the part of government attorneys. Yet, while compliance with executive policy should be the norm, a compelling need exists in this society—as in others that have come before it—to mitigate the harshness of the law through individualization of justice.

Jack B. Weinstein & Gay A. Crosthwait, *Some Reflections on Conflicts Between Government Attorneys and Clients*, 1 Touro L. Rev. 1 (1985).

Consider the following example discussed by Professor Jesselyn Radack:

> A client asks his lawyer a question: During an interrogation of a suspected terrorist, how much pain can I legally inflict?
>
> The lawyer should:
>
> a) Explore every legal avenue available for his client, including all possible defenses should criminal charges be filed.
>
> b) Give legal guidance but add advice on the wisdom and morality of what the client is considering.
>
> c) Tell the client to take a walk.
>
> The lawyers at the Department of Justice who prepared the so-called "torture memos"—a series of United States government legal opinions holding that the torture of terrorism suspects might be legally defensible—have come under fire in the legal community for choosing option "a" above. The Department of Justice's Office of Legal Counsel ("OLC"), which "writes legal opinions considered binding on federal agencies and departments" and maintains a longstanding tradition of dispensing objective legal advice to its clients in executive-branch agencies, authored the most incendiary of the interrogation memoranda—the infamous "torture memorandum" of August

1, 2002, which advised the CIA and White House that torturing al Qaeda terrorists in captivity abroad "may be justified," and that only "serious physical injury, such as organ failure, impairment of bodily function, or even death" constitutes torture.

"It is well known that the 2002 Opinion was used for guidance by the Defense Department to justify interrogation practices, including abusive ones . . . ." In June 2004, the White House renounced the controversial document, calling it "over-broad and irrelevant," but only once the Abu Ghraib prison abuse scandal broke and the memorandum became public. The Justice Department did not put out a replacement memorandum for more than six months. On December 30, 2004, the original memorandum was "formally repudiated by the administration the week before [then-White House Counsel Alberto] Gonzales's appearance before the Senate Judiciary Committee for confirmation as attorney general."

The Justice Department issued a new memorandum on acts that constitute torture, which states that the memorandum "supersedes the August 2002 memorandum in its entirety." However, the very existence of the rescinded memorandum, which became one of the most criticized policy memoranda drafted during President Bush's first term, still begs for a reexamination of the proper role for the government lawyer acting in an advisory capacity in the war on terrorism.

Tortured Legal Ethics: The Role of the Government Advisor in the War on Terrorism, 77 U. COLO. L. REV. 1, 1-4 (2006) (footnotes omitted).

Professor Radack proposes clearer ethical rules for government attorneys:

Rule 2.2: Special Responsibilities of a Government Attorney in an Advisory Role

The government attorney in an advisory role shall:

>   (a) not give advice that is either illegal or unethical;
>
>   (b) refrain from rendering advice that the attorney knows is likely to lead to a violation of existing law;
>
>   (c) give an accurate, complete and balanced analysis of the law that:
>
>>   (1) makes the majority legal position known when advocating a minority, close, contrary or novel legal position;
>>
>>   (2) makes adverse case law known;
>
>   (d) add advice on the wisdom and morality of what the client is considering, especially when the advice is unlikely to be subject to judicial review.

This proposed language would ensure that government lawyers advising on morally perilous questions would give advice that is legal, ethical, moral, complete, balanced and unlikely to lead to a violation of current law. Yet it would also leave government attorneys free to render advice that is not completely supported by existing law when an agency has determined that existing law should be challenged. The government lawyer just has to be transparent about doing so . . . .

[T]he Model Rules should adopt a provision governing the special responsibilities of government lawyers acting in an advisory capacity so that moral consideration will be required and not optional, and carry consequences, not excuses. Id. at 42-43, 48.

> **Exercise 9.9** As deputy state's attorney, you have been assigned to a high profile case that your boss wants you to prosecute. You firmly believe that the defendant police officer, charged with murdering his girlfriend, should not be prosecuted. The evidence supports the officer's claim that he acted in self-defense, although there is a history of the officer abusing his girlfriend. Your boss is known for aggressive prosecution of domestic violence cases, especially when they involve members of the police force. You are convinced that he will not like your conclusion. What are your options in this instance? What considerations should influence your decision?

Reflecting on the Relationship Between Work and Values

One discipline that can be easy to lose sight of is the process of checking the work you do against what you believe you should be doing. Many lawyers become absorbed in attempting to achieve what the organization or the individual client expects without stopping to evaluate whether the objectives and approaches are consistent with their values and professional goals. As you progress in your professional development, regularly assess the relationship between the work you do and your own goals and values.

An excerpt from the February, 2004, ABA Journal suggests the challenge, and the rewards, of synthesizing your values and your work:

> When Howard Vogel arrived at the Minnesota Supreme Court building
> in September, he came with Atticus Finch on his mind.

Vogel, a professor at Hamline University Law School in St. Paul, was one of 12 people there to address the court on an issue they believed went to the very heart of what it means to be a lawyer.

He told the justices that he uses Harper Lee's *To Kill a Mockingbird* to help his students understand the concept of professional identity. On a recent occasion, he said, he asked his students what most stood out to them about Atticus.

"We had a wide-ranging discussion," he recalled, and a student who had been rather quiet up until then said that what struck her was the fact that Atticus is the same everywhere he goes. "He's the same when he's at home and when he's at church. He's the same when he talks with Calpurnia, who takes care of his children, and when he visits with neighbors. He's the same when he goes to the state legislature, and when he goes to represent a black man against a rape charge."

The student's point, and the message Vogel came to make to the court, was simple but weighty: Finch was a whole person. "You have a complete range of skills rooted in your humanity . . . and you will bring those to your work, as did Atticus."

Steven Keeva, *CLE for the Whole Person: Minnesota Supreme Court Gives Full Credit for Classes Emphasizing Self-Reflection*, 90 A.B.A.J. 76 (2004).

That is not to say that the whole person of Atticus Finch is without controversy. A bevy of articles have been written about his limitations. One of the articles, by Professor Monroe H. Freedman, is the most provocative and captures the gist of these critiques in these two paragraphs:

Consider, then, the moral truth that [Atticus Finch] tells to the children when they experience the lynch mob outside the jail. Walter Cunningham, a leader of the mob, is "basically a good man," he teaches them, "he just has his blind spots along with the rest of us." It just happens that Cunningham's blind spot (along with the rest of us?) is a homicidal hatred of black people . . . . What are we to make of this fatuousness? That a lynch mob is not a lynch mob because it's "made up of people?" That because Cunningham is "still a man," he has no moral responsibility for attempted murder? . . . Lest anyone miss the point, this contention is derived from cultural relativism. This is a philosophy that rejects the idea that there are any moral values that are absolute . . . . Slavery? Apartheid? Lynching? Sacrificing babies? . . . [T]here are prima facie principles of right and wrong (which can be called Natural Law), which each of us is capable of recognizing by the use of experience, intellect, and conscience.

. . . Finch "hoped to get through life without a case of this kind." It means that Atticus Finch never in his professional life voluntarily takes a pro bono case in an effort to ameliorate the evil—which he himself and others recognize—in the apartheid of Macomb, Alabama. Forget about "working on the front lines of the NAACP." Here is a man who does not voluntarily use his legal training and skills—not once, ever—to make the slightest change in the pervasive social injustice of his town.

Atticus Finch—Right and Wrong, 45 Ala. L. Rev. 473, 476-477, 481 (1994).

Professor Freedman also makes the point that dedicating one's entire professional life to fighting for social justice is "too easy to preach and too hard to practice." *Id.* at 480. For example, consider the work of Bryan Stevenson. In an article about Stevenson, a lawyer who has devoted his life to fighting injustice in general and the death penalty in particular, Walt Harrington likens Stevenson to *lamed-vovniks*, thirty-six righteous men in an ancient Jewish legend "who were sent by God to live and work among us, always poor, unnoticed and without glory, unaware of their own perfection." *How Can Anyone Do Anything Else?*, Wash. Post, Jan. 6, 1991, (Magazine) at W12. Stevenson, a graduate of Harvard Law School and the John F. Kennedy School of Government, rejected lucrative alternatives to head the Alabama Capital Representation Resource Center, which is involved in some way with most of the death-row inmates in Alabama. Harrington reported that Stevenson works seven days a week, often from 8:30 a.m. to 11:30 p.m. His work style is fueled by his passion to alleviate the injustice he sees on death row: "I could go through the South's prisons and put together five death rows of men not condemned whose crimes were far more vicious. The people who end up on death row are always poor, often black. And almost always they had bad lawyers—real estate lawyers who never handled a capital case and who had to be dragged screaming into the courtroom." Bryan Stevenson is currently a Professor of Clinical Law at New York University; he continues his previous work through the Capital Defender Clinic in Alabama and as the Executive Director of the Equal Justice Initiative in Alabama.

The level of analysis that the fictional character of Atticus Finch has provoked underscores the particularized responsibility of those of us who choose to equip ourselves to be lawyers and the challenge of understanding how to weave that responsibility into the lives we need to live. Returning to what Professor Vogel's student observed, you bring your humanity to your work and that should make the necessary difference.

> **Exercise 9.10** What roles do lawyers fulfill in society? What were your goals when you came into law school? Were those goals tied to a specific area of legal practice? Have those goals changed or been refined? In what ways? Why? How connected are those goals to what you believe is right? Which lawyers have had an impact on your aspirations as a lawyer?

Conclusion

Your externship will provide you with material to reflect upon as you explore your place in the legal system and lay the foundation for building expertise. It is important that you tie your experiences to the experiences of others. Where do you fit in? How should you relate to your clients? How should you interact with the other players in the system? How will your values guide your practice? How should you practice law? The discipline of *reflective lawyering*, begun now, will serve you well throughout your professional life.

FURTHER READING

Carwina Weng, *Multicultural Lawyering: Teaching Psychology to Develop Cultural Self-Awareness*, 11 CLIN. L. REV. 369, 375-376 (2005).

Harold I. Abramson, *Mediation Representation: Advocating in a Problem-Solving Process* (NITA 2004).

Bryan Stevenson, 2006 Commencement Address, Bard College, http://www.bard.edu/commencement/2006/stevenson_speech.shtml

FILM

A FEW GOOD MEN (Sony Pictures 1992).

PHILADELPHIA (Sony Pictures 1997).

TO KILL A MOCKINGBIRD (Universal Studios 1962).

Chapter 10

Creative Problem Solving

Linda Morton & Janet Weinstein

For every complex problem there is a solution that is
simple, neat, and wrong.

—H.L. Mencken

You are externing in a small firm. Your supervising attorney has asked you to prepare an alibi witness, the defendant's girlfriend, for a forthcoming trial. In your first meeting with the witness to go over her testimony, you realize her presentation is very weak; she speaks too quickly and seems very nervous about testifying. Moreover, her alibi testimony that the client was with her on a specific date two years ago is almost too detailed to be believable. The trial is on Monday. It is the Wednesday prior, and your supervisor is out of town until Friday morning. You are anxious to do a good job to impress your supervisor. What will you do?

You are an attorney representing an inner city hospital, and you have proudly negotiated a partnership contract with a suburban hospital. There is only one item holding up the signing of the contract. Both hospitals have agreed they need an MRI machine and that, due to the expense of the machine, it would be necessary to share it between the two hospitals; however, each hospital wants the machine housed in its facility. The suburban hospital, through its lawyer, maintains that the machine will increase profits if housed at its facility, because its wealthier patients will pay for the service. Your client, the urban hospital, believes that it should house the machine, based on its larger and more needy patient base. You clearly want to finalize the partnership between the two hospitals by resolving the placement of the MRI. Where will you start?

You are a new attorney, who just started working at a mid-size firm three months ago. You have been working very hard, including lots of late nights and week-ends. It is Friday, 4 p.m., and you are packing up to head off for the weekend to attend a friend's wedding, a few hours drive from the office. A partner enters your office and asks that you stay in town until Saturday morning to work on a very pressing research project. You have done some work for this client, but nothing related to this current project. The attorney tells you that if you can have it on her desk by Saturday at 9 a.m., she'll come in, take a look, and not keep you more than another hour or two. The wedding is Saturday afternoon. You would likely make it, but would miss the pre-wedding activities Friday night and Saturday morning. What will you tell her?

A law firm partner, Nancy Zeluski Berg, explains, "We tell our associates that anybody can figure out a lawsuit. Our task is to look at the entire problem and serve clients by helping them find the solution, whether it be a lawsuit, legislation or family therapy."

The problems outlined above are typical of those lawyers encounter in their work. "Problem solving" is a term used to express the broader ways experienced lawyers think about and ultimately resolve such issues. When faced with a problem, such as those described above, the brain looks quickly for "tried and true," or patterned, solutions. As a result, a lawyer can react too quickly to uncomfortable issues by engaging in familiar yet potentially unproductive responses. If the brain does not find a familiar pattern of response, it may default to a fight or flight mode by avoiding the issue (flight) or immediately confronting the problem makers with a strong response (fight).

For example, in the first scenario above, a law student might decide quickly to put the witness problem aside until the supervisor gets back (flight). In the second scenario, a transactional lawyer for the inner city hospital may engage in a patterned advocacy response and try to persuade the other hospital to relinquish its interest in housing the MRI machine (fight), ignoring more creative solutions and potentially jeopardizing the partnership. In the third scenario, a law student or lawyer might dismiss the partner's behavior in asking her to work Friday night and Saturday as "unhealthy" (flight), give in to the partner's request without expressing her needs (another form of flight), or stand up for her own values (fight).

see▷ Chapter 17 *on Work-Life Balance*

None of these solutions is necessarily the best or even appropriate under the circumstances. An extern's avoidance of a problematic issue in the first scenario will likely vex the supervising attorney and surely not make the best impression about the extern's potential as a problem solver. In the second scenario, although one's reputation as a zealous advocate is important, it may not serve the client's interest to approach the contract negotiation in an adversarial manner. While maintaining life balance is a significant value, the third problem may have solutions that do not involve the trade-offs the more rapidly formed solutions have. There may be many creative ways to resolve these issues, once the problems are thought through and better understood.

Off-the-cuff or rapidly formed solutions are not likely to be the most effective. A more conscious problem-solving process will produce more useful and creative solutions. Law students are trained to use analytic, logical, linear thought processes—processes of narrowing thinking to prove a specific point. In contrast, the problem-solving process broadens the approach to problems and thus enlarges the potential solution base.

A brief introduction to how the brain works explains why individuals may panic or jump to conclusions when faced with a problem. This information also provides a theoretical foundation for the problem-solving model discussed in the following section.

The Brain as a Problem-Solving Mechanism

The purpose of the brain, as well as the body's other organs, is to ensure the organism's survival. This functioning is automatic; the brain reacts to any external or internal event that appears to threaten the well-being of the organism. Problem solving is a basic mechanism for survival; more sophisticated and conscious brain functions continue to be rooted in problem solving. While people living in modern society generally do not experience ultimate survival issues, such as being attacked by wild animals, or being without food or shelter, they regularly experience threats to their sense of well-being. In the context of being a legal extern or an attorney, these threats might take several forms, such as the fear of being embarrassed by not knowing what to do or making a mistake, fear of not being offered a job, or fear of losing a job or a client. This fear may not necessarily be rational—as in an externship when students are there to learn, even by their mistakes, and supervising attorneys are supposed to provide constructive feedback. Nevertheless, the fear arises, and as a result the body (including the brain) moves into a defensive strategy that relies primarily on familiar, patterned solutions, including the more primal fight or flight mode. This is one of the reasons it is difficult to be creative, or even to learn, in a highly stressful environment. Positron Emission Tomography (PET) scan images of the brain have demonstrated that the frontal lobes, which are responsible for planning and "executive functions" necessary to problem solving, are not fully activated during times of fear and anger; they are most activated when a person is happy.

Patterns of behavior are created by neural pathways, or connections, in the brain—pathways that are reinforced by use. These pathways are formed by early childhood experiences and, to some degree, throughout life. The more frequently a person does a particular thing, thinks in a particular way, or reacts to events in a similar fashion, the stronger the neural connections responsible for those actions, thoughts, and feelings become. Thus, while everyone is born with similar genetic material, the neural pathways established through repeated behaviors play a major role in determining how an individual approaches life—how he does things, how he feels and thinks, and how he solves problems. Throughout life the brain continues to build upon these connections established in early childhood. When a person ceases to use particular connections, those neural pathways may be lost, or "pruned."

Law school does not transform students into problem solvers. People problem solve naturally, because it is a requirement for survival. Every law student solved problems before coming to law school. Every law student brought to law school some patterns of behavior (based on established pathways created through life experience) that enhanced or inhibited his or her problem-solving skills.

Problem-solving skills developed in traditional legal education may differ from those developed prior to law school. The problem-solving skills required in law school include the following: reading legal opinions and ascertaining the rules of law contained in them; identifying relevant facts that led the courts to their conclusions; learning by memory the important rules, facts, and policies; analogizing those facts to the case at hand; understanding the nature of policy considerations; anticipating arguments that can be made by both sides; clearly and succinctly writing and speaking in a way that demonstrates all of the above. This set of knowledge and skills, which is reinforced many times throughout law school and which is determinative of "survival" (whether that be simply passing or making law review), have become well-worn neuropathways that can be used, fairly automatically, to solve legal problems.

Real-life legal problems do not necessarily fit into the law school exam pattern. Problems in real life tend to be ill-structured, not well-defined, and often presented with missing pieces. One lawyer describes a family coming to her office in tears after its apartment was destroyed by fire to ask her help in finding them a place to live. Although the family did not present a legal issue, upon further questioning the lawyer learned that the son had been forced to jump out the window to escape the fire and was suffering from severe spinal cord injuries. Subsequent investigation revealed that the landlord had not installed proper fire escapes.

For example, the role of apology in settling lawsuits is gaining increased recognition. Research has shown that patients injured by medical malpractice are more appeased by hospitals' acknowledgment of wrongdoing and assurances that mistakes will not happen again than by compensation alone.

Because law students' and lawyers' brains have been so well trained in the narrow range of problem solving required for law school exams, these individuals tend to solve problems using the familiar, more narrow and expeditious legal approach. Although absolutely necessary to law practice, a purely legal approach to problem solving can have adverse effects on more general, complex, or ill-structured problems. Such an approach can alienate clients, who may feel their true needs are not being met, or can hinder help by other professionals who might respond adversely to a purely legal approach. Moreover, when the brain cannot find a pathway that "fits" the problem at hand, it will resort to the more primal fight or flight instincts, often exacerbating rather than ameliorating the problem.

Exercise 10.1 Struggling with a problem for which we see no clear resolution can arouse fear that triggers the fight or flight instinct. When the fight or flight response is triggered, a number of physiological reactions, including shortness of breath and rapid heartbeat, automatically initiate to increase the chances of survival. The next time you are feeling anxious or afraid, observe your physiological reactions. If you notice shortness of breath or rapid heartbeat, you might try the following: Make a purposeful effort to slow down your breathing by taking slow, deep breaths, inhaling into your diaphragm and then gently contracting your abdominal muscles as you exhale. You will find that the anxiety will decrease, allowing you to attend to the problem in a less frantic way.

To be effective in solving real-life legal problems, it is necessary to learn how to handle them more broadly, rather than adhering solely to linear legal training or allowing the more primal instincts of fight or flight to inappropriately dictate a course of action. One of the major challenges to becoming an effective legal problem solver is to expand one's knowledge and skills and to practice these until they also become strong pathways that can be relied upon when facing new problems.

A Problem-Solving Model

Models help translate thoughts into action. Following a model may help to strengthen underutilized neural pathways in the brain and create new ones to help work through problems. Some models, like the one presented below, provide an overview of the complete process, as opposed to detailed pieces of it, thus serving as a convenient reference as the brain attempts to learn and implement new ways of thinking and acting. Models can be used as guidelines to ensure all aspects of the problem and its possible solutions have been considered. Models can be dangerous if one tries to follow them in an overly rigid, formulaic, or simplistic way. To counter these pitfalls, a problem solver must maintain awareness of the interests, values, and needs each problem presents. It is important not to proceed in lockstep progression with each phase. Problem solving frequently demands a return to or expansion of prior phases, or development of tangents outside of the model. The model below is simply a convenient reference point and a way to begin to engage in a more thoughtful method for solving problems. From this more generic example, individuals can develop more specific models suitable to their own work.

This problem-solving model has seven different stages, expressed visually below. Each stage involves a series of questions that serve the dual functions of slowing down and expanding the process. During all stages of the problem-solving endeavor, one is likely to acquire information that will be useful but will not fit necessarily into the questions asked at each stage. For example, in discussing the problem with others, one is likely to learn about personalities, behaviors, systems characteristics, environmental influences, etc., that will affect one's approach to the problem. In gathering facts and answering the questions posed in the model, it is important not to discount these other factors that may influence a resolution. Problem solving requires certain skills, attitudes, and values, depicted in the center of the model because they permeate the entire process. These core skills, attitudes, and values are discussed in further detail in the section, *infra*, on Attributes of Effective Problem Solvers.

A VISUAL MODEL OF PROBLEM SOLVING

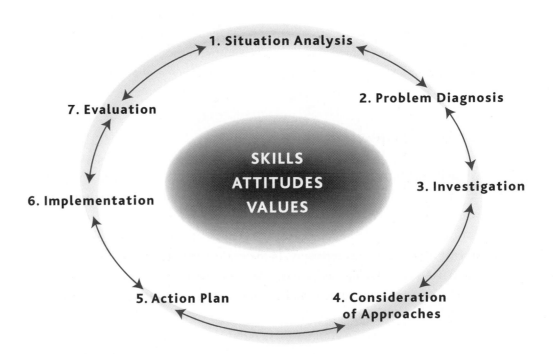

♦ Stage one, **Situation Analysis**, grounds the problem solver in what is happening at the moment the problem presents itself and helps him or her move forward. In this stage, the following questions help assess the circumstances:

- What is wrong with the current situation? How is it affecting me?
- What is the preferred situation?

- What should I do now?

- Have I experienced something like this before? If so, what did I learn that might be useful here?

♦ Stage two, **Problem Diagnosis,** offers a preliminary definition and context for the problem by posing the following questions:

- How would I define the problem at this point?

- Who else can help in identifying the problem?

- What are their roles/interests/objectives?

- Whom/what does the problem affect?

- What are their interests/values/objectives?

- Who/what is responsible for the problem?

- Is the problem part of a larger problem?

- If so, which should be addressed first?

- Could the problem have been prevented?

♦ Stage three, **Investigation,** looks outside the problem context to understand what additional information is needed and who might help provide it. This stage encourages the problem solver to consider redefining the problem as a result of the investigation. Some questions to help with this process include the following:

- What additional information is needed (facts? feelings? legal issues?)?

- Who/what can help?

- Who is the appropriate person/entity to fix this problem?

- Are there cultural issues to be considered?

♦ Stage four, **Consideration of Approaches,** helps the problem solver develop a variety of approaches, legal and non-legal, to address the problem as most recently defined. This stage also provides fertile ground for creative thinking techniques, described later in this chapter. Potential questions to be answered are as follows:

- What approaches does the law provide?

- What other approaches might there be? Would creative thinking help?

- Whose interests, values, and objectives does each approach reflect?

- What would the client like to do?

- What new problems might each approach create?

- Can any potential new problems be prevented?

- Which approaches might be most effective?

♦ After thinking through a variety of approaches, the problem solver decides on an **Action Plan** in stage five. The action plan might involve one or several approaches. The process for implementing the action is also an important component to be considered in this stage. Potential questions are as follows:

- What is the best course of action?
- Who should be involved?
- Who will implement the action?
- Who is responsible for it?
- How should decisions be made?
- What new problems might be created, and what steps should be taken to prevent them?
- Given the above and all the information available, is this still the best path?
- What has been learned?

♦ After careful consideration of the Action Plan, **Implementation,** stage six, begins. Important questions for this stage include the following:

- Am I following my Action Plan? If not, why not?
- Is the Action Plan producing the expected results?
- Do I need to change my Action Plan and, if so, how?

♦ The seventh and final stage, **Evaluation,** is an effort to assess the course of action and to reflect on one's learning from the problem-solving process. It is a simple but essential step, which takes place continuously, before, during, and after the Implementation stage. Evaluation questions also are built into the process in most of the other stages. The following questions are relevant to the evaluation that follows implementation:

- Has the problem been solved?
- What, if any, new problems have been created?
- Was the Action Plan appropriate? Is there anything I would change in hindsight?
- What did I learn? (If working in a group, what did we learn?)

In applying this model to a problem, it is important to remember that the process does not always flow as simply as the model's stages might portray. Going back to redefine the problem, collect more facts, consult with other disciplines, or adjust the process are all common tacks one might take in problem solving. It is essential to adopt an expansive, flexible approach.

The next section applies the model to the first two scenarios presented earlier. There are no right or wrong answers to the questions each phase poses. Depending on the problem, some questions may be unnecessary, inapplicable, or redundant; if so, it is fine to skip them or go back to them in a later phase. The purpose of the model is to slow down, as well as to expand, one's thinking, not to do superfluous work.

Application of the Model

A demonstration of how the model might be applied to the first two scenarios is provided below. The last stage of the model involves the evaluation of an action plan, which can only be accomplished after an action plan is executed. In applying the model, specific questions were omitted if they were redundant or not applicable.

Example 1 *The Alibi Witness*

♦ **Situation Analysis**

What is wrong with the current situation? How is it affecting me?

> *I'm feeling very anxious about doing the right thing. I've been given an important assignment, and it's not turning out as planned. I want to impress my supervisor by letting him see he can rely on me, but I am not sure it is true. Our key witness is very nervous and not believable, and my supervising attorney is out of town. I'm not sure what to do next. I'm on my own.*

What is the preferred situation?

> *The witness is articulate and credible, and I do such an impressive job coaching her that my supervising attorney lets me do the direct exam at trial.*

What should I do now?

> *I'm going to calm down and think this through. I'll talk to some people and then develop a plan by the end of the day.*

Have I experienced something like this before? If so, what did I learn that might be useful here?

> *I know that I have a tendency to panic when I have to do something new and important. I know I can't think clearly when I'm feeling panicked.*

I remember that, when I took a course in Client Interviewing and Counseling, I got some feedback that I do not ask questions very clearly. Maybe I need to make sure that I'm being clear with this witness.

♦ Problem Diagnosis

How would I define the problem at this point?

I am responsible for our key witness, who talks too fast, is very nervous, and does not seem credible. My supervising attorney is not available to help me prepare this witness. I do not want to ruin the defendant's chances for a "not guilty" verdict, and I must remain ethical at the same time.

Who else can help in identifying the problem?

Maybe someone else could interview the witness and tell me if my suspicions are correct. Other lawyers, law professors, or staff here at the office might help, though I must keep in mind rules protecting client confidentiality. The client should be able to help, too.

What are their roles/interests/objectives?

Some who might be willing to help are altruistic; they want to help us out. The client and those involved with the case surely want to win by achieving a "not guilty" verdict.

Whom/what does the problem affect?

The client, most of all, and no doubt the witness, but also the office, my supervising attorney, and me, in terms of our reputations for quality advocacy and professionalism. The problem also affects the alleged victim and the justice system generally.

What are their interests/values/objectives?

The client's interests are in a not guilty verdict—justice.

The witness's interests are the above, perhaps her continuing relationship with the client, and her ego as well.

Also, there are societal interests in maintaining a fair justice system. The alleged victim wants justice, as well.

Who/what is responsible for the problem?

Maybe we should have talked to the witness earlier.

Maybe I am too inexperienced to be left alone with this kind of responsibility.

Maybe our client has convinced this witness to lie.

Maybe the witness's nervousness is affecting her performance.

Is the problem part of a larger problem?

There are issues of ethics, such as how much to coach the witness.

Another problem might be that my supervisor spends too much time out of town.

I don't have enough experience to handle something this difficult. My supervising attorney is giving me too much responsibility.

If so, which should be addressed first?

I need to address the immediate problem and plan to discuss the other problems with my supervising attorney at another time.

Could the problem have been prevented?

Next time, I'm going to talk to all witnesses earlier. I also will clarify my responsibilities with my supervisor when he gets back.

♦ **Investigation**

What additional information is needed (facts? feelings? legal issues?)?

I need to assess better how bad the problem is and figure out what my ethical duties are. I also need to figure out if there is any way I can reach my supervisor.

Who/what can help?

I've talked about this above, but I will list some names now.

Who is the appropriate person to fix this problem?

I am, with some help from others.

> **Additional Facts:** The witness relates to you, somewhat incoherently and much too rapidly, a very detailed story of what she and her boyfriend were doing the afternoon the crime was committed. She even describes the kind of tea they drank that afternoon, the specific errands they ran together, and what they had for dinner that evening. When you call your client at his job site that afternoon about the witness's "million-dollar memory," your client reminds you that he was arrested shortly afterwards and that it was not hard to remember what they had done together a week prior. He also confirms that the alibi witness, his girlfriend, does have a terrific memory for every-day facts and is telling the truth. You learn that the paralegal will be in touch with your supervising attorney Thursday afternoon. The paralegal has offered to help you in any way he can, although he is very busy. You asked him to have a short meeting with the witness, and he agreed with you that she is difficult to understand. You checked out the local rules on ethics and, at this point, are aware that you would be traversing dangerous waters only if you know your witness to be lying while testifying. Your bigger issues at this point are the witness's extreme nervousness, rapid speech, and potential lack of credibility.

♦ Consideration of Approaches

What approaches does the law provide?

> *Apparently it would be fine for me to help the witness prepare for the hearing so that she can be understood by the jury and so that her testimony sounds more credible.*

What other approaches might there be?

> *I could talk to the witness about my concerns and then have her practice with me.*

> *I'm thinking that a quick counseling session could be useful, at least for helping the witness feel more comfortable speaking in court. It might be difficult to find someone to do this on such short notice.*

Whose interests, values, and objectives does each approach reflect?

> *Logically, it would seem that the client, the witness, my supervising attorney, and I all share the same interests, values, and objectives—making sure the client does not get convicted. However, the witness may be offended or embarrassed at the suggestion that her speech is not clear and her testimony is not credible. This also might upset the client. The witness's need to protect her self-image could create defensiveness or a self-consciousness that might make her testimony even worse.*

What would the client like to do?

The client wants us to use any means possible to achieve a "not guilty" verdict. He also wants me to make these suggestions to his girlfriend in a way that will not offend her. He wants to talk to her, too.

What new problems might each approach create?

Potential ethical issues may arise if the coaching gets into the substance of what the witness would say.

A counseling session also would be an expense to the client, which could be a problem for him. There is the possibility that the girlfriend would get mad, embarrassed, or angry at her boyfriend and refuse to testify.

Can any potential new problems be prevented?

I have to make sure that whoever does the counseling session understands that there is an ethical problem if the counselor coaches the witness about the substance of her testimony.

Maybe I can talk to a counselor to get some ideas about how to approach the witness in a way that avoids offending her. Maybe the client would be able to help me talk to her.

Which approaches might be most effective?

I like the idea of talking to other professionals, but I am not sure I can get anyone to help me with so little time. The most effective thing would be to talk to the client first.

♦ **Action Plan**

What is the best course of action?

I will talk to our client again to discuss our options and see if he has any suggestions about how to talk to his girlfriend.

Who should be involved?

The client and I will have this conversation. If he thinks it would be best for me to talk to his girlfriend alone, I will do that. If he thinks it would be good to have a counseling session for her, and if she agrees, I'll arrange that.

Who will implement the action?

I will, but I hope I am not going beyond what my supervising attorney would approve. I will have the paralegal discuss this with my supervising attorney when they speak by phone.

Who is responsible for it?

Really, my supervising attorney is responsible, because he's the one with the license. However, I have been given this assignment, so I'm responsible for getting it done right.

How should decisions be made?

I should get the OK from the client, consult with the paralegal, and have the approval of my supervisor.

What steps should be taken to prevent further problems?

I need to be tactful and communicate clearly. Mostly, I need to make sure I don't overstep my authority.

Given the above and all the information available, is this still the best path?

I think the plan is good, but I think I need to talk to my supervising attorney personally, not through the paralegal.

What has been learned?

I need to stop panicking in difficult situations.

I need to be more assertive of my needs with my supervising attorney.

I need to trust myself that I am capable of solving legal problems.

I think I have a tendency to jump to conclusions too quickly and not to give people the benefit of the doubt.

♦ Implementation

Am I following my Action Plan? If not, why not?

I did speak with my supervising attorney, and he agreed that I should follow my action plan.

I spoke with the client and he felt that I should speak with his girlfriend about my concern. He is pretty sure she is going to be very embarrassed and upset.

I tried to contact a counselor to get some advice about how to approach the problem with the girlfriend, but I have not been able to reach anyone who has time to do it.

I spoke with the girlfriend, and she was very embarrassed and angry. She said she does not want to testify.

Is the Action Plan producing the desired results?

No, I might have lost my witness.

Do I need to change my Action Plan? If so, how?

Yes, I have to find a way to work with the witness so that she can feel more comfortable testifying and so that she sounds credible. It seems like I've made things worse.

I think I will need to spend more time with her. I need to be more careful about what I say and to apologize for offending her. Maybe I can let her know that I believe what she is saying and that I know that she and I have the same goal—to make sure her boyfriend is not convicted.

Am I following my new Action Plan? Is it producing the desired results?

I met with the witness for a couple of hours and she calmed down. I think I developed a good rapport with her. She seems more relaxed. She will testify.

♦ **Evaluation**

Has the problem been solved?

The problem has been partially solved in that the witness is not as nervous about testifying. I am still nervous about her testimony being credible. I'm not sure if she is prepared for the kind of cross-examination she will encounter. I need to work with her on this.

What, if any, new problems have been created?

I am worried that my supervising attorney is going to think I got too involved with this witness. I know I have not coached this witness on the substance of her testimony, but I worry whether I have overstepped my bounds in working with her.

Was the Action Plan appropriate? Is there anything I would change in hindsight?

The action plan was appropriate in theory, but I do not think that my skills in working with the client and the witness were as good as they needed to be. I would like to have my supervising attorney actually supervising me through something like this so I could get the feedback I need.

What did I learn? (If working in a group, what did we learn?)

I need to pay more attention to my interpersonal skills, particularly expressing empathy and helping people to relax.

Example 2 *The MRI Machine*

This problem was adapted from a problem developed by Professor Bryan Liang in his article, *Understanding and Applying Alternative Dispute Resolution Methods in Modern Medical Conflicts,* 19 J. Leg. Med. 397 (1998).

♦ Situation Analysis

What is wrong with the current situation? How is it affecting me?

There is some tension between the hospitals at this point. Each feels that the location of the MRI machine at its facility is non-negotiable. This disagreement is setting a bad tone for the partnership. Both institutions have expressed concerns about future dealings if we cannot resolve this issue.

My role as representative of the urban hospital is tricky. I want to keep the hospital as a client and impress my managing partner with my dealmaking skills.

I need to advocate on our client's behalf, but I also need to figure out a way to make both hospitals happy so the partnership goes through.

This conflict is delaying the actual purchase of the MRI, as well as the partnership deal between the two hospitals.

I am a bit nervous.

What is the preferred situation?

We need to resolve this in a way that everyone will be happy and we can move forward with the partnership. I also want to look good in the eyes of my firm's client and my managing partner.

What should I do now?

I will do further research on MRI machines, consult with our hospital staff, and then talk to the suburban hospital's lawyer about a process for resolv-

ing this. We may be able to do it on our own, or we may need to form a joint committee to work on the issue. We also may need to call in a neutral facilitator to help us.

♦ Problem Diagnosis

How would I define the problem at this point?

We have agreed to purchase an MRI; both hospitals want the equipment placed at their respective sites.

We cannot afford two MRI machines.

It's important to the welfare of the new partnership that these hospitals work collaboratively, but this conflict is disrupting the potential partnership relationship.

Who else can help in identifying the problem?

I will need to work with the other hospital's lawyer, as well as consult with administrators, doctors, and MRI technicians of both hospitals. I will probably need to get some information about the patient needs from hospital social workers. Maybe I will look at partnership agreements of other hospitals or institutions to see how they share resources.

Whom/what does the problem affect?

The problem affects the administrators, investors, staffs, patients, and caretakers of patients at both hospitals.

It affects each hospital's finances and ability to care for patients. It also affects the perceived level of services the hospitals offer and, thus, their standing within the community.

What are their interests/values/objectives?

The interests involved are better healthcare and more convenience for hospital patients, more prestige for the hospital that has the equipment, and potentially more profits.

I think there are genuine concerns about patients' welfare, as well as some monetary and ego/prestige concerns on the part of the physicians and hospital administrators.

The suburban hospital is more interested in increased profits, while my client is most interested in better patient service. However, both hospitals want to resolve this conflict so that the partnership agreement goes through.

Who/what is responsible for the problem?

In one sense, the partnership would be responsible for the problem because there will be two hospitals under the same umbrella, vying for the equipment.

A lack of finances to afford two machines also might be responsible.

The decision to purchase the MRI machine created this problem.

On another level, the need to provide modern services to patients, both to improve diagnoses and to compete with other providers, drives this problem.

Issues of transportation between the two hospitals also might be responsible for the problem.

Is the problem part of a larger problem?

A larger problem is the high cost of healthcare technology, as well as the need for hospitals to make a profit while providing quality patient services.

Also, the disparity of income between the patients generally seen at the two hospitals is part of the larger social issue regarding distribution of wealth. The suburban dwellers and inner city dwellers may feel uncomfortable visiting a hospital not in their community for a variety of socio-economic reasons.

The transportation infrastructure is weak, thus creating difficulties for people who need to travel between the inner city and the suburbs by public transportation.

If so, which should be addressed first?

I do not think we can address the general socio-economic disparity issue in the country, nor the need for hospitals to make a profit while providing quality services. However, the transportation issue is something to keep in mind as we work on the more narrow issue.

Could the problem have been prevented?

The problem might have been prevented by deciding not to purchase the MRI equipment, but that decision would have had other negative consequences.

It might have been prevented if the MRI had been bought by one of the hospitals before the partnership was discussed.

A more far-reaching discussion about how resources would be shared might have been part of the preliminary partnership discussions.

♦ Investigation

What additional information is necessary? (facts? feelings? legal issues?)

What transportation is available between the two areas?

What kind of facility is necessary to house an MRI machine? Can the equipment be mobile? Could it switch locations on a regular basis?

Which hospital population is likely to use the machine more?

Does one of the hospitals feel more strongly about the machine location than the other?

Which medical community (urban or suburban) is more likely to send other (non-hospital) patients to use the equipment?

Are there crime problems in the inner city that might inhibit our suburban patients from making use of the equipment? Are there possible liability issues here?

How do the suburban patients actually feel about having to go into the inner city for services?

Is there any way to buy another machine?

Where do the patients from both hospitals go to get an MRI now?

Is there another expensive and necessary piece of equipment that we may be purchasing in the foreseeable future that might be used as a tradeoff for the placement of the MRI? Is there something else that might be a tradeoff?

Who/what can help?

Most of this information should be available from the hospital administrators, MRI technicians, doctors, patients, and social workers. Perhaps other hospitals might help us.

Who is the appropriate person to fix this problem?

I am in collaboration with the other attorney and administrators of both hospitals.

Exercise 10.2 Read the additional facts presented below and complete Stages 4 and 5.

Additional Facts: You are aware that the objectives of your urban hospital are focused on serving as many patients as possible while attracting more responsible and skilled physicians to its staff. The administrators of the hospital believe that an MRI machine located at the hospital would help attract those physicians. The suburban hospital is particularly interested in increasing profits, while continuing to offer its patients a very high standard of medical care. Its staff of physicians is considered to be top-notch. The attorney for the suburban hospital, though both affable and altruistic, is worried about potentially falling profits from this partnership and therefore is fairly staunch in her position.

The MRI machine is not mobile. Once in place it is difficult to move it without creating a risk of damage to the equipment. The hospitals cannot afford two MRI machines currently, but may be able to in the future, should revenues increase. Hospitals tend to make a 30% profit annually over the amortized cost of the MRI equipment. The only other hospital in the area with an MRI machine is equidistant from both hospitals, about 20 miles away. There are four other hospitals within a 10-mile radius of the urban hospital and two other hospitals within a 10-mile radius of the suburban hospital. There are about the same number of medical practitioners in the urban and suburban areas. The hospitals' records indicate that approximately the same number of patients from each hospital have been sent for MRIs in the past five years, although the urban hospital has serviced far more patients during that time. Currently there is bus service between the two hospitals; it involves one transfer and the trip takes approximately 45 minutes each way. A more efficient and economical public transportation system will help link the two hospitals, but its construction is several years away from completion. A shuttle service is in the plan for the partnership; its cost and details have yet to be worked out.

There are no current plans to purchase another piece of expensive equipment in the near future. An informal poll of the suburban patients indicates that they would be willing to travel to the urban hospital for an MRI, but would prefer not to. The suburban patients are particularly concerned about the lack of parking facilities near the urban hospital and neighborhood safety. Recent area crime statistics indicate that, although it is not a particularly dangerous neighborhood for an urban area, there is a higher rate of theft and assaults than in the suburban neighborhood.

As mentioned earlier, the process rarely proceeds exactly according to the model. Adaptation of the model may require going back to earlier stages, rethinking the problem, getting more information, or trying new approaches. Paying attention to the process is an essential factor in the skillful application of the model.

Exercise 10.3 Reread the third scenario and offer your immediate response. Then apply as many stages of the model as you can to the issue. If necessary, supply your own facts so you can reach the end of the process. Did you reach an approach different from or even better than your initial approach?

A Problem-Solving Model for Quick Decisions

Sometimes lawyers need to make decisions quickly and do not have the luxury of thinking through each question using the complete model. For such decisions, the following abbreviated model is more appropriate:

◆ Problem Diagnosis

What is the precise problem?

Whom does it affect?

◆ Investigation

What other information is needed?

Who can help?

◆ Consideration of Approaches

What are possible legal and nonlegal approaches?

Do I need to do some creative thinking?

◆ Action Plan

What is the best action?

How can negative consequences be avoided?

◆ Implementation & Evaluation

Am I getting the results I want?

Was this the best plan?

Did it create any new problems?

What have I learned?

Exercise 10.4 Think of a simple, current dilemma you have faced in the last day or two, such as communication problems with your supervising attorney, issues in your office environment, problems with a co-worker, workload, etc. Recall your solution. Now, apply the problem-solving model for quick decisions. Did you arrive at a different conclusion? How long did the process take you?

Attributes of Effective Problem Solvers

As the model illustrates, problem solving requires a flexible, multidisciplinary approach involving numerous core **skills, attitudes,** and **values**. Some of these are developed as a result of life experience; some are learned in law school. These attributes are detailed below, with particular emphasis on those that may be less familiar to traditionally trained lawyers.

The **skills** involved in problem solving include listening, collaborating, empathizing, working in teams, seeing the big picture, fact-finding, communicating, consensus building, making good judgments, creative thinking, assessing needs, working with other disciplines, and asking the right questions.

Listening and questioning. Often, lawyers assume they know how to listen, as it is a behavior they perform every day. Listening in the context of working with others and solving problems is something different from ordinary listening. It requires full attention to the speaker and an interest in truly understanding what the speaker is trying to communicate. Sometimes it means hearing things that the speaker is not verbalizing, or "reading between the lines." In the context of work with clients, this kind of listening helps develop rapport and allows one to *empathize*, thus building trust and a good working relationship that encourages clients, witnesses, opposing counsel, and others to be forthcoming. Listening is an essential skill for defining the problem, understanding its impact on the client, and clarifying what the client *needs*. Most important, good listening requires that problem solvers do not do most of the speaking. Instead, their job is to encourage others to communicate fully and to ask appropriate *questions* where needed.

For example, a client asked an attorney to help him sue his neighbor over his neighbor's American flag, which breached a "no flag" covenant. As he listened to the client, the attorney realized it was not the flag itself that bothered the client, but the fact that the flag blocked the client's view. In this case, although the legal solution favored his client, the attorney suggested, more simply, that the client request that the neighbor use a shorter flagpole to solve the problem.

Collaborating and working with others, including those from other disciplines. Collaboration is a skill not often fostered during law school. Law students usually have at least one opportunity to collaborate during law school, perhaps during a moot court exercise or in a trial practice course, but usually no direction is provided regarding how to collaborate successfully. Also, students may prefer to work on their own, having more of a sense of control over the work. Problem solving, however, often involves working with other people, sometimes in teams; the skills involved in doing so do not necessarily come naturally. Collaboration and "teamwork" require clear "communication" and a shared sense of responsibility, including a commitment to meet deadlines. Lawyers frequently work with professionals from other disciplines—work that, in turn, raises a number of other issues. For example, unspoken hierarchies among a variety of disciplines or personality issues may give rise to struggles for power or control within a work group. There may be communication problems, because each discipline has its own language and approach for solving problems. Most important, work with professionals from other disciplines requires shared respect that comes from an understanding of what each discipline has to contribute to the problem-solving endeavor. "Consensus-building" skills are essential to effective teamwork; they are, in turn, dependent on each team member's ability to listen, empathize, and communicate to others on the team.

Seeing the big picture and exercising judgment. One of the consequences of legal training is that lawyers tend to become very focused on specific legal questions, frequently framing problems as issues of "rights." This has become an efficient method for problem solving during law school (lawyers' brains have become "wired" for this process), because it reflects the nature of the casebook approach to training for work within the adversarial system. In the real world, problems are not packaged so precisely. In addition to legal rights, there often are relationship, health, environmental, and economic interests involved. Emotions such as embarrassment, shame, anger, revenge, and fear may play a part. Moreover, other people and interests may be impacted beyond the parties represented. There may be family members, friends, and community groups, as well as less tangible interests, affected by the problem. Understanding the breadth of the problem and its impacts is important to effective problem solving. Rather than take a "band-aid" approach by a narrow focus on legal issues, understanding the "big picture" allows problem solvers to consider a wide variety of solutions that go beyond the traditional adversarial approach and may prevent future problems. The decisions lawyers make with clients can reflect a more sophisticated exercise of "judgment" when they expand their considerations in this way.

Criminal defense lawyer Gerry Spence contends that "creativity is the single most important ability a trial lawyer—and probably any lawyer—can bring to the table."

Creative thinking. Law schools do provide some training in creative thinking; they encourage students to create new arguments within the framework of statutory and case analysis. Even within this context, there are techniques for creative thinking that can assist in developing new arguments. If lawyers are interested in problem solving beyond the adversarial process, or with more focus on the "big picture," creative thinking techniques can help their brains make new, helpful connections.

Anyone can think creatively; the process does not require artistic talent. Many think most creatively when their brains actually take a "break" from focusing on the problem at hand. Going for a walk or taking a shower, for example, frequently can stimulate creative ideas. These activities are examples of a creative-thinking technique known as **relaxation** or **incubation**.

The lawyers practicing family law at the firm of Walling, Berg and Debele are encouraged to look at their cases through the lens of different types of lawyers—criminal or tort lawyers, for example.

Another creative-thinking technique, **changing lenses**, involves shifting one's mental framework. Lawyers and law students can practice this by looking at a problem through the lens of another profession. For example, in the hospital scenario, a doctor, patient advocate, or businessman might view the problem of the placement of the MRI very differently from the way a lawyer might.

Exercise 10.5   Consider how a patient advocate might approach the MRI machine problem.

Word, picture, and object games also can stimulate creative thinking. There are a variety of word games. One method is to change a word or two in a stated problem. This can create a different perspective and lead to alternative resolutions. For example, if a lawyer is focusing on the poor verbal skills of a *witness*, perhaps she should focus instead on her own verbal skills. Perhaps the problem is the *extern's* overuse of legalese or use of demanding tones, which intimidates the witness.

A variation on word games is to use **random words, pictures, or objects** as a way to divert the brain from its ordinary ways of considering the problem. Any word, picture, or object will do.

Exercise 10.6 Think of a problem regarding your externship. Perhaps you would like more challenging work or more feedback from your supervisor. How have you considered resolving the problem?

Now, think of a word completely unrelated to the problem. If you have trouble thinking of a word, try "bicycle." Or, look at the picture of the flamingo in relation to the same problem.

What are the characteristics of the word or picture? Are there aspects of it that you can relate to your problem? What does the bird in the picture represent for you? Jot down the words and thoughts that come immediately to mind—this is not intended to be a logical thinking process but rather free association. Does this picture help you think about the problem in a different way? Does it help you arrive at other possible solutions?

Another technique to encourage creative thinking is **visualization**. What would the world look like if this problem did not exist? How might one achieve this dream? For example, if the lawyer imagines an MRI machine going back and forth between hospitals, he or she might imagine a mobile facility, such as a trailer or van, housing the machine. The mobile facility could be stationed at each hospital according to patient need and economic interests. On the other hand, if a mobile facility is not possible, the lawyer might reframe the problem, not as the transportation of the *machine*, but the transportation of the *patients needing the machine*. Considering the problem in this manner, the hospitals could investigate providing a patient shuttle service between the two facilities that would allow for greater sharing of resources. Or, the lawyer could imagine the problem being the transportation of profits from the machine, and a profit sharing clause could be drafted for the situation. Of course, these are only approaches to be considered. Certainly, potential problems with each of these approaches must be explored before choosing an action plan.

Exercise 10.7 For the third scenario, visualize what the situation would look like without the problem. Visualize enjoying yourself at the wedding festivities. What would have to happen to make that possible?

As lawyer and author Steven Keeva states "[c]reativity can not only lead to superb results for clients, but also [can] enhance well-being and enjoyment at work."

Several books and articles describe additional creative techniques useful to lawyers and other professionals. A main premise is that anyone can use them. Using creative techniques helps to create new neural connections and to revive and nurture the underutilized neural pathways in the brain, which can then offer broader solutions to problems. Solving problems creatively also can provide lawyers with more satisfaction in their careers.

Important **attitudes** for problem solving are being open-minded, resilient, persistent, patient, non-judgmental, humble, respectful, curious, trusting, aware of one's perspective and bias, able to accept criticism, willing to change, willing to deal with ambiguity, if not fear, and willing to explore and stretch one's limits.

With some overlap, these attitudes generally fall into two groups. First, certain attitudes help lawyers work effectively with others. These include being non-judgmental, humble, respectful, trusting, aware of personal biases, and able to accept criticism. Clearly, the absence of any of these attitudes would be a problem for collaborative or team work. The second group of attitudes, which includes being open-minded, resilient, persistent, patient, and curious, allows individuals to do the hard work involved in being an effective problem solver. Because the brain "wants" to use tried and true methods for solving problems, it is often uncomfortable and difficult to do something new; the stress threatens the sense of well-being. Thus, the brain struggles to resolve problems quickly, making it difficult to maintain an open mind and to be resilient and persistent. An attitude of curiosity may be helpful in overcoming this resistance and may provide some room for patience, as one allows the problem solving process to uncover something new.

> **Exercise 10.8** Do a personal inventory of your problem-solving attitudes. How open-minded are you? Are you persistent? Are you aware of your biases? Think of particular situations in your externship setting that exemplify these attitudes. What are your strengths? Your weaknesses?

Values, which certainly overlap with skills and attitudes, include respect for relationships, respect for differences, respect for culture, respect for others' knowledge, appreciation for decentralized decision making, willingness to admit one's limitations, inclusiveness, creativity, self-awareness, and self-reflection. These values encourage collaboration and persistence, and inhibit the tendency to jump to quick conclusions or freeze in a panic when faced with a new problem.

Exercise 10.9 Do a personal inventory of your problem-solving values. How comfortable are you with values such as inclusiveness and self-reflection? Are you creative? Are you self-aware? Think of particular situations in your externship setting that exemplify these values. What are your strengths? Your weaknesses?

Why Problem Solving is Important: the Changing Face of Law Practice

With increasing competition for jobs and clients, rapidly changing technology, and expanding globalization, lawyers no longer can rely simply on analysis of precedent and succinct brief writing to be successful.

New approaches to helping clients can aid lawyers in this time of transition. Collaborative lawyering, therapeutic jurisprudence, conflict management, preventive lawyering, and transdisciplinary work are examples of these more recent approaches to solving client dilemmas. For example, many businesses now have ombudspersons within their organizations to prevent issues from escalating. Some institutions have incorporated a series of staged problem-solving mechanisms within their organizations, beginning with dialogue and coaching and extending to mediation and formal arbitration.

As one of these new approaches, the process of creative problem solving certainly offers to those who use it a less conventional methodology for solving legal issues. Moreover, the process reinforces a broader perspective on attorneys' role in society. It expands lawyers' focus beyond the normative legal rules to a broader calling—including promotion of social justice, awareness of values, efforts at problem prevention, and critical self-reflection. In sum, creative problem solving involves a broader, more humanistic approach to the law than the traditional advocacy model demands. Although the problem-solving process accepts the practical approach to lawyering, it rejects a more narrow pragmatism as the essence of law practice. Drug treatment courts in the United States are a very successful example of this practical approach. These collaborative systems are designed to remedy the root of the problem, namely the defendant's drug addiction, by encouraging the prosecutor, defense attorney, judge, and probation officer to work together with the defendant to resolve the root issue.

In taking such a problem-solving approach, the lawyer negotiating the MRI transaction might think about the effects of her decision making on larger societal

Edward Stead, former vice-president and general counsel at Apple Computer, complains, "An awful lot of lawyers are in a rut, and just keep doing the same thing over and over again. Businesses can't do that. I don't know why lawyers think they can." Attorney Sam Guiberson, who runs a renowned eight-lawyer firm in Texas, argues that only the open, adaptable, creative lawyer will thrive in today's world.

Therapeutic Jurisprudence examines the ways in which the law, either substantively or procedurally, impacts human beings and looks for ways to make human encounters with the law healing experiences.

needs, or how her values might differ from those of the patients and hospital administrators. The lawyer might reflect critically on the terms of the partnership and evaluate how the current disagreement could have been prevented. The lawyer could reflect on new, creative ways to heal the rift and prevent further conflict. For example, the lawyer could suggest the use of focus groups of the impacted populations to discuss how to approach future issues, or those involved more directly with the conflict could create a dispute resolution process to discuss issues that might arise in the future.

It is this expanded form of thinking that ultimately can separate the great lawyers from the good ones. Developing the skill of problem solving helps lawyers better serve their clients and results in greater personal satisfaction for the lawyers themselves.

FURTHER READING

On Problem Solving

California Western School of Law maintains an excellent bibliography on problem-solving materials at http://www.cwsl.edu/content/library/problem_solving.pdf.

On the Brain

Patricia Smith Churchland, Brain-Wise: Studies in Neurophilosophy (2002).

Antonio R. Damasio, Descartes' Error: Emotion, Reason, and the Human Brain (Quill Edition 2000).

Antonio Damasio, The Feeling of What Happens: Body and Emotion in the Making of Consciousness (1999).

Elkhonon Goldberg, The Executive Brain: Frontal Lobes and the Civilized Mind 2 (2001).

Daniel Goleman, Emotional Intelligence: Why It Can Matter More Than IQ (1995).

Steven Pinker, The Blank Slate (2002).

Matt Ridley, Genes, Experience, and What Makes Us Human: Nature Via Nurture (2003).

The quotations from practitioners reproduced in the margins were taken from two articles by Steven Keeva: *Creative Passion*, 91 ABA J. 88 (2005) and *Opening the Mind's Eye*, 82 ABA J. 48-49, 55 (1996).

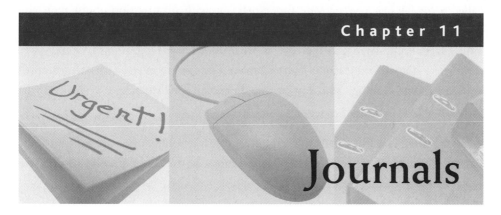

Chapter 11

Journals

J.P. Ogilvy

Boswell: I mentioned that I was afraid I put into my Journal too many little incidents.

Johnson: There is nothing, sir, too little for so little a creature as man. It is by studying little things that we attain the great art of having as little misery and as much happiness as possible.

— Boswell's *Life of Dr. Johnson*

Experience without reflection does not lead to learning or growth. You can spend a semester or an entire year at an externship and fail to derive much benefit from the experiences and tasks you are asked to perform. To learn experientially, you must be an active observer of the concrete experiences of the externship and reflect on these observations and experiences. Only through the cycle of experience, observation, reflection, abstraction, and action is new knowledge created.

Reflection on experience takes many forms. You can have a dialogue with a colleague, a fieldwork supervisor, your faculty supervisor, a friend, or a family member. You can write an essay. You can do a self-evaluation. You can keep a journal.

During your externship, your faculty supervisor may ask you to maintain a reflective journal on a regular basis or to write reflective essays on a periodic basis to assist you in processing what you are learning. The journal can be used to record ideas and work through thoughts that ultimately will form the basis for the reflective paper.

DO
REFLECT
PLAN   INTEGRATE
DO
REFLECT
PLAN   INTEGRATE
DO
REFLECT
PLAN   INTEGRATE

A common use of a journal during an externship experience is to record for later use the details of your experiences. A journal used for this purpose is often called a log. A log may provide the supervisor with information about how you spend your time in the externship. It may be used as an adjunct to a time sheet or as a time sheet itself, when time increments are included in the log. A log also may serve simply as a diary of experiences that, when read months or even years later, can provide fascinating reading. Your log becomes a sort of time capsule of your life at the time the log was made.

As valuable as the recording of experience is, it is only one way to use a journal. In this chapter, we want to explore the range of uses for a journal so that you will see how you can benefit.

The Uses and Benefits of Journal Writing

Cognitive Skills

Improving Higher Order Thinking Skills

The study and practice of law requires the practitioner to use an increasingly complex array of thinking skills. Throughout your years of formal education, you have developed the building blocks of sophisticated thinking skills. As with any other skill, the skills of critical thinking are improved upon and developed best through guided practice. A journal is a place for such guided practice of higher order thinking skills.

What do we mean by higher order thinking skills? The American psychologist Benjamin Bloom and his colleagues developed a taxonomy of thinking skills that describes a hierarchy of thinking tasks or skills that has been very influential in education. Bloom's taxonomy presents thinking skills in terms of a pyramid with the most fundamental skills at the bottom and the most complex skills at the top. Almost everyone is capable of displaying learning at the most fundamental level, which Bloom calls knowledge, but learning the higher order thinking skills is more difficult. The higher order skills also are less frequently demonstrated as products of learning, even in formal educational settings. In many undergraduate courses, students are rarely required to demonstrate the ability to think above the level of knowledge, that is, the recall of facts. In law school, however, most final examinations require the student to display competence by demonstrating some of the higher order thinking skills, especially those of comprehension, application, and analysis. Synthesis and evaluation also may be demanded.

Knowledge is demonstrated by recall or recognition of specific information. For example: *Which courts make up the federal judicial branch of government?*

Comprehension involves the ability to make some limited use of knowledge. In Bloom's scheme, someone who comprehends a fact or an idea can translate it by transforming the knowledge from one form to another, interpret it by being able to explain it, and interpolate from it by identifying certain, but not necessarily all, implications and consequences that arise out of but extend beyond the information provided. *Explain the difference between personal and subject matter jurisdiction.*

Application is the ability to solve new problems by using the products of knowledge and comprehension. This level of thinking skill is most frequently tested in law school by the task of solving a hypothetical by, for example, applying case law to the facts of the hypothetical. *Given a set of facts, discuss the legal rights and remedies of the parties to the transaction.*

Analysis, in Bloom's taxonomy, involves breaking down information into its constituent parts so that the relationship among the parts is made clear. *Given a problem of personal jurisdiction, articulate and discuss the elements of the doctrine of minimum contacts that the court may find persuasive in resolving the issue.*

Synthesis requires pulling together a variety of ideas, viewpoints, problems, or concepts and placing them in a single framework or pattern so as to constitute a structure not clearly there before. Problems that require a student to categorize, combine, organize, or reorganize often test the skill of synthesis. *Draft a motion for summary judgment, which requires the selection and presentation of relevant facts together with a persuasive explanation of the applicable rules of law.*

At the top of Bloom's pyramid is *evaluation*. Evaluation implies mastery of the preceding levels of knowing, comprehending, applying, analyzing, and synthesizing. At this level of thinking, the student is capable of evaluating the information presented and making sound judgments about the use, value, and implications of the information. *Advise a client with respect to a settlement offer.*

Keeping a journal should assist you in exercising any of the six levels of thinking skills in Bloom's taxonomy. As the tasks that you are called upon to perform require more frequent use of the higher order thinking skills, the need to record the products and processes of thinking becomes more acute. Because of the limits of short-term memory, truly in-depth thinking about any subject requires memorialization in written form to preserve a record and to enable you to engage in complex inquiry.

Learning about Learning

Learning is a life-long endeavor. Law students cannot in three or four years of law school learn all that is necessary for them to function as attorneys over an entire career. Law schools, like medical and other professional schools, are designed to help students *learn how to learn* and to assist them in becoming self-directed learners. This necessarily includes helping the students to become more aware of their preferred modes of learning, to become more aware of their strengths and weaknesses as learners, and to become more efficient at self-evaluation.

Becoming a self-directed learner also involves learning to take more responsibility for your own learning, to foster the habit of moving continually from the general to the specific and back to the general, to develop the practice of formulating and recording questions to be investigated and answered, learning to look carefully, learning to record observations accurately and completely, to tolerate ambiguity, and to develop independent wondering, questioning, and connecting.

Each of these topics or tasks is appropriate for journal entries and can assist you to improve your capacity for learning from experience, which is, undoubtedly, an important goal of your externship.

Writing to Learn

Much research by educational psychologists regarding the writing process has revealed that writing enhances learning, perhaps because the process of writing is continuously reinforcing. In writing, visual, cognitive, and kinesthetic (physical drafting) processes all converge, with learning further reinforced by the resulting concrete record. Writing does more than merely record or communicate knowledge that the learner already has assimilated. Rather, writing is an integral part of the process of knowledge creation through observation, analysis, and critical thought. Writing is inseparably related to thinking and learning in a number of identifiable ways. Here are some sample conclusions from one study:

- "Writing seems to help learners run thoughts through their minds repeatedly, a cyclic activity that often results in embedding or engraving the new information into the existing cognitive structure."

- Writing is a "stepping stone to further thought and an instrument for making connections. Writing sharpens the learner's powers of observation, as well as awareness, both as a causative factor and as a consequence."

- Writing "serves as a valuable attention-getting or focusing device." Writing has the capacity to force the learner to maintain a focus on the problem under investigation and to encourage the learner to be precise.

- Writing "triggers systematic follow-up." It permits the learner to "clarify thoughts, reach conclusions and search for alternatives, as well as to initiate and pursue the enterprise of critical thinking." By writing down what he or she is doing and recording concurrent thoughts, the learner can open the door to new thoughts and techniques. Vera H. Goodkin, *The Intellectual Consequences of Writing: Writing as a Tool for Learning* (1982) (Ph.D. dissertation) (University Microfilms International, 1986), pp. 314-15.

Other than note taking, outlining, and a few lawyering skills exercises (the open memo, closed memo, advice letter, and brief), law students rarely have an opportunity to write until the final examination. Journal writing can contribute to developing a range of thinking and learning skills without committing an enormous amount of time to the product, such as might be required for other opportunities to improve writing skills, like a seminar paper.

Cognitive theorists believe that the complex process of learning requires learners to relate new information to what they already know. The process of writing requires this same kind of connecting and organizing. Properly used, the journal is a space for you to record both what you think that you know and the gaps in your understanding. You are able to test your understanding by committing your tentative conclusions to a concrete record, a record that may be reviewed for misunderstandings and gaps in your knowledge base. The journal has the added benefit of permitting a dialectical examination of understandings with the instructor who is reading and reacting to the same concrete record.

Law students who have used journals recognize this link between writing and thinking/learning:

> I found doing the journal entries helped me to understand rules or concepts I was having trouble with. In a lot of my entries I took a rule and broke it down into sections and analyzed it. I think this technique really helped me because I am the type of person that has to write things down in order to memorize and understand them. Seeing, for example, rule 13 [of the Federal Rules of Civil Procedure] on paper in my own words helped me work it through in my head so that I understand it better. Sometimes just reading the rules or cases is enough for me to grasp the meaning of what is being said, but often times doing a journal was almost necessary. [A.B.]

Affective Skills

Relieving Stress

Journals can be, and often are, therapeutic. A common use of journals is to blow off steam about events in your daily life, both at the externship and in other aspects of your life.

For most students, law school is an intense and stressful experience. Students often write in their journals about an anxiety provoking experience and many find that by writing about their anxiety they are better able to deal with it. This is how one first-year law student expressed it:

> Your idea of having us write journals was great. It took time, but it was valuable because we could use it to talk to you, ask questions, give opinions that—for lack of time or appropriateness—we couldn't do in class. It also served as a pressure valve, at least for me. But that may be because I'm used to doing it. I have been writing journals off and on since I was 13—and sometimes they were lifesavers. They've helped me sort out my thoughts on topics, weigh decisions, displace anger, frustration or confusion when there wasn't someone to talk to about something. If there's any time when a person needs to air frustration and anxiety, it's first year. [B.C.]

Functional skills

Enhancing Observation Skills

see Chapter 12 *on Observation*

A great deal of learning in an externship comes through observation. Whether you are watching a court proceeding or the interpersonal dynamics of office politics, lawyering behavior is being modeled and is available for your observation, reflection, and analysis. By taking contemporaneous notes during an observation and by rewriting those notes into a journal entry soon after the observation is completed, you can maximize the opportunities for learning presented by observation. Note taking increases the amount of data that you can retain for later analysis. Rewriting the raw data into a more complete journal entry not only provides a fresh opportunity for recall of additional data but provides another opportunity to analyze the data. Making a concrete product of your observation serves to preserve the data for repeated analysis and synthesis as more data is obtained.

Reflecting

The journal allows a place for you to reflect about both the products and the processes of learning. Donald Schön's influential body of work on learning by professionals has demonstrated that the best practitioners in various professions develop their skills through continual reflection about the uncertainties, complexities, and value conflicts that confront them in practice situations. Journal writing is a powerful tool for both immediate and long-term, self-provided reflective feedback.

see Chapter 9 on Reflective Lawyering for a discussion of Donald Schön's work

Aiding Communication with Your Faculty Supervisor

Journals provide an excellent mechanism for a two-way communication with the faculty supervisor responsible for overseeing your externship. A journal is not a substitute for personal communication, but it can supplement in-person communication in meaningful ways.

A journal entry gives you the opportunity to frame carefully a specific question to which you would like an answer from the faculty supervisor. A journal provides the faculty supervisor with information about your externship and can help the supervisor design helpful learning interventions to improve your experience. In addition, detailed entries about your experiences at the externship can help the faculty supervisor to counsel future externs about opportunities at the externship. Your entries may provide the supervisor with more information about the nature and quality of experiences of particular externships than is otherwise available.

Improving Writing

Journal writing can be an effective tool for improving written communication skills. A journal permits you to improve your writing by (1) encouraging you to focus on the writing process rather than on the product, (2) emphasizing the expressive and personal nature of writing, (3) providing a record of thought and expression that is available for rereading and possible revision, and (4) providing an opportunity to engage in a meaningful writing opportunity.

Journals also can be helpful in improving your formal writing, such as academic papers, essays and articles, and legal documents such as memoranda and briefs. First, journal writing assists you in planning, text generation, and revision in an appropriately supportive environment. Second, journal writing may be a good starting place for new writers, or in the context of law students, writers of new types of writing. Formal writing requires attending to many complexities, such as audience, the spelling rules, punctuation and grammar, and the internal consistency of the text. Journal writing, because of its informality, reduces the demands of the writing task. Third, journal writing may prevent or minimize writer's block. The range of appropriate journal topics and strategies for generating something to say about these top-ics make it very difficult for students to believe they are incapable of generating ideas. Finally, journal writing emphasizes the use of your own language. Much legal writing is wooden and formalistic, the result of students trying to write like lawyers, without any real sense of what that means. Legal educators often deplore the unwill-ingness of students to speak in a voice that is uniquely theirs. Journal writing allows the writer to re-experience intensely the event written about and permits the writer to breathe his or her own life into the writing.

Law students who have used journals recognize the value of keeping a journal to improve written communication skills; here is how one student put it:

> As to journals being used to enhance and sharpen writing skills, I think this is a very crucial element of their success. Certainly in our classes here at school and in the profession we are undertaking, the written word carries great significance. One way in which to enhance and hone this skill of writing is by constant use and practice. [C.D.]

Problem Solving in the Externship

Keeping a journal can help you to problem solve during your externship. Problem solving involves problem identification, goal setting, information gathering, generation of alternatives, evaluation, decision making, and review. A journal may be used profitably at any stage of the problem-solving process as a place to record ideas, to brainstorm, and to think on paper.

A person's short-term or working memory generally is capable of holding up to seven chunks of information. Depending upon how the chunks are constructed, the amount of information held during processing can vary significantly. As problems begin to get more complex, the working memory is easily overwhelmed by the pro-cessing tasks. Alternative modes of holding information for processing become nec-essary. Symbolic representations of the information by, for example, formulas, dia-grams, schematics, outlines, or narratives serve as memory and processing aids.

Exercise 11.1 Try this: look around the room in which you are now seat-ed reading this book. Take about 60 seconds to record mentally as many of the room's features as you can. Now leave the room and list the features you can remember. Go back into the room and see how you did. How many more features could you have recorded if you had sat in the room and made a list without relying on your short-term memory?

Exercise 11.2 Your fieldwork supervisor has given you an assignment to research. For example, the supervisor wants to know whether the firm's client, a contract employee of a janitorial company, is a seaman for purposes of the Jones Act. The client was injured while cleaning rooms aboard a cruise ship that has been converted into a hotel and casino and is permanently moored in Baltimore harbor. Without stopping to evaluate their usefulness, think of all of the possible resources you might use to research the question. Have a colleague record your suggestions. After you exhaust the possibilities, prioritize your suggestions without referring to the list your colleague created. Now have your colleague share the list with you. Did you remember all of the suggestions that you had articulated? Is it easier to evaluate and prioritize the suggestions with the written list in front of you? As you reviewed the list, did any other possibilities come to mind?

Unless you generated only a very short list of possible resources, you should see that recording the suggestions facilitates evaluation, prioritization, and idea generation.

There are many other benefits to be gained from keeping a journal. We suspect that you will discover personal benefits beyond what we describe here, but this short recitation of uses and benefits of journal writing should be enough to get you started. We now want to focus your attention on some of the practical aspects of journal writing.

The Specifics of Journal Keeping

How Should You Keep Your Journal?

There is no single best way to create journal entries. Your faculty supervisor may have specific instructions and guidelines. If not, we want to provide you with some basic guidance with respect to how you should write, how much you should write, and about what you should write.

A good journal contains frequent entries. The more often you write, the greater number of critical events you will record for later reflection. Writing frequently can make writing easier because the craft more quickly becomes a habit.

What is a journal?

- A place to work out ideas, concepts, and processes discussed in class or in assigned reading; an individual record of your experiences with a course; a place to practice personal writing; a place to engage in a dialogue with the faculty supervisor; a place to evaluate the course; and more.

What should you write?

- personal reactions to your externship experiences, to class, your fieldwork supervisor, other students
- informal jottings, notes, clippings
- explorations of ideas, theories, concepts, problems
- reactions to readings, TV, events, public policy questions
- anything you want to explore or remember
- specific journal topics suggested in class
- an evaluation of each week's classes reviewing what you learned (or did not learn), problem areas.

When should you write?

- as often as possible
- any time; early in the morning, late at night, on the bus
- when you need to practice or try something out

How should you write?

- however you feel like it
- without interruption
- without worrying about formal language conventions including spelling, punctuation, and grammar
- by taking risks

A good journal contains a mix of short and long entries. The more writing you do at a single sitting, the greater the chance of developing a thought or of finding a new one. Short entries tend to be superficial.

A good journal is organized in a way that is systematic and chronological. Even if you do not write every day, your entries should be in chronological order, with the date and time of entry clearly indicated. There is real value to you in writing every day. You have a better chance of capturing critical incidents in your externship from which you can learn, and your reflection on the events you record contemporaneously is much more likely to be rich in detail.

How Should You Write?

The point of the journal is to think on paper. Therefore, do not worry too much about spelling, punctuation, and grammar. Write as correctly as possible, but you should not interrupt your writing to edit. You should use language that feels natural and expresses your voice and style. Do not try to write as you think a lawyer might. Remember that the audience for your journal is you and your faculty supervisor. Be aware of the minimum amount of detail that you must provide in order to have your writing understood.

What Should You Write About?

A journal is a place to write about everything related to your externship, your study of law in general, your struggles to grow personally and professionally, and your efforts to cope with the stress created by the need to balance school, work, and personal life. Your faculty supervisor may have established some ground rules particular to your program. Keep in mind that you must be careful not to reveal any client confidences or secrets to which you are privy. You want to be able to discuss situations that occur in your externship in order to get feedback from your faculty supervisor but do so in a way that does not compromise your duties of confidentiality.

Technical Aspects

You may wish to experiment with formats, unless your faculty supervisor requires a particular format. One simple but useful format is to divide each page of the journal into two parts. On the left side of the page, describe your externship experiences over a period of time. On the right side, reflect on an event or expand on a topic referenced in the description. This double-entry format ensures a descriptive record of your externship and encourages you to engage in higher order thinking skills.

You may wish to purchase a looseleaf notebook to hold your journal pages. Use dividers to separate the notebook into sections, especially if you decide to keep a separate journal in one or more of your other classes. Even if you decide not to keep a journal in your other classes, you may want to reserve a section in your journal notebook for private entries that are not shared with your faculty supervisor. These entries may be removed before you turn in your entries.

Privacy

As distinguished from a diary, which is usually written with the understanding that no one but the author will read it, the journal must necessarily be read by at least one other person, the faculty supervisor. Unless you are notified otherwise by your faculty supervisor, your journal will be a private dialogue between you and the faculty supervisor. You control what you let the supervisor read and the supervisor promises to keep strictly confidential all journal entries that you share. Absent your explicit permission, your faculty supervisor will not share your journal with any other person. You may, however, choose to publish your own journal excerpts in any way you wish, such as in an essay for the school newspaper, in your memoirs once you become famous, or as a book. A journal for this purpose was used by Scott Turow, the author of *One-L: An Inside Account of Life in the First Year of Harvard Law School* (1988).

Sharing Journal Entries

Sharing journal entries with colleagues can promote collaborative learning. It can help to build a sense of a learning community by modeling entries from which others can learn. It promotes dialogue and discussion. From time to time, your faculty supervisor may ask your permission to share one of your journal entries with the class. Your faculty supervisor should tell you the privacy guidelines for your class. Even if you grant permission to publish an entry, it can be edited if necessary to protect your anonymity or to preserve confidentiality.

Getting Started

Some students have difficulty providing more than an account of the day's events in their journals. If this is a problem for you, try including the following sections in your journal entry:

- First, record a log of the day's events.

- Next, prepare a list of three or four questions raised by the day's events.

- Then, make a record of your perceptions: What happened during the day?

Practical requirements (subject to your faculty supervisor's course specific instructions)

- purchase an 8-1/2" x 11" looseleaf notebook

- turn in only the pages containing new entries; do not hand in the entire notebook

- date each entry (include the time at which you are writing)

- write long entries as often as possible to help develop ideas fully

- make lots of entries; quantity is the single best means to a useful journal

- use a computer, or a pen (pencils smear)

- do not include your class notes in your journal; however, you may include your reactions to classes and to class discussion

- turn in your journal entries according to the published schedule

- retain a copy of every entry you turn in

Privacy

- retain entries you prefer not to share with the faculty supervisor

- be assured that what you share will be kept in confidence

- be cognizant of the need to protect the secrets and confidences of the placement

What did you see? What patterns are beginning to emerge in the course of your externship? What did you observe about the legal system?

- Record how you felt about your observations.

- Imagine yourself in the role of players in the legal system whom you have observed (e.g., other lawyers, judges, clients, witnesses, court personnel, support staff); how might they have perceived the same events differently?

The following are two lists of suggestions for journal entries. The first is more general and is intended to give you the maximum flexibility to generate your own journal topics. The second list provides more directed suggestions for journal entries. Your journal will be most useful to you when you write about events that interest you, but nearly everyone, at one time or another, experiences writer's block, the seeming inability to get started on a writing project. These suggestions may help you if you get stuck for a topic about which to write.

General Topics

Look for this icon throughout the book for additional journal topics.

- Explain the new concepts you learned as if you were explaining them to a non-law student friend or spouse.

- Write a letter to a client explaining a topic you are having trouble understanding.

- Explain the new concepts you learned by showing how they fit in with something you already know. Give examples.

- Find similarities between something you learned today and something you already knew.

- Think about what you learned today. Was it important? Why?

- Question what you do not understand. What is confusing you? What information would help you understand?

- List the most important facts you learned today and write your opinion of each.

- Copy into your journal a word, phrase, or sentence from your textbook or from today's class discussion, then write what you think about it.

- Explain step-by-step how you are solving a problem as you work on it. Make up other problems that could be solved this way.

- Prepare for a test by asking yourself questions and writing answers to them.

- Write nonstop about a particular concept or discussion. Do not worry about style, grammar, or organization.

- Assume the role of a judge, juror, opposing counsel, client, or legislator and react to something you learned today.

- What are your strengths and weaknesses in this subject? What could you do to improve?

- Reread last week's journal. Write a reaction to what you wrote.

- Write in reaction to your faculty supervisor's comments on a journal entry.

Specific Topics

- **Selecting an externship.** Discuss your observations about and reactions to your work in selecting an externship. Explain how you identified the organization and the contact person. Describe your interviews with any externships you considered and your reactions to the experience. What were your first impressions of the organization(s) and the people? If you looked at more than one organization, explain how you made your selection.

- **The history of the organization where you are working.** Learn something about the history of the organization where you are working as an extern. When was it established, by whom, and why? How has it changed over time? (If you were working at the Department of Justice, for example, you might discover that in 1859 the Office of the Attorney General had only five professional employees.) Record what you learn in your journal, and discuss how, if at all, your understanding of the operation of the organization is affected by its history.

- **What is the institutional mission or purpose of the organization where you are working?** Is the institutional mission (in your opinion) useful or important? Why or why not? How well is that mission being accomplished? What leads the organization to do its work well or poorly? Consider the relationship of the mission of the organization where you work as an extern to your own professional goals. What do you wish to accomplish during your professional life and why? Are your thoughts about this affected by your current experience at your externship?

- **Diversity—difference and sameness.** What is the demographic composition of your organization? How do sex, race, sexual orientation, age, national origin, religion, education level, physical appearance, family background, home location, and other differences affect people's roles in the organization and relationships with one another? How are the persons with whom you most closely work in the organization different from you? In what ways are they similar? How does your awareness of differences and similarities affect your work within the organization?

- **Sizing up your supervisor.** Evaluate your supervisor as a professional role model. You might reflect on the quality of supervision, work style, effectiveness as a lawyer, talents, and shortcomings. Also, consider how your supervisor conceives of his or her professional role.

- **Evaluating your own abilities.** Discuss your perception of your talents and shortcomings as a soon-to-be-lawyer, what you do well or poorly, how you are perceived, how you feel about your own performance. What does your current externship offer by way of opportunities to work on filling gaps in your skills?

- **Ethics in practice.** Identify an ethical quandary or decision that occurred during the semester. Explain the issue, how it was resolved, and whether you think the resolution was proper and why.

- **Your externship and your future.** How does this externship experience fit into your future plans? What have you learned that will help you to make decisions about future employment?

- **The stress of getting comfortable in a new work environment.** What stressors are present in a new work environment? How do you react to stress of this type? What can you learn from observing your response to stress? Have you seen others react to this stress? How did they behave? What can you learn from observation of others experiencing stressors similar to yours?

- **The effects of a partisan role on your perception, interpretation, and analysis of data.** How does your participation in an event affect your perception and analysis of that event? How might your perceptions and analyses differ if you were a neutral observer? In which situation are your observations more or less accurate?

- **The impact of other people's reactions and behaviors on the lawyer and his or her activities.** How does your supervising attorney respond to the praise or criticism given by others, such as judges, colleagues, superiors, subordinates, and clients? How would you evaluate the responses?

- **The stress of having responsibility for making decisions.** Describe the stressors involved in having the responsibility for making decisions. Write from personal experience or from observing your supervising attorney or others in the work environment.

- **How to balance professional and personal lives.** Describe how you balance your professional (school and work) and personal lives. What changes in either might make both more satisfying? What do you believe the challenges of balancing your professional and personal lives will be after graduation? Will it be easier or harder than now? Why?

see **Chapter 17**
on Work-Life Balance

- **The impact of interpersonal relationships on lawyering.** How do interpersonal relationships impact on the quality and quantity of lawyering done at your externship? What interpersonal relationships are involved? Are there positive and negative impacts? Elaborate on several.

- **The nature of authority relationships in the legal system and legal profession.** What authority relationships have you observed in your externship? How does authority impact the lawyering at the externship?

- **How to give guidance to client while respecting client autonomy.** If you deal with clients at your externship, describe how you or a lawyer in the office balances giving guidance and advice to a client, while respecting the client's right to make decisions. How do you avoid steering the client to what *you* view as the right solution?

- **The place of honesty in relations with the court, clients, and other attorneys.** Describe a situation where you thought that a lawyer at your externship behaved honestly or dishonestly with the court, a client, or another attorney. Were you surprised by the actions of the attorney? Would you have behaved similarly in a like situation? Why or why not?

- **Manipulation by lawyers, clients, staff, or others.** Describe a situation in which you observed a lawyer or a client attempt to manipulate someone. What was done? Was the behavior appropriate or inappropriate? Why?

- **How it feels to make decisions where there is no right answer and, often, insufficient data.** Describe a situation in which you or a lawyer at your externship made a decision where there was no clearly right answer or where a decision was made with less data than was desirable. How did you or the lawyer feel about the decision? Why was there no right answer that could be found? Why was there insufficient data?

FURTHER READING

Keeping Journals

TOBY FULWILER, THE JOURNAL BOOK (1987). This book is a collection of short articles that describe the use of journals in a wide variety of academic settings.

THOMAS MALLON, A BOOK OF ONE'S OWN: PEOPLE AND THEIR DIARIES (1984).

TRISTINE RANIER, THE NEW DIARY: HOW TO USE A JOURNAL FOR SELF-GUIDANCE AND EXPANDED CREATIVITY (1989).

Published Journals by Lawyers

MARIO CUOMO, FOREST HILLS DIARY: THE CRISIS OF LOW-INCOME HOUSING (1974). Chronicles Cuomo's fight on behalf of low income tenants in New York.

FELIX FRANKFURTER, FROM THE DIARIES OF FELIX FRANKFURTER (1975). Excerpts from the diary of one of the most respected justices of the United States Supreme Court.

OLIVER WENDELL HOLMES & MARK DE WOLFE, ED., TOUCHED WITH FIRE, CIVIL WAR LETTERS AND DIARY OF OLIVER WENDELL HOLMES, JR. 1861-1864 (1969).

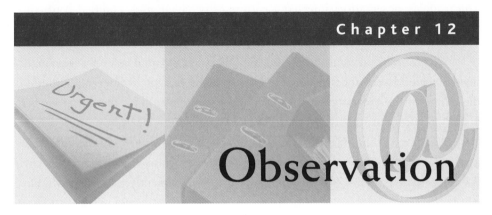

Chapter 12

Observation

J.P. Ogilvy

> What really teaches man is not experiences, but observation. It is observation that enables him to make use of the vastly greater experience of other men, of men taken in the mass. He learns by noting what happens to them. Confined to what happens to himself, he labors eternally under an insufficiency of data..
>
> — H. L. Mencken

Watching others is a primary mode of learning. From birth, children are careful observers of their environment. They learn by observing and then imitating the behaviors of their parents, siblings, and others in their environment. Learning from observation does not end in childhood but continues throughout life. Learning through observation continues to be important even though you are spending much of your time in formal learning settings. Consider how you learn about someone you meet for the first time. You observe how the person dresses and with whom the person speaks. You listen to what the person says and also to how the person says it. Your initial, and perhaps final, impression of this person is formed through your initial observation.

Whether we are conscious of it or not, we constantly learn from our environment. In law school, whether in a classroom or in an externship, you are bombarded with a continuous stream of data from your observations. You learn information, behaviors, and values from observation of teachers, classmates, and supervisors.

In a typical law school classroom, the primary mode of teaching may take the form of a modified Socratic dialogue. You observe that the professor calls on the students in the row in front of you one after another. You detect a pattern and begin to relax a little, believing that the professor will not discover how unprepared you are. You made an observation, inferred a pattern of behavior, and modified your emotional state in response to your observation and interpretations.

What else might you observe during this particular dialogue? By listening to the dialogue between the professor and the students you might discern a pattern in the nature of the professor's questions. Conscious reflection on the questions may better prepare you to answer the professor's questions when your turn comes. Understanding questioning patterns may enable you to focus your reading of the assigned materials as you prepare for the next day's class. For example, in Civil Procedure class, you might notice that the professor frequently asks what will happen in the case after this decision. As you prepare for subsequent classes, you note not just "who won" but also what happened next. To add another dimension, you may learn modes of behavior and values of which you are not aware, or of which you become aware only years later. For example, the manner in which the professor relates to the students in the classroom provides a model that may affect the way you relate to clients after you enter practice. How does the professor respond to student questions? With enthusiasm? With impatience?

> I recently was in court observing students who, as part of their externship, were trying cases for the county prosecutor of a local jurisdiction. During a lull in the court's activities, I witnessed an interaction between a public defender and his client. The client, whose case was on the docket for a plea or trial that afternoon, was clearly anxious. On several occasions, he approached his attorney to inquire about the status of his case. At one point, his attorney told him sharply, "When I know something, you will be the first to know." I was struck by the tactlessness of the attorney's remark and by his demeaning tone. Waiting for a case to be called is a routine, oft-repeated event for the attorney, but is important and nerve-wracking for the client. Why did the attorney snap at his client? What had been the model for his behavior? Perhaps this lawyer had a professor who saw a faceless person who had asked the same, inane question every year for the past twelve years rather than the individual student asking a question that the student thought was important to his understanding. [J.P.O.]

Much of your time at your externship will be spent in formal and informal observation of persons and events. Your externship will provide a golden opportunity to learn by observation. You should not squander this opportunity by hoping that somehow you will know what is important and how to interpret it. You will be bombarded by information from your experience in the workplace. To make the best use of this information you must have a framework to organize and interpret it. This chapter offers techniques for improving your observation skills so that you may use your observation time more effectively.

How can you learn to be a better observer? Lawyers often critique the observational skills of others—their clients, opposing parties, and both lay and expert witnesses:

> At your deposition you said that the defendant was about 5'8" tall, but now you say that the defendant was over six feet tall. During your deposition, here on page 234, you state that the defendant was dressed in blue jeans and a tee-shirt. Today your testimony is that the defendant was dressed in chino slacks and a long-sleeve shirt. You don't really remember what the defendant looked like, do you?

Lawyers less often critique their own observational skills. There is a paucity of material in the legal literature or in law school textbooks to prepare law students to improve their own ability to learn from their observations of their environment.

There is some legal literature that reports on the results of observations, but nothing that discusses how law students can become better observers and consequently learn better from observation. One of the most famous examples of a law student's observation of his environment is Scott Turow's book, *One-L: An Inside Account of Life in the First Year of Harvard Law School* (1988), which describes his experiences as a first-year student at Harvard Law School. There are other examples of institutional or systemic critiques based, in part, on the observations by law students of a specific legal environment. (See the list of suggested readings at the end of this chapter.) Lessons in observation also can be drawn from other disciplines in which, like the legal profession, observation is an important part of client assistance, professional self-improvement, and research. These include anthropology, psychology, sociology, and teacher education.

This chapter addresses a number of related topics: How should you plan for the observation? What are your purposes for the observation? Which events, subjects, and settings would be most useful for your purposes? Should you observe from the perspective of the *participant observer* or the *outside observer*? What are the differences between the two types of observer? When is the appropriate time for conducting your observations? How can you most effectively record your observations? How can you learn from reflection on your observation? What are some of the ethical issues involved in conducting observations?

Planning for Observation

Much of the learning that you do through observation is completely unplanned. Think about the last time you were in a group of people most or all of whom you did not know. A common example is when you overhear conversations of persons near you in a restaurant or theater. Another example is being introduced by a mutual friend to a group of people you do not know. Think about the conversation that was going on. You may have learned something about the setting in which the conversation took place. You probably learned some information from the conversation, but you also undoubtedly learned something about the people involved in the conversation as well. Who seemed to be a leader in the group? Who used humor to achieve his goals? Who offered new alternatives? Even though you did not actually join the group or actively seek to learn information from it about the people or the setting, through your unplanned observations, learning occurred.

You can enrich and deepen your learning from unplanned observation by reflecting on your observations after they occur. If you did as we suggested above and thought about the last time that you interacted with a group of people you did not know, it is likely that recalling the event and thinking about what you learned may have increased your learning from the event. Now that the event is in your consciousness, you may generalize from the experience and explore what you have learned. This can lead to additional learning.

Although you can learn from unplanned observations, you can learn more from planned observations. Because your experiences are so full of observations, you cannot attend to and evaluate them all. To avoid having data just flow by, we recommend that you build several planned observations into your externship experiences. By improving your observational skills, you will internalize the process. Even your unplanned observations will become richer learning opportunities. While pausing to observe attorneys in action while you are in the courthouse has some value, planned observations can be much more intellectually nourishing. We now turn to planning for observations and introduce you to the concept of a *reflective observation cycle*, which involves a continuing cycle of planning, observing, recording, reflecting, and sharing.

Planning for an observation involves asking familiar questions: why, who, what, when, where, and how. Why to observe (how is the data from the observation going to be used), whom to observe, what to observe, when to observe, where to observe, and how to observe.

In this situation, like every other in your externship, the cycle of learning starts with an articulation of goals. Why you are observing—what are your purposes for the observation?

What do you want to learn? How will you use what you learn from the observation? Your answers to these questions will influence your answers to the other planning questions.

There are many purposes for which you might undertake an observation in an externship. You may want to improve your performance of a specific lawyering skill such as conducting a direct examination of an expert witness. To begin work on this skill, you may want to observe someone whom you regard as an expert conduct a direct examination. Or you may want to improve your skills in policy analysis by investigating how a court-annexed mediation program works for low-income people. You may wish to observe how the participants in the process are treated by judges, court personnel, mediators, attorneys, and opposing parties.

More generally, you may undertake planned observations to make concrete some abstract problem you are struggling to understand and thereby to provide additional information that can assist you in solving the problem. You may wish to observe others in order to step out of your own experience in an attempt to understand the values and assumptions that others bring to a situation or problem. You may wish to compare information that you have acquired in textbooks and classroom discussions with information acquired in the field.

Perhaps you can use observation to further one of your goals for your externship. If so, you can refer to the goals that you developed in Chapter 2. Which of the goals and objectives you identified can be pursued through focused observation?

> **Exercise 12.1** Using your goals and objectives as a guide, make a list of topics for which focused observation could lead to the achievement of one or more of your learning objectives for your externship.

Use Table 12.1 on the next page to outline some of your major learning goals and objectives and then to identify some of the opportunities for learning from observation in your externship. Once you have decided on the purposes of your observation, you can answer the other questions. Table 12.2 provides an organizational tool for planning your observation.

What should be observed? Once you have identified topics or settings for focused observation, choose one or more of the topics for further reflection. Consider the complexity of the topic, how accessible the setting is to you, your time constraints in conducting the observation, and the extent of preparation required before you can begin your observations. Write down your concerns.

How many observations do you need to make? How many actors in the setting do you wish to observe? What is the time frame over which the observations will occur? How many different types of observations do you need to conduct? To what extent can the detail of the events be observed and recorded? What questions do you want the observation to answer?

Table 12.1 Worksheet for Identifying Opportunities for Learning from Observation

Learning Goals	Objectives	Opportunities for Observation
A. *Improve interviewing skills*	1. *Establish client confidence and build rapport*	a. *Initial attorney client interviews* b. *Paralegal-client interviews* c. *Listen to phone interviews*
	2.	a. b. c.
	3.	a. b. c.
B.	1.	a. b. c.
	2.	a. b. c.
	3.	a. b. c.
C.	1.	a. b. c.
	2.	a. b. c.
	3.	a. b. c.

Table 12.2 Planning for an Observation

What are my purposes for conducting this observation? (See Table 12.1)	1. Improve interviewing skills 2. 3.
What should be observed?	1. Initial meeting with a new client 2. 3.
Who should be observed?	1. Attorney Jones 2. Client Harris 3.
Where should I conduct the observations?	1. Attorney Jones's office 2. 3.

How should I observe?
— as a participant
— as a non-participant
  – directly
  – indirectly
	If I am a participant, I may be more accepted by the client, although depending on my level of involvement, I may have fewer opportunities to make observations.

When should I observe?	Whenever the intitial client meeting is scheduled, I should try to observe several initial meetings to get a broader perspective of the behaviors I am interested in observing.
What ethical issues are involved? — do I need special permission — are there confidentiality issues — etc.	Must be sensitive to protect the secrets and confidences of the client; I will certainly need the permission of Attorney Jones; Attorney Jones may wish to seek the permission of the client, depending on my role.

For example, assume one of your learning objectives is to improve your ability to deliver an opening statement in a criminal case. Among the tasks that leads to the achievement of that objective may be the observation of an experienced and well-respected criminal law practitioner giving an opening statement in an actual trial. Although this topic is not without complexity and richness, it is not nearly as complicated a situation as one that involves the investigation of how the drafting of tax legislation can be influenced by meetings with congressional staff. (Do you take your client with you? Do you do the talking or does the client? Should there be a memorandum explaining why your client wants the changes? Do you warn the staff why others will be opposed? Do you try to get their agreement in principle and then offer to draft language? Do you take your proposed language with you to the meeting? Do you wait for the staff to ask for something in writing?)

Whom to observe. Deciding whom to observe may be easy. There may be only one opportunity for an observation that involves just one person. If you are doing an investigation of a systemic problem, you may need to observe dozens of actors in the setting. It may be something in between. For example, you may want to observe how the drug is identified and placed in evidence in a prosecution for drug possession by attending several trials involving drug charges.

If you plan to observe only one person, then the decision is made and you move on to the other questions. It is rare, however, that your opportunities for observation are so limited. When several alternatives are available, you must decide which of the alternatives to select. As is true of most problems where the answer is not certain, you must decide what factors will influence your selection of the subject of your observation and then prioritize those factors in some fashion.

Think of a topic, situation, or problem from your externship experience that you might want to investigate at least in part through formal observation. If you are an extern in a litigation setting, you might want to learn how the attorneys in the office prepare a witness to testify. If you are in a judicial externship, you may want to investigate how the judges in your court prepare for trial. If you work for a government agency, you might want to understand better how the hierarchical structure of the office affects the production of work. If you work for a solo practitioner, you may want to observe the assignment and flow of work within the office to learn about efficient administration of a small law office. What factors may influence your choice of the person or persons to observe? Use Table 12.3 to list the factors you think would influence your decision. Then rank the factors according to their relative importance in your judgment.

Table 12.3 Factors Influencing Decision of Choice of Person(s) to Observe

Ranking	Factor	Comments

What factors were important to you? Here are some possibilities:

• When can you fit the observation into your schedule?

• When is the subject of the observation available?

• Do you want to observe a subject who is *the best* at the task or one whose performance is *adequate*?

• Which of several possible subjects is most likely to perform in a manner *typical* of the situation?

• Would the subject be available for questions after the observation?

• How accessible to you is your subject?

• How close can you get to the subject?

• Do you need to get permission for the observation?

• Do you need to disclose to the subject the fact that you are conducting an observation?

• How important to your observation is it that you be unobtrusive?

• Will a single observation suffice for your purposes?

- Do you need multiple opportunities to observe the same subject?

Where to observe. If your subject can be found in only one place, the answer is easy. If the subject may be observed in more than one place, consider the following possibilities:

- where you are most likely to get close enough to the action to get the most data without being too intrusive;

- whether the time required to secure permission to observe in a particular setting outweighs the benefits to be derived from observing in that setting over an alternative for which permission is not required;

- which setting offers the most opportunities to observe the persons or activities that are of most interest to you;

- where you will have the best opportunity to make contemporaneous field notes of your observation.

How to observe. You may be a participant observer or a non-participant observer. If you are a non-participant observer, you may observe the situation directly (by being physically present) or indirectly (by viewing a videotape or listening to an audiotape of an event). A "participant observer" is involved in the activities that are being observed. For instance, your supervisor might ask you to participate in the deposition of a witness. The supervisor might ask you to take notes, to evaluate the witness, and to assist with the documents that will be shown to the witness during the deposition. This will provide an excellent opportunity for observation, but as a participant your ability to observe is constrained. Some constraints are physical; you cannot both give your full attention to the tasks assigned to you and at the same time take detailed descriptive notes on the deposition. Other constraints are ethical; your obligation to perform the tasks assigned to you will limit your ability to concentrate on your personal learning goals.

see Chapters 4-7
on Ethics

As a non-participant observer, you may have fewer physical limitations on your ability to conduct your observations, but ethical constraints are still present. You may need special permission to observe some situations. One example is an *in camera* conference among the judge and attorneys. Your ability to report on your observations may be restricted, even if you have the necessary permission to observe. For example, your supervisor might invite you to sit in on a client interview just to observe. You have the necessary permission to observe, but you cannot report some of what you learn from your observation to third persons because you must protect the confidences and secrets of the client. When you are a non-participant observer, you want to be close enough to the action to hear the words spoken and to see the facial expressions and body postures of the actors, but not so close as to interfere with what is going on because they can see *your* facial expressions and body postures. Even the fact that you are taking notes will make some people nervous, so you may have to take notes unobtrusively or rely on memory and make notes after the observation.

Whether you are a participant or non-participant observer, you may want to interview some of the people that you observed to clarify and deepen your understanding of the event that you observed. For example, suppose you observed closing arguments in a non-jury trial. You made extensive notes and gave some thought to what elements of each argument you thought effective or ineffective. After the judgment is entered, you might try to interview the judge, both counsel, the clients, the court clerk, or others about their perceptions of the effectiveness of the arguments. You might learn how the arguments affected the decision maker, what each attorney's goals were for her argument, and whether and how those goals were achieved. You can compare and contrast the perceptions of several participants with your own to more fully understand the event.

When to observe. If your observation is part of a course, your instructor may impose a deadline. Schedule your observations well in advance of the deadline for turning in a written report to allow for sufficient time to reflect on the observations, to draft the report, and to revise it. Your own schedule and other commitments will limit your ability to schedule observations. Your biological clock also may influence the timing of your observations. If you are a morning person, you should schedule your observations before noon if possible. The timing of your observation also will depend on the availability of your subject. If you need to observe a specific individual performing a task, then your observations must be timed to coincide with the time of performance by that individual. On the other hand, if you plan to observe a situation in which there are many actors, the timing of your observations may depend on such things as when the most actors are present, when the most representative sample of actors or events are present for observation, whether there is a need for repeated observations, and so on.

Recording Observations

Without some effective way to record your observations, the exercise, though perhaps entertaining, will be of minimal value as a learning experience. Our memories are too unreliable for anything more than general observations. You can use one or more of the following techniques to assist in recording your observations.

- *Narrative description* involves writing down what the observer saw and heard as fieldnotes and then constructing a narrative report using the fieldnotes to recall detail.

- *Time samples* are used to record information that is being observed at regular intervals. Through a time sample, you can take verbal snapshots of a subject's behavior over the course of the observation.

- *Checklists* contain a series of behaviors the observer expects to see during the observation. The observer may want to note the frequency over time that the subject performs the behavior. For example, how many times does an attorney object during the deposition.

- *Interaction* reports record what subjects say or do to each other. You might select one person as the focus of the observation, and record everything that the subject says or does for a specified time period.

- *Rating scales* require the observer to rate behavior, generally on the basis of prevalence, for example, from *always* to *never,* along a continuum of values.

Each of these techniques has strengths and weaknesses. For example, a time sample might require recording fewer events than an interaction report, but would not generate as much data. Checklists may be easy to use if the behaviors being recorded are not complex, but they risk missing important interactions or events that are not clearly included on the checklist. Interaction reports provide very detailed data of the interaction being observed, but require constant attention and very precise note taking techniques. Rating scales have some of the same advantages as checklists but suffer from the same limitations. In addition, rating scales frequently add room for error through inter-rater inconsistencies. The technique or techniques that you choose to use will depend on a number of factors, but most important are the intended use of the data and the amount of time you have to prepare for the observation.

In most cases you will use narrative description to record your observations contemporaneously or as soon after the observation as possible. Each narrative description may contain a number of features that can be observed in the situation you are observing. Ethnologist James P. Spradley listed the following features or dimensions in his book *Participant Observation* (1980):

space—the physical place or places;

object—the physical things that are present;

actor—the people involved;

act—single actions that people do;

activity—a set of related acts people do;

event—a set of related activities that people carry out;

time—the sequencing that takes place over time;

goal—the things people are trying to accomplish; and

feeling—the emotions felt and expressed.

Here is a sample narrative written by Spradley. In this excerpt from a set of field notes, Spradley describes the presentation of a witness to a grand jury on which Spradley sat.

There was an air of anticipation, a few minutes during which the members of the grand jury sat in silence and the prosecuting attorney searched through his files. Then he said, "I've got two cases to present this morning. I'll have to rush. We have ten witnesses." He spoke fast and conveyed a strong impression that we would have to move quickly throughout the morning.

"This is a case of felonious theft by retention. It means retaining property of at least $2500, retail market value on the date of the offense. Here is a summary of the case. One day in July a van was broken into and a revolver was stolen. Then later there was another robbery of stereo equipment from a stereo store. The police, making an investigation of a house, recovered the revolver, three Pioneer receivers, one Teac tape deck, two JBL speakers. There were three people in the house at the time, and the police found the prints of one of them on some of the stereo equipment."

The prosecuting attorney spoke rapidly, and when he came to this point he looked up at a clerical assistant and motioned to him. He got up and left the grand jury room, I looked at the people on the grand jury and they were now whispering to each other, all looked very interested.

"We now have our first witness," the prosecuting attorney said as the clerk returned with a middle-aged man dressed in a blue business suit. The clerk pointed to a chair, the man sat down, the clerk asked him to raise his hand and proceeded to administer an oath: "Do you swear to tell the truth, the whole truth, and nothing but the truth, so help you God?" "I do."

"What is your name?" the prosecuting attorney asked. "Bob Johnson." "Would you spell your name and give your address?" "B-O-B J-O-H-N-S-O-N, 42 East Alder, Center City."

"On July 14 did you report a theft?"

"Yes, a .38 Colt was stolen from my van. I had purchased it in February of 1972, paid $118 for it. At the time I worked for the Center City Police Department and I have a permit to carry the revolver."

"As of July 10, do you have any opinion about the retail value of the .38 Colt?"

"Yes, about $140, because it had gone up about $20 more than the purchase price."

The prosecuting attorney turned abruptly to the grand jury and asked: "Any questions?" He paused for a total of three seconds, turned to the witness, and said, "Okay" and the clerk quickly ushered him out of the grand jury room.

This incident, and others that he observed, led Spradley to reflect on the prosecutor's emphasis on speeding up the process of presenting cases to the grand jury. He sought to understand how the prosecutor speeds things up, including techniques that the prosecutor has to keep the jurors from asking questions and ways to hurry witnesses in delivering their testimony. He also noted events that can slow down the process, hindering the prosecutor's quest for speed.

> **Exercise 12.2** Review the excerpt and see how many of the dimensions of narrative description you can identify in Spradley's recorded observation. Spradley's observation of the grand jury process was unplanned. Since he was called to grand jury duty like any other citizen, presumably, he did not set out with a research agenda to study a grand jury. However, because of his training and interests, he was able to apply his skills of observation and analysis to an event in which he found himself. As you become more skilled in observation, you also will be able to find more learning opportunities in unplanned events.

Since you cannot transcribe everything that occurs during an observation, detailed note taking is critical. Especially when you are a participant observer, your notes may be quite condensed. You can prepare for note taking by creating a template containing the nine dimensions described above with space near each dimension label for notes about it. The notes themselves may be no more than single descriptive words or short phrases that capture the observation. These can jog your memory when you later write an expanded narrative account of your observation. For example, if you were observing a pretrial conference in the judge's chambers, your notes might look like this:

actors—judge Brown, attorney Smith, attorney Jones, reporter, clerk

activities—welcoming, setting tone, describing process, clarifying, giving instructions, outlining, cajoling

What you record depends on what you want to observe.

Where possible, record conversations verbatim, especially when your goals include the study of your subject's rhetoric. Use concrete descriptive words. Avoid generalization and characterization. For example, instead of saying that the attorney appeared to be late for another appointment, record what she said about her schedule, that "she glanced at her watch repeatedly during the observation, and that she hurried from the room." Instead of saying that the witness appeared nervous, identify the specific observations that led you to that conclusion. "The witness sweated profusely throughout the cross-examination, his eyes darted around the room, he gripped the sides of his chair so hard that his knuckles whitened." The key to recording data for later analysis is to expand, fill out, enlarge, give specific detail. You can add interpretations of it later. Condensed notes should be expanded into a fuller account as soon as possible after the observation ends. Any delay in recording leads inevitably to a degradation of the detail that can be recalled.

Reflection on Observation

The final stage in the observation cycle is reflection. In thinking about what you saw, you should refocus some attention on your learning goals and objectives. Reflection should lead to deeper, more complex learning about a skill, an event, or a system. It also can lead to asking more precise questions and making more focused observations.

We recommend that some of your reflection on observation be done in writing, through the use of fieldwork journals or in reflection papers. The exercise of committing your reflections to paper permits you to write to learn. Perhaps you have had the experience of being asked to write on a topic about which you thought you had little to say (like an unexpected examination question), only to find that as you began to outline an answer, you were able to write your way to a good response. The process of writing focused your attention and assisted your recall of what you knew about the topic. Similarly, writing your condensed notes into an expanded version will trigger memories from your observation and provide more data for analysis and interpretation. As you review the material, you will perceive new connections. Rewriting your expanded field notes into a journal entry or reflection paper provides an additional opportunity to recall more detail and to begin to analyze and interpret the data from which insights will occur.

Interpretation of data is never value free. As you try to learn from your observations, you must provide constant checks of the process to guard against misinterpretation. Three areas for particular vigilance include observer bias, non-representativeness of the observation, and errors introduced by the mere fact that the subjects know they are being observed.

Observer Bias

As an observer you may have prejudged in some fashion the actors or events that you will observe. For example, assume that you have chosen to observe a particular defense attorney engage in plea negotiations with the prosecutor. You have been told that this particular defense attorney frequently engages in conduct that is questionable ethically. Because of this information you may filter your observations of the attorney's conduct through a fine mesh that assumes unethical conduct when, in fact, none may be present.

A *halo effect* is a lingering effect of a particularly strong positive (or negative) reaction to something that occurs. It causes the observer to interpret more of the data from the observation favorably (or unfavorably) than is justified. Suppose you encounter one of your professors in the checkout line at the grocery store. The professor does not acknowledge your presence, even though you brush elbows as you set your purchases down. If you know this particular professor to be stereotypically absentminded, you may attribute his failure to greet you to this idiosyncracy, rather than to an attitude that students should not exist outside the classroom. The professor gets the benefit of your previous knowledge of the professor's personality.

Your interpretation also may be biased if the limits on your own frame of reference retard your ability to appreciate fully what was observed. We have all had an experience in which what we thought we heard turned out to be quite different from what was actually said. Our minds try to make sense out of imperfectly perceived data and sometimes produce a logical, but inaccurate, picture of the actual communication. Suppose you just came out of a class during which you were engaged in a heated, but friendly, debate with another student. In the hallway you overhear the student say to a classmate your name and the word "unreasonable." You might assume that the student was telling your classmate that you were being unreasonable during the debate. In fact, the student may have said, " . . . knowing that's her position really makes me think twice; I have never found [her] to be unreasonable."

Another significant source of interpretive error is the effect of making generalizations from a small or non-representative data set. You probably would not make a career decision on the basis of the recommendation of a single family friend. Likewise, you should be cautious about drawing conclusions about actors, events, or systems from limited observations. Assume that you are an extern in a government agency. You have chosen to investigate whether the agency is fulfilling its designated mission. During your observation of the work of the agency, you notice that a number of the staff attorneys leave their desks and go into a nearby conference room to talk and drink coffee. You wonder whether the attorneys are conducting personal business during work hours and neglecting their work. This interpretation may be correct, or it may reflect observer prejudgment. Perhaps you believe that lawyers who work for the government do not work very hard. This may lead you to assume that because coffee is being consumed, no work is being done. Even if the lawyers were gossiping and not working, you may have observed an atypical event and assumed it to be common.

What are some other examples of misinterpretation from a small or non-representative data set? Let's assume that you come into the office a bit earlier than usual one morning and see a secretary making coffee that you know everyone in the office will drink throughout the day. Based on this single observation, you may assume that the secretary in this organization, being the low person in the hierarchy, is tasked with making coffee for everyone else. It may be the case, however, that the task of making coffee is rotated among the entire staff, including the attorneys, and on the day you observed the secretary making coffee it was simply his turn.

Similarly, you are scheduled to interview at a government agency at 4:00 p.m. on a Friday. When you arrive you notice that fully half of the attorney offices are unoccupied and dark. You may assume that these government lawyers snuck out because it is Friday afternoon. The fact may be, however, that the occupants of the empty offices are on flextime and scheduled to work from 7:30 a.m. to 3:30 p.m.

You also should be cognizant that your subject's awareness of your observations may cause the subject to alter the behavior that you are planning to observe so that it is no longer typical. It is not uncommon for someone engaged in a task to alter the performance of the task when the person knows someone is observing. Performance could be enhanced; the subject might prepare more carefully to avoid errors that might otherwise be caused by inattention. Performance could be diminished; the subject's anxiety might disrupt the activity.

If it is important that the behavior you observe be unaffected by the subject's awareness, you will need to conduct unobtrusive observations or multiple observations of the behavior so that the observation awareness effect is diminished by familiarity or a sense of trust between you and the subject.

To some extent you can avoid or reduce the misinterpretation of data. Where possible, conduct multiple observations of the same phenomenon. Repeated observations greatly reduce the odds that the data are non-representative. You can seek additional data from sources other than your own observations. You can test the reliability of your observations by comparing them with those of others observing the same event. There may be possibilities for this in your extern seminar if several students observe the same event, record their observations, and compare the results. Through a technique called triangulation, you can attempt to confirm your observations through informant interviews involving multiple perspectives and through the collection and use of artifacts (documents, pictures, physical objects) employed in the situation observed. Just as scientists can locate any spot on the surface of the earth by recording the point of intersection of the data streams from three satellites in high earth orbit, the technique of triangulation in reflective observation allows the observer to make interpretations more accurately than is possible from data drawn from only one perspective.

Ethical Issues

Any activity involving interaction among lawyers and third parties may involve ethical conflict. The observation by law students of lawyers at work is no exception. By observation you may become more sensitive to the ethical issues that arise in the situations that you are observing and in relation to your role as observer. Watch for examples of the problems described as you learn through observation of lawyers at work.

see Chapter 5 *on Confidentiality*

Confidentiality. When you act as a participant observer, be aware of your obligation to protect the confidences and secrets of the clients on whose behalf you are working. Although you are not yet a lawyer and may not be subject to formal sanction by the licensing authority in your jurisdiction, the firm or organization for whom you work may be subject to sanction if you fail to protect the confidences and secrets of clients. Moreover, you may jeopardize your admission to the bar if you fail to act in a professionally responsible manner. Before you share with others what you have learned from observation, consider whether your report would violate the client's trust. If you are observing otherwise private lawyer-client interactions, but you are not part of the lawyer's firm, your presence could result in a waiver of the attorney-client privilege for communications between the lawyer and the client.

Conflict of interest between your role as observer and your role as student lawyer. Whenever you work on behalf of an externship, you provide service to the client or organization *and* provide a learning opportunity for yourself. At times these dual purposes may conflict. Consider this example: You have been asked to assist your fieldwork supervisor with the deposition of the opposing party in a lawsuit. You are to assist in handling the documents that will be used during the deposition, take notes, and observe the deponent's general demeanor and credibility. This is the first deposition that you have ever attended and you want to be able to make a detailed observation of the entire event. You want to be attentive to all of the dimensions of the observation opportunity, including space, objects, actors, acts, activities, event, goals, time, and feelings to learn as much as possible about the taking and defending of a deposition. In this situation, your first obligation is to the client on whose behalf you are participating in the deposition. Therefore, you must subordinate your personal learning objectives to the discharge of your assigned tasks. This is not to say that you should jettison completely your personal learning objectives. Since part of your assigned role is to observe the deponent, you probably can observe and record other features of the event at the same time, without jeopardizing the client's interests. You may never report your additional observations to your fieldwork supervisor because they are tangential to your assignment. You may simply use them for further reflection and learning.

On some occasions you might ask to observe persons or events even when you will not produce a product for the externship. For example, assume you have researched a motion that is being argued next week. Your learning objectives would be furthered by observing the hearing on the motion, but your fieldwork supervisor has not assigned you any responsibilities with respect to the hearing. If permission is granted for you to attend, the balance between producing work for the externship and satisfying your personal learning objectives shifts markedly toward your objectives for the time you spend observing the hearing. The observations, done by you for your benefit, also could be made available to the organization as a bonus.

In addition to the special ethical issues raised by the role of participant observer, there are other more general ethical issues that you must consider when doing any type of fieldwork observation. Perhaps the foremost consideration in any observation is concern for the privacy interests of those observed. Before you share your observations with your faculty supervisor or classmates in your fieldwork seminar, consider the privacy interests of the participants in any setting that you observe. The more public the setting, such as an in-court observation of litigation not involving juveniles, the less expectation of privacy the participants will have. As you move your observations into more private space, such as the meeting rooms of the organization for which you are doing your externship, the expectation of privacy by the participants in the settings that you observe increases dramatically. The concern for the privacy interests of the participants should lead you to consider whether information, such as names, identifying characteristics, criminal charges, or relevant strategy issues about the participants or the setting should be withheld or changed in any report you make to third persons about your observations.

In any situation where you conduct an observation anonymously, you should consider whether you need special permission. It may be preferable to disclose your presence and your purposes for observation where possible. Although disclosure may cause participants to be more self-conscious and to change their behavior in response to your observation, disclosure will be critical if your presence or activities are inquired into for some reason. Participants will be less likely to feel that they were spied upon.

If you anticipate using your observations for purposes beyond achieving your personal learning goals and objectives, such as turning your observations into a published research paper, consider whether you need to disclose this possibility and ask permission. The American Anthropological Association offers guidelines for persons engaged in observation for research purposes.

In both proposing and carrying out research, anthropological researchers must be open about the purpose(s), potential impacts, and source(s) of support for research projects with funders, colleagues, persons studied or providing information, and with relevant parties affected by the research. Researchers must expect to utilize the results of their work in an appropriate fashion and disseminate the results through appropriate and timely activities. Research fulfilling these expectations is ethical, regardless of the source of funding (public or private) or purpose (i.e., "applied," "basic," "pure," or "proprietary").

Anthropological researchers should be alert to the danger of compromising anthropological ethics as a condition to engage in research, yet also be alert to proper demands of good citizenship or host-guest relations. Active contribution and leadership in seeking to shape public or private sector actions and policies may be as ethically justifiable as inaction, detachment, or noncooperation, depending on circumstances. Similar principles hold for anthropological researchers employed or otherwise affiliated with nonanthropological institutions, public institutions, or private enterprises.

A. Responsibility to people and animals with whom anthropological researchers work and whose lives and cultures they study.

1. Anthropological researchers have primary ethical obligations to the people, species, and materials they study and to the people with whom they work. These obligations can supersede the goal of seeking new knowledge, and can lead to decisions not to undertake or to discontinue a research project when the primary obligation conflicts with other responsibilities, such as those owed to sponsors or clients. These ethical obligations include:

• To avoid harm or wrong, understanding that the development of knowledge can lead to change which may be positive or negative for the people or animals worked with or studied

• To respect the well-being of humans and nonhuman primates

• To work for the long-term conservation of the archaeological, fossil, and historical records

• To consult actively with the affected individuals or group(s), with the goal of establishing a working relationship that can be beneficial to all parties involved.

2. Anthropological researchers must do everything in their power to ensure that their research does not harm the safety, dignity, or privacy of the people with whom they work, conduct

research, or perform other professional activities. Anthropological researchers working with animals must do everything in their power to ensure that the research does not harm the safety, psychological well-being or survival of the animals or species with which they work.

3. Anthropological researchers must determine in advance whether their hosts/providers of information wish to remain anonymous or receive recognition, and make every effort to comply with those wishes. Researchers must present to their research participants the possible impacts of the choices, and make clear that despite their best efforts, anonymity may be compromised or recognition fail to materialize.

4. Anthropological researchers should obtain in advance the informed consent of persons being studied, providing information, owning or controlling access to material being studied, or otherwise identified as having interests which might be impacted by the research. It is understood that the degree and breadth of informed consent required will depend on the nature of the project and may be affected by requirements of other codes, laws, and ethics of the country or community in which the research is pursued. Further, it is understood that the informed consent process is dynamic and continuous; the process should be initiated in the project design and continue through implementation by way of dialogue and negotiation with those studied. Researchers are responsible for identifying and complying with the various informed consent codes, laws and regulations affecting their projects. Informed consent, for the purposes of this code, does not necessarily imply or require a particular written or signed form. It is the quality of the consent, not the format, that is relevant.

5. Anthropological researchers who have developed close and enduring relationships (i.e., covenantal relationships) with either individual persons providing information or with hosts must adhere to the obligations of openness and informed consent, while carefully and respectfully negotiating the limits of the relationship.

6. While anthropologists may gain personally from their work, they must not exploit individuals, groups, animals, or cultural or biological materials. They should recognize their debt to the societies in which they work and their obligation to reciprocate with people studied in appropriate ways. [Code of Ethics of the American Anthropological Association (Approved June 1998).]

This brief list does not exhaust the issues that will arise when doing observations. For instance, if you were to do *studies* on individuals for research, you would need to obtain authorization from the university. Universities have guidelines for the use of human subjects in research that establish rules, including the requirements for disclosure to participants and the obtaining of informed consent. This list, however, should sensitize you to some of the more common and more significant issues that can arise. As ethical questions surface during preparation for your observations and during the observations, you are encouraged to share your concerns with your faculty supervisor and, when appropriate, with your fieldwork supervisor and resolve fully your concerns before you proceed.

Exercise 12.3 In order to prepare for fieldwork observation, take a few minutes to do one or more of the following observation exercises, then reflect on your observations in your journal. Your journal entry should not merely be a rewriting or an expansion of the contemporaneous notes that you took during the observation even though you will find that you are adding detail to your notes as you revisit the observation. Your entry should contain a record of the experiences, ideas, concerns, mistakes, insights, and problems that arise during fieldwork observation. Use your journal to reflect on the personal side of fieldwork, including your reactions to the persons and events that you observe and your perceptions of the feelings of others.

- Observe a person engaged in an activity for two minutes. Take notes about as many dimensions of the situation as you can. Expand your notes into a narrative description of what you have just observed.

- Observe two persons interacting for five minutes. Take notes about as many dimensions of the situation as you can. Expand your notes into a narrative description of what you have just observed.

- Write a detailed description of a physical space (classroom, faculty office, attorney's office) that you were in recently. After writing the description, return to the same room and conduct an observation. This time take notes of your observations. Expand your notes into a narrative description of what you have just observed. Compare and contrast the two descriptions.

- Pair yourself with a classmate and watch a short segment of a film or conduct a two-to-five minute observation of a situation. Compare and contrast your recorded observations. What did your classmate observe that you did not? What did you observe that your classmate did not? What did each of you record that the other did not? What might explain the differences in what was observed and what was recorded?

FURTHER READING

JAMES P. SPRADLEY, PARTICIPANT OBSERVATION (1980).

Susan D. Bennett, *"No relief but upon the terms of coming into the house" — Controlled Spaces, Invisible Disentitlements, and Homelessness in an Urban Shelter System*, 104 YALE L.J. 2157 (1995). The article was written from data collected by a group of community activists and law students who spent time in the waiting room of a municipal office that provided emergency shelter and support services to homeless persons. The observers were present to provide basic information and assistance to homeless families applying for overnight shelter and to note how these families were being treated in the application process.

Barbara Bezdek, *Silence in the Court: Participation and Subordination of Poor Tenants' Voices in Legal Process*, 20 HOFSTRA L. REV. 533 (1992). The article describes a court watching project by law students. The students observed interactions among litigants, attorneys, and court personnel in landlord-tenant court.

COUNCIL FOR COURT EXCELLENCE, COMMUNITY OBSERVATION OF THE UNITED STATES DISTRICT COURT FOR THE DISTRICT OF COLUMBIA (August 2004). This publication reports the findings and recommendations of the Council for Court Excellence's third Court Community Observers Project. Appendix II contains a sample court observation form. The document is available on the Council's website: www.courtexcellence.org/publications/reports.shtml.

Judicial Externships

Mariana Hogan & J.P. Ogilvy

Law Clerks are not merely the judge's errand runners. They are sounding boards for tentative opinions and legal researchers who seek the authorities that affect decision. Clerks are privy to the judge's thoughts in a way that neither parties to the lawsuit nor his most intimate family members may be.

— Judge Alvin B. Rubin, *Hall v. Small Business Administration*, 695 F.2d 175, 179 (5th Cir. 1983).

Introduction

You are in the courthouse. You have access to the judge's chambers. You are in the well, perhaps even behind the bench, of a courtroom. Short of donning robes yourself, you are as close as it gets to seeing the court system from the judge's perspective. The opportunity you have to be a participant-observer of the judicial process is something few of your law school classmates will experience in their careers in the law.

While you will learn a great deal by doing the research and writing assignments the judge and law clerks give you, the opportunity to learn from observing cases in the courts may be even more valuable. If you are attentive, exposure to courtroom advocacy can help you develop your advocacy skills. Observation of the judge and the other players at the courthouse is a learning bonanza. To realize the potential of these opportunities for observational learning at the courthouse, refer especially to Chapter 12, Learning from Observation, and Chapter 9, Reflective Lawyering.

As with any externship, the greatest benefits from the judicial externship will come from reflecting on the big picture. To capitalize on your access to the courts, look beyond individual cases and assignments. Use the materials in the second part of this chapter (beginning at page 251) to explore how your judge and her court fit into our judicial system and to give yourself a framework for analyzing the work your judge does and the relationship between the courts and society. Reflecting on the wider implications of your experience at the courts will make you a better lawyer.

Preparing for the Judicial Externship

Other sections of this book provide information on learning from supervision, developing skills, and addressing ethical issues. This chapter begins by supplementing those materials with information that is unique to judicial externships, including sections on special ethical concerns for judicial externs, the cast of characters at the courthouse, and the research and writing assignments that most frequently arise in judicial externships.

Ethics for Judicial Externs

Significant ethical responsibilities accompany the extraordinary opportunities of a judicial externship. For the purposes of understanding and negotiating the ethical constraints on a judicial extern, you should regard yourself as a law clerk employed by the judge for whom you extern. Federal court law clerks are guided by the Code of Conduct for Judicial Employees (1986), including Advisory Opinions issued by the Advisory Committee on the Code; the Ethics Reform Act of 1989 and Judicial Conference regulations promulgated under the Act; and any local court rules or guidelines of the clerk's own judge. State courts have comparable sources for resolving ethical questions. Before beginning work in chambers, it is your responsibility to familiarize yourself with the guidelines that apply in your jurisdiction and any other sources called to your attention by your faculty supervisor or chambers' personnel.

see> Chapters 4-7
on Ethics

Whichever venue is the site of your judicial externship, three of the most significant ethical issues you are likely to face are confidentiality, conflicts of interest, and decision making on the record. Refer to Chapters 4-7, Ethical Issues in Externships, for a more extensive treatment of ethics issues for all types of externs.

Confidentiality:
What Goes on in Chambers Stays in Chambers

Perhaps no other single ethical issue is as important as understanding the need for and the extent of preserving the confidentiality of the work of chambers. The relationship between the judge and the judge's clerk is many faceted—at times teacher-student, at other times colleague-colleague. The relationship often is a close and confidential one. This is necessary for many reasons, not the least of which is the need for the judge to feel free to explore with the clerk the judge's most personal thoughts about matters before the judge for decision. If the judge is not confident that he or she can share questions, soul searching, and preliminary ideas leading up to a publicly-declared decision, the judge may keep these thoughts internalized, and the decision-making process, made possible only through a free ranging exploration of ideas, is seriously impaired.

In addition, telling tales out of chambers runs the risk of harming the reputation of the judge and undermining public confidence in the judiciary. All rigorous decision-making processes tend to be messy, and judicial decision making is no exception. The judge initially may consider factors that ultimately are discarded as irrelevant, inappropriate, or without sufficient merit, and a snapshot view of that process could easily be misinterpreted and turned against the judge and the courts.

There is also a more personal reason for respecting the confidentiality rules of chambers. Discretion is a highly valued trait in the legal profession. You do not want to gain a reputation early in your legal career as a lawyer who is unwilling or unable to maintain secrets and confidences.

Conflicts of Interest

Be vigilant to actual and potential conflicts of interest between your past, current, and future work as an employee, extern, or volunteer, or simply as someone with knowledge of people or facts, and the work of the court to which you are assigned as an extern. Your goal is to avoid any appearance of impropriety. Therefore, if you suspect that there may be a conflict of interest with respect to a matter on which you have been assigned to work, or on which you *may* be assigned to work, you should tell your judge immediately. In most cases the actual or potential conflict of interest can be avoided by reassigning work to another extern or to the judge's clerk and ensuring that you have no further involvement in or access to the matter.

The most common sources of conflicts of interest include work you may have done in the past on a case that is now before the judge for whom you are externing, matters in chambers that involve a law firm to which you have applied for employment or wish to apply for employment in the future, and matters about which you have personal knowledge of the facts, parties, or attorneys.

Decision making on the record

A law clerk is constrained by the factual record developed by the parties and is not permitted to conduct any investigation to more fully develop the factual record, except as to facts of which the court may take judicial notice. Therefore, you may not visit the scene in order to gather information on which the judge might base a decision in the case or otherwise communicate facts to the judge not developed by counsel but known to you because of familiarity with the events or locations of the case or obtained through factual research that you have conducted. Rather, you are to research the law to be the applied to the issues and facts in the case as presented by the parties. Thorough research includes checking the authorities cited by the lawyers to determine the relevance and the accuracy of the citations and independent research to determine whether the lawyers have overlooked controlling precedent or authority that may be helpful even if not controlling.

The Courthouse Players

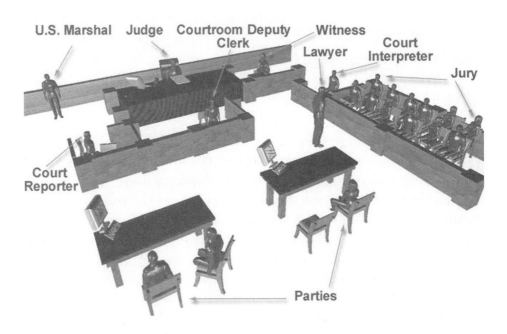

Source: Federal Judicial Center website http://www.fjc.gov/federal/courts.nsf/

Who Does What in the Courtroom

Although it is natural for you to focus your energy and attention on the judge, you also can learn from other personnel in the courthouse. In this section, we will review the players in the courthouse dramas that happen on a daily basis, describe their roles, and suggest opportunities for learning through your interactions with many of them.

The cast of characters differs depending on whether you are placed with a federal court, state court, or administrative tribunal, at the appellate or trial court level. Even where the roles are similar, titles may vary from jurisdiction to jurisdiction. Because there is more commonality among the federal courts, we will focus our descriptions on the federal courts, but if you are in a state trial or appellate court system, you should be able to recognize the players from these descriptions. Under current Judicial Conference policy, courts of appeals judges can hire up to five people as law clerks or secretaries; district judges can employ up to three people; bankruptcy and magistrate judges, up to two people. The judge decides how to allocate these positions to best accomplish the work of chambers.

During your externship you are likely to work most closely with the staff in chambers. Typically, the judge has a **Judicial Assistant** or **Secretary** and one or more law clerks. The secretary is the receptionist in chambers and usually has principal responsibility for answering telephone calls and forwarding calls to the law clerk, docket clerk, or judge, as appropriate. The secretary also prepares correspondence and other documents not prepared directly by the law clerk or the judge and may be responsible for keeping the judge's files in chambers and the judge's calendar of appointments outside of her court calendar. The judge's secretary can show you how to navigate chambers, introduce you to other courthouse staff, and schedule time with the judge for you to discuss your work.

The **Law Clerks** are lawyers who do legal research and writing for the judge and perform other tasks as directed by the judge including, especially in chambers with fewer employees, many of the tasks performed by the secretary, courtroom deputy, and bailiff. In most chambers, law clerks are appointed for a term of one year, although some are employed for two years and others may be permanent employees with no set termination date. Most courts have one law clerk although some will have more than one. Your role at court will be most like that of the law clerk and in some chambers your primary supervisor may be the judge's law clerk rather than the judge. In many chambers, you will collaborate with the clerk on projects for the judge. Consult the materials in Chapter 15, Management Skills, for guidance on working collaboratively.

see Chapter 15
*on Management
Skills*

In addition to the law clerk or clerks working directly for the judge in chambers, there may be other clerks available to all of the judges in the courthouse. In federal district courts with a heavy docket of filings from prisoners, the court may appoint *pro se* **law clerks** to review civil cases filed by prisoners and other parties.

The *pro se* clerks assist the court by screening the complaints and petitions for substance, analyzing their merits, and preparing recommendations and orders for judicial action. *Pro se* clerks usually are long-term employees of the court. At the appellate level, the federal circuit courts employ staff attorneys. Although the tasks assigned to **staff attorneys** vary from circuit to circuit, generally they include reviewing correspondence from *pro se* litigants to determine the legal sufficiency of the correspondence as an appeal or request for *writ of mandamus*, reviewing appeals and applications for *habeus corpus* involving collateral attacks on state or federal criminal convictions, preparing memoranda of law and recommending disposition of the issues raised by motions; and assisting in case management and settlement procedures.

It is also important for you to understand the roles of the judge's courtroom staff. Most judges have a **courtroom deputy** or "minute law clerk" or "case manager." The deputy is an employee of the clerk of court's office, although the deputy serves the judge to whom the deputy is assigned. In trial courts, nearly all courtroom deputies record the minutes of the court and assist the judge with scheduling trials or hearings on motions. The deputy's duties may include administering oaths to jurors, witnesses, and interpreters; maintaining custody of trial exhibits; maintaining the court's docket; serving as liaison between the judge's chambers and the clerk of court's office; and other duties as assigned by the judge. Because the courtroom deputy handles the judge's calendar and case records, she can help you to locate files and documents and give you information on the status of cases and scheduling. Many courtroom deputies work in the courtroom so they can be good sources regarding the judge's courtroom practices and preferences.

Many judges also have a **Bailiff** or **Crier** who attends sessions of court and announces openings of court, recesses, and adjournments. The bailiff maintains order in the courtroom under the direction of the judge and is responsible for conducting the jury to and from the jury room. Except in a few courts where recording devices are in use, when the court is in session there is a **Court Reporter** or stenographer present who creates the official record of all court proceedings that are required to be recorded and prepares a written transcript when requested by the court or the parties. The court reporter is the person to contact if you need to make reference to the record of a court proceeding.

In federal courts, courthouse security is provided by the **United States Marshals Service** sometimes in conjunction with private contract court security officers. The U.S. Marshals also move prisoners; supervise the department's Witness Security Program; apprehend federal fugitives; and execute writs, process, and orders issued by the court. In many places, the marshal or marshal's deputy is in complete charge of the jury. The marshals will be able to tell you when a defendant or witness who is in custody will be produced in the courtroom, and they can help you to locate prisoners.

From time to time other players will appear in the courtroom, often to assist the judge by providing information necessary to the judge's work. Each federal district court has a **Probation Office** whose officers conduct pre-sentence investigations and prepare pre-sentence reports on convicted defendants; supervise probationers and persons on supervised release; oversee payment of fines and restitution by convicted defendants; and conduct investigations, evaluations, and reports to the Parole Commission when parole is being considered for an offender or when an offender allegedly violates parole. Some courts may have a separate **Pretrial Services Office** whose officers assist the judge in making bail determinations on criminal cases and supervising defendants who are released pending trial. Finally, anytime a non-English speaking party or witness appears in court, an **interpreter** attends to provide translation.

In certain cases, judges require specialized assistance. Under Federal Rule of Evidence 706 the judge may appoint a **court appointed expert** witness to help the court and jury understand complex matters outside the common understanding of the court and lay jurors, including helping to understand the often conflicting testimony of the parties' own experts. Federal Rule of Civil Procedure 53 authorizes any district judge before whom an action is pending to appoint a **special master** as an impartial expert designated to hear or consider evidence or to make an examination with respect to some issue in a pending action and to make a report to the court.

There are two groups of attorneys who appear regularly in the federal courts, United States Attorneys and public defenders. In all cases in which the United States is a party, a representative of the Department of Justice is the attorney for the government, usually the **U.S. Attorney** or an Assistant U.S. Attorney for the district in which the case is pending. The counterparts in state courts are local prosecutors and attorneys from the state attorney general's office. The Criminal Justice Act of 1964 (18 U.S.C. §3006A) requires each federal district court to have a plan to ensure that federal defendants are not deprived of legal representation because they cannot afford it. This need may be met by assigning cases to private attorneys or, in districts where at least 200 appointments are made annually, by establishing a **public defender organization**. State and local governments may have comparable systems in place.

Once we move from the courtroom to the remainder of the courthouse, there are two significant resources that you may use as an extern and, later, as an attorney: the Clerk's Office and the library. **The Clerk of Court** in a federal district court serves as the chief operating officer of the court, implementing the court's policies and reporting to the chief district judge. The clerk's responsibilities include maintaining the records management system to safeguard the official records of the court, accepting for filing pleadings and other papers required to be filed with the clerk, issuing subpoenas, and managing the jury selection process. Each chief clerk is assisted by one or more deputy clerks and clerical assistants. Depending on the size of the jurisdiction, deputy clerks and assistants may have specialized duties. By familiarizing yourself with the workings of the clerk's office you can learn a great deal about the intricacies of filing cases, serving documents, obtaining court orders, and finding court records. The understanding you develop can be invaluable in your legal practice.

As an extern you undoubtedly will find your way to the library in the court-house. The **librarian** can expose you to resources and techniques that will make your work more efficient and reliable. Later, knowing what resources are available to the Judges and their law clerks should inform your advocacy.

As a judicial extern you are likely to come into contact with most if not all of the persons described above, but there are others employed in the courthouse, sometimes less visible but nevertheless serving important functions, with whom you may interact. Your interactions with any of the members of the courthouse community are important opportunities for reflection.

Exercise 13.1 Prepare a Chart (see example) of the Players in the Courthouse in which you are externing. Describe the duties of each person, noting where the duties vary from the brief description above. In the final column, make a list with respect to each person of some things that you might learn about the work of the court from speaking with and observing the work of the person.

Title	Duties	Opportunities for Learning
Judge		
Chief Clerk		
Bailiff	Announces the opening of court, recesses, and adjournments. Maintains decorum in the courtroom and is responsible for conducting jurors to and from the jury room.	Compare how these employees are treated with the treatment accorded the judges; note especially how you treat these individuals. Observe the gender and racial composition of the workforce; compare to the other categories of workers.

Research and Writing for Judges

The primary players at the courthouse are the judges, and just as the supporting cast described above work to assist the judge, much of your experience (and learning) will revolve around helping the judge. In almost all courts, judicial externs will do some research and writing. This section identifies some of the idiosyncratic writing products that judicial externs may be asked to prepare and provides some general advice about research and writing in judicial chambers. For additional assistance on developing your research and writing skills refer to Chapter 14, Skill Development.

Opinions are of varying complexity and length. "Full-dress" opinions are those that require structured discussion of the facts, legal principles, and governing authorities. **Memorandum opinions** are used where the decision does not require a comprehensive, structured explanation but still needs some explanation of the rationale. They are generally brief and informal and may or may not be published. **Per curiam opinions,** issued in the name of the court as a whole and on which no single judicial author is identified, generally are included in this category. **Summary orders** simply state the disposition of an issue or the case, sometimes with a brief statement of findings and conclusions, but often with little or no explanation. Summary orders usually are not published.

Orders are many and varied in complexity and form, from an Order of Judgment disposing of a case after a jury verdict to an order granting an unopposed request for an extension of time. Some orders of judgment may be as detailed as a full-dress opinion, such as where a complex matter was tried to the court sitting without a jury. Other orders are so routine in nature that they are prepared by the office of the clerk of court rather than in chambers. In some jurisdictions, the parties prepare the draft orders and the judge just signs them.

A **voting memorandum** presents the view of a judge on a panel to the other members of the panel. It is usually more succinct than the related bench memorandum and typically will reflect the view of the case that was developed at oral argument.

A **bench memorandum** typically is a brief document prepared for the trial judge or appellate judge to orient the judge to the facts of the case, the arguments of the parties, and the applicable law. It may be prepared by the parties or by the clerks. In a trial court, it may be as short as a page or two in length and include the facts as presented by the parties, the applicable law, an analysis, and a conclusion or recommendation to the judge. In an appellate court, the bench memorandum typically is longer, as it must deal with all issues raised by the parties' arguments. For the appeals court judge, the memorandum is most often a summary of the briefs of the parties, together with an analysis of the validity of the respective positions of the parties, and an identification of issues that require further inquiry at oral argument.

see Chapter 14
on Skill Development

A **single-issue memorandum** is a research memorandum that deals with a single issue that arises during trial, often as a result of inadequate preparation by counsel, an unexpected development during trial, or the judge's wish to pursue an aspect of the case not fully developed by the attorneys.

Some trial court judges may ask clerks or externs to draft **case summaries** of recent appellate court decisions to keep the judge apprised of current developments without the judge having to read the entire opinion.

Rarely will the clerk or extern be asked to prepare routine **correspondence** for the judge's signature. On occasion, however, when the person responsible for routine correspondence is not available to prepare it, the task may fall to the clerk or, less likely, an extern. Correspondence may be prepared by the clerk or extern, but always will be signed by the judge because the clerks and externs should not have any contact with the parties or their attorneys unless directed to communicate with them by the judge.

General Advice—Research

Regardless of the nature of the written product you will be asked to prepare, it is likely that some research will be necessary to gather together the facts and law required to prepare the document. Chapter 14, Skill Development, contains additional material to help you become more proficient at research.

Clarify the assignment

Whether the assignment is simple or complex, a clear understanding of the research and writing tasks involved is essential to doing an effective and efficient job. Asking for answers to fundamental questions after receiving the assignment but before leaving the clerk's or the judge's office to begin organizing the task often can save hours of fruitless work and dead ends. At a minimum you should know the answers to these questions: In what format should the project appear when turned in? Are there any examples (where you are unfamiliar with the format) that you can review? What is the deadline for the project? Are there any sources or resources that you should use or be aware of in working on the project?

Organize the project

Upon receiving the assignment, establish a work schedule and a work plan. Usually the first step is to collect all of the materials needed to commence researching the project. For example, if you are drafting an order granting or denying a motion, you will want to collect all of the papers filed by the parties in support of or in opposition to the motion as well as any notes created by the judge that reflect the judge's thinking on the outcome.

Check for conflicts

As soon as you can after receiving the assignment, familiarize yourself with the parties involved in the matter you are being asked to research. Determine whether you have an actual or potential conflict of interest because of your relationship to the matter or one or more of the parties. Discuss the potential conflict with the clerk or the judge and resolve the question of conflict of interest before proceeding any further with the project. For example, the physician whose expert opinion's admissibility is in dispute may be your aunt, or next door neighbor, or former employer.

Do background research

For issues where you have little familiarity with the basic law involved, you cannot begin to research the issue adequately until you familiarize yourself with the area of law. You can perform a preliminary survey of the field utilizing secondary sources such as specialized treatises and texts, casebooks, law review articles, loose-leaf services, ALR annotations, or legal encyclopedias. You may want to ask the law clerk, the judge, or a reference librarian for suggestions. After the judge and judge's clerk, the most important and helpful person in your life at chambers may be a good reference librarian.

Keep a research log

It is wise to employ a research log or journal during your research, especially for long-term, complex research tasks. A research log provides a detailed trail of your (re)search through all of the materials you consult while researching your assignment. By faithfully maintaining a research log, you keep a record of where you have looked in your research so that you can avoid repeating your efforts if there is a time lapse between research sessions. A research log also can be very useful to someone to whom you may need to pass off your assignment—such as the law clerk or another extern at the end of your stay in chambers—and can form the basis for you to discuss any problems that you are experiencing with your research strategy. You may wish to develop your own research log format, but a simple form would identify each resource you consult, describe the search path used within the resource, record the relevant results of the use of the resource, and describe any limitations or problems with the resource.

General Advice - Writing

Know the audience

As you turn from the research task to the writing task, you want to be clear about the format for the document and its intended audience. A bench memorandum is for the judge's eyes alone, but should be in a familiar format so that the judge easily can find the information needed. An order disposing of a routine motion is addressed to the lawyers for the parties and, to a lesser extent, the parties themselves. The language used should reflect this audience. Opinions are written primarily for the litigants and their lawyers, but opinions also serve to guide the future action of others: lawyers, lower courts (appellate opinions), agencies, and the general public. The broader the intended audience the more important the appropriate tone, language, and detail of fact and analysis.

Keep it simple

Your written product should be clear, concise, and logical. To ensure that everything pertinent is included in your draft, prepare a sentence or topical outline before beginning to write. In general, less is almost always preferable to more: fewer words are better than more words; shorter words are better than longer words; shorter sentences are better than longer sentences. The use of abstract or obscure words and phrases, flowery language, or complex literary devices may interfere with the reader's ability to understand the point. Leave flourishes to the judge.

Adopt the judge's preferences

Learn the judge's personal style preferences and use them. For example, the judge may prefer to write plaintiff and defendant or *the* plaintiff and *the* defendant or to substitute the name of a party (Smith) or a descriptive term (tenant) for plaintiff and defendant.

Know which style manual to use. Although you may be most familiar with one style manual, such as *The Bluebook*, the court may use another. Your citation style should conform to that used by your judge.

Proof and edit your "draft"

Your draft is a final product. Even though the clerk or the judge may ask for a *draft* memorandum, what you provide to the clerk or to the judge should be your best effort. For all but the most basic documents, you probably will be asked to do a second draft after receiving the input and edits from the clerk, the judge, or both.

Nonetheless, every document you prepare for the judge should be your best effort at preparing a final product. This necessarily means that you have employed the proper format for the document, that your references are appropriate and accurate, and that you have subjected the document to a thorough proof read to catch all spelling and grammatical errors and typos. Using the spell check function of your word processing program is necessary, but not sufficient. If you can do so without violating the rules of confidentiality, ask a colleague to proofread your document before submitting it.

Check in with the clerk or judge

Throughout the research and writing process, do not hesitate to ask questions of the clerk and the judge if you need further guidance on the assignment, help in doing research, or suggestions in writing. Nevertheless, be mindful of their limited time for your questions and try to bundle several questions that can be asked at one time rather than asking each separately. Learn the times of day when interruptions are least disrupive, and approach the clerk or judge with questions at those times unless the question is so urgent that you cannot wait to ask it. Consult additional resources.

Context for Analyzing Your Judicial Externship Experience

see Chapter 12 *on Observation*

There are many ways you might improve your research and writing ability during law school, but where, other than a judicial externship, could you observe a judge at work? Understanding the work of the judge and the implications of the judge's approach to her work potentially has a huge payback that transcends all other gains you may make during your semester at the court. Using your time in the courthouse to observe and analyze the judicial process and its implications in real cases is bound to make you a better advocate. Analyzing your judicial externship experience in the broader context of the judicial system also will give working with an individual judge, in single courtroom, in just one courthouse, in a specific jurisdiction, more universal meaning and value.

The Work of a Judge

What are the elements of the judge's work? Typically, we picture judges hearing legal arguments, reading briefs, researching, and analyzing the law all in order to render a well-reasoned written decision. Certainly, opinion writing is central to the judge's role, but the work of a judge, particularly a trial judge, includes making a variety of decisions beyond the published written opinions that are so familiar to law students. Decision making is just a part of the judge's work. In addition to rendering written and oral decisions on a range of issues, they engage in a fair amount of what has been called "case management"—all of the other work that goes into managing and resolving a large docket of cases.

The Judge's Role as Decision Maker

When we think of what a judge does, decision making is likely the first thing that comes to mind. In fact, the verb form of the word "judge" is synonymous with the words "decide" and "determine." The essence of the judicial role is deciding things; yet, the process by which judges make decisions is difficult to discern. Cardozo noted that even judges have difficulty describing how they make decisions:

> The work of deciding cases goes on every day in hundreds of courts throughout the land. Any judge, one might suppose, would find it easy to describe the process which he had followed a thousand times and more. Nothing could be farther from the truth. Benjamin N. Cardozo, *The Nature of the Judicial Process* 9 (1921).

So how can we start to determine how judges make decisions? Cardozo attempted to further the inquiry:

> What is it that I do when I decide a case? To what sources of information do I appeal for guidance? In what proportions do I permit them to contribute to the result? In what proportions ought they to contribute? If a precedent is applicable, when do I refuse to follow it? If no precedent is applicable, how do I reach the rule that will make a precedent for the future? If I am seeking logical consistency, the symmetry of the legal structure, how far shall I seek it? At what point shall the quest be halted by some discrepant custom, by some consideration of the social welfare, by my own or the common standards of justice and morals? Into that strange compound which is brewed daily in the caldron of the courts, all these ingredients enter in varying proportions. *Id.* at 10.

Understanding the way a particular judge brews the "strange compound" to make a decision is a skill that good advocates cultivate. You can use your time at the court and your interactions with the judge to begin to develop that talent.

Judges are confronted with different types of decisions. It is possible to categorize them in any number of ways, including by type: findings of fact, statutory interpretations, and application of standards or rules. Some judges distinguish between decisions based on their level of difficulty. Cardozo describes three types of cases:

> Of the cases that come before the court in which I sit, a majority, I think, could not, with semblance of reason, be decided in any way but one. The law and its application alike are plain. . . In another and

considerable percentage, the rule of law is certain, and the application alone doubtful. A complicated record must be dissected, the narratives of witnesses, more or less incoherent and unintelligible, must be analyzed, to determine whether a given situation comes within one district or another upon the chart of rights and wrongs. . . . Finally there remains a percentage, not large indeed, and yet not so small as to be negligible, where a decision one way or the other, will count for the future, will advance or retard, sometimes much, sometimes little, the development of the law. *Id.* at 164-65.

Does your experience at the court confirm Justice Cardozo's assessment that the majority of cases present only one possible result? How do judges decide that small number of very meaningful cases that move the law? Cardozo suggests that a judge must

> . . . balance all his ingredients, his philosophy, his logic, his analogies, his history, his customs, his sense of right, and all the rest, and adding a little here and taking out a little there, must determine, as wisely as he can, which weight shall tip the scales. *Id.* at 162.

Exercise 13.2 Take a difficult issue in one of the cases before the judge with whom you are externing and analyze the judge's decision making on that issue. What "ingredients" did the judge consider? Of those, were some more meaningful to the judge than others? How, if at all, did the judge reveal her inclinations to the lawyers? How effective were the lawyers' arguments, written and oral, in recognizing those "ingredients" and their relative importance to the judge?

Justice Cardozo was reflecting on the judge's decision-making process at the appellate level. Many of you are placed in trial courts. Trial judges are called upon to do more fact finding than appellate judges. In one classic text on judging at the trial level, Jerome Frank distinguishes fact finding from other types of judicial decision making. He refers to facts as guesses and notes that the judge, in finding facts, is subjectively judging the testimony of witnesses. Jerome Frank, *Courts on Trial* 22 (1950). Frank suggests that the trial judge's ability to find the facts plays a determinative role in many cases all the way through appeal. Does that shed a different light on the importance of the trial judge's findings of fact?

Exercise 13.3 Do you always agree with your judge's assessment of witnesses' credibility and her determination of the facts of the case? Pay particular attention to the testimony of a witness at a hearing where the judge will be making findings of fact. Develop your own findings of fact based on the testimony of the witness. Compare it to the facts as found by the judge. If your findings of fact are different, analyze the application of the law to the facts as you found them. Is your result different from the judge's? Why?

Finally, to what extent do judges bring their personal beliefs into the decision-making process? Even Cardozo, a judge renowned for his legal reasoning, recognized that "the likes and the dislikes, the predilections and the prejudices, the complex of instincts and emotions and habits and convictions, which make the man" influence judges' decisions. Cardozo, *op. cit.* at 167. Most judges try to resist the temptation to substitute personal preferences for principles. Is it realistic to expect that judges can make purely principled decisions? Judge Frank seemed to think it was not possible: "[the trial judge's] decisional process, like the artistic process, involves feelings that words cannot ensnare." Frank, *op. cit.* at 173. If that is the case, what does that teach you about how lawyers should approach legal arguments?

The Judge's Role as Case Manager

The sheer volume of cases requiring decision has the potential to overwhelm the judiciary. Courts struggle to reduce, or at least control, persistent backlogs. How can the courts, which seem to be swimming against the tide, hold their ground and offer judges the opportunity to make reasoned, not rushed, decisions?

Exercise 13.4 Analyze the caseload your judge is handling. How many cases are on the judge's docket? How old is the oldest case? If your judge holds regular "calendar days," how many cases does she typically have on the calendar in a single day? How long, on average, does she spend on each case? How many cases does she close each month? Compare this to the number of new cases added to her docket each month. How many of those are newly filed cases and how many are cases being transferred from another docket?

The past several decades have seen an increased focus on judicial case management. Some have argued that aggressive judicial case management techniques have contributed significantly to managing effectively the increasing number of case filings. Not everyone credits case management with improving the pace, much less the quality, of justice. One federal judge, criticizing legislation aimed at moving civil cases through the federal courts more expeditiously, summed up the challenges:

> There is little consideration of quality control, as such, but the judge, wearing two hats—quality control and assembly line monitor— knows that both aspects of the case are her concern. Moving the case along without concern for the substance of what is happening is not only a useless act, but it just doesn't work. Images of *I Love Lucy* with Lucy on the assembly line in the candy factory come to mind. Judge Marjorie O. Rendell, *What is the Role of the Judge in Our Litigious Society?*, 40 Vill. L. Rev. 1115, 1126 (1995).

What does the judge's role as case manager entail? Case management takes many forms—judicial involvement in discovery, scheduling, and settlement are all types of judicial management. Even mundane matters like the frequency of and length of time between adjournments leading up to the trial are management issues. Some judges like to call the attorneys and parties into court frequently while others prefer to let the cases proceed largely outside the courthouse and only calendar the most significant case markers like the pre-trial conference and the trial itself. Whom does the judge want to see in court at each of these adjournments? Some judges require an attorney or party with settlement authority to appear each time the case is on the calendar, while others routinely excuse the parties in civil matters requiring only the lawyers be present. Noticing how your judge "manages" cases and thinking about the implications of the management decisions she makes will make you a better advocate.

Court systems and individual judges also have different approaches to the flow of cases. Does the judge routinely grant extensions of deadlines and adjournments on the consent of the parties or is he largely unyielding? Some of the more aggressive means of judicial management include setting hard and fast trial dates and restricting discovery. Courts routinely using more aggressive management methods have earned names like the "rocket docket" or are termed "fast track" courts. Even judges whose courts have not earned such monikers sometimes resort to those tactics to move a particular case forward or at the request of one of the parties.

As you spend time at the courthouse, be alert to the management techniques in use. Pay particular attention to when and how your judge becomes involved in cases and who initiates the judge's involvement, the judge or the parties. Think about whether any of the methods of case management your judge uses potentially have a disparate effect on different kinds of litigants or attorneys. As an advocate you will need to know about the management policies of the judges and courts in which you appear, and you should think about whether there are ways to use the policies to your clients' advantage in litigation. Careful lawyers use their understanding of case management techniques to inform strategy decisions at every stage of a case, beginning with the decisions of what kind of case to bring and where to file it.

> **Exercise 13.5** Many judges have their own rules and procedures that they provide to attorneys and litigants at the beginning of each case. Find out if your judge has individual pre-trial practices. If so, how does she convey them to attorneys and litigants? Go to www.uscourts.gov and follow the links to your local federal district court's website. Explore it, paying particular attention to the information individual judges have posted. You are likely to find a variety of individual practices that the judges expect attorneys appearing before them to follow. Print out one example and compare it to your judge's practices.

The Judge's Role in Settlement

Settlement before trial has become an essential case management tool available to judges. Judges make choices regarding the role they will play in the process. There are a wide range of views on the appropriate role of the judge in facilitating settlement. One prominent critic of settlements contends that the judge's role is not "to secure the peace, but to explicate and give force to the values embodied in authoritative texts such as the Constitution and statutes: to interpret those values and to bring reality into accord with them. This duty is not discharged when the parties settle." Owen M. Fiss, *Against Settlement*, 93 Yale L.J. 1073, 1085 (1984). Proponents of settlement see benefits when judges use the settlement process selectively to craft quality solutions, not simply to clear the docket. Each judge has her own viewpoint about the role she should play in the settlement process ranging from those who disdain involvement to those who aggressively pursue settlement.

The judges who eschew a role in the settlement process do so for a variety of reasons. Participation in the settlement process arguably calls into question the judge's impartiality. It may be difficult for a judge who has actively participated in settlement negotiations to preside impartially over later proceedings if the settlement talks fail. Some argue that judges cannot easily set aside the opinion of the case they formed during settlement talks. To avoid the impartiality problem some judges have their law clerks oversee the negotiations. Does this resolve the problem? Others believe that any urge to settle should come from the parties rather than being imposed upon them.

Among the judges who view encouraging settlement as part of their role, there are a range of techniques and styles. Some judges actively analyze the merits of the case, suggest an appropriate figure, or formulate proposals not contemplated by the lawyers. Other judges encourage compromise without endorsing a number or assessing the strength or weakness of the respective cases. Judges may require attorneys and their clients to attend the settlement conference. Some judges even bypass the attorneys and advocate settlement directly to the litigants. Another technique favored by some judges is meeting with each attorney separately to discuss settlement. Do you see any potential problems with these meetings? Other judges use more indirect means of encouraging settlement such as setting a quick or unmovable trial date or alluding to the weakness of a key motion made by the attorney for a recalcitrant litigant. Attorneys who anticipate and understand how the judge is likely to encourage settlement can use the judge's participation to their clients' advantage. For example, an attorney who recognizes that a particular judge is likely to encourage settlement by moving the case to trial quickly will be certain to prepare for trial early so that the judge's technique will not put undue pressure on him to settle and an attorney who knows that the judge is prone to argue settlement directly to the parties by noting the weakness or strength of a pending motion will take pains to impress upon the judge the relative strength of any motion he has pending during a settlement conference.

A wide range of techniques are acceptable, but there are limits. The law "does not sanction efforts by trial judges to effect settlements through coercion." *Kothe v. Smith*, 771 F.2d 667, 669 (2d Cir. 1985). In *Kothe*, the U.S. District Judge had threatened to impose sanctions on the party rejecting his recommended settlement if a comparable settlement was reached after the trial started. The parties settled the case one day into the trial and the judge imposed the sanction on one of the defendants. The appellate court vacated the sanction as coercive.

Exercise 13.6 Think about the settlements you have seen during your externship. What role has the judge or her clerk played? What techniques does the judge or clerk use? Are any of the techniques arguably coercive?

Analyze a particular settlement you have seen. Do you think the settlement was "fair" to both sides? Was justice served by settlement? Do the parties seem satisfied?

Have you ever seen the judge voice concern over the fairness of a settlement? Describe the circumstances.

Plan how you would approach a settlement conference with your judge or her clerk, if you represented a plaintiff in a case.

Watch the settlement conference in the movie *The Verdict* or read Judge Saxe's fictionalized depiction of a settlement negotiation in a medical malpractice case. David B. Saxe, *Anatomy of a Settlement*, 79 A.B.A. J. 52 (1993). Compare and contrast the settlement negotiations you have seen at the court.

The Judge's Role at Trial

For that small percentage of cases that does not settle, there will be a trial. For judges, presiding over trials is a complex, and sometimes frustrating, function. In a frequently quoted passage, the United States Court of Appeals for the Second Circuit adopted the trial judge's view that he "need not sit like a 'bump on a log' throughout the trial." *United States v. Pisani*, 773 F.2d 397, 403 (2d Cir. 1985). Yet, in the adversary system, the attorneys have the more apparently active role in trying a case. What is the judge's role during a trial and what are the limits of judicial intervention?

In a jury trial, the judge typically structures the selection of the jury, instructs the jury on the law, controls the flow of the trial, and admits the evidence. In a non-jury trial, the judge also evaluates the credibility of witnesses and assesses the evidence to "find the facts." The judge is expected to produce a just, speedy, and economical trial. It sounds straightforward, and many judges make it look easy, but presiding over a trial while maintaining impartiality is a difficult task.

Think about the number and variety of decisions the judge must make during the course of a trial. The pace of trial often requires instantaneous rulings from the bench on legal and evidentiary issues. Throughout the trial, not just during the charge, the judge instructs the jury on the law. Knowing many areas of the law is only one part of the decision-making process. Frequently, the judge has to make a factual determination before making a legal ruling, so that even in a jury trial, the judge acts as a fact finder. The decision-making process is complicated. To determine the facts the trial judge must evaluate witnesses:

> He must do his best to ascertain their motives, their biases, their dominating passions and interests, for only so can he judge of the accuracy of their narrations. He must also shrewdly observe the stratagems of the opposing lawyers, perceive their efforts to sway him by appeals to his predilections. He must cannily penetrate through the surface of their remarks to their real purposes and motives. He has an official obligation to become prejudiced in that sense. Impartiality is not gullibility. Disinterestedness does not mean child-like innocence. If the judge did not form judgments of the actors in those court-house dramas called trials, he could never render decisions. Frank, *op. cit.* at 414-15.

The judge also controls the flow of the trial. The procedural rules leave the judge broad discretion in controlling the conduct of trials within her courtroom. Judges may determine the structure and length of the *voir dire*, the order and number of witnesses, the length of witness examinations and attorney argument, and the structure of the trial itself (for example, Fed. R. Civ. P. 39, 40, 42, 47, and Fed. R. Evid. 611). Trial judges may even call witnesses and may question witnesses whether called by the court or by a party (for example, Fed. R. Evid. 614). Judges also have inherent power to control the conduct of attorneys, parties, and witnesses during trial. In addition, the judge controls seemingly mundane matters such as where attorneys may stand when questioning a witness, how evidence and exhibits will be handled, when and how matters will be discussed outside the presence of the jury, and how objections may be made. All of these elements of the conduct of the trial may affect the outcome, particularly if an attorney has not anticipated them when planning trial strategy. During your externship be attentive to the varying abilities of counsel to exploit, or at least cope with, the judge's direction of the trial.

To get a feel for the dramatic impact a judge's ruling on the structure of the trial can have on a case, read Jonathan Harr's book, *A Civil Action*, chronicling the litigation of a mass tort case in a federal district court.

Exercise 13.7 Some judges provide trial attorneys with a list of trial conduct rules they expect the attorneys to follow. Think about what sorts of trial procedures your judge employs and how she communicates them to attorneys. Consider how the judge's control and structure of a trial you have observed affected the lawyering or the outcome of the trial.

During your externship, watch the judge's conduct in front of the jury with a critical eye. Even the fairest judge sometimes gets caught in the conflict between attempting to provide a fair trial and an economical one. And, given human nature and the number of attorneys who appear in most courts, judges are bound to run into attorneys whose temperament or style they find antagonistic. Watch carefully how the judge deals with an attorney who tries her patience. Does her treatment of the attorney vary depending on the presence or absence of the jury in the courtroom?

Judges must perform all these trial functions impartially. What constitutes impermissible partiality? Jerome Frank sums up the quandary "[T]here can be no fair trial before a judge lacking in impartiality and disinterestedness. If, however, 'bias' and 'partiality' be defined to mean the total absence of preconceptions in the mind of the judge, then no one has ever had a fair trial and no one ever will." Frank, *op. cit.* at 413. Whatever opinions the trial judge holds, she must be careful not to signal to the jury bias toward any party. Judges who call or question witnesses, comment on witnesses or testimony, or repeatedly rebuke counsel in front of the jury, sometimes find their behavior the subject of appellate review. The bar is high for overturning a verdict based on the judge's intervention at trial. The party asserting the claim of improper bias by the judge must show not only that the judge in fact displayed bias to the jury but also that serious prejudice resulted from the showing of bias. Appellate courts reviewing allegations of bias based on a judge's questioning of witnesses during trial often note the trial judge's obligation to interrupt the presentations of counsel in order to clarify potential misunderstandings. Reversal is only warranted in extreme circumstances. For example, the appellate court reversed a judge whose lengthy and vigorous examination of a defendant in a criminal trial obviously sought to impeach his testimony. *U.S. v. Mazzilli*, 848 F.2d 384 (2d Cir. 1988). Appellate courts often refuse to reverse based on regrettable comments towards counsel or witnesses, noting the trial judge's duty to manage trials to prevent them from becoming needlessly protracted and costly. In other words, only the most egregious intervention by the trial judge is likely to result in reversal.

Exercise 13.8 Do you think the judge's manner or participation at a trial you have watched has hurt or helped one side? Did the attorneys do anything to provoke the judge? Could they do anything to blunt the impact of the judge's behavior on the jury? If the judge's participation has arguably helped one side, did the attorneys for that side capitalize on the judge's favor? Is it appropriate to take advantage of a conflict between the judge and your adversary?

Selection and Evaluation of Judges

After reviewing all of the elements of the judge's role and the myriad ways judges control and shape the judicial process, you can see why savvy lawyers like to know about the judges before whom they appear. The judge's background and experience prior to donning the black robes may inform a lawyer's advocacy. Similarly, the judge's experience, his route to the bench, and his term of office provide externs with important context for evaluating and analyzing their experiences at the court.

Qualifications

The federal Constitution and the constitutions and statutes of each state set out the qualifications for judges. Typically, these qualifications are sparse. Not all jurisdictions require the judges in all levels of their courts to be lawyers; and, in those that do require their judges to be licensed attorneys, many do not require any minimum number of years in practice before a lawyer may take the bench. The federal courts and many state courts do not have mandatory retirement, and in those states that do, retirement age ranges from 70 to 75 years of age. Perhaps even more surprising, most states have no minimum age for members of their judiciary.

Consult the materials compiled by the "Judicial Selection in the States Project" on the American Judicature Society website at www.ajs.org for a summary of judicial qualifications in your state.

What are the qualities that we ought to look for in candidates for judicial office? Alexander Hamilton, writing in *Federalist 78*, sets a high standard:

> . . . there can be but few men in the society who will have sufficient skill in the laws to qualify them for the stations of judges. And making the proper deductions for the ordinary depravity of human nature, the number must be still smaller of those who unite the requisite integrity with the requisite knowledge.

A recent ABA report suggests five criteria for judicial selection: experience, integrity, professional competence, judicial temperament, and service to the law and contribution to the effective administration of justice. The ABA standard recommends a minimum of 10 years admission to the bar, and its definition of professional competence includes "intellectual capacity, professional and personal judgment, writing and analytical ability, knowledge of the law and breadth of professional experience." The ABA standard says judicial temperament includes, "a commitment to equal justice under law, freedom from bias, ability to decide issues according to law, courtesy and civility, open-mindedness and compassion." There are also many qualities that the standard does not mention, such as decisiveness, organization, and management skills, to name just a few. ABA Standing Committee on Judicial Independence Commission on State Judicial Selection Standards, *Standards on State Judicial Selection* (July 2000).

Exercise 13.9 Create a list of the qualities you think are most important in our judiciary. Compare your list to the ABA standards. How would you rank the ABA standards in order of importance? Would the nature of the court where the judge was to preside (trial, appellate, or administrative) or the types of cases she was to hear (for example: criminal, family, or civil) affect your list or rankings?

Research the background and experience of the judge with whom you work as an extern. Do your own analysis of the qualities and qualifications that suited her to judicial service. Redo the analysis using the ABA qualifications. Compare the two.

Selection

The judicial selection process can be controversial. The crux of the controversy is the tension between ensuring judicial independence and maintaining judicial accountability. Reduced to the simplest terms, judges are either elected, in partisan or non-partisan contests, or appointed, but there are countless variations on both processes, and all seem to have imperfections. Frequent elections maximize accountability while lifetime appointment enhances independence. The myriad methods of judicial selection in effect throughout the country are all attempts to balance these competing interests.

Exercise 13.10 How did the judge you work with get on the bench and how long will she serve? Answering these questions may be complicated by the fact that in some states and counties, and even within some courthouses, there are multiple routes to the bench, each with different terms of office. What are the implications of the selection process that put your judge on the bench?

Elections

Popular election of judges takes many forms. The first distinction is whether the judicial elections are partisan or non-partisan. Non-partisan elections attempt to insulate the electoral process from politics by having the judge run without party affiliation. In partisan elections, the process for nominating judicial candidates varies and may involve nomination by a county political leader or through a party convention. Political nomination processes open the door to allegations that spots on the ballot are bestowed as political favors.

Campaign Finance and Free Speech

Whether the elections are dubbed partisan or non-partisan, judges running for office have to face the issue of campaigning. Given the role of judges as fair and impartial interpreters of the law, judicial campaigns are potentially unseemly. The problems posed by the need to finance political campaigns generally are seen as more critical in judicial elections, because the most likely contributors to judicial campaigns are the lawyers and potential litigants in the jurisdiction where the judge is seeking election. Restrictions on contributions, however, may limit judicial candidates to the wealthy, jeopardizing the goal of a diverse bench of the most qualified candidates. Mandatory disclosure of campaign contributors and publicly financed judicial campaigns are two frequently proposed solutions that ameliorate but do not completely resolve this problem.

In order to preserve the impartiality of the judiciary and the public's confidence in the impartiality of their judges, most states have prevented judges and judicial candidates from expressing their views on disputed legal or political issues. The various ethical provisions prohibiting judges from announcing their views insulate judicial candidates from feeling bound by statements they might otherwise make during the course of a campaign, but the provisions also deny voters some meaningful information upon which to base their votes. The Supreme Court's 5-4 decision in *Republican Party of Minnesota v. White*, 536 U.S. 765 (2002) freed judicial candidates from some of these ethical restrictions on free speech grounds. That decision has left the states grappling with the limits on judicial campaign speech.

Exercise 13.11 If the judge with whom you extern is elected, research her campaign to see what statements she made while campaigning. Did they give an indication of the way she would decide any types of cases or issues? Is her behavior on the bench consistent with her campaign statements? If you were appearing as an attorney before your judge do you think knowledge of those statements would be helpful to your preparation?

The designation "popular election" may be a misnomer when applied to judicial elections. Many judicial elections are not contested; even in contested elections, voter turnout is typically low. One commentator estimates that typically eighty percent of the electorate does not vote in judicial elections and cannot even identify the candidates for judicial office. Charles Gardner Geyh, *Why Judicial Elections Stink*, 64 Ohio St. L.J. 43, 54 (2003). This suggests that most voters know little about their choices in judicial contests which makes it likely that name recognition and information provided by the ballot, such as affiliation with a political party, play a large role in judicial voting.

More than one hundred years ago, Roscoe Pound asserted that judicial elections had "almost destroyed the traditional respect for the bench." Roscoe Pound, *The Causes of Popular Dissatisfaction with the Administration of Justice*, 29 REP. A.B.A. 395 (1906), *reprinted in* 35 F.R.D. 273 (1964). The passage of time indicates that the situation was not that dire, but the controversy continues. Do you think the democratic value and judicial accountability attributed to judicial elections outweigh the potential detriment?

Appointment

The hallmark of an appointment process is that the executive—the President, Governor, Mayor, or County Executive—has the authority to make appointments to the bench. There are variations on how each executive informs his selections. Some processes, including the system for appointments to the federal courts, involve confirmation of appointees by the legislative branch. Judicial appointment may take the judicial candidate off the campaign trail, but it is difficult to claim that the appointment process is not political. The controversies over federal judicial appointments have been continuous, often culminating with Democrats and Republicans in the Senate squaring off over appointees. Appointment processes in states and localities frequently involve their own brands of local politics.

Much of the controversy surrounding judicial appointments stems from how the executive chooses appointees. Appointment by a single person is susceptible to accusations of cronyism. Executives who seek input only from their own staff or other leaders in their own party may appear to be doling out political favors. There is also the fear that, once appointed, the judge will feel he owes allegiance to the person or party who appointed him.

The least controversial appointment processes involve bi-partisan or multi-partisan screening panels that include a diverse group of lawyers and non-lawyers selected by a wide variety of politicians, bar leaders, law school deans, and citizen groups. The panel reviews candidates' qualifications and makes recommendations to the executive. The executive appoints judges from among the candidates recommended by the panel. This sort of process is touted as a "merit selection" process. In one variation, sometime after appointment (usually a year), the judge faces the electorate in what is called a retention election. Most often, the judge runs unopposed and the retention election acts as a sort of referendum on her performance by the electorate.

The merit selection system with a retention election combines the best features of merit appointment with the accountability of elections, but even this system has flaws. Judges who have made unpopular decisions prior to the retention election have been subject to ruthless ouster campaigns and studies have shown that absent noisy campaigns, retention elections are subject to voter apathy. Malia Reddick, *Merit Selection: A Review of the Social Scientific Literature*, 106 Dick. L. Rev. 729 (2002).

Does Independence Trump Accountability?

Which system offers the best hope of promoting public trust and confidence in the judicial system while at the same time putting the most qualified judges on the bench and ensuring their independence and impartiality? Elections appear to offer accountability but at a cost to independence and the appearance of impartiality. Moreover, the accountability provided by elections is arguably illusory given the apathy of voters and the dearth of information available to them on the candidates. Appointment by a single executive also compromises independence and impartiality unless the executive relies on a diverse, non-partisan screening committee committed to seeking out the most qualified candidates. Ultimately, the best test of a judicial selection system is the quality of the judges selected.

Evaluation of Judges

Since 1987, several organizations, including the National Center for State Courts, the Judicial Conference of the United States, and the American Bar Association, have recommended or issued guidelines for the evaluation of judicial performance. The result has been the development of court-sponsored evaluation plans in many jurisdictions. Local bar associations also have stepped in to evaluate judges, particularly where the courts do not sponsor an evaluation plan.

Courts and bar associations implementing an evaluation system confront a daunting task. Threshold questions include determination of who should conduct the evaluation and where they should get their information. Generally, it is agreed that obtaining balanced information requires assembling a diverse group of stakeholders to design and implement the process. No one interest group should control the evaluation process. To avoid results tainted by rumor or heavy media coverage of a few notorious cases, it makes sense to survey only those with firsthand knowledge of the judge's performance. That includes the attorneys who have appeared before the judge, litigants, witnesses, jurors, and court personnel who have seen the judge in action. Do non-lawyers possess sufficient understanding of the judge's role to evaluate judicial performance? Can litigants fairly evaluate judges? Anonymous evaluations may encourage forthright responses, but does anonymity risk unfair comments? The challenges are formidable.

Exercise 13.12 There are countless evaluation forms in use throughout the country. Find out if there is an evaluation process for judges in your jurisdiction and get a copy of the evaluation form attorneys complete. Complete the form using your courtroom observations of the judge with whom you work. Review your completed evaluation. Do you think it conveys an accurate assessment of the judge? How would you improve the evaluation form? Do you think the judge could or would benefit from seeing the evaluation? If there is no evaluation form available in your jurisdiction use the evaluation form provided in the Appendix 13.1.

Most evaluation forms do not rank the importance of each quality relative to the others. Are all of these qualities of equal significance? After having observed your judge in action, which qualities do you find most critical to "good" judging?

Judicial Oversight

Elections and evaluations are not the only ways to hold judges accountable. The trial courts and the intermediate level appellate courts are accountable for their legal reasoning through appellate review. Frequent reversals may motivate a judge to decide cases differently. Even the highest appellate courts in each jurisdiction may be reversed by the legislature in some cases. If a judicial decision is unpopular, the legislature may "correct" the law through new legislation.

Judicial conduct commissions oversee other forms of judicial behavior. Under the Judicial Improvement Act of 2002 (28 U.S.C. §§ 335-364), anyone may file a written complaint against a federal judge who they believe has engaged in "conduct prejudicial to the effective and expeditious administration of the business of the courts" or "is unable to discharge all duties of office by reason of mental or physical disability." The states have comparable oversight systems to investigate allegations of judicial misconduct, although there is variation in the composition of the oversight body, the investigatory process, whether and to what extent the proceedings are confidential, and the appeals processes.

One frequent complaint about our judicial system is its lack of efficiency, including judges' productivity. A court system's administrative office may monitor judges' productivity by recording and publishing statistics on caseloads, such as the number of cases each judge resolves, the average number of days before each judge renders a decision on a motion, the number of cases pending on each judge's docket; the average age of the cases on the judge's docket, and the like. The court administration may react to an individual judge's statistics by reassigning the judge to a different court or altering the number or types of cases the judge is assigned.

The American Judicature Society's website has a wealth of information on judicial oversight with links to specific information for each state. http://www.ajs.org

> **Exercise 13.13** Does the court where you are externing keep case statistics? Who keeps the statistics? Are they kept by individual judge? Are the statistics available to the public? Are the statistics conveyed to the judge? Think about the impact the statistics have on the judge.

Finally, citizen groups, bar associations, and the media use a variety of methods to hold judges accountable. Citizen groups sometimes send court watchers to monitor what is happening in the courts. Bar associations may survey their memberships and produce reports on judges in the jurisdiction. The media report on cases of note and instances of egregious judicial conduct. In some jurisdictions the media is not limited to sending reporters to the courthouse; cameras bring televised proceedings into viewers' homes.

Cameras in the courtrooms are another possible avenue for judicial oversight. Cameras may or may not be permitted in courtrooms in the jurisdiction of your placement. If they are, their use is likely to vary from judge to judge and, perhaps, even case to case. Despite decades of experience with cameras in the courts, there is no consensus on whether the behavior of judges, lawyers, and witnesses improves under the camera's watchful eye. There is some concern that conduct deteriorates because participants "play to" the cameras. Other concerns include whether cameras in the courtroom discourage knowledgeable witnesses from coming forward and whether televising court proceedings enhances public understanding of the courts or, because of the sensational trials that attract public attention, contributes to skewed notions of the judicial process.

While much of the media coverage of the judiciary furthers the goals of public access to the courts and judicial accountability, some forms of public criticism of judges threaten judicial independence. It is difficult to defend *ad hominem* attacks on judges as productive, but where is the line between harsh, but permissible, criticism and personal attack? When a judge is subject to unfair or inaccurate criticism, what is the proper response, and who should respond? Judicial ethics rules in many jurisdictions strictly limit the judiciary's response to criticism of judges' decisions. Should judges who anticipate a public reaction to a decision take greater pains to explain their reasoning when they rule? What role should the bar associations play in defining the limits of permissible criticism and responding to improper criticism of judges and the judiciary?

Exercise 13.14 If there is media coverage of a case you are familiar with through your externship, read or watch the coverage with a critical eye. Write a journal entry analyzing the accuracy of the coverage and the effect, if any, of the media scrutiny on the judge, lawyers, witnesses and parties. What effect do you think the media coverage might have on public opinion of judges and our judicial system?

Judges, Courts, and the Public

Another of the benefits of a judicial externship is the opportunity to reflect on the role of judges and courts in our society and the public perception of that role. By doing a judicial externship, you become an insider in a major cultural and political institution that much of the public sees only through the filters of media coverage or pop culture, as litigants represented by lawyers, or as jurors fulfilling a specific function. As an attorney you will represent clients who will impose their expectations of the judiciary and the courts on you and your handling of their legal problems. If you become a litigator, you will argue your clients' cases to jurors who bring to that role certain expectations of the court system. Your image will be colored by the image of the system itself.

Exercise 13.15 Take the opportunity at the beginning of your placement in chambers to assess your own image of the courts in your community. What do you know about the particular judge for whom you will be externing? Start by completing the short survey found in Appendix 13.2. Compare your responses to the responses of members of the general public about their perceptions of the courts in their communities, which are contained in David P. Rothman, et al., *Perceptions of the Court in Your Community: The Experience of Experience, Race and Ethnicity* (final report) (National Center for State Courts 2003), http://www.ncsconline.org/WC/Publications/Res_AmtPTC_Perceptions Pub.pdf. At the end of your placement, come back to the survey and take it again. Reflect on any changes in your responses.

What is the Public Perception of Courts and Judges?

Since 1977 most of what is known about the public perception of courts and judges is through public opinion surveys that have been conducted over the years on both the state and national levels. A 2003 report by the National Center for State Courts reviewed many of the previous state and national surveys and reported findings from those surveys and concluded that there was an "apparent lack of significant change in public opinion about courts" over the years covered by the surveys. The authors of the Report note that "[t]he core public image of state and local courts is a stereotype—one that seems to change little over time or differ from state to state or locality to locality." The stereotyped images have both negative and positive facets.

The positive images include the perception that "judges are honest and fair in making case decisions, that they are well trained, that the jury system works, and that judges and court personnel treat members of the public with courtesy and respect."

The negative images center on perceptions of limited access to the courts due to cost and complexity, delays in the processing of cases, unfairness in the treatment of racial and ethnic minorities, leniency toward criminals, and a lack of concern about the problems of ordinary people. Specific concerns include a perception of leniency in sentencing in criminal matters and favoritism toward the corporate sector and the wealthy in the civil justice system. There also is strong evidence of public concern that political considerations, especially related to campaign fundraising, exert an undue influence on the judiciary.

The authors of the 2003 Report noted that "distinctive views of the courts are associated with race and ethnic groups. African-Americans tend to have distinctly lower evaluations than do Whites of the performance, trustworthiness, and fairness of courts. Latinos emerge as generally holding the most positive assessments of the state courts, but present a mixed picture in terms of specifics. . . ."

 **Chapter 16**
on Bias

Exercise 13.16 Differing perceptions of the courts along racial, ethnic, or gender lines within our society raise concerns about the fairness of the courts to different segments of society. Bias or the perception of bias in the courts runs counter to the core values of our judicial system. Over the last several decades most state and federal courts have studied the issue of fairness to diverse segments of society and issued reports. Do you see any evidence of bias in your court? Look at any reports on bias in the courts issued in your jurisdiction. The National Center for State Courts has collected the data and has links to many of the reports on their website http://www.ncsc.online.org. The federal circuits also have done reports, many of which are available through the Circuit Executive at the court. Compare your own observations with the results presented in the reports.

Exercise 13.17 If you have an opportunity to watch a jury trial, try to put yourself in the shoes of the jurors. How have they experienced the court system? How do you think their experience has affected their view of our judicial system? Here are two fascinating first-person accounts of jury service by former jurors that reflect frustration and ambivalence: D. Graham Burnett, *A Trial by Jury* (2001) and William Finnegan, *Doubt*, The New Yorker, January 31, 1994 at 48. Is frustration inherent in the nature of the jury's task? Can you identify some ways the judge could limit any frustration jurors seemed to experience during your observation?

How are Public Perceptions of Judges and Courts Formed?

How do people form their perceptions of their local courts? Several studies have attempted to answer that question. A 1999 national survey by the National Center for State Courts interviewed 1826 randomly-selected Americans. Approximately 53% of the respondents indicated some personal involvement in the courts, with almost one-half of personal experience taking the form of jury service. About half (48.7%) of the respondents felt they knew "some" about the courts, but only 14.1% felt they knew "a lot."

The sources identified by the respondents as regularly providing information to them about the courts were as follows: some personal involvement with the courts (53%), electronic sources (59%), and print sources (50%). Interestingly, TV dramas and comedies were identified by 25.6% of the respondents as regularly providing information about the courts, and TV reality shows (for example, *Judge Judy* or *People's Court*) regularly provided 18.3% of the respondents with information about the courts.

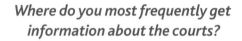

Where do you most frequently get information about the courts?

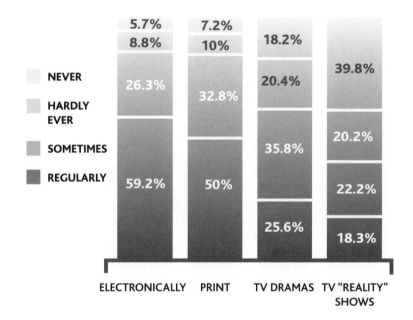

The survey analyzed in the 2003 Report only asked for sources of information that contributed to an overall impression of how courts in the community worked from respondents who indicated that they or a member of their household had any personal involvement in the courts in the preceding 12 months. seventy-one percent rated their experience in court as a very important source of information. Further down the list was TV news (23%), newspapers (27%), and TV reality programs (8%). Generally, the three identified racial and ethnic groups, African-Americans, Latinos, and Whites, reported similar patterns of information sources. African-Americans, however, were most likely to cite personal experiences in court (77%) compared to Whites (70.4%) and Latinos (55%), and Latinos were more likely to cite TV reality shows (21%) than African-Americans (15%), and Whites (3%) as important sources of information about the courts.

Percent Rating Source as "Very Important" on Overall Impression of Courts

	Whites	*African Americans*	*Latinos*	*All Respondents*
• Your experience in court	70.4	77.0	55.0	71.0
• Experience by a household member	59.0	63.0	53.0	58.0
• Your lawyer	61.0	66.0	59.0	62.0
• Experience by a close relative	46.0	65.0	54.0	49.0
• Experience of a friend	39.0	41.0	33.0	38.0
• Experience of someone you work with	29.0	32.0	28.0	32.0
• Your job	41.0	61.0	53.0	46.0
• What you see on TV news	21.0	33.0	42.0	23.0
• What you read in newspapers	25.0	34.0	46.0	27.0
• What happens during TV Judge Program	3.0	15.0	21.0	8.0

By contrast, a 1978 survey by the National Center for State Courts found that respondents reported learning the most about the state and local courts in their state through formal education (24%) and personal experience with courts (23%), followed by print media (17%), TV news (14%), and TV entertainment programs (6%).

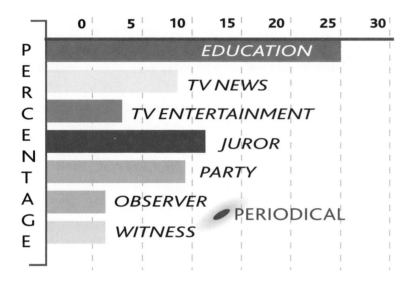

Overall, the more recent data suggest that roughly 50% of Americans have had some personal experience with the courts that is used to inform their images of the judiciary and judges, but even those with personal experience also report relying on TV news and newspapers for a significant amount of information about the courts. The other 50% of the population necessarily relies on media sources, such as sensational news stories and TV dramas, for much of its information about the courts. As the surveys since 1977 demonstrate, the public's attitudes about the courts and judiciary are quite impervious to change in part because of the limited exposure of most members of the public to the courts in any meaningful ways and in part because of the atypically sensational nature of the news stories and TV dramas from which many citizens derive their perception of the courts.

Courts Adapting to Change

The static nature of public perception of the courts may be a manifestation of the public's belief that the courts do not change. There is value to stability and predictability in a judicial system, but constancy does not preclude modernization to improve delivery of services. Technology is a good litmus test for innovation. Be alert to the use of technology (or the lack thereof) in the court where you are externing. To what extent is technology in use in the courtroom and the clerk's office?

Compare your perceptions of the court in which you are externing with those of the general public as reflected in these data. What similarities and differences emerge? Can you think of any suggestions for your judge or for the administrators of the court system in which you are working that they can undertake to improve the public's perception of them?

Technology is a boon to court clerks and lawyers craving paperless litigation. E-filing, the filing and storage of court documents in an electronic format rather than on paper, has many benefits. E-filing offers obvious savings on paper, copying, postage, couriers, and staff time. Electronic documents also are easily accessible and searchable. E-filing is in place through PACER (the Public Access to Court Electronic Records system) in most federal courts and in an increasing number of state court systems.

The accessibility of electronic court records gives new meaning to the notion of public access to the courts. To examine traditional court papers, an individual would have to travel to the court and request the one physical set of court records on a matter from the court clerk. Electronic records can be available online to anyone with Internet access. The wider access to electronic records and the ability to search electronic records with a keystroke raise confidentiality and privacy concerns for lawyers and courts. Identity theft, corporate espionage, and unfair competition are some of the potential misuses of information in court files. Courts are grappling with ways to strike a balance between the privacy concerns presented by Internet access and the fundamental right of public access to the courts.

Exercise 13.18 Look at the court file for one of the cases before the judge. Is there information in the file that you would characterize as "private"? What makes the information "private"? Could the information be used to embarrass or harm someone, for an illegal purpose such as insider trading, or for a commercial purpose? Weigh the privacy concerns you have isolated against the three fundamental values of public access to court records, monitoring the court system to promote fairness and honesty, protecting public health and welfare, and allowing the media to report on matters of public interest and concern.

The potential for use of new technology in the courtroom to present and argue cases is vast, but most courtrooms are ill-equipped. In 1993, the National Center for State Courts and William & Mary Law School unveiled Courtroom 21, a courtroom designed to experiment with the use of technology to improve the legal system. Since then, a number of jurisdictions have opened showcase high-tech courtrooms with innovations such as real-time court reporting facilities; real-time streaming video to other locations; interactive whiteboards; touch screen monitors in the witness box; integrated electronic podiums and benches; personal computer docking stations at counsel tables, the witness box, and on the bench; equipment and monitors for presentation of electronic evidence; and wireless Internet access points.

Despite the increase in availability of courtroom technology, in most jurisdictions, trial attorneys who want to use technology bring their own laptops loaded with presentation software, overhead projectors, and the like. The cost of outfitting and, in many instances, retrofitting courtrooms is an impediment to rapid deployment of new technology. In addition, there are questions about reliability, access, and training to consider. As anyone who has used presentation software knows, one must be prepared to go forward with a low-technology presentation when the high-technology hardware or software fails at the last minute.

Conclusion

This quick overview of the courtroom as classroom should be viewed as a starting point for your adventure. Your opportunities for learning are limited only by your imagination. The courts are a rich resource for learning about lawyering. *Carpe diem.*

What technology is available in your courtroom? Are additional resources available in your courthouse? During your externship was technology used in the courtroom? Did it enhance the presentation of evidence to the judge or jury?

■ Appendix 13.1

NEW HAMPSHIRE JUDICIAL BRANCH

TRIAL COURT

JUDICIAL PERFORMANCE EVALUATION QUESTIONNAIRE

The New Hampshire Supreme Court is committed to improving performance of judges through regular performance evaluations. Your candid responses to this questionnaire will assist an Administrative Judge in assessing the performance of the judge named below. Narrative comments are very helpful: please use the "Comments" section at the end of this questionnaire to make additional observations about the judge's performance. To preserve confidentiality, please do not sign this questionnaire.

Judge/Master: _____

Court: _____   Date: _____

Please fill in the circle O that best reflects your opinion of the judge's performance in each area.	1 Excel-lent	2 Very Good	3 Satis-factory	4 Fair	5 Unsatis-factory	6 Not Applic-able
PERFORMANCE						
1. Ability to identify and analyze relevant issues.	O	O	O	O	O	O
2. Judgment in application of relevant laws and rules.	O	O	O	O	O	O
3. Giving reasons for rulings, when needed.	O	O	O	O	O	O
4. Clarity of explanation of rulings.	O	O	O	O	O	O
5. Adequacy of findings of fact.	O	O	O	O	O	O
6. Clarity of judge's decision (either oral or written).	O	O	O	O	O	O
7. Completeness of judge's decision.	O	O	O	O	O	O
8. Punctuality.	O	O	O	O	O	O
9. Resourcefulness and common sense in resolving problems arising during the proceeding.	O	O	O	O	O	O
10. Credibility of the judge's settlement appraisals.	O	O	O	O	O	O
11. Decisiveness.	O	O	O	O	O	O

	1 Excel-lent	2 Very Good	3 Satis-factory	4 Fair	5 Unsatis-factory	6 Not Applic-able
TEMPERAMENT AND DEMEANOR						
12. Fostering a general sense of fairness.	O	O	O	O	O	O
13. Absence of coercion, threat or the like in settlement efforts (if less than adequate or poor, please explain in comments section).	O	O	O	O	O	O
14. Courtesy to participants.	O	O	O	O	O	O
15. Open-mindedness.	O	O	O	O	O	O
16. Patience.	O	O	O	O	O	O
17. Absence of arrogance.	O	O	O	O	O	O
18. Maintaining order in the courtroom.	O	O	O	O	O	O
19. Demonstration of appropriate compassion.	O	O	O	O	O	O
JUDICIAL MANAGEMENT SKILLS						
20. Effectiveness in narrowing the issues in dispute, when appropriate.	O	O	O	O	O	O
21. Moving the proceeding in an appropriately expeditious manner.	O	O	O	O	O	O
22. Maintaining appropriate control over the proceeding.	O	O	O	O	O	O
23. Allowing adequate time for presentation of the case in light of existing time constraints.	O	O	O	O	O	O
24. Appropriateness of the judge's settlement initiatives (if less than adequate or poor, please explain in the comments section).	O	O	O	O	O	O
25. Thoughtfully exploring the strengths and weaknesses of each party's case in settlement discussions with the attorneys.	O	O	O	O	O	O
26. Skill in effecting compromise.	O	O	O	O	O	O
LEGAL KNOWLEDGE						
27. Knowledge of relevant substantive law.	O	O	O	O	O	O
28. Knowledge of rules of procedure.	O	O	O	O	O	O
29. Knowledge of rules of evidence.	O	O	O	O	O	O
ATTENTIVENESS						
30. Attentiveness.	O	O	O	O	O	O
31. Ability to really listen.	O	O	O	O	O	O

	1 Excel-lent	2 Very Good	3 Satis-factory	4 Fair	5 Unsatis-factory	6 Not Applic-able

BIAS AND OBJECTIVITY

32. Absence of bias and prejudice based on race, sex, ethnicity, religion, social class, or other factor (if less than adequate or poor, please explain in the comments section).   O   O   O   O   O   O

33. Even-handed treatment of litigants (if less than adequate or poor, please explain in the comments section).   O   O   O   O   O   O

34. Even-handed treatment of attorneys (if less than adequate or poor, please explain in the comments section).   O   O   O   O   O   O

DEGREE OF PREPAREDNESS

35. Doing the necessary "homework" on the case.   O   O   O   O   O   O

36. Rendering rulings and decisions without unnecessary delay.   O   O   O   O   O   O

COMMENTS Narrative comments are very useful in this evaluation process. Please use the space below, or attach a separate sheet of paper, to provide narrative comments. The narrative comments will be provided to the judge either verbatim or in summary form; however, to preserve confidentiality, anything in the comments that may identify the person making the comment will be removed.

BACKGROUND INFORMATION

The background information requested on this page is voluntary and will be kept in strict confidence. The judge being evaluated will not be supplied with any information which could identify the evaluator.

37. Please indicate approximately how many times you have appeared before or observed this judge in the last three years.

O	O	O	O
Less than 5	5-10	10-25	More than 25

38. If you are a lawyer, how many years have you practiced law?

O	O	O	O
Less than 5	5-10	10-25	More than 25

39. If you are a lawyer, what percentage of your time and practice is within this judge's jurisdiction?

O	O	O	O
Less than 5	5-10	10-25	More than 25

40. If you are a lawyer, is your practice
principally conducted in the county in
which this judge presides?   O Yes   O No

41. Types of cases in which you generally appear before or observe this judge:

     O Juvenile   O Marital   O Domestic violence petitions

     O Guardianship of minor   O Criminal non-jury

     O Adoptions   O Criminal jury   O Termination of parental rights

     O Civil / equity non-jury   O Other   O Civil jury

■ Appendix 13.2

PERCEPTIONS OF THE COURTS SURVEY

1. On a scale from 1 to 5, with 1 being least favorable and 5 being most favorable, how would you rate how you feel **in general** about the courts in your community? If you feel neutral, use 3.

2. How often do you think people receive fair outcomes when they deal with the courts? Would you say (1) always, (2) usually, (3) sometimes, (4) seldom, (5) never receive fair outcomes, or (6) don't know?

3. How often do you think courts use fair procedures in handling cases? Would you say the courts are (1) always, (2) usually, (3) sometimes, (4) seldom, (5) never fair, or (6) don't know?

4. For each of the following statements about courts in your community, indicate how strongly you agree or disagree with each.
Would you say you   (1) strongly agree,   (2) somewhat agree,
(3) somewhat disagree,   (4) strongly disagree,   (5) don't know

    a. The courts are concerned with people's rights.

        (1) strongly agree,   (2) somewhat agree,
        (3) somewhat disagree, (4) strongly disagree,   (5) don't know

    b. The courts treat people with dignity and respect.

        (1) strongly agree,   (2) somewhat agree,
        (3) somewhat disagree, (4) strongly disagree,   (5) don't know

    c. The courts treat people politely.

        (1) strongly agree,   (2) somewhat agree,
        (3) somewhat disagree, (4) strongly disagree,   (5) don't know

d. The courts make decisions based on the facts.

> (1) strongly agree,   (2) somewhat agree,
> (3) somewhat disagree,   (4) strongly disagree,   (5) don't know

e. The judges are honest in their case decisions.

> (1) strongly agree,   (2) somewhat agree,
> (3) somewhat disagree,   (4) strongly disagree,   (5) don't know

f. Courts take the needs of people into account.

> (1) strongly agree,   (2) somewhat agree,
> (3) somewhat disagree,   (4) strongly disagree,   (5) don't know

g. Courts listen carefully to what people have to say.

> (1) strongly agree,   (2) somewhat agree,
> (3) somewhat disagree,   (4) strongly disagree,   (5) don't know

h. Courts are sensitive to the concerns of the average citizen.

> (1) strongly agree,   (2) somewhat agree,
> (3) somewhat disagree,   (4) strongly disagree,   (5) don't know

i. Court cases are resolved in a timely manner.

> (1) strongly agree,   (2) somewhat agree,
> (3) somewhat disagree,   (4) strongly disagree,   (5) don't know

5. Some people say that the courts treat everyone equally, while others say that the courts treat certain people differently than others. How often are each of the following groups of people treated worse than others by the courts? Do they always, often, sometimes, rarely, or never treat . . . worse than they treat others?

A. An African-American?

(1) always, (2) often, (3) sometimes, (4) rarely, (5) never , (6) don't know

B. A Latino or Hispanic?

(1) always, (2) often, (3) sometimes, (4) rarely, (5) never , (6) don't know

C. A Non-English speaker?

(1) always, (2) often, (3) sometimes, (4) rarely, (5) never , (6) don't know

D. Someone with a low income?

(1) always, (2) often, (3) sometimes, (4) rarely, (5) never , (6) don't know

6. How important to you are the following sources of information to your overall impression of how the courts in your community work? Are they (1) very important, (2) somewhat important, or (3) not at all important?

    A. Your prior experience in court?`

    (1) very important,   (2)somewhat important,
    (3) not at all important, (4) don't know

    B. Court experiences by a member of your household?

    (1) very important,   (2)somewhat important,
    (3) not at all important, (4) don't know

    C. Court experiences of a close relative?

    (1) very important,   (2)somewhat important,
    (3) not at all important, (4) don't know

    D. Court experiences of a friend?

    (1) very important,   (2)somewhat important,
    (3) not at all important, (4) don't know

    E. Court experiences of someone you work or go to school with?

    (1) very important,   (2)somewhat important,
    (3) not at all important, (4) don't know

    F. Your past or current educational experiences?

    (1) very important,   (2)somewhat important,
    (3) not at all important, (4) don't know

    G. What you see on television news?

    (1) very important,   (2)somewhat important,
    (3) not at all important, (4) don't know

    H. What you read about court cases in newspapers?

    (1) very important,   (2)somewhat important,
    (3) not at all important, (4) don't know

    I. What happens during t.v. programs such as Judge Judy or Judge Joe?

    (1) very important,   (2)somewhat important,
    (3) not at all important, (4) don't know

The previous questions asked your perception, in general, of the courts in your community. Now consider your preliminary perceptions and understanding of the court and judge for whom you will extern. Identify at least five significant roles that your judge performs as part of his or her official duties:

1. _____

2. _____

3. _____

4. _____

5. _____

How would you rate the competence and judicial temperament of the judge for whom you will extern? Use a scale of 1 to 5 with 1 being the lowest and 5 the highest rating; use 3 if you feel neutral.

1.　　Does the judge possess a general working knowledge of the substantive law in the fields that are likely to come before the judge?

2.　　Does the judge possess a good working knowledge of the procedural and evidentiary law of the jurisdiction?

3.　　Are the judge's decisions well reasoned and well thought out?

4.　　Does the judge ask relevant, perceptive questions about matters before him or her?

5.　　Does the judge issue timely rulings and judgments?

6.　　Does the judge generally start trials on the first day they are scheduled to start?

7.　　Is the judge consistently courteous in his or her dealings with others, including counsel, litigants, jurors and staff?

How would you rate the integrity of the judge for whom you will extern? How would you rate the competence of the judge for whom you will extern? Use a scale of 1 to 5 with 1 being the lowest and 5 the highest rating; use 3 if you feel neutral.

1.　　Does the judge decide cases on the facts and law, without consideration of public appeal?

2.　　Does the judge recuse himself or herself whenever his or her impartiality might reasonably be questioned?

From what primary sources do you draw your information for your ratings on competence and integrity?

1. _____

2. _____

3. _____

4. _____

5. _____

Skill Development

Lucia Ann Silecchia

Using the Externship for Skill Development

There are many reasons for doing an externship, and some or all of these reasons may have motivated you. An externship is an excellent way to gain knowledge of a substantive area of law in which you may wish to practice. Likewise, an externship can facilitate your entry into a field of practice by acquainting you with experienced practitioners and by allowing you to experiment in several different work settings to determine where you believe you may be most professionally effective and personally satisfied. An externship is also a good introduction to the legal workplace where you will, perhaps for the first time, deal with many issues of professionalism and on-the-job challenges that will characterize your professional life.

Equally as important, if intelligently selected and diligently pursued, an externship also offers an excellent opportunity to develop professional skills while still in law school. Externships are similar in some respects to the traditional way in which many attorneys were educated prior to the twentieth century—by working in a practitioner's office to learn essential skills. Although American legal education has moved away from this apprenticeship model as the primary means of educating lawyers, this "hands on" learning continues to offer substantial benefits that you will experience in an externship.

Although there are many legal skills that you may wish to sharpen at your externship, this chapter focuses on legal writing and research skills. You are likely to use these two fundamental skills in any type of externship you do. In addition, both of these skills are critical to professional excellence in virtually any type of legal practice. Before turning to writing and research skills, we will discuss some general considerations about learning legal skills at your externship.

Selecting Skills to Develop

Your selection of an externship should be influenced by your consideration of the substantive area of law involved and the skills that a particular externship will allow you to develop. Equally important, you should consider carefully the types of skills you hope to hone during the externship. Some externships will allow you to gain significant experience or practice in

- legal research,
- legal writing,
- legal drafting,
- client interviewing and counseling,
- discovery planning and execution,
- oral advocacy (particularly if you extern in a jurisdiction that provides for supervised law students to represent clients in court),
- policy development,
- witness preparation,
- victim assistance,
- legislative/administrative interpretation, and
- legislative/administrative drafting.

Consider the competencies you hope your externship will help you develop. There are numerous questions you should ask yourself as you analyze your potential externship for the skills training it will provide. Specifically, just as you would ask yourself about the substantive area of law handled at the externship, consider many of the same issues when you evaluate the skills training you will receive there:

- Which skills do you or others perceive as your weakest and, therefore, in the most need of further development?

- Which skills are you least likely to acquire in your other courses in law school?

 Chapter 2
on Setting Goals

- Which externship will provide you with the most direct supervision and feedback as you practice these skills?

- Do any of the placements you are considering have an organized skills training program? What does the formal training program entail and, as an extern, will you be allowed to participate fully?

- Which skills do you most enjoy using and want the opportunity to use more often?

- Which skills will be most valuable to you in the substantive area and practice setting in which you hope to work after graduation? If you are not sure about your post-graduation plans, will the externship offer you training in a wide range of transferable skills that you will be able to use in a variety of settings?

- Which externships will train you in skills that complements those you used at previous externships, anticipated future ones, or both?

As you assess these issues, discuss your concerns with students who have previously externed at places you are considering. Ask them how much of their work time was spent using the skills that interest you the most. How much flexibility were they given in selecting their projects? Were senior employees receptive to teaching and assisting externs? What training—formal or informal—was provided when they were asked to perform an unfamiliar task? What type of feedback and critique was available? Discuss your ideas with your professors—particularly those who teach in the skills curriculum. They will be able to give you their perspectives on the type of training you will need in particular practice areas and whether you will receive it at the externship you are considering.

Exercise 14.1 In 1992, the American Bar Association's Section of Legal Education and Admission to the Bar published a report titled, *Legal Education and Professional Development: An Educational Continuum.* This document, available at http://www.abanet.org/legaled/publications/onlinepubs/maccrate.html, is often referred to as "The MacCrate Report" after Robert MacCrate, the chairperson of the task force that wrote the report. The MacCrate Report discusses, among other things, the place of legal skills in the education of American attorneys. Chapter 5, "The Statement of Fundamental Lawyering Skills and Professional Values," attempts to enumerate the drafters' assessment of the most significant legal skills. Review the Overview of Skills and Values at Chapter 5(B), and reflect on the following questions:

To what extent do you agree that this is an accurate enumeration of the most important skills for attorneys to possess? Are there any skills you would delete from the list or add to it?

To which of the skills on the Overview of Skills and Values have you already been exposed in your law school classes? To which have you had no introduction? Will this affect your choice of externship? Should it?

In your opinion, what should be the role, if any, of law schools in teaching skills and values? How can they best accomplish this? How does your law school teach skills and values? How effective is this training? Where, beyond law school, might legal skills and values be effectively taught?

What opportunities does your law school provide to enable you to further develop the skills you will learn at your externship? If you were to make curricular recommendations to enhance your law school's skills training, what would you suggest and why?

Exercise 14.2 Interview three attorneys from various types of practice and at different stages in their careers. Obtain information from each of them about developing legal skills:

What legal skills have they found to be the most important for their success? See if their answers vary by practice type and if they mention any "skills" that you have not yet thought of as legal skills.

How did they learn the skills they needed? Through law school courses? Law school extracurricular activities like moot court? Practice experience? A mentor or advisor? Continuing legal education courses? Trial and error? Which activities did they find most helpful in acquiring the necessary skills for their practices?

If they were in law school now, what advice would they like to receive about developing skills while in law school?

As they observe entry-level attorneys, what are the skills they believe are most lacking, and what recommendations do they have for acquiring them? How do they assist new attorneys in enhancing their practice skills?

Once you have selected an externship and considered the skill development opportunities it will provide, your next task is to ensure that you receive adequate training in the skills you wish to develop. An essential component of this requires eliciting effective supervision, which is discussed in Chapter 3. There are, however, a number of steps you can take independently to ensure that the skills training you receive at your externship fulfills your needs and expectations. Although your fieldwork supervisor should play a large part in this, *you* should take the initiative to ensure that you will not be disappointed in the skills training you receive.

see Chapter 3
on Getting Supervision

First, review the skills you listed as priorities when seeking your externship. Ask yourself whether the externship you selected is a realistic place in which to develop them. Early during your externship, share your list with your fieldwork supervisor. Both of you should identify one or two projects that you can undertake to practice each skill. Your assignments will vary as the externship progresses and you are required to respond to the needs—anticipated and unanticipated—of the office. Be realistic in your expectations of how your needs and the needs of your office are best balanced.

Although it may not be possible at your first meeting to earmark a project for each of the skills in which you have an interest, it is still important to make the list so that you can watch for opportunities. Moreover, your preliminary list will change as the needs of the office change and as new opportunities arise. By preparing this informal skills "syllabus," you and your fieldwork supervisor will be more sensitive to opportunities and more aware of whether the mix of assignments you receive is well suited to the skills training you desire.

After your plan is in place and you begin working on your projects, make sure that you are getting both guidance and feedback. *Guidance* is the advice and counsel you receive as you are working on your projects. Although the ability to work independently is a valuable skill, it is also important to receive appropriate guidance. Ask yourself the following questions:

see Chapter 3
on Getting Supervision

- When given an assignment, do you get sufficient clarification of the assignment? Do you ask questions about the scope of the task, the time frame in which you must work, the major pitfalls about which you should be aware, the work others in the office already have done on the project, and the substantive background you might need? Keep in mind that the openness of supervisors to fielding questions may depend on the workplace's culture and the amount of work that must be handled. See if you can sense how questions will be received by your supervisors as you plan the ways in which you will seek their guidance.

- Do you know when and where your fieldwork supervisor will be available to answer questions about your project as they arise? Is there anyone in the office other than your supervisor who might offer you guidance?

- Are there any logical pieces into which you can divide your project so that you can make an interim progress report to your fieldwork supervisor?

- Are you keeping notes about your progress so that you can discuss them later with your fieldwork supervisor? For example, maintaining a record of people you consulted for information, theories you explored and then discarded, and research sources you reviewed, will make it easier for you to receive guidance from your supervisor. Always keep a record of where your research has taken you. This will help you to avoid repeating yourself if time elapses between different stages of your research, be extremely valuable if you pass your project to someone else when you leave the externship, provide clues if you run into a "dead end," and protect you if anyone raises questions about the adequacy of your research. Careful research notes can also help you avoid the frustration of having the "perfect" answer, failing to make a note of it, and lamenting to your client or supervisor, "I *know* I saw it *somewhere*!"

Over time, you will begin to develop instincts that will guide you as to when you should be able to do a project independently and when this independence should be tempered with necessary requests for guidance and assistance. The externship is intended to be an educational experience for you. Thus, you should generally err on the side of requesting more guidance rather than less.

In addition to guidance, you should receive appropriate *feedback*. Although there is some overlap between guidance and feedback, feedback is the honest appraisal of your work after it is essentially completed. Seeking this critique may be difficult at times, particularly if you are not pleased with your work or if it was part of an unsuccessful effort on behalf of a client or cause. You should try to get as much information from your supervisor as you can about the quality of your work in order to improve it.

Schedule regular meetings during the externship so that you and your fieldwork supervisor can discuss the development of your skills. Outline your questions in advance and ask what you can do to improve future work rather than merely review completed projects. Also, focus on learning about trends in your performance. Are old problems improving? Are you discovering new skills you did not know you had? Are there additional areas in which you would like experience that you had not anticipated?

In most law school classes, the syllabus is presented to you by an instructor who has already defined the educational goals and the means for achieving them. In an externship, planning the syllabus is, to a large extent, your responsibility. It will be your plan, made in conjunction with your fieldwork supervisor, that will determine whether you have achieved your goals. So be serious as you undertake this "curricular design."

Exercise 14.3 You have just received the following assignment from a supervisor:

Our client, Mary Murphy, signed a covenant not to compete when she left her dental practice. This agreement provided that she would not open another dental practice within fifty miles of the former one for ten years after leaving the practice. Mary has moved forty-five miles away and wants to open a part-time cosmetic dental practice. She is afraid this may cause some problems with her former practice group, but she still wants to go ahead and do it. Let us know if Mary can do what she wants to do.

List any additional information or guidance you would seek before beginning this assignment. What else should you know before proceeding? Is the project so vague that it needs clarification before you begin your work? If so, how?

Connecting Skills Training at the Externship with Skills Training in the Classroom

You will not be doing your externship in an academic vacuum. It will be surrounded by semesters in which you have no externship experience. Most likely, you will also be taking other more traditional law school courses during the semester you do your externship, and/or you may be taking a practicum course in conjunction with your externship. Your externship credits may represent a numerically small percentage of your overall law school experience, despite the externship's significance to you personally and professionally.

As you plan your skill development at the externship, examine your law school's skills curriculum to see what courses will complement or supplement the skills learned at your externship. Your review may lead you to select an externship that exposes you to skills that are not introduced in your law school classes. You may decide, instead, to pursue an externship that will allow you to build on a set of skills in which you already have talent or training. Whichever way you choose, recognize the importance of integrating your externship with your law school studies and viewing the externship in context.

- Thus far, what skills-based courses have you taken?

- What skills did those courses aim to teach?

- How confident do you feel about your abilities in those skill areas to which you have been exposed?

- What type of personalized feedback have you received in your previous skills classes?

- Which skills will you have the opportunity to refine at your externship?

- What additional skills-based courses does your law school offer that you have not taken?

- What skills do these additional courses aim to teach?

- Which of these courses, if any, are you planning to take? In what sequence?

- Will these courses introduce you to skills that your externship did not cover or give you a post-externship opportunity to refine skills introduced by your externship? Which is more important to you?

- Are you planning to do any additional externships, in-house clinics, or simulation courses in later semesters? Is there any particular order in which you should take these courses to ensure that you gain the most from them and do your best work at each one?

Among the skills used by practicing attorneys, the most common (in the sense that most attorneys use them) and the most fundamental (in a foundational sense) are legal writing and legal research. The remainder of this chapter focuses on those two critical skills.

Using an Externship to Develop Legal Writing Skills

Almost any externship will expose you to the skills required for effective written communication. Attorneys write in many different genres and careful selection of your externship will help ensure that you gain experience writing a variety of documents such as office memos, briefs, motions, wills, statutes, regulations, advice letters, legal publications, correspondence, and judicial opinions, to name but a few.

You are likely to enter your externship after completing a legal writing course in your first year of law school. Therefore, these materials will not review in detail the fundamentals covered there but will give you some pointers on ways in which you can gain the most from your practice in writing at your externship. Every project you do will be different, but the basic qualities of good writing will remain constant.

If your first-year background was solid, your externship will sharpen these skills and make them more sophisticated in the way that only practice can. If you feel that your skills in this area are weak, use your externship experience to find a writing mentor to assist you in becoming a critical editor of your work product. There also are some excellent legal writing texts that can assist you in becoming a clear and effective legal writer. Some of these are listed in the suggestions for further reading at the end of this chapter.

The writing you do at your externship may be of many different types. You may be asked to do objective, **analytical writing** in which you address a subject and, in a nonpartisan way, fully address the legal issues involved and provide an unbiased discussion of the legal issue. Or you may be asked to do **advocacy writing** in which you take a position on behalf of your client and argue it forcefully. Alternatively, you may be asked to engage in **legal drafting**. In drafting, you create a document that will have some legal effect—a contract, a lease, a will, a set of interrogatories. You may often be called on to write more informal—yet critically important—documents in the form of interoffice e-mails or memoranda. Whether these documents are printed in "hard copy" on letterhead or transmitted in an e-mail, they deserve your professional best. As you write all these types of documents, the following checklists might help you to become your own best editor.

Checklist for Objective Analytical Writing

In objective analytical writing, regardless of its level of formality, your central goal is to evaluate an issue by presenting a full analysis of the issues without arguing the position of either party to a dispute. In critiquing your objective writing, ask yourself the following questions *before* submitting your draft to your supervisor:

- Does the document have a theme? What is its goal? Is the organizational scheme chosen the best way to accomplish that goal? Are there any ideas that logically should be discussed in sequence, in groups, or chronologically? If so, has this been done?

- Are the component parts of the paper raised in an order that makes sense? Do the parts follow logically from each other so that the transitions between them are smooth and clear?

- Generally, is the more important information in the beginning of the paper? That is, does the beginning of the piece give enough background to put the rest of the discussion in context? Does it avoid giving too *much* background, or information best left for fuller discussion later?

- Does the opening paragraph(s) make the paper's main point clear? Does it establish the thesis, goal, or argument of the paper? In legal writing, readers generally appreciate knowing where they will be led.

- Is there any overlap in the coverage of various sections? Are any of the sections redundant?

- Is the difficulty or detail level of the material presented appropriate to the audience?

- Is there adequate authority to support each section? Does any section have any unsupported assertions?

- Are transitional sections provided as necessary?

- Are the subheadings detailed enough to be effective signposts to a reader traveling through the paper? Are the subheadings consistent? Is the same grammatical structure and the same letter or number system used for all the subheadings? Is the punctuation in the headings and subheadings correct?

- Is the typeface—font size? underlining? bold? italics? plain?—consistent throughout?

- Does each individual paragraph have a single, clear purpose? Is that purpose established in a lead sentence? Is the lead sentence a good *roadmap* for the rest of the paragraph? Conversely, does the lead sentence provide a jarring signpost such as, "This paragraph will discuss . . . ." Be clear, but be subtle.

- Do all of the sentences in each paragraph help to support the main idea of the lead sentence or do they address other tangents?

- Do any paragraphs attempt to discuss too many unrelated ideas? Should any be divided? Conversely, should any be combined with an earlier or later paragraph?

- Do any paragraphs end abruptly without a clear finish?

- Is each paragraph appropriately placed within the paper? Is each preceded by and followed by appropriate transitions to guide readers from one thought to another?

- Is each paragraph properly divided into sentences? Do the sentences vary in length? Are there any run-on or incomplete sentences?

- Are quotations used judiciously? Are they overused, misused, unattributed, or cut-and-pasted? Are any taken out of context? Is the punctuation surrounding the quotation correct? Is the quotation accurately taken from the primary source? Is anything paraphrased too closely to the original? Sources for *ideas* must be cited even if the *text* is not closely paraphrased.

- Are pinpoint cites used appropriately? If a string cite is used, are all authorities in the proper order and with the proper signals?

- Is the tone appropriate to the subject matter and consistent throughout the paper? Is anything written in a way that is too informal or casual?

- Is the vocabulary used appropriate to the subject, genre, and audience?

- Are there any exaggerations? Is your opinion expressed appropriately and correctly identified as opinion rather than fact?

- Are there any sentences that are simply awkward and should be reworked? When read aloud, do the paragraphs sound logical, well-ordered, and grammatical?

- Are there any "sentences" that lack a subject, a verb, or the ability to stand on their own as independent sentences?

- Are there any sentences that should be divided because they contain too many clauses?

- Are there any unnecessary words? Avoid being verbose, and try to be as succinct as possible.

- Is there any unnecessary jargon, legalese, or technical language? When legal terms of art are necessary, are they used correctly and accurately?

- Are commas used appropriately? Is the spelling and punctuation correct? Remember, computer spell checking programs and grammar checks will not catch all of your errors. (In fact, they may generate new errors!) You *must* proofread your work manually.

- Do subjects and verbs always agree?

- Is the often misused apostrophe used correctly? It is *not* used to make plurals; it *is* used to show possession.

- Are all typeface conventions correct?

- Is *The Bluebook* form followed perfectly?

- Are any words overused or misused? Are the clearest words always used? Are there times when one active word will express the same idea as multiple words?

- Are there any cliches or colloquialisms? Are there any contractions? These typically are *not* appropriate in formal legal writing.

- Is there always parallel structure?

- Have you used double negatives? These should be eliminated for the sake of clarity.

- Are there capital letters where appropriate and small letters when those are appropriate?

- Are the required formalities—font size, margin size, page limits, court clerk requirements, etc.—strictly followed?

- Has your supervisor expressed any preference as to stylistic or formatting issues that may be relevant to the document you are preparing? If so, have you complied with those requests?

Checklist for Advocacy Writing

In contrast to objective analytical writing, advocacy writing entails taking a position and arguing it from the perspective of a particular client seeking to achieve a specific goal. Within the constraints of legal ethics, the boundaries of applicable law, and the form of the documents that you are creating, your advocacy writing should convince a reader to adopt your position. As you edit your own advocacy writing, ask the following questions:

- Which pointers in the "Checklist for Objective Writing" apply with equal force to persuasive advocacy writing? Many of them do. Have you complied with them?

- Almost every part of an advocacy document can be used to advance your position. Have you left any sections bland and neutral?

- Are there careless errors, technical inconsistencies, or poor style in your document? These can undermine your credibility with those you wish to persuade.

- If your document includes an account of the facts of the dispute, have you

  — presented the facts in the light most favorable to your position?

  — complied with your ethical responsibilities to avoid factual misrepresentations or material omissions?

  — selected the words you use carefully? Words are powerful tools in the hands of a skilled wordsmith. Consider, for example, the very different effects these two accounts of the same event have:

    Defendant sped around the dark corner by the playground and plowed into seven-year-old Alyson Hills as she attempted to cross Park Street.

    Plaintiff was struck by defendant's vehicle at the intersection of Howe and Park streets.

How is the impact of each different?

- Is your argument well-organized so that you have an effective argument at the beginning as well as a powerful conclusion?

- Have you used authority effectively? Refer to the facts of your case to demonstrate how the law you claim should be applied in a certain way will apply to your facts. You are not writing a detached scholarly article on the subject but are trying to guide a decision maker to a particular resolution of an actual controversy. Have you bridged the gap between the applicable law and your facts?

- Have you done anything to undermine your credibility such as exaggerate, use authority out of context, or attack your adversary before establishing your own position? You can be persuasive only if you win the trust of your reader.

- Have you used point headings effectively to assert affirmatively the salient points of your argument?

- Have you clearly identified the relief that you are seeking on behalf of your client?

- Is your tone appropriate—an effective blend between forceful advocacy and calm, respectful, rational analysis?

For further guidance on the particular challenges of argumentative writing, you may find the suggestions for further reading at the end of this chapter to be helpful.

Checklist for Legal Drafting

Legal drafting is a type of writing in which the documents themselves have legal effect. You may still be creative in drafting, but within significantly greater constraints than other types of legal writing. Attorneys often consult form books (in hard copy or online) as a starting place for their drafting projects, but they must be careful not to over-rely on them. Form books may not provide samples that comply with all the current requirements of the law in your jurisdiction. They may not meet the clients' specific needs, offer the clearest wording for particular provisions, or make provisions for unusual or complex circumstances. A good drafter looks at form book forms critically and edits or tailors them for particular uses.

As you review or undertake a drafting project, consider the following:

- Are you familiar with the substantive law in the field and your specific jurisdiction's legal requirements for the documents you are drafting?

- Have you used form books and boilerplate judiciously? Form books do not present legally binding versions of any documents. These models generally are drafted by employees of publishers and may not comply with the statutory requirements. In addition, because the law may change quickly, an outdated form book can create serious drafting problems.

- Do you fully understand the special needs or wishes of your particular client? Does the document you are drafting accommodate those specific needs and wishes?

- Have you been cautious about re-using portions of any documents used in a previous project? The law can change quite rapidly, making older documents obsolete. Furthermore, the needs of a previous client may be slightly and subtly different from your present case so that there will not be a good "fit" between the language in the old document and the one you are currently drafting.

- Have you compared your document to the current statutory or legal requirements of your jurisdiction to ensure that it accomplishes its goals?

- Without sacrificing accuracy or precision, is the document written in a clear and straightforward style that can be easily understood by lay readers?

- Do the terms of the document resolve all problems that you anticipate? Does it contain any ambiguities that may lead to future conflicts or litigation?

- Finally, are there any pointers in the "Checklist for Objective Writing" or "Checklist for Advocacy Writing" that apply with equal force to drafting? Have you complied with them?

You should note that many of these pointers may apply to the context of legislative or administrative drafting as well. For further guidance in document drafting, check the suggestions for further reading at the end of this chapter.

Being an Ethical Writer

Lawyers have ethical obligations with respect to all of their work, including written documents. Thus, attorneys must learn not merely how to be skilled legal researchers and writers but also how to be ethical and professional ones. In the practice of law, these obligations include honesty to the tribunal, client, and others in matters of fact and law; accuracy and fairness in representing the state of the law; thoroughness of research; clarity of expression; communication appropriate to the level of the intended audience; professionalism and decorum in written communication, particularly to adversaries; fairness in characterization of facts; complete citation to authority where appropriate; and attention to the details of the craft of writing.

Your ethical responsibilities will affect your drafting of a variety of documents, including motions, briefs, contracts, leases, letters to clients and adversaries, interoffice memos, settlement agreements, discovery requests, interrogatories, and fee agreements. As you work at your externship, be conscious of these issues and explore them with your supervisors.

Exercise 14.4 Select an argumentative paper that you have written for your externship, a moot court competition, a law school class, or a legal job. With appropriate consideration of client confidentiality (if the document you are using is a "real" one), exchange this paper with another student. Edit each other's work, using the questions on the checklist above as the basis for your critique.

Exercise 14.5 Repeat Exercise 14.4, working with an objective, analytical piece of writing.

Exercise 14.6 Take the very last legal document you have drafted—a project for your externship, a law school examination, a course paper, a law review note, etc. Select any five pages from it and line-edit it carefully to see how you might improve your writing style. You may well have written the original document under the pressures of time and deadlines. Free of those pressures, see how much editing it takes to create your best possible work.

Exercise 14.7 Return to the problem of Mary Murphy's covenant not to compete, described in Exercise 14.3. Assume now that you are the person who drafted the original covenant, rather than the one assessing its merits. Draft a covenant not to compete that 1) provides the dental partnership with the most protection permissible in your jurisdiction to prohibit former partners from competing and 2) avoids as much future litigation as possible. Then review your draft using the guidelines in the checklist to see how successful you were.

Exercise 14.8 Obtain a copy of the ethical rules governing attorneys in the jurisdiction in which you are working. Review it to see how many of its provisions govern lawyers' conduct in their writing activities.

Using an Externship to Develop Legal Research Skills

A significant part of your externship experience may be spent conducting legal research. Your knowledge of the underlying substantive law will come only from the ability to do good legal research. Although your law school studies will have familiarized you with many fundamentals of the substantive law, the issues you will encounter at your externship are likely to be far more focused and detailed, and will require research into highly specialized, fact-specific questions you have not previously considered. In practice, unlike in law school, your research will be accompanied by constraints on time and costs that will require you to aim for efficiency as well as accuracy and reliability. Another difference you may find is that, in practice, collaborative research is encouraged rather than prohibited. You may find that much of your research comes from other people as well as the library. Use your externship to develop your basic research skills and to explore the differences between academic research and research in a "real world" setting.

Before you begin your externship, review your legal research skills to refresh your memory of legal research techniques that you may not use often, and familiarize yourself with research tools you may not have learned about in your basic research course. Some texts listed in the suggestions for further reading at the end of this chapter may be useful references for you as you do this.

Once you are comfortable with the basics of legal research, remember that you will not do your work by using specific legal resources in a vacuum. Rather, you should create a research plan for each of your projects. Such plans ensure that in the course of your research you have consulted all those sources that are likely to bring you to the correct answer within the time constraints imposed on you. In addition, a good research plan will ensure that you are being efficient. An effective research plan is synergistic, with each reference you consult leading you to others. Thus, planning the order in which you consult various sources also is important. It is also critically important to understand any limitations on research imposed by your supervisor, due to the cost of various specialized research tools.

The research plan you follow will vary from project to project. Seek the guidance of those with whom you work to learn their techniques and ask them for effective shortcuts. For example, there may be a deskbook or a practice guide consulted regularly by local practitioners, or a treatise geared to your jurisdiction. Similarly, if at your externship you are doing a lot of work in a specialized area—tax, environmental law, international law, securities law, to name just a few—there will be many specialized sources heavily used by practitioners in those fields to which you may not have had much exposure. Devote some time early in the externship to learning about these sources:

- Plan a meeting with one of your colleagues or fieldwork supervisors to discuss research techniques frequently used in the practice and ask for guidance.

- If there is a law librarian employed at your externship, ask the librarian for a tutorial on sources unfamiliar to you.

- Consult your LEXIS® or WESTLAW® account representative to see if there are any specialized online research seminars offered in your area. Both companies sponsor topical training sessions for students and may hold free classes that will assist you.

- As you receive a new project, ask if your supervisor has any research leads for you. Five minutes spent in such a discussion may save you hours in research time lost by false leads or dead ends.

- Learn how to use the Internet effectively. The explosion of information now available through the Internet is quickly changing the face of legal research. Some materials are available only online or are more current online. To the extent you can, use your research experience during your externship to use Internet research in a practice setting and discover when its use is beneficial. Also, learn how to be critical of the information you find online. While Internet sources certainly increase the *quantity* of information available, they also make available much information that is of dubious *quality*. Thus, as you conduct your research, learn how to sort the reliable information from that which is inaccurate and unreliable.

LEXIS® and WESTLAW® are probably the most used and misused research tools. In contrast to your law school, the office in which you do your externship will not have free access to either system. An important part of your task is to discover how to use them cost-effectively, how to determine when manual research will be more effective, and how to use computer-assisted legal research ("CALR") to supplement—but not to replace—your manual research. In addition, you also should consider whether there are any free online resources that may be useful and economical.

While at your externship, keep two caveats in mind as you use CALR. First, the LEXIS® and WESTLAW® passwords you received at school are for educational use only. Legal and ethical responsibilities limit your ability to use these passwords to school-related activities. Be wary of supervisors who may pressure you to use your student password for their business uses. Second, do not use either system until you know what policy governs the use of CALR in your office. Some externships may encourage frequent use, while others may require pre-approval or authorize use of these systems only after other research leads have been exhausted.

Once you have done a preliminary review of the research methods with which you should be familiar, be conscious of your research techniques as you create a plan for each project you undertake. Use your externship to develop your research skills by focusing on the process of research and the results. Create a research plan as you begin each project and then, armed with your plan, set out to do the research necessary. The following sample research plan outlines the various elements of legal research.

Phase One: Factual Research

Before you begin a legal research assignment, be sure that you have a complete grasp of the facts surrounding the problem for which you will be doing your research. There are many ways to explore facts. For example, you can

- review all documents relevant to the project. As an extern, it is very likely that you will work on cases that arose before you began your work. The attorneys with whom you work will be familiar with the prior record in the case. Ask if you can review the documents underlying the dispute, client correspondence, litigation documents filed in the case, and, if this is an appeal, the lower court records.

- interview clients, witnesses, potential experts, and others. As you gather information, be aware of the "spin" and bias each person is likely to put on the event. Be careful not to disclose confidential information in conversations with non-clients.

- learn as much as you can about the factual debate that may underlie the legal research you are undertaking. For example, if you are working for a public interest environmental law firm attempting to have a new animal added to the Endangered Species list, learn how to do the scientific research needed to ascertain the correct facts about current threats to the animal's habitats. What sources are the most accurate? Which resources are non-partisan and scientifically neutral? Which sources will be most persuasive to your adversaries?

Phase Two: Background Information

Generally, good research should begin with research into the primary sources of law. The primary sources are the only ones that will be binding, and you will want to review them without being unduly influenced by the views of others. If you are new to the field, however, it may be helpful to gather some information about the substantive law so that you know the relevant terminology and are better able to identify potential legal issues. You also may want to read through some of these resources prior to starting your externship so that you can be a more active participant in the discussions at and activities of your office. Some places you may look for this background information include the following:

Familiarizing yourself with **legal encyclopedias** will be easy since they are similar in structure and purpose to traditional encyclopedias. They are comprised of multi-volume sets of alphabetically arranged articles about various legal subjects that can provide helpful overviews of the relevant areas of law. Note that the articles contained in legal encyclopedias are rarely in-depth or analytical. Encyclopedias may state a general rule that is not applicable to your jurisdiction or outline a rule that is too broad to be particularly helpful. Nonetheless, these articles can help acquaint you with a new field of law and provide cross-references to primary sources in the field. There are two major legal encyclopedias, both published by Thomson-West, with which you should become familiar: CORPUS JURIS SECUNDUM and AMERICAN JURISPRUDENCE. In addition, many states have their own encyclopedias (for example, N.Y. JUR.).

A **treatise** is a scholarly commentary about a particular area of law that is written by an expert in the field. These treatises can be single volume or multi-volume. They may address a very broad area of law or a very narrow topic. They may be old classics in the field or new commentaries on a developing area of law. In any event, they can help provide background information about a particular field and outline the case law and statutory law so that you will have a place to begin your work. While treatises are secondary sources and should never be confused with binding authority, some treatises and their authors are highly respected. When you use treatises, be sure to look to your library's most current edition. Some treatises are updated with pocket parts. Keep in mind that there can be considerable lag time between when a book is written and when it is published. A law librarian or a professor in the relevant substantive field can acquaint you with the most authoritative and relevant treatises in your particular practice niche. Some treatises are available online as well.

Legal periodicals may be more current than other sources. Periodical articles, particularly law review articles, tend to be well researched and contain footnotes that can lead you to other sources. The key to using legal periodicals effectively is mastering the indices that will lead you to relevant articles. There are three major ways in which to find legal periodicals: use of the *Index to Legal Periodicals*, use of the *Current Law Index*, and use of the online databases of LEXIS® and WESTLAW®. In addition, some of the indices appear on CD-ROM, which may be more convenient or current. Acquaint yourself with these different methods of locating articles. In addition, a general Internet search may uncover some relevant secondary materials—albeit in a more haphazard way.

A.L.R. Annotations are, essentially, compilations of cases on various topics organized in annotated notes that collect summaries of decisions from assorted jurisdictions on a single legal topic. If you find an A.L.R. annotation that addresses the legal issue you are researching, it can be a good research lead that will save you time. The quickest way to see if there is an A.L.R. annotation for your topic is to look up your subject in the "Index to Annotations," a set of bound volumes that provides a subject matter list of all annotations from all sets of A.L.R. Be sure to check the most recent supplements that you can find, so you can insure that the cases you find are current. A.L.R. Annotations also are available online, and you may search for a relevant A.L.R. Annotation online as well.

Your externship will be an excellent opportunity to familiarize yourself with **looseleaf services**—sources used often by practitioners in highly specialized fields, but more rarely in academic research. Essentially, looseleaf services are a "hybrid" research tool, containing both primary and secondary sources. These services are devoted to specific subject areas of law and are designed to give practitioners in that field a comprehensive compilation of source material. A looseleaf service, unlike more traditional sources, will contain cases from different jurisdictions, administrative decisions, regulations, legal commentary, and proposed regulations. Looseleaf services can be confusing to use until you become familiar with them. Take the time to acquaint yourself with the organization of those services that you are likely to use most often. A good way to learn how to use a particular looseleaf is to read the "How to Use This Service" section, which usually appears in the front of the index to the service. Many of these looseleaf services also are available online, where they may be more frequently updated.

By exploring some of these resources, you should become equipped to move on to the heart of your research: the search for the primary research that will let you know what the law governing your problem is and what will be binding in your jurisdiction.

Phase Three: Primary Law Research

Research should include, where relevant, the following primary areas of legal authority:

- Constitutions: Federal and State

- Statutes: Federal, State, Local

- Cases: Federal, State, Local

- Local Ordinances

- Administrative Regulations: Federal, State, Local

- Administrative Adjudications: Federal, State, Local

- Procedural Rules: Civil, Criminal, Administrative, Probate

- Treaties

Many primary materials are available through different sources, including online, so you must understand the different places to find these laws and determine which ones are easiest to access, best indexed, most current, and most economical to use.

Phase Four: Update and Verify

As you know, the law that was current yesterday may no longer be good law today. Therefore, a substantial part of your research responsibility lies in ensuring that the law you find is still binding and reflects the most current version of the law. This requires you to be diligent about updating your research through the use of pocket parts, *Shepard's Citations* (available for cases, statutes, administrative regulations, legal periodicals, ordinances), computer assisted case citators, "lists of sections affected" tables in the regulatory codes, and other methods for updating.

You always must update your research at the very last stage to account for any last minute changes in the law, but it is also wise to update as you go along. This will help you to avoid wasting time developing a theory based on law that is no longer valid.

Phase Five: Secondary Sources

While you may consult secondary sources early to give you some background in the field, you should do your substantial secondary research after you have a good handle on the primary sources. Return to the sources discussed earlier and do a diligent search through the secondary sources on your topic. This will help you find other primary sources, such as cases you may have overlooked. It will also provide you with different perspectives and opinions on the law that you may not have considered.

Phase Six: Non-legal Research

In your legal writing course you may have mastered the use of a law library and the tools of legal research. Skill in this area is essential for successful practice, but not all the answers you need will be available in the law library. Non-legal research may be required. For example, in a products liability case you may have to do engineering research. To prepare for a criminal prosecution, you may have to make psychiatric inquiries. In legislative drafting, you may have to do some social science research. In negotiating a real estate contract, you may have to do architectural research. As you do your research, keep searching for ways in which material from outside the law library may help you make or bolster a point. Because you may have less training in non-legal research than in legal research, this phase of your research will benefit particularly from the assistance of librarians and outside experts.

Phase Seven: Update and Verify Again

Your research will vary significantly depending on the substance and scope of your problem. At the same time, many of the basic essentials will be uniform. A well-designed research plan should move you in a circle, with each source referring you back to sources you have already consulted. When you reach this point, you may conclude that your research is close to completion.

Exercise 14.9 Write out a research plan that you might use for any one of the following projects. Be as detailed as possible:

You are externing for an appellate judge in your state court system. An attorney is appealing a lower court order of sanctions against him for misconduct during the trial. To assist the judge in deciding the appeal, you want to know the standard of review for such sanctions. What research might you do?

[handwritten note: westlaw law library]

You are externing in a solo practitioner's office. You have been asked to research the extent to which the board of directors of a condominium association may make emergency repairs to a privately owned unit in the building and finance it through the association's funds. What research might you do?

[handwritten note: go to condo to find documents + contacts]

You are externing for the legal department of a national trade association representing chemical manufacturers. Your supervisor has asked you to prepare a ten-page summary of "last year's major legal developments of concern to our members." What research might you do?

[handwritten note: look for similar documents in the office prepared in the past]

You are externing for an insurance company's legal department. The company provides the malpractice insurance for a physician who made a serious surgical error while operating under the influence of an illegal intoxicant. You have been asked to research whether the insurance company may deny coverage for the incident. What research might you do?

[handwritten note: westlaw]

You are externing for a large firm's litigation department, assisting in the defense of a product liability case in which your client has been accused of selling paint that contains solvents that pose a health risk to children. You have been asked to find an expert witness. What factual *and* legal research might you do?

[handwritten note: doctors who have testified before]

Select a project that you have been assigned from your externship. What research might you do?

As your research nears completion, you may find yourself concerned about the amount of time your research is requiring. Your first forays into research in a new area will take more time than you might have anticipated and, perhaps, more time than your colleagues, clients or supervisor expect. As a general rule, because your externship is a learning opportunity for you, direct your attention to learning *accuracy* and *thoroughness* in research. With time, *efficiency* will follow, particularly if you do subsequent projects in the same field. Reflect at the end of each project about how you might have approached it differently.

Be wary of the temptation to research too quickly. Rushing can lead to incorrect answers that will call into question the integrity of your work. Even if you are lucky and make no apparent mistakes, you may lay the foundation for shoddy research habits that will be hard to change. With this caveat in mind, you might still use your externship to begin exploring research efficiency. To assist you in being more efficient, consider the following:

- When you get a new research project, ask your fieldwork supervisor or another colleague what sources they would consult first. Very often specific areas of law have particular resources that can be wonderful timesavers but that you would not know of unless you worked in that area.

- If there are law librarians at your externship, get to know them as soon as possible. They can assist you in developing an effective research plan. The librarians at your law school library might also be able to offer you advice and guidance on research in particular substantive areas of law.

- Keep track of the actual time you spend on your research. After you have completed your research, discuss with your supervisor or a trusted colleague both the steps you took in your research and the amount of time it took you. Ask for suggestions on improving your efficiency.

- Identify any specific type of research with which you had particular difficulty, such as computer-assisted legal research, the Internet, legislative history, or a specific looseleaf service. Try to arrange additional training in the use of that particular resource.

Conclusion

Your externship may provide an opportunity to learn or further develop your legal writing and research skills, as well as a panoply of other skills. No two externship experiences will be the same, and each will provide you with a very different educational opportunity. With planning and a commitment to take the initiative required, you should leave your externship closer to your goal of being a skilled and competent practitioner.

FURTHER READING

Legal Writing and Analysis

MICHAEL A. BERCH, *et al.*, INTRODUCTION TO LEGAL METHOD AND PROCESS (4th ed. 2006). Although this text is not, strictly speaking, a text in legal writing, it offers a helpful and highly readable introduction to legal reasoning skills, which underlie successful legal writing.

JOHN BRONSTEEN, WRITING A LEGAL MEMO (2006). This succinct little book provides a full introduction to writing a successful legal memorandum. Since this is a legal document quite likely to be among a junior attorney's first assignments, this may prove to be a helpful reference source for an entry-level externship.

CHARLES R. CALLEROS, LEGAL METHOD & WRITING (5th ed. 2006). An excellent writing text, this book explores in detail the basic principles of legal writing as well as the writing of specific documents such as office memoranda, pleadings, motions, briefs, contracts, and advice and demand letters.

VEDA R. CHARROW, *et al.*, CLEAR & EFFECTIVE LEGAL WRITING (3d ed. 2001). This text progresses from a general discussion of written legal materials, to a broad overview of basic principles of writing, to instruction on creating specific types of legal documents. It is particularly recommended as a "self-help" resource for legal writers because of its extensive set of exercises and appendix of exercises on sentence structure and grammatical proficiency.

BRADLEY G. CLARY & PAMELA LYSAGHT, SUCCESSFUL LEGAL ANALYSIS AND WRITING: THE FUNDAMENTALS (2d ed. 2006). This text includes helpful chapters on legal writing for both "prediction" and "persuasion." It is particularly useful in the extensive treatment it gives to citation form.

LINDA H. EDWARDS, LEGAL WRITING: PROCESS AND ANALYSIS (2003). This comprehensive guide to legal writing contains two particularly helpful sections: one on writing "predictively" (analytically) and one on writing "persuasively." For each of these units, the author provides comprehensive details about each aspect of predictive and persuasive documents, as well as an extensive set of exercises to assist the reader in active learning. The book also includes a very helpful collection of appendices that contain sample documents that will be of assistance to novice legal writers. In addition, this text includes sections on the legal system, writing formalities, and oral advocacy.

ANNE ENQUIST & LAUREL CURRIE OATES, JUST WRITING: GRAMMAR, PUNCTUATION, AND STYLE FOR THE LEGAL WRITER (2d ed. 2005). This text provides an excellent overview of many technical aspects of legal writing. It also includes a special section for legal writers for whom English is a second language.

ELIZABETH FAJANS, *et al.*, WRITING FOR LAW PRACTICE (2d ed. 2006). This text includes sections (complete with exercises) that cover basic writing skills, as well as sections devoted to in-depth coverage of complaints, answers, motions, letters of various types, office memoranda, trial and appellate briefs, judicial opinions, legislation, contracts, and wills. It is particularly helpful for those preparing for externships in that it covers documents that are not frequently covered in the basic law school legal writing class.

MARGARET Z. JOHNS, PROFESSIONAL WRITING FOR LAWYERS: SKILLS AND RESPONSIBILITIES (1998). This book, geared to practitioners rather than to students, is organized around legal documents and contains chapters devoted to offering guidance on an array of common legal documents, including the office memorandum, client letters, demand letters, complaints, motions, and appellate briefs. Much attention is devoted to questions of professional responsibility and to the oft-neglected art of rewriting legal documents.

TERRI LECLERCQ, GUIDE TO LEGAL WRITING STYLE (3d ed. 2004). A reference book for both students and practitioners, this guide includes materials on common stylistic issues.

RICHARD K. NEUMANN, JR., LEGAL REASONING & LEGAL WRITING: STRUCTURE, STRATEGY & STYLE (5th ed. 2005). In addition to providing a detailed discussion of office memoranda, law school examinations, motions, and trial briefs, this text describes the differences between objective and persuasive writing. In addition, it contains a clear and succinct guide to "24 Rules of Punctuation," helpful for both novice and experienced legal writers.

DIANA V. PRATT, LEGAL WRITING: A SYSTEMATIC APPROACH (4th ed. 2004). This text provides in-depth instruction in writing a number of types of legal documents: office memoranda, trial briefs, and appellate briefs. Also included is an appendix providing sample documents.

MARY BARNARD RAY, THE BASICS OF LEGAL WRITING (2006). An easy-to-follow text that can serve as an excellent review for those whose legal writing skills are weak, or those for whom it has been some time since their basic legal writing course. This book contains many examples and exercises to foster interactive learning.

MARY BARNARD RAY & BARBARA J. COX, BEYOND THE BASICS: A TEXT FOR ADVANCED LEGAL WRITINGS (2d ed. 2003). Unlike many of the other basic texts, this book includes guidance on writing such documents as jury instructions, pleadings, interrogatories, opinion letters, wills, trusts, and research papers.

MARY BARNARD RAY & JILL J. RAMSFIELD, LEGAL WRITING: GETTING IT RIGHT & GETTING IT WRITTEN (4th ed. 2005). This reference book contains concise discussions of common writing questions and errors arranged alphabetically.

NANCY L. SCHULTZ & LOUIS J. SIRICO, JR., LEGAL WRITING AND OTHER LAWYERING SKILLS (4th ed. 2004). This text provides an introduction to basic legal writing style, with a helpful overview of oral advocacy as well. It is particularly useful for providing detailed guidance on specific legal documents such as case briefs, memoranda, opinions, letters, settlement agreements, pleadings, discovery requests, motions, jury instructions, and appellate briefs.

HELENE S. SHAPO *et al.*, WRITING & ANALYSIS IN THE LAW (4th ed. 2003). This succinct writing text is particularly helpful for the guidance it provides on organization of legal discussions, focusing attention on both "large scale" organizational issues and "small scale" stylistic concerns.

MICHAEL R. SMITH, ADVANCED LEGAL WRITING: THEORIES AND STRATEGIES IN PERSUASIVE WRITING (2002). This highly theoretical text will be of interest to those wishing to learn more about the classic rhetorical theories that underlie modern legal writing.

ROBIN WELLFORD SLOCUM, LEGAL REASONING, WRITING, AND PERSUASIVE ARGUMENT (2d ed. 2006). An excellent, client-centered approach to legal writing, this text presents guidance on legal writing in a variety of contexts in which an attorney may be required to prepare a document on behalf of a client.

EUGENE VOLOKH, ACADEMIC LEGAL WRITING (2d ed. 2005). This text, unlike most practice-oriented legal writing books, is geared to those who are writing academic papers and law review articles. It includes particularly helpful checklists for effective writing, and contains some excellent guidance on use of sources and citations.

MELISSA H. WERESH, LEGAL WRITING: ETHICAL AND PROFESSIONAL CONSIDERATIONS (2006). This book includes an excellent discussion of—and selection of cases and rules illustrating—the ethical requirements that govern legal writers who prepare memoranda, letters, complaints, briefs, and other documents. It combines important lessons from both legal writing and professional responsibility courses into one practical guide.

Legal Drafting

SUSAN L. BRODY *et al.*, LEGAL DRAFTING (1994). One of the most complete legal drafting texts available, this book devotes a great deal of attention to outlining basic drafting principles and to *applying* those concepts in specific contents such as estate planning documents, contracts, pleadings, and legislation.

SCOTT J. BURNHAM, DRAFTING CONTRACTS (2d ed. 1993). This text combines a brief summary of contract law principles with a discussion and demonstration of how those principles can be used in drafting contracts.

BARBARA CHILD, DRAFTING LEGAL DOCUMENTS: MATERIALS & PROBLEMS (1988). This text focuses on broad principles of legal drafting, with a great deal of attention to the "plain English" movement in legal drafting.

THOMAS R. HAGGARD, LEGAL DRAFTING: PROCESS, TECHNIQUES, AND EXERCISES (2003). This text includes both general background on legal drafting techniques and specific guidance for the drafting of contracts and legislation. It includes abundant drafting exercises, as well as stylistic pointers and ethical guidelines for drafters.

GEORGE W. KUNEY, THE ELEMENTS OF CONTRACT DRAFTING WITH QUESTIONS AND CLAUSES FOR CONSIDERATION (2003). This text explores the elements of effective contract drafting and includes both general principles and guidance on specific types of contract clauses.

ROBERT J. MARTINEAU, DRAFTING LEGISLATION & RULES IN PLAIN ENGLISH (1991). This text includes an excellent overview of the legislative process and both stylistic and substantive advice on drafting effective legislation. This will be particularly useful for those at legislative or administrative externships.

WILLIAM P. STATSKY, LEGISLATIVE ANALYSIS AND DRAFTING (2d ed. 1984). Particularly useful for those whose work involves legislative or regulatory materials, this text includes material on understanding and interpreting statutes.

Legal Research

Cathy Glaser, *et al.*, The Lawyer's Craft: An Introduction to Legal Analysis, Writing, Research, and Advocacy (2002). Although the legal analysis section is the highlight of this book, it contains a helpful guide to legal research basics and offers this research guidance in the practical context of effective legal writing.

Christina L. Kunz *et al.*, The Process of Legal Research: Successful Strategies (6th ed. 2004). This comprehensive book includes detailed presentation of both traditional research methods and CALR. It makes an excellent reference book as well, because it contains many illustrations and a focus on the *process* of research.

Michael D. Murray & Christy H. De Sanctis, Legal Research and Writing (2005). This comprehensive book includes three distinct sections. The first includes general chapters on legal method and basic writing; the second includes chapters on all aspects of legal research and citation; the third section includes chapters on specific types of legal documents.

Bonita K. Roberts & Linda L. Schlveter, Legal Research Guide: Patterns and Practice (5th ed. 2006). This compact book is a useful desktop reference because of its "checklists" and "computer notes" sprinkled throughout. While it lacks some of the in-depth material on research strategy that is available elsewhere, it is a useful reference work and a helpful tool for brushing up on basic research techniques.

Amy E. Sloan, Basic Legal Research: Tools and Strategies (3d ed. 2006). This text offers a basic, yet comprehensive, overview of legal research methods. It begins with a discussion of "secondary source" research, which is very helpful for students or externs involved in a project where they are unfamiliar with the substantive law. It then progresses through a discussion of individual research tools, with extensive use of illustrations and samples pages. Particularly helpful is the final chapter on developing a research plan. This book will be particularly useful for those who seek some background contrast between print resources and electronic resources, as Prof. Sloan illustrates the advantages and disadvantages of each in her comparative approach. In addition, each chapter ends with a "checklist" of research pointers that can provide a quick review for those whose research skills are already well honed.

Chapter 15

Management Skills

Lucia Ann Silecchia

Your law school education, and your externships, should provide you with basic training in legal research and writing as well as exposure to various other skills such as oral advocacy, interviewing, negotiation, drafting, and trial practice. Depending on your talents and interests, you should do all you can to acquire the skills necessary to enable you to take the substantive knowledge you spend three or four years acquiring and use that knowledge in a way that will have practical benefit.

Effective lawyers are more than merely the sum of the discrete skills and knowledge they possess. To practice law effectively, an attorney also must possess management skills. Without these skills, a lawyer may have a repertoire of useful abilities but will lack the focus and organization to use those abilities effectively. Just as computer application programs are of no value without a powerful operating system, individual legal skills are best used when you have the ability to run them effectively. It is this set of overall management skills that this chapter will explore. These skills include

- developing time management and planning skills,

- delegating tasks,

- working collaboratively,

- communicating effectively with colleagues and legal professionals,

- communicating effectively with clients, and

- being creative.

As should be obvious from this list, lawyers do not have a unique need for these skills. These skills are essential for effective professional life in most fields.

The challenges of legal practice require that these skills be well developed. Ironically, these skills are often "invisible" and seem to be either so obvious or so broad that they get little or no attention in legal education. Law students with prior work experience may understand the critical importance of these skills, but they often are not addressed in academic settings. Because of the importance of these skills, this chapter will help you cast some light on these invisible skills and reflect on their importance in your practice.

> **Exercise 15.1** Think about three people—not necessarily lawyers—whom you admire professionally. They may be people you know personally or people about whom you have heard others speak well. Ask yourself what these individuals have in common and whether you can identify a common trait that accounts for their success. In addition to the skills that they share, what are the unique skills that make each individual particularly effective?

Developing Time Management and Planning Skills

Attorneys, like most busy people, often have more to do than time would seem to permit. Juggling the urgent demands of multiple clients or supervisors is not an easy task. As a law student, you are probably all too familiar with the "so much to do, so little time" problem. Developing time management skills can help you to meet your professional obligations, ensure that you have enough time for quality work, and guarantee that you have at least some time left over for healthy relaxation.

see> **Chapter 17**
on Work-Life Balance

Of course, your externship will not be the first time you have had to manage your time. Being successful at your previous jobs and managing to juggle your academic responsibilities with other demands on your time have always required good time management. Now that you are doing an externship, examine your time management skills conscientiously and explicitly. Begin to explore such questions as these:

- Do you often leave important tasks to the last minute? Do you procrastinate when faced with unpleasant or difficult tasks? Why? How well do you do these tasks under pressure? How often do you find yourself completing your work at the last possible moment? What is the impact of this on the quality of your work?

- Can you or do you break large tasks into smaller, more manageable jobs so that you can begin accomplishing them?

- Do you prioritize the demands on your time so that you have enough time to devote to important ones, or do you spend large amounts of time on insignificant matters and then rush through important work?

- How often do you fail to meet deadlines at your externship? At school? Socially?

- Do you maintain a daily, weekly, or monthly schedule of your obligations to help you keep track of your projects? How effective is your scheduling system?

- How do you see your failure to manage time negatively affect others (for example, support staff)? How, if at all, have you been successful at mitigating these impacts?

- What, if any, projects have taken you unusually long to accomplish? Do you have any ideas about why this is so?

- When you receive assignments, do you ask your supervisor for a realistic deadline for completing the project? Do you keep your supervisor informed of unexpected hurdles that threaten the timely completion of the project?

- Are there certain times of the day during which you are the most productive? The least productive? Do you schedule your most challenging work around your most productive hours?

- How efficient are you at using short periods of time effectively?

- When you are facing a particularly busy time at work or school, does this have negative consequences in other areas of your life (for example, sleep, health, personal relationships, etc.)?

As you attempt to answer these questions, realize that these are challenges faced by people in all lines of work. The particular pressures of law practice, the time-based billing system and the tight deadlines, make lawyers' mastery of time management particularly essential. Your externship should introduce you to people who are good time managers—and perhaps to poor ones. Discuss these issues with them (tactfully with the poor ones, of course!), and ask for guidance. At the very least, your externship can expose you to a variety of approaches that may help you develop your own management style.

Exercise 15.2 In private practice, it is typical for attorneys to keep time sheets for recording in six-, ten- or fifteen-minute blocks the tasks they perform. This enables attorneys to bill clients for the time devoted to the services rendered and provides a detailed description of work accomplished. You already may have kept such time sheets in a previous legal job, or you may be required to do so for your externship. Whether or not you have to keep such a record for business purposes, recording what you do can be an effective way to assess your time management skills and observe your work habits. Pick two typical days of any given week. For each day, keep a written time sheet. In fifteen-minute intervals, record the amount of time you spend in transit, eating, on the telephone, in classes, at work, studying, with family and friends, watching television, surfing the net, reading and answering e-mail, handling household tasks, exercising, doing volunteer work, participating in religious activities, sleeping, etc. At the end of the two days, review your time sheets. See what they can tell you about how you manage and spend your time. Consider, particularly, whether there are any surprises and whether there are any significant differences between the way you *think* you spend your time and the way you actually *do* spend it.

The first step in becoming an effective time manager is to understand how you spend time. After completing Exercise 15.2, ask yourself about any surprises you have found in the allocation of your time. Consider whether you might be more effective in the way you manage your time.

If you are surprised by the amount of time you spend on e-mail, consider whether you should devote a set time each day to e-mail rather than returning repeatedly to your messages.

Ask yourself whether certain tasks are taking longer than they should because you are "multi-tasking" rather than devoting your full energy to the task. (For example, how many instant messages did you respond to while trying to read your cases for class?)

Consider whether you have sufficient time for the non-work-related activities and relationships that are important to you. Consider how you might reallocate your time in a way that may lead to greater satisfaction.

Evaluate whether you are getting sufficient sleep, or if drowsiness is impairing your ability to perform as well as possible. Studies have shown that sleep is critical to the learning process. Likewise, ask yourself whether you are eating well and exercising sufficiently, or whether unhealthy habits are impairing your productivity.

Consider whether the tasks you *actually* complete are the same as the ones you *planned* to complete when you began your day. If they are not, ask yourself whether this represents a judicious flexibility or repeated diversion from your priorities by tempting distractions.

Use your externship to learn how you manage time and how you might do so more effectively. As your time management skills continue to develop you will reap the benefits: more effective and efficient achievement of your professional obligations; fewer mistakes arising from last-minute work and rushed deadlines; more control over the pace of your work life; more time available to do the things most important to you; more collegial relationships with other professionals who rely on your commitments; and the reduced stress that comes from being in control of rather than controlled by time.

Delegating Tasks

Closely related to the question of time management is the skill of effective delegation. Tasks are generally accomplished best and most efficiently if the person most suited to it is doing that task. At times, this will mean that you should do an entire task yourself because your skill or background has made you best qualified for that task. For example, if you have done all the research for a motion, perhaps you should write the first draft of that motion, prepare the exhibits, and do the necessary revisions. There may be times, however, when it is not best for you to do all aspects of a project. Good professional judgment sometimes requires that you delegate parts of a project when others are better qualified, or when your time is needed for something else.

As an extern, you are more likely to have work delegated to you rather than be in a position to delegate it to others. Nevertheless, you may have some opportunity to delegate. For example, you may be working with support staff or undergraduate interns who have been asked to assist you with your projects. Your externship will give you an opportunity to observe others delegating work. In addition, being in the position of "delegatee" gives you a special perspective on the subject. Take advantage of that perspective, and observe when you believe work has been effectively delegated to you.

As you prepare for professional situations that will provide you with delegating responsibilities, consider what factors will make delegation successful. Before you can delegate, you must have colleagues you trust to whom you can delegate work. When you become an attorney, you may need to train colleagues for the tasks you will ask them to do. You will have to develop judgment to determine when to trust others to work independently and when—and to what extent—your supervision is required. No matter how much you delegate, the ultimate responsibility for your work product will be yours.

As you receive each new project at your externship, assess it to see if it is easily divisible into tasks that can be delegated to others without overlap or inefficient repetition. If there are people at your externship to whom you might delegate tasks—other externs, paralegals, secretaries, undergraduate interns, research librarians, or attorneys with a particular specialty—do so wisely. Because the practice of law often involves the performance of many different types of tasks, not all of which require legal training, providing legal services requires attorneys to act with the assistance of support staff who have significant responsibilities. Use your externship to observe attorneys who delegate tasks well to others. Reflect on what you learn about effective delegation. Ask yourself such questions as these:

- Is the person to whom I am delegating this task well suited to it and well trained for it? Is this an accepted part of this person's job? Has this person expressed willingness or ability to assist with this task?

- Can I delegate this task with a realistic deadline, or have I waited until the last minute to delegate? If the latter, is my attempted delegation fair?

- Are others making demands on the same person whose assistance I am soliciting? Have I coordinated schedules? Are my expectations reasonable?

- Am I in a position to supervise the person to whom I have delegated the task? Am I prepared to be responsible for the work that is done? Will I have sufficient time to review it?

- Have I given sufficient guidance as I delegate the project, and have I made myself available for questions as they arise? Have I been clear in setting my expectations?

- Have I been respectful of others as they assist me? If there is criticism to be made of their work, have I done so appropriately, and privately?

- If there is an unpleasant task to be done, have I weighed the benefits of delegating the task to someone who will find it less onerous than I? Should I do the task myself to set an example about pitching in and sharing the less attractive parts of practice?

- If the person to whom I have attempted to delegate a project balks at doing it, or neglects to complete it, how can I effectively handle the situation?

Exercise 15.3 Consider these questions with respect to delegations by others that you have observed in the externship — particularly in those circumstances where tasks were delegated to you. What did the person delegating the project do well? What might the person have done differently? If, at the end of your externship, you are asked to evaluate your placement, be sure to consider the delegation skills of your supervisors.

Working Collaboratively

Legal practice often involves collaborative efforts in addition to delegation of duties. In law school, many tasks you accomplish are done individually. The outcome of what you do, usually in the form of a grade, is assessed solely on your individual efforts. Indeed, collaboration may even be forbidden so that your instructor may evaluate your *individual* progress. This is often not the case in law practice. A team effort frequently is required, and the final outcome may be determined more by how well you work with others than by your individual work. As discussed above, some projects may require teamwork in the form of delegation, others require teamwork in the form of collaboration. Collaboration involves working with others in a way that enhances the quality of the ultimate work product.

Collaboration may happen in simple, casual ways such as a discussion with a colleague about your legal theory or a quick proofreading of another's brief. Collaboration also may be more substantive or formal. For example, a team of attorneys may work on a case in which one does the oral argument, another is the primary brief writer, still another solicits and maintains contact with the client, and a fourth (usually junior) colleague handles much of the background research. Collaboration results not only from the division of tasks but from the communication about various pieces. Alternatively, several attorneys and paralegals may share the task of responding to a subpoena as they sift through thousands of documents together. In yet another scenario, attorneys handling the same issues might meet regularly to update each other on developments in that legal field.

As an extern you may engage in some collaborative lawyering. As you do so, observe how the attorneys at your placement work together and consider whether the collaboration is effective. You may find, for example, that the attorneys in your office are isolated and do not share work. Conversely, you may find that they spend a lot of time talking together that might be better spent in more independent thought. You might find that the collaboration is hierarchical, with senior attorneys dominating shared ventures. The collaborative structure may change dramatically from project to project or from supervisor to supervisor.

As your externship progresses, reflect on the positive and negative aspects of the collaborative setting in which you find yourself. Reflect, too, on your role in this scheme and your ability to perform well in that working model. Consider which settings you prefer, and what skills you must develop to become a better collaborative attorney.

Exercise 15.4 Think back on a collaborative legal project you have worked on, at your current externship, a previous job, or a law school project such as a moot court team or a study group. Ask yourself the following:

What collaborative model was used? Was it casual? Was it hierarchical? Was work evenly divided? Was there a "leader" of the group? How was that "leader" chosen?

What were the model's strengths and weaknesses?

How well did you contribute to that collaboration?

What skills would you like to improve to enhance your ability to be an effective collaborator?

Exercise 15.5 Alicia, Nathan, and Yvette are in the same property class. As the semester reaches its midpoint, they decide to form a study group to review their property cases, construct a joint outline, and practice taking old property examinations. They have heard all about study groups that failed because one person ended up doing all the work, members failed to meet their commitments, meetings started late, or the study sessions became social events. The three want to keep the group informal, but they would like to be effective. Draft a set of rules for Alicia, Nathan, and Yvette that will provide the framework for running a successful collaborative study group. What did you seek to achieve with your set of rules, and what problems did you seek to avoid? How did you outline the rights and responsibilities of each person? To what extent would these same rules apply in a professional work setting?

Communicating with Colleagues and Professionals

At your externship, examine the style in which you communicate in the legal workplace. Evaluate how you can be most productive. Consider the following qualities of effective workplace communication:

- honesty and accuracy in the substance of what is said;

- discretion about what one should communicate, to whom, in what format, and when;

- sensitivity to the knowledge and personality of the audience and the ability to tailor communication to that particular audience;

- ability to listen to others effectively;

- maturity in handling differences of opinion and criticism;

- prudence in the selection of the means of communication (for example, formal memo? e-mail? telephone call?);

- ability to be articulate and clear in conveying information;

- confidence in thinking on one's feet and responding to issues as they arise, coupled with the ability to know when an off-the-cuff response is premature;

- strength in defending one's position when it is correct and willingness to admit when it is not;

- respect for confidentiality when needed;

- diligence in documenting communications when appropriate;

- civility and cordiality, particularly under pressure; and

- patience with those who do not grasp what is being communicated.

Obviously, these qualities of effective communication are not unique to the law office nor to communication with legal professionals, but they are crucially important in this context because the legal profession is based on the ability to communicate ideas, theories, arguments, and strategies. As discussed above, these skills are particularly important because law practice often is a collaborative enterprise. In addition, attorneys often are judged—initially at least—by their communication abilities. It is, after all, communication skills that allow attorneys to translate the knowledge they possess into a form that can be used by others.

There are also some issues that arise specifically when working with attorneys that may be worth particular consideration as you begin to develop your professional "persona" for communicating in a legal setting. For example, in a legal workplace you may find yourself under pressure to deliver information very quickly. You may need to develop the ability to gather and disseminate information more quickly than you may be accustomed to doing.

In a legal workplace, you have the options to communicate through in-person meetings, e-mail, memoranda, faxes, telephone conversations, and voice-mail messages, to name a few. Part of your task will be to decide which mode of communication is appropriate. Consider whether the type of communication you have chosen is

- **efficient for disseminating the information to all those who should have it.** If you are preparing a report for a litigation team of seven people, it may be better to use e-mail rather than telephone calls to ensure that all possess the same information at the same time.

- **expedient for communicating quickly.** You may not have the time to write a full memorandum analyzing an issue if a motion must be filed the next day.

- **discreet and safe for retaining client confidences.** A fax machine used by many people or an e-mail easily forwarded should not be used for transmitting highly confidential information.

- **permanent, if the communication is to be preserved, and disposable if the communication is something about which there should not be extensive files.** If you will be leaving your externship at the end of the semester, it may be appropriate to make a permanent and detailed record of your work so that the project may be passed on to the extern who replaces you; alternatively, your early, subjective impressions about a client's liability may not be something about which there should be permanent records.

- **appropriate for responding to questions and inviting discussion.** If your research results indicate that a particular area of law may be unsettled, an in-person meeting or telephone call may be the most effective method of communication because it offers an opportunity to discuss the issues with others and explore complexities and open questions.

- **consistent with the culture of your workplace.** If your office is very e-mail oriented, refrain from sending paper copies of your work unless you have a good reason for departing from the office tradition.

- **required by the rules of your organization.** Your firm or organization may require you to keep certain types of communication, such as client files or expense records, or to put information in a certain form.

- **cost-effective.** If your office will be billing clients for word processing time, consider whether a formal, typed document is required for the task.

- **necessary for providing the service your clients need.** If your client provides you with essential information, consider how and if that information must be preserved.

- **prudent to protect you and/or the firm from liability.** Assume, for example, that you have given your client advice and that client has decided to reject it. Consider how this should be documented in the event that negative consequences follow your client's decision to disregard your advice.

You may be more at ease with certain types of communication than others. Some people are comfortable communicating orally but uneasy about their written communication skills. Others may be shy or reluctant about oral communication but express their thoughts well on paper. Part of being an effective communicator is to assess your strengths and weaknesses, to learn how to improve your ability in the areas in which you do not feel comfortable, and to use your strengths whenever you can. Of course, the other side of the communication question is learning which type of communication your supervisor prefers and adapting your style to fit.

Exercise 15.6 Think back to the last job you had, or the last time you were responsible for carrying out a task in cooperation with others. List the various ways in which your co-workers and others communicated with you and with each other. Evaluate each type of communication to consider which was most effective and when; which was most effective for achieving a quick response; which was best for preserving information; and which you felt more comfortable using.

Communicating with Clients

If your externship provides you with any client contact, use the opportunity to develop your client communication style. Even if you are not asked to work directly with clients, see if you may observe client interviewing or counseling sessions conducted by experienced attorneys. This will provide some exposure to different styles and a chance to observe some of the problems that may arise when dealing with clients.

Establishing a good working relationship with your clients — whether they are individuals, institutions, or a combination of both — is essential for a successful attorney. You should understand and explain to clients the confidentiality rules governing legal counsel so they understand the care with which you will retain their confidences. The discussion of professional responsibility in Chapter 5 will give you some guidance on these issues. Another communication skill to develop is the ability to obtain necessary information from the client. Often, this involves work before a client interview so that you are prepared to ask probing, relevant questions. Do not hesitate to ask and re-ask important questions if you have not received a complete answer. Do not gloss over sensitive questions. Unless you have a complete and accurate statement of the facts, you will be unable to serve the client effectively. In addition to your focus on getting hard facts from your clients, do not undervalue the importance of allowing clients the opportunities to communicate to you their more subjective concerns, worries, hopes, and goals. Emphasize the client's obligation to tell you the truth, and reiterate your duty to keep the information confidential. Keep careful records of the answers your client provides to you.

Consider, as well, your role as an educator of your clients. Remember that a client is entitled to an explanation, in lay terms, of the law that governs the matters in question. A client also is entitled to receive answers to any questions relevant to the matter for which you are providing representation. It is irresponsible to mislead a client, tell half-truths, promise what you are not sure you can deliver, or create a false sense of security concerning the outcome of the legal matter. Any information you provide should be accurate, cautious, and understandable.

As an extern, or a new attorney, be careful not to make misrepresentations as to what your supervisors will be doing, and do not act beyond the boundaries of what your supervisors have authorized you to do. Do not hesitate to tell a client that you need to consult other attorneys at your office before you answer a professional question.

Exercise 15.7 You are assisting your supervisor in planning for a meeting with an elderly client who wishes to rewrite her will—a document she has not revised since her husband died twelve years ago. Make a list of ten questions you want to ask this client at your first meeting with her before you take on the drafting task.

Exercise 15.8 In class, pair off into groups of two. For five minutes, both of you should think about a legal problem or dispute in which you have been involved. This can be anything from a traffic ticket, to a warranty dispute, to a conflict over insurance coverage, to the terms of an apartment lease. (Do not select a matter that should be kept confidential.) In your pairs, spend a half hour interviewing each other. For the first fifteen minutes assume the role of the attorney and interview your partner to glean the details of his or her problem and plan a course of action. For the second fifteen minutes become the client and have your partner play the role of the attorney you have retained to help you solve your problem. After your interviews are completed, ask yourself the questions below. You might videotape the interview you conduct and review the videotape with your faculty supervisor and/or your partner and assess the strengths and weaknesses of your interview.

Did you obtain all the factual information needed to begin understanding your client's legal problem?

Were there any difficulties in getting the information you needed? If so, what were they, how could they be avoided, and how did you resolve them?

Did your client feel comfortable discussing the legal issues?

Were you able to answer the questions your client asked?

How comfortable did you feel in the role of attorney?

When you were in the role of the client, what did you like most and least about the way your attorney conducted your interview? What put you at ease and what made you less willing to share information?

Exercise 15.9 During the course of your externship, you may observe several attorneys in their personal dealings with clients. Reflect on the differences in their styles, and critique the efficacy of each approach. Identify the traits that make particular attorneys highly effective and the traits that make others less effective.

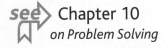

see ▷ Chapter 10
on Problem Solving

Being Creative

Creativity is a quality expected in artists, musicians, playwrights, and poets; it is equally important for successful lawyers. Although lawyers are bound by statutes, precedents, rules, and regulations, a lawyer's work is, at heart, to help clients in solving problems. Lawyers are also in the business of facilitating their clients' attempts to do complex tasks in compliance with the law. If you have not yet thought of the legal profession as an inherently creative one, begin to think of yourself in the role of creator and use your externship to consider how you might become more creative in your legal practice.

Clearly, lawyers "create" many things: contracts, settlement agreements, regulations, briefs, oral arguments, motions, articles, wills, memoranda, legislation, leases, letters, and policies, to name but a few. Obviously, many of these products are creative in the sense that they are specifically made to respond to particular problems and meet unique needs of individual clients.

A truly creative lawyer will:

- consider alternatives to traditional litigation;

- employ non-legal solutions to legal problems;

- be aggressive in preventive lawyering, anticipating problems before they arise;

- make good faith arguments for changes in the law;

- generate novel theories of recovery to advance;

- argue less obvious causes of action, alternative theories, or both; and

- work out novel trade-offs in their negotiations and settlements.

As the law becomes more complex, there is an increasing need for lawyers who can approach problems in new ways. Cultivating creativity takes a lifetime, but your externship can be a good time to begin thinking about the ways in which you can be creative in law practice.

A short list of readings about creativity appears at the end of this chapter. As you read through these materials, you may be surprised to see how much they have to teach you about the importance of creativity in areas other than the arts. The readings share several common themes that can be applied to your externship.

There are many different types of creativity or intelligence to explore. Hence, as you evaluate your creativity think as broadly as you can about the areas in which you are creative and how you might define creativity more comprehensively than you previously have.

Creativity often involves taking risks and having a willingness to try new approaches to old problems. Consider how often you approach problems in a novel way or when the last time was that you tackled an issue unconventionally.

There are things that can block creativity—perfectionism, pressure, and pessimism to name but a few. Part of being creative is being able to identify what inhibits your creative energy and why. As you work through your projects both at your externship and elsewhere, see if you can detect any times or situations in which you find it particularly difficult to be creative.

Creative people work in many different ways. As you meet more and more professionals in your work, study their work habits and thought processes to see in what ways they are similar to and different from each other.

A very important part of creativity consists of things often not considered to be productive, such as recreation. Consider how and to what extent such activities can assist you in being more creative and effective when you turn your attention back to your work.

Exercise 15.10 Think back to a time when, in a non-legal context, you came up with a solution to a problem that you or others thought was creative. What did you do to reach that solution? What about it was creative?

Conclusion

This chapter highlights the basic management skills that are crucial to creating a system in which all of your other skills will operate. Although these skills rarely receive explicit attention in the law school classroom, knowing how to use them effectively will enhance your ability to use your legal skills and knowledge to serve your clients' needs more effectively and assist you in being the most productive attorney you can be.

FURTHER READING

The following books are not particularly law-related because the skills addressed in this chapter are not the exclusive province of lawyers. Instead, these books may provide you with practical advice for developing important personal management skills, with a particular focus on time management.

Time Management

STEPHEN R. COVEY, THE SEVEN HABITS OF HIGHLY EFFECTIVE PEOPLE (1989). A well known and popular volume, this book reviews several strategies for becoming more efficient and effective at tackling many diverse demands successfully.

Communicating with Clients

ROBERT M. BASTRESS & JOSEPH D. HARBAUGH, INTERVIEWING, COUNSELING, AND NEGOTIATING SKILLS FOR EFFECTIVE REPRESENTATION (1990). This text combines a lucid discussion of the theory behind the skills of interviewing, counseling, and negotiating with illustrative problems that put the interpersonal skills into an authentic context.

DAVID A. BINDER *et al.*, LAWYERS AS COUNSELORS: A CLIENT-CENTERED APPROACH (2d ed., 2004). This classic book provides a description of the objectives of legal interviewing and counseling processes and the basic techniques that are needed for legal interviewing and counseling.

ROBERT F. COCHRAN *et al.*, THE COUNSELOR-AT-LAW: A COLLABORATIVE APPROACH TO CLIENT INTERVIEWING AND COUNSELING (2d ed. 2006). This text contrasts the authoritarian, client-centered, and collaborative models for legal counseling, and focuses primarily on the latter. In particular, it offers extensive practical advice on involving clients more fully in their legal affairs.

ROGER S. HAYDOCK *et al.*, LAWYERING: PRACTICE AND PLANNING (1996). This very practical book provides a thorough overview of the various aspects of legal practice, with extensive attention paid to the functions of interviewing, counseling, negotiating, and investigating.

Creativity

STEVEN KEEVA, TRANSFORMING PRACTICES: FINDING JOY AND SATISFACTION IN THE LEGAL LIFE (1999). An excellent, thoughtful book that discusses the sources of attorney dissatisfaction and the ways in which a creative and spiritually oriented view of practice can re-energize the profession.

Other

JOSEPH G. ALLEGRETTI, THE LAWYER'S CALLING: CHRISTIAN FAITH AND LEGAL PRACTICE (1996). A reflective book, this text offers perspectives on integrating spirituality with law practice, with particular emphasis on what this means for client service and relations with adversaries.

ELIZABETH DVORKIN *et al.*, BECOMING A LAWYER: A HUMANISTIC PERSPECTIVE ON LEGAL EDUCATION AND PROFESSIONALISM (1981). This text is an interesting collection of short readings on various aspects of legal practice, with attention to questions of lawyer professionalism and satisfaction.

ALEX J. HURDER, *et al.*, eds. READINGS FOR LIVE CLIENT CLINICS (1997). This anthology of essays is primarily designed as a resource for law students in so-called "live" client clinics. However, with its collections of essays on such topics as "Lawyer-Client Communication," "Goal Setting, Decision Making, & Planning," "Advocacy in the Legal System," and "The Public Role of the Lawyer," this book contains much to offer with regard to legal practice.

Chapter 16

Bias in the Legal Profession

Stacy L. Brustin

A Personal Reflection

I had been out of law school for about a year. I spent most of my days in our local trial court and was just beginning to feel like a lawyer, albeit an inexperienced one, when I had my first professional encounter with bias.

I was sitting in a settlement conference at which the judge hearing the case was attempting to broker a settlement between my client and the other party. Every time my opposing counsel addressed me, she referred to me as young lady. "Listen young lady," "what do you mean young lady," "now, young lady . . ." She was not saying it in the good-hearted, encouraging way older people sometimes refer to those who are younger. She was using it to make me aware of my status and it was working. "Why does she keep saying 'young lady'?" I thought to myself, trying to keep focus on the issues at hand. Finally, I could not stand it any longer. "Would you please stop referring to me as 'young lady'?" I asked. The judge looked up and the other attorney calmly replied, "Okay, older lady, what do you think about this proposal?" The judge did not say a word. I was fuming inside, but did not want to let the other lawyer know it. I ignored her comment and continued with the negotiation.

During that same year, I was appearing before a different judge in a family law matter. The courtroom was packed. My co-counsel and I were presenting arguments to the judge on a procedural issue. When we finished, the judge turned to the other attorney and asked for his response to our arguments. While arguing his point, the opposing attorney referred to us as "lovely young ladies." The judge interrupted him in mid-sentence and ordered him to approach the bench. Although the judge tried to make her comments inaudible to the rest of the courtroom, everyone heard the admonishment. She told the attorney that "while your opposing counsel may be lovely and may be young, you better not ever use that kind of inappropriate language again in my courtroom."

In both situations, as soon as the attorneys uttered their comments, I felt unnerved and upset. The comments seemed inappropriate, but, I thought to myself, maybe I was being too sensitive. Perhaps the attorneys did not mean anything by what they were saying. Yet it felt as though they were trying to use their status to intimidate or belittle me as a young, female attorney. Should I react in these situations, or should I just let these types of comments go? Does the judge have a responsibility to put a stop to the behavior? How severe or blatant does the bias need to be in order for a judge to react? The two judges in these situations handled similar behavior in very different ways. Did it make a difference that one incident was in chambers and the other in a more public setting? The one thing that was clear to me was that my legal education had not prepared me to deal with these issues. [S.L.B.]

Issues of bias will arise in legal practice. It is likely that you either will be the target of biased behavior or biased behavior will occur in your presence. It is also possible that unless you examine your own beliefs and assumptions, you may unintentionally engage in biased behavior that can negatively affect your professional relationships and your practice.

The legal profession is undergoing a period of self-examination. Lawyers and judges around the country are pointedly questioning whether the profession and the justice system as a whole are tainted by bias. Since 1982, at least 65 state and federal courts have published reports analyzing this question. These reports have documented racial, ethnic, gender, and sexual orientation bias in jurisdictions throughout the United States. Studies conducted of law schools suggest that students perceive similar bias in the law school environment.

Concern about bias in the legal profession has caused several jurisdictions to adopt rules of professional conduct prohibiting judges and attorneys from engaging in biased behavior. These rules vary in scope, but they are designed to ensure that lawyers and judges are held accountable for their behavior in and out of the courtroom. These disciplinary rules supplement existing state and federal laws that prohibit employment discrimination and tortious behavior. All attorneys, including those who are about to enter the legal profession, need to understand these rules.

Some behavior does not rise to the level of actionable discrimination or violation of a disciplinary rule but is inappropriate nonetheless. The court and bar commissioned reports indicate that inappropriate behavior is prevalent throughout the profession. Will you recognize it when you see it? How will you respond if, during your first year of practice and in a professional setting, someone makes an inappropriate comment to you based on your age, race, ethnicity, gender, disability, sexual orientation, socioeconomic status, or religion? What if the comment is directed toward a colleague? Will you make clear your disapproval, or will you let the comment slide?

The legal work force increasingly reflects the diversity of the larger workforce. In practice, you will encounter judges, attorneys, administrators, support staff, and clients whose race, gender, physical abilities, learning abilities, age, religion, sexual orientation, or socioeconomic class differ from yours. How will you develop solid professional relationships? How can you ensure that you are not inadvertently engaging in behavior or making decisions based upon negative stereotypes or biased assumptions?

What happens when you become a supervisor or managing attorney and you bear the responsibility for ensuring that neither you nor the institution with which you are affiliated tolerates biased behavior? Will you know how to protect your organization? Will you be able to supervise a diverse group of employees? Even if, as a manager, you have ensured that your law office or organization is free of illegal, discriminatory practices, is that sufficient? How can you foster a positive working environment in which all employees are productive and feel that they are part of the team?

This chapter encourages you to grapple with some of these issues during your externship—before you officially enter the legal profession. If you have not previously considered the issue of bias, then an externship provides an excellent opportunity to develop your awareness. For those of you who are all too familiar with the impact of biased or discriminatory behavior, an externship offers an opportunity to explore and refine how you will address these issues, as lawyers, in a legal setting.

Manifestations of Bias in the Legal Profession

Exercise 16.1 When you hear the term bias, what images come to mind? Take a couple of minutes and think about whether you have ever been in a situation in which you felt someone made an assumption about you or you were treated differently because of some characteristic or trait you possess: for example, because you are short or tall, because you are male or female, because you are young or old, because you are Irish or Italian, because you have straight hair or curly hair or no hair, because you are Baptist or Jewish, because you are from the Midwest or the South, because your family had a lot of money or no money, because you are African-American or Asian American, because you went to an Ivy League school or a state school.

The offensive conduct might not have been as blatant as refusing to rent an apartment to you or refusing to give you a job promotion, but it bothered you nonetheless. Why did it bother you? What assumptions were being made about you? What was it about the behavior directed at you that felt unfair or stereotyped? What did you do about it? Did you confront the person? Ignore the comment? Make a joke? Deliver a sermon?

Now take a couple of minutes to think about a time in which you were present when a joke was told or a comment made that was not directed at you but depended on a racial, ethnic, gender, or other stereotype. How did you feel? What did you do? Did you walk away? Say something? Show approval or disapproval?

While these are questions that every person might reflect upon, attorneys, as officers of the court, are responsible for understanding the law and seeking justice. They have a particular responsibility for ensuring that the legal system and legal practice remain untainted by discrimination, bias, or the perception of bias.

The concept of bias and its subtleties are best understood in the context of real life stories. The following excerpts explore bias in the legal profession from the perspectives of lawyers and judges who have directly experienced it. As you read these excerpts consider whether you believe that the behavior described constitutes bias or discrimination. If so, what do you believe is motivating the behavior? If there is none, why might it appear as biased behavior? If you had been in the situation(s) described by the authors, how would you have responded to the behavior?

Thomas S. Williamson, Jr., a partner at Covington and Burling in Washington, D.C., discusses the challenges African-American lawyers face when they begin practicing in large law firms.

Thomas S. Williamson, *Transcript of the Boston Bar Association Diversity Committee Conference: Recruiting, Hiring and Retaining Lawyers of Color*, 44 B.B.J. 8, (May/June 2000).

. . . Often there are no other blacks in your entering class of associates; there may not be others in the whole firm, or, at best, there will be a token scattering. Depending on which floor in the firm you're on, you may not see any black professionals for weeks or months at a time. Many firms have no black partners, and those that do only have one or two . . . . The people of color who work in these firms are concentrated in support positions, at secretarial desks, in the mail room, pushing the carts around with audio/visual equipment, or in janitorial services. The firm's clientele rarely, if ever, include any black organizations or any black individuals.

It may be an overstatement to say that this is a culture shock, but it is a particularly stressful entry experience. New black lawyers who have gone to these predominantly white firms understand the unwritten law that says you must be an expert, an expert in making white people feel comfortable, and, from the first, you are expected to act delighted and pleased that you are in such a "great firm." If you fail to follow that rule, fail to adhere to that law, there will be severe repercussions for your professional career . . . .

Partner critiques and supervision of black lawyers are awkward, at best. Partners are the authority figures in law firms. They hand out the assignments; do the evaluations; decide who will become a partner. Minority lawyers, especially black lawyers, understand, that many white partners at the large law firms have low or skeptical expectations about the abilities of minority lawyers. Those low expectations inevitably affect the types of assignments and the types of evaluations black lawyers receive . . . .

White partners are generally very uncomfortable critiquing black lawyers for fear that aggressive criticism will be interpreted as racial animus. Even when a black lawyer does well, white supervisors are reluctant to push the good black lawyer to excel further, fearing it might be viewed as some kind of racial bias. This, of course, is very important for one's partnership prospects. Most firms expect their lawyers to be good, but the associates who want to make partner must show they can be excellent. Thus, black lawyers are shortchanged at the very time in their careers when they are most open to learning and most in need of advice and guidance . . . .

. . . The success mantra at law firms today is that you have to learn how to find clients and serve the clients if you want to get ahead. Minority lawyers face special obstacles in making their mark developing client relationships. Although a firm might provide a positive and nurturing environment for black lawyers, there's no assurance that the clients are eager to entrust their problems to people of color . . . .

Partners, of course, have to be realistic and business oriented and make careful calculations about how to foster client confidence. Will a client think a white partner is giving his company's problem top priority if the partner assigns an African-American lawyer to handle the matter? Some clients are reluctant to believe that black lawyers are smart enough to handle a difficult and sensitive problem. I have had personal experience with this "business sensitivity" in my own career, and my unpleasant experiences have not just been limited to my associate years.

I had been a partner for two or three years when a client telephoned another partner and said, "We're going to have a very sensitive board meeting and I know Tom is supposed to be there. But there are a couple of white southerners on the board, and I don't think he would be the right person to do this." The partner made it clear to the client that if Covington & Burling was to continue representing his organization, I would be the lawyer at the meeting. One of my African-American partners, a woman who is a stellar lawyer, recently reminded me that when she was an associate I had asked her to work on a matter, and she had expressed reluctance. She thought the client would be troubled because he and his colleagues would have to rely on two black lawyers as the only lawyers on the case. I acknowledged that she may be right, but insisted that she accept the assignment, since I had already informed the client that he was extremely lucky to have one of the top associates in the firm on the case.

My examples of the special burdens and challenges of being an African-American lawyer in a large law firm are not intended to be comprehensive, but simply illustrative of the fact that racial integration in the law firm setting is not simply a matter of white people opening doors with good intentions . . . .

Marta-Ann Schnabel served as president of the Louisiana State Bar Association and is a former president of the New Orleans Bar Association. She addresses the question, are women still a minority?

Marta-Ann Schnabel, *Diversity in the Legal Profession: A Look at the Present and the Future . . . Are Women Still a Minority?*, 53 LA Bar Jnl.. 114, (August/September 2005).

The National Association for Law Placement reports that women comprise 43 percent of the associate or staff attorney positions, but only 16.8 percent of the partners.

It's this last set of numbers, of course, that gets to the heart of the issue and strips "opportunity" to its more practical core. Plenty of women train to become lawyers, and most graduate with every intention of finding a firm at which they can learn their trade, grow, prosper, and perhaps become a partner. Yet, a great many flee from the traditional firm structure within a few years of hiring on . . . .

. . . Typically, when women lawyers are asked about gender bias, their first instinct is to tell a funny story about some form of past treatment by judges, colleagues, partners . . . . [M]y favorite story of this genre comes from a domestic lawyer who runs a successful two-person practice in a rural parish. In about the sixth month of her second pregnancy, when she stood to make an appearance before the court on a pending motion, she was greeted from the bench by the exclamation, "So, your husband knocked you up again, eh?"

We rattle these stories off, to some measure, to avoid having to say what we really think. The female managing partner of a satellite office of a New Orleans firm told me that she was not sure how to offer a meaningful answer to my question without sounding like a "Pollyanna." Likewise, my friend who had been "knocked up" said she was far more focused on keeping her practice a float [sic] and her children out of trouble than she was on what it was like to be a woman lawyer. She didn't consider herself less professionally respected than men (after all, she had won that motion!). On the other hand, she admitted that she was constantly tired, over-committed, worried about her children and physically run-down, but she wasn't at all sure that her problems were any different from those of the average small-town practitioner, regardless of gender.

Many of the women with whom I spoke felt an immediate need to describe themselves as having chosen the "mommy" track. This was often said in a self-denigrating manner, as though a judicial clerkship or a staff or corporate position were somehow an admission of second-class status. One judicial law clerk in north Louisiana spoke of fleeing private practice and its "blatant gender discrimination." She went on to compare herself to a well-known woman partner in a local firm by saying, "maybe I have just been easier to beat down."

Yet, a lot of women veterans of that "predatory" world have a different view. Those of my vintage (that is, a tad over 40) wanted to talk about younger women. Many were quizzical about the attitudes of the young. A prominent woman litigator from Baton Rouge dismissed the issue of gender bias against "chick lawyers" and instead wished to focus on the generation gap amongst women lawyers. The youngsters, she noted, have no compassion or understanding for those who came before them—those who were compelled to behave like "tough broads" to make inroads. Now these young women criticize the older, successful women as being "bitter and mean." Another prominent practitioner from the Northshore of New Orleans echoed these views, commenting that younger women lawyers did not appear to have "nearly the awareness of gender" that older women lawyers do and that "often they learn the hard way."

. . . A case in point: about five years ago, I was the only woman partner in a medium-sized New Orleans law firm. A young woman associate sought the advice of one of my partners about how to handle a case assigned to her. During the course of the conversation, she reported that the opposing counsel "intimidated" her, and she sought some tips on how to handle him. Although he answered her questions, my partner also sought me out immediately. In a hushed voice, he told me he was worried that this young woman would never become a good litigator because she allowed herself to become "intimidated." My first reaction was a flash of anger—because, of course, the associate had been foolish enough to tell a partner what she was feeling. I certainly would have known better than to say that when I was an associate! Surely this young woman should have had more sense! But, indeed, she was not constrained by worry—much less conscious appreciation—that her world view was not the world view by which she was being judged. This young woman did not understand that she was supposed to copy a man's behavior. Instead, she did what women tend to do: she sought advice and began to process a reactive strategy. It goes without saying she managed the opposition rather well. She also never became a partner, choosing instead to retire and raise a family.

In the end, the pertinent issue may well be what we as a profession model as success and treat with respect. Women of a certain generation bemoan the "Superwoman" image while secretly believing that they are better people and true pioneers for having returned to the telephone, dictaphone or megaphone within hours of giving birth. There could be no question about their equality. Yet, there has also been little question of the toll that it took. Those who followed have begun to build a model that does not require a woman to be the clone of a man in order to feel comfortable in her own success. But we still have a long way to go. There also needs to be room for family, for external support rather than external competition, and for mentors of both genders who value good lawyering and recognize that good lawyers make the best client contacts. Of course, along the way, we need to be able to make a living.

And in the meantime, the answer is: Yes, women are still a minority . . . but watch your back!

A lawyer in San Francisco who has not disclosed his sexual orientation to colleagues in his law firm, discusses his experience as a "closeted" attorney.

Anonymous, *Truth and Consequences: Journal of a Closeted Attorney*, 2002 San Francisco Att'y 44 (June/July 2002).

Of the 400+ lawyers in the firm, there are six "known" queer associates, of whom five are out. We have lunch every other month. There are no gay partners. The one left last year for a friendlier atmosphere.

In the three years that I've worked here, I've been present three times when the fag jokes started. These jokes were told by successful and intelligent people whom I generally liked, but who didn't know I was gay. The truth is that I didn't speak up. Plaintiff attorneys tell me I could file a sexual harassment claim, but it's not my style, and frankly I wasn't hurt by the jokes. I was hurt by my silence, but not by their stupidity.

I used to be out before I became a lawyer. In my previous job, I supported domestic partnership and made a point of being matter-of-fact—if not in-your-face—about being gay.

Things began to change when I decided to go to law school. On my applications to schools, I was out in some of the essays I submitted and not in others. Was it coincidence that I only got into schools where I wasn't out? Maybe.

. . . When I applied for jobs at prestigious law firms, the experience replicated itself. I looked over the literature at my school's career center and some of it quite clearly recommended that gays and lesbians do not come out on their résumés. The message was pretty clear: Being out negatively affects your legal career. I bought into that.

I never lied about being gay. If asked, I'll tell the truth. However, I avoid the question, "Do you have a girlfriend?" by avoiding social situations. I say to myself that I'm just a private person and not dishonest, but I'm a good enough lawyer to know an omission is as much a fib as an outright lie. At times I wish that someone would ask, so I could be tested for truthfulness and hopefully pass.

. . . The truth is that being closeted doesn't help my career, either. By avoiding social situations, I'm not being part [of] the collegial atmosphere that is a big part of corporate law—teamwork and drinks after work. By taking myself out of that part of the game, I'm out of a big part of the career life. I know in my heart that I'll never make partner being closeted like this, either.

At this point, I don't see a win-win way out of my deceit. Come out and torch my career, or stay in the closet and lament my own cowardice. I could always go into employment law, a traditional safe haven for gay lawyers. However, unlike many people, I actually like corporate law. If I were out at work, would I be part of the board meetings that make up a big part of a corporate law practice? I could be wrong, but I doubt it.

I know that the answer to my external stress is to come out, and I expect to do that sometime soon by bringing a boyfriend to dinner or by sending some equally obvious signal. But I'm enough of a realist to know that coming out has ramifications. Being a gay boy automatically excludes you from the old boys' network. In my view, coming out means getting out of the business of corporate law. Once I get my résumé in order, I'll make that move.

The final excerpt examines obstacles that lawyers and judges have had to overcome and the challenges they continue to face on account of a disability.

Ann W. Parks, *Disability as a law firm diversity issue*, The Daily Record, May 19, 2006, at 1B, *available at* http://mddailyrecord.com

[Scott] Labarre, who is blind, says people are always shocked to find out that he practices law. "I've shown up to many bar association conferences where other lawyers thought I must be lost," he said, adding that there are anywhere between 600 and 1,000 blind attorneys in the United States. When I explain that I'm actually a lawyer, they're kind of taken aback."

. . . .

James E. Scarboro, a partner in Arnold & Porter's LLP's Denver office, practiced law for 25 years before he went blind as the result of an operation. Rather than take disability, he chose to come back to the firm. Scarboro has a computer that talks, readers to help him read and the luxury of being in a large firm, so that when he tries cases they can be staffed with more than one person to help him. (Incidentally, Labarre, who is also blind, is a sole practitioner, using screen-reading software and an assistant to read things like mail and faxes.)

"I think people with disabilities have a lot of trouble [in terms of getting employment] because we're all naturally afraid of something that's different," said Scarboro. However, he insists his situation is not nearly as difficult as someone who has a disability from the outset. A prospective employer "has to overcome that sense of 'Oh, my gosh, this person is not going to be able to do the job,'" Scarboro said. Michael A. Schwartz, a Syracuse University, College of Law professor who is deaf, was harsher. "Many legal employers cannot see beyond the disability," he said, asserting that it is much easier to obtain employment and reasonable accommodations in public service than in the private arena. "Then all they can see once they've recovered from the shock is, 'How much is this gonna cost me?' That kind of traditional thinking I call 'stinking thinking.'" Still, every experience is different. [Andrew] Levy, who uses a wheelchair, got offers from three out of five firms he interviewed with for summer positions during law school (he graduated in 1982, with honors) and the firm he chose eventually hired him on a permanent basis. "I was sort of an exotic quality," he said. "I was obviously different but that intrigued some of the firms, and others were more put off by it."

Since the term "lawyers with disabilities" is extremely broad, the particular disability may not be readily apparent. While one might think that would make things easier in terms of bias—because people don't always have to know about it—people with "hidden" disabilities face their own particular challenges, according to Andrew J. Imparato, the president and CEO of the American Association of People with Disabilities in the District of Columbia. "It's very common to be either put into a category where the disability is like a hangnail—'it's not significant enough to matter, so don't go there with me'—or the disability is so significant that you're not desirable for whatever it is you're trying to do," said Imparato, who was diagnosed with bipolar disorder/manic depression after graduating from law school . . . . "The stuff that you have to say to show that it's real, to get over the hangnail test, often gets used against you when people are trying to figure out whether they really want to hire you," he said. "In my experience, you never really know who is going to react positively or negatively," he noted. "We have allies in lots of strange places [where people have had] personal experiences with disabilities themselves or with their families, and we have enemies in lots of strange places, including places that hold themselves out as advocates for people with disabilities."

. . .

Exercise 16.2 Record in your journal or in a reflection paper your reactions to the above readings. How would you define bias? Is the bias that these legal professionals describe different in any way from bias that occurs to non-lawyers or those not involved in the legal profession? Are the stresses that the lawyers describe attributable, at least in part, to stresses intrinsic to the practice of law regardless of race, gender, sexual orientation, or disability? Do any of these excerpts, though intended to illustrate bias, inadvertently perpetuate stereotypes as well?

Defining and Assessing Bias

What is bias, and how does it impact the legal profession? There are many different definitions of bias found in statutes prohibiting discrimination, task force reports studying bias, and in scholarly articles. Bias generally can be defined as intolerance, prejudice, differential or disparaging treatment toward an individual based on stereotypes or perceptions of inferiority related to the individual's race, ethnicity, gender, age, sexual orientation, socioeconomic status, religion, disability or other cultural characteristic or trait. The Final Report of the Task Force on Gender Bias for the District of Columbia Courts (at pages xiv-xv) gives examples of biased behavior in the gender context:

- when people are denied rights or burdened with responsibilities on the basis of gender;

- when stereotypes about the proper behavior, relative worth and credibility of men and women are applied to people regardless of their individual situations;

- when men and women are treated differently in situations because of gender where gender should not make a difference; and

- when men or women are adversely affected by a legal rule, policy or practice that affects members of the opposite sex to a lesser degree or not at all.

Although these examples are set in the context of gender bias, the concepts apply to other forms of bias as well. Bias may be manifested in the behavior of individuals or may become institutionalized in an organization's policies and procedures.

Some forms of discrimination are obvious and illegal. Firing an employee when she becomes pregnant, for example, or refusing to promote an associate in a firm because he has a foreign accent are obvious forms of illegal employment bias. Bias also can come in more subtle or elusive forms. While one person might interpret an incident as clear-cut bias, another person viewing the same situation may not see it at all.

Rather than relying on anecdotal tales of individual and institutional exclusion, bar associations and courts have taken a more systematic look at the issue. These task forces and commissions have gathered data through surveys, individual interviews, focus groups, review of court decisions, review of personnel records, and testimony at public hearings. The studies examine numerous areas including judicial decisions and jury verdicts in civil and criminal cases; judicial and jury decisions in criminal cases; numbers of minority law students, lawyers, litigants, court clerks, and judges in a particular jurisdiction; patterns of promotion in courts, the private and public sectors; availability of legal services; reports of discrimination, harassment, unwanted advances, disparaging comments or "jokes"; attorney disciplinary hearings; composition of court-appointed committees; court contracting and procurement practices; and court appointment of counsel in criminal cases. These reports not only compile raw statistics, but attempt to capture perceptions of those who interface with the legal profession and the justice system.

For example, the American Bar Association Commission on Racial and Ethnic Diversity in the Legal Profession issued a report assessing the representation of African-American, Hispanic, Asian-American, and Native-American law students and lawyers in the legal profession as of August 2004. It analyzes the obstacles impeding these groups from enjoying full participation in the legal profession and offers recommendations for improvements.

Elizabeth Chambliss, *Miles to Go: Progress of Minorities in the Legal Profession* 66-67 (American Bar Association Commission on Racial and Ethnic Diversity in the Legal Profession 2004).

In 1983, two thirds of the largest U.S. law firms had no black partners; more than 75% had no Hispanic partners; and many had no black or Hispanic lawyers at all. As late as 1987, over one third of the nation's 250 largest law firms had no Asian American or Hispanic lawyers. Such figures make current statistics—20.3 percent of law students, 14.6 percent of associates, and 4.0 percent of partners—seem worthy of celebration.

Nevertheless, there are miles to go. Compared to ten years ago, there has been little progress in the racial integration of the profession. Although nationally minority representation has increased slightly since 1990, and minority lawyers have made incremental gains in most employment settings, the pace of integration has slowed considerably since the 1980s and early 1990s. Total minority enrollment in law school hit 20 percent in the mid-1990s and has hovered at 20 percent ever since. Native American enrollment is stagnant and African-American enrollment has dropped. And minorities continue to be grossly underrepresented in top legal jobs.

Moreover, the legal profession is significantly less racially integrated than other, comparable professions. Accountants, engineers, architects, doctors: despite their similar histories of racial discrimination and exclusion, all of these groups currently have higher minority representation than lawyers. Minority representation among physicians and surgeons is 25 percent—about the same as minority representation in the civil labor force generally. Yet minority representation among lawyers remains less than 10 percent.

The American Bar Association Commission on Women in the Profession also has undertaken a comprehensive analysis of the participation of women in the legal profession. As excerpts from the Commission's report demonstrate, although women participate in the legal profession at every level, there is great disparity in the representation of women in management positions in law firms, the judiciary, and law school faculties.

Deborah Rhode, *The Unfinished Agenda: Women and the Legal Profession* 8 (American Bar Association Commission on Women in the Legal Profession 2001).

. . . Over the last dozen years, the number of women law partners, general counsels, and federal judges doubled. At the turn of this century, women accounted for almost a third of the nation's lawyers, and for the first time constituted a majority of entering law students.

Yet despite substantial progress towards equal opportunity, that agenda remains unfinished. Women in the legal profession remain underrepresented in positions of greatest status, influence, and economic reward. They account for only about 15% of federal judges and law firm partners, 10% of law school deans and general counsels, and five percent of managing partners of large firms. On average, female lawyers earn about $20,000 less than male lawyers, and significant disparities persist even between those with similar qualifications, experience, and positions. Studies involving thousands of lawyers find that men are at least twice as likely as similarly qualified women to obtain partnerships. The under-representation of women of color is still greater. They account for only 3 percent of the profession and their small numbers limit the information available about their experience. However, what data are available find significant inequalities in pay and promotion for lawyers of color, as well as for lesbian and disabled attorneys.

The problems are compounded by the lack of consensus that there are in fact serious problems. In the ABA Journal's 2000 poll, only about a quarter of female lawyers and three percent of male lawyers believed that prospects for advancement were greater for men than for women. Most attorneys equate gender bias with intentional discrimination, and the contexts in which they practice produce few overt examples. Yet a wide array of research finds that women's opportunities are limited by factors other than conscious prejudice. Major barriers include unconscious stereotypes, inadequate access to support networks, inflexible workplace structures, sexual harassment, and bias in the justice system.

Based on the data and information collected, the task forces have concluded that racial, ethnic, gender, and sexual orientation bias—or the perception of such bias—exists in varying degrees in the U.S. legal system. Some of the findings of the reports include disparities in hiring and promotion of court personnel as well as appointment and promotion of judges; differential outcomes in criminal and civil law cases attributed to bias, and disparaging treatment of court personnel, attorneys, court reporters, litigants, and witnesses by attorneys, judges, and supervisors. For example, the Final Report of the Judicial Council of California on sexual orientation fairness states that one in five court employees has heard derogatory statements or disparaging jokes about gay men and lesbians in open court. These remarks were most frequently made by judges, lawyers, and court employees. See Sexual Orientation Fairness Subcommittee, Judicial Counsel of California, *Sexual Orientation Fairness in the California Courts* 4 (2001), http://www.court info.ca.gov/programs/access/documents/report.pdf.

see Chapter 13 *on Judicial Externships*

In addition, studies have found that women and racial/ethnic minorities perceive bias in the legal system more frequently than those in majority groups. In 2003 the National Center for State Courts issued a report entitled "Perceptions of the Courts in Your Community: The Influence of Experience, Race, and Ethnicity." This report released results of a national study that found significant differences in perceptions of unequal treatment in courts. African-American and Latino respondents were more likely to believe that unequal treatment occurs frequently in the courts than White respondents. All groups agreed, however, that low-income individuals from all racial and ethnic groups receive the worst treatment in the courts.

The task force and commission reports contain wide ranging recommendations for addressing the problem of bias. Some of these recommendations include changing hiring and promotion policies in courts and law firms to ensure equal opportunity; adopting institutional measures for strengthening diversity within law firms such as tying compensation to diversity initiatives; enhancing mentoring programs, conducting multicultural training for court personnel, attorneys and judges; improving communication between workers and managers; increasing the number of employees who speak languages other than English; increasing the number of women/minorities on court-appointed committees; improving the use of minority contractors; developing sexual harassment policies; enhancing the data collection and research conducted on diversity within the legal profession; instituting flexible work schedule policies; ensuring diversity in law school admissions as well as in law faculty hiring and promotion; incorporating discussions of the history of exclusion in the legal profession into the law school curriculum; and improving disciplinary proceedings for attorneys and judges.

While bias studies and task force reports have been lauded for recommending needed institutional changes, they also have generated criticism. See, for example, Laurence H. Silberman, *The D.C. Circuit Task Force on Gender, Race, and Ethnic Bias: Political Correctness Rebuffed*, 19 Harv. J.L. & Pub. Pol'y 759 (1996); Kari M. Dahlin, *Actions Speak Louder than Thoughts: The Constitutionally Questionable Reach of the Minnesota CLE Elimination of Bias Requirement*, 84 Minn. L. Rev. 1725 (2000). Critics argue that the task force recommendations threaten judicial independence and free speech. Some believe, for example, that the desire to bring about racial or gender equality is being used as a justification for changing substantive outcomes in civil and criminal cases. As a result, discretion is removed from judges to interpret the law based on the particular set of facts before them. There is also concern that the enactment of disciplinary rules prohibiting biased conduct, recommended in some of the reports, may prevent lawyers from expressing their personal opinions outside of the courtroom or might inhibit lawyers from zealously advocating on behalf of their clients inside the courtroom if the strategy they use depends on appealing to the biases of the decision maker. Other critics suggest that outgrowths of these studies such as mandatory continuing legal education courses on diversity or bias infringe upon lawyers' free speech rights (the government cannot coerce individuals into speaking or listening to messages with which the individual disagrees) and constitute thinly veiled attempts to fulfill an agenda of political correctness.

Whatever your views of the work of the task forces, you will likely observe and experience changes in court practice, personnel policies in the private and public sectors, judicial decision making, and disciplinary rules brought about as a result of task force recommendations.

Exercise 16.3 How should the judicial system cope with the effects of bias that is prevalent in the culture at large? Should reforms be implemented based upon the perception of bias? How do you account for the differences in perceptions between minority groups and majority groups? Are there situations in which zealous advocacy on behalf of your client requires you to appeal to stereotypes or engage in biased behavior?

Recognizing Cultural Lenses and Developing Multicultural Competence

From early childhood, each of us sorts our world into categories based on our experiences. Stoves are hot; snow is cold. Candy is good; brussels sprouts are not. Our view about people and the categories into which they fall are similarly shaped by our experiences and by others around us. We acquire attitudes from parents, the media, teachers, peers, and a host of other external sources. From these early experiences, we develop lenses through which all of our perceptions are filtered. How have you developed your view of those who are different from you? Examining your experiences, beliefs, and assumptions may help you better recognize and avoid making inappropriate or inaccurate assumptions about clients, colleagues, judges, support staff, and others with whom you come into contact on a professional basis.

For a lawyer, developing the ability to communicate and work with individuals of varying backgrounds serves several important purposes. First, and most importantly, lawyers have the obligation to remedy injustices and ensure that laws are applied and enforced fairly. Attorneys who remain unaware of their own assumptions about those who are different from themselves cannot effectively carry out their responsibilities. Failure to recognize assumptions or personal biases may lead to ineffective client interviewing or counseling, imprecise and inaccurate use of language in oral or written advocacy, incomplete legal analysis, and unintentionally offensive behavior with colleagues or staff. Secondly, as bar associations and law firms are increasingly recognizing, multicultural competence makes business sense. An ability to work effectively with individuals of differing backgrounds enables lawyers and law firms to attract diverse clients, appeal to diverse juries, retain better lawyers, and develop more creative, comprehensive solutions to complex legal problems. As one study demonstrated, clients who perceive their lawyers as culturally sensitive are more likely to view their lawyers as competent. See Robert F. Cochran, Jr., John M.A. DiPippa & Martha M. Peters, *The Counselor-At-Law: A Collaborative Approach to Client Interviewing and Counseling* (2d ed. 2006).

Exercise 16.4 Write down three "facts" about yourself on a piece of paper. These facts might include personal traits, characteristics, likes or dislikes. However, one of the three "facts" should be inaccurate or untrue. Break into pairs and reveal your personal facts to your partner. Your partner must try to guess which "fact" is false. After the exercise, use the following questions to discuss how we develop our understanding of other cultures and make assumptions about people based on these understandings.

On what basis did you decide that a particular "fact" was false?

If you were correct in your guess, discuss whether you made any assumptions in arriving at your conclusion. Were these assumptions accurate? Can you envision a situation in which such assumptions might not hold up? How can you protect against automatically adopting such assumptions since they will not always be true?

If you were incorrect in your guess, did you make any assumptions that led you to your conclusion? What caused you to make this assumption? What steps can you take to prevent yourself from making inaccurate assumptions?

Social science and, increasingly, legal literature recognizes, as law professor Carwina Weng points out, that "cultural self-awareness is . . . the key to multicultural competence, because awareness of one's own culture allows more accurate understanding of cultural forces that affect the lawyer, the client, and the interaction of the two." Carwina Weng, *Multicultural Lawyering: Teaching Psychology to Develop Cultural Self-Awareness*, 11 Clin. L. Rev. 369 (2005). This awareness also allows lawyers to improve their communication and collaboration with judges, colleagues, court personnel, and others in the legal profession.

A lawyer is more likely to be aware of the need to consider cross cultural differences when representing a client or interacting with a colleague who was born in another country or who does not speak English as a first language. However, cultural competence comes into play whenever a lawyer interacts with someone whose background differs from the lawyer's in a significant way whether because of race, religion, education, socioeconomic status, gender, sexual orientation, disability, or age. It is important to recognize that a person will not be wholly defined by one of these characteristics and may be significantly influenced by a confluence of factors, such as both race and gender. Similarly, there are tremendous differences within cultural groups. Individuals who may identify themselves as Latino or Asian, for example, hail from a host of countries that have their own unique histories, languages or dialects, foods, religions, and customs. "A broad definition of culture recognizes that no two people can have exactly the same experiences and thus no two people will interpret or predict in precisely the same ways." Susan Bryant, *The Five Habits: Building Cross-Cultural Competence in Lawyers*, 8 Clin. L. Rev. 33, 41 (2001).

Without conscious recognition that one's own culture is a filter through which information is channeled, a lawyer may not be able to recognize that someone else has a valid, yet different, interpretation or reaction to the same set of facts, law, or circumstances. Common sense is not enough. As Professor Bill Ong Hing points out, "common sense, without training, is dangerously fashioned by our own class, race, ethnicity/culture, gender, and sexual background. What we think of as common sense may make little sense or even be offensive to someone of a different identification background. Thus, the opportunity to learn and discuss different approaches with the help of different perspectives from readings, the opinions of others, and self-critique is unique." Bill Ong Hing, *Raising Personal Identification Issues of Class, Race, Ethnicity, Gender, Sexual Orientation, Physical Disability, and Age in Lawyering Courses*, 45 Stan. L. Rev. 1807, 1810-11 (1993).

Exercise 16.5 Write responses to the following questions in order to assess and reflect on your own cultural values, assumptions, preferences. You will not turn in your responses to your instructor. Please be honest and direct as you respond. This checklist is not exhaustive but is an attempt to illustrate some of the component parts of one's cultural lense.

- How would you define your cultural background?

- What have you been taught about the value of money, work, family, or religion?

- How have you learned about members of other racial, ethnic, or religious groups?

- Do most of your friends have a similar cultural background (race, religion, socioeconomic status)?

- Even if you do not subscribe to them, were you taught certain biases or prejudiced beliefs about groups or individuals who are different from you?

- How does your socioeconomic level affect your attitude toward people of other economic groups?

- Do you consider yourself extroverted and sociable, introverted and shy, or a little of both depending on the situation?

- How much personal space or distance do you need when you speak with someone?

- Do you prefer to work in groups or alone?

- To whom do you turn when you need support?

- How do you make important decisions in your life? Do you consult with others? Do you make these decisions independently?

- In your view, what type of body language demonstrates honesty? Dependability? Professionalism?

- In your view, what constitutes professional success?

- Do you believe that one can achieve success through individual effort?

- Are you a linear thinker who can tell a story from beginning to end or do you think more abstractly, going from one topic to another until eventually you weave a story together?

Of course, the answers to some of these questions will be fluid and change with time and experience—yet identifying your responses to these questions can help you understand some of your values, beliefs, and preferences. Have these values or beliefs influenced your decision to choose law as a career? How might some of your preferences affect your professional interactions or influence the way in which you make professional judgments in your legal work? The next exercise is designed to help you answer some of these abstract questions in a more practical context.

Exercise 16.6 Consider the following scenario: A woman comes to your law office seeking legal assistance. She is a grandmother interested in petitioning for joint custody of her grandchild because she believes her daughter, the nineteen-year-old mother of the child, is too young to responsibly make decisions for the child. The grandmother understands that her daughter is legally an adult, but she worries that because her daughter has not received a college education (though she is a high school graduate) she will never be able to adequately support the child. The mother of the child works in a retail store and the grandmother feels that the mother uses her paycheck to buy unnecessary household items such as a DVD player rather than saving money for an emergency or for the child's education. The grandmother is also very concerned that the mother is an atheist and does not plan to provide the child with a religious identity.

Imagine that you are the lawyer that has just conducted the initial interview with this potential client. You are not familiar with the standards for joint custody or the rights of grandparents in your jurisdiction. You will have to do more research on the legal issues. What are your initial impressions of the factual situation? Have you begun to develop views or concerns based on the little information you have received? How do your own values concerning money, work, family, and religion influence your initial views? Is it appropriate to use your own cultural views or perspective when assessing a legal problem or fashioning legal advice? How can you ensure that your own cultural values do not interfere with your ability to give sound legal advice— advice based on the potential client's values or objectives? What steps might you take to identify and understand the grandmother's values?

Developing self awareness is an important initial step toward becoming a culturally competent lawyer. However, it is then necessary to find ways to educate and check oneself to ensure that a lawyer's "lense" is not obscuring facts and leading one to arrive at inadequate or offensive judgments. As professors Lorraine Bannai & Anne Enquist point out, "[t]o be effective advocates in the 21st century . . . [law students] must learn to recognize cultural bias in language and analysis. Realizing that words are the tools of their trade, they need to be particularly attentive to their spoken and written language and examine it for imprecision, stereotyping, and any potential for unintended offense. Realizing that legal analysis and legal argument are the professional services they will offer, they need to probe for cultural bias that leads to faulty reasoning." Lorraine Bannai & Anne Enquist, *(Un)examined Assumptions and (Un)intended Messages: Teaching Students to Recognize Bias in Legal Analysis and Language*, 27 Seattle U. L. Rev. 1 (2003).

So, how does a lawyer develop cultural competency? Like many other lawyering skills, the ability to interact and communicate with individuals from a variety of cultures takes practice and conscious effort. An externship offers opportunities to hone these skills. The following is a list of concrete methods to use with colleagues, clients, court personnel, or others in the profession in order to uncover assumptions, determine whether an assumption is accurate, challenge negative judgments, communicate clearly, and correct mistakes that you inadvertently make.

- Stay in information gathering mode, LISTEN CAREFULLY, ask questions rather than making statements or making assumptions.

- Try to identify or imagine circumstances under which an assumption you are about to make is not true or does not hold up. If you can identify such circumstances then do not make the assumption until you have gathered more information.

- Before commenting or reacting, repeat back or summarize what you have understood the other person to say in order to ensure that you accurately received the intended message.

- Be aware of your own cultural beliefs, values, customs, and biases.

- Do not assume the normalcy of your life. Do not measure a client's reaction, a court employee's comment, or a colleague's decision using your own beliefs, customs, and values as a yardstick.

- Do not assume that all people from a particular cultural group are the same or share the same values and priorities. Ask questions. Listen. Reflect before reacting or commenting.

- Before making a negative judgment about someone, try to come up with at least three or four possible explanations for the other person's reaction or behavior.

- Identify areas of commonality you have with those you determine to be different from yourself and use these similarities to build rapport.

- Identify areas of difference and try to anticipate where areas of miscommunication might arise, plan to ask more questions or gather more information.

- Be extremely careful with humor. Ensure that jokes do not rely on inappropriate bias or prejudice. If you are not sure, DO NOT TELL THE JOKE.

• Think about your choice of language in both face to face interactions and in writing. Reflect on which titles and terminology you should use to address or describe individuals of varying ages, races, ethnicities, gender. If you are not sure, check.

• Clarify that your view or opinion is your individual view, using phrases such as "I think," "I believe," "My view is . . . ," rather than making global statements suggesting that there is only one reasonable position or view on an issue.

• APOLOGIZE if you make a mistake. If it is not appropriate or possible to apologize or correct the mistake immediately, then find the next available opportunity to do so.

These suggestions are adapted from numerous sources, including, Stacy L. Brustin, *Cross Cultural Communication,* in *The Impact of Domestic Violence on Your Legal Practice: A Lawyer's Handbook* 70 (Margaret B. Drew, Lisae C. Jordan, Donna J. Mathews & Robin R. Runge eds. 2004); Susan Bryant, *The Five Habits: Building Cross-Cultural Competence in Lawyering,* 8 Clin. L. Rev. 33 (2001); and Paul R. Tremblay, *Interviewing and Counseling Across Cultures: Heuristics and Biases,* 9 Clin. L. Rev. 373 (2002).

Exercise 16.7 Choose a person or a group of persons with whom you come into contact at your externship (your supervisor, the lawyer in the next office, a member of the maintenance or secretarial staff, witnesses in a hearing you observe, criminal defendants awaiting arraignment) and observe their interactions with others. For example, you might observe interactions between your supervisor and subordinates, interactions among lawyers at your externship, interactions among lawyers and support staff, interactions among lawyers and judges, or interactions among lawyers and clients. See Chapter 12 for techniques for observation. Record any interactions that you believe demonstrate biased attitudes based on cultural assumptions *or* that demonstrate effective multicultural communication. For each example, reflect on how you believe the interaction was perceived by those involved. Do you think the actor was aware of how his or her actions were perceived by others. What do you think caused the person to engage in such behavior? What was the response to the conduct, if any? What would you have done if you were in the situation?

Now undertake the same analysis with written communications you have received or reviewed during the course of your externship.

You could use documents such as office memos, e-mails, pleadings, correspondence, training materials, or legal briefs. Can you identify a written document that uses biased terminology or makes arguments based on unexamined cultural assumptions? Analyze the impact of such language on the overall quality of the document. How would you revise the language or the argument? Can you identify a written document that uses precise language, culturally appropriate terminology, and arguments based on solid information gathering rather than untested assumptions? How does the language contribute to the quality of the communication? (If you are required to discuss this exercise with your instructor or with student colleagues, be sure to maintain an appropriate level of confidentiality and discretion.)

Developing cultural competency is a challenging, yet critical, process for lawyers to undertake. There are many legal resources, as well as literature in other disciplines, that offer insights into this process. In addition, there are clinical opportunities and numerous continuing education trainings in which law students and lawyers can further develop this important lawyering skill.

Strategies for Dealing with Bias

During the course of your legal career you may witness or become the target of biased behavior. How do you respond? You may not be certain that what you are seeing or experiencing is bias, but you perceive that something is not quite right. A comment an associate at your firm makes may bother you. A reaction of a judge to lawyers or litigants may take you by surprise. A policy of the organization in which you are working may seem unfair. In certain circumstances, the bias or discrimination you experience may be so severe and blatant that you decide to resort immediately to formal channels of redress such as reporting an ethics violation to the court or bar, requesting that a judge impose sanctions, lodging a grievance with an employer, or filing a lawsuit. There are federal laws, state laws, and organization policies designed to address egregious forms of discrimination or abuse. In many instances, however, it can be difficult to identify more subtle forms of bias and even more difficult to determine how to respond to them. It is important to develop strategies for addressing biased behavior whether you are on the receiving end, a witness, or a supervisor who becomes aware of a particular problem. This section discusses a variety of informal and formal ways to do so.

A Personal Reflection

One of the most difficult moments of my first year of law practice involved what I believed to be a situation of racial and ethnic bias. My client's first language was Spanish. Although she spoke a fair amount of English, my client was much more proficient in Spanish, particularly when it came to talking about the emotionally charged issues involved in a divorce trial. Opposing counsel repeatedly questioned the need for a court interpreter. While the judge permitted my client to use an interpreter, the judge seemed impatient and made it clear that he considered the interpreters an inconvenience.

At one point in the trial, a new interpreter came in to replace an interpreter who was about to take a break. The opposing counsel jumped up and asked for a sidebar with the judge. She told the judge that according to her information, the interpreter, who was Hispanic, had herself been through a messy divorce from an African-American man and could not be trusted to interpret the proceedings accurately because our case also involved a Hispanic woman seeking a divorce from an African-American man. I was outraged. I objected strenuously to the attorney's comments. I suggested that she was simply trying to disrupt the proceedings and deflect the court's attention from the substantive issues at hand. I waited patiently for the judge to chide the attorney for bringing such inappropriate, biased, unsubstantiated claims into the proceeding. Instead the judge asked questions of the interpreter until he was assured that she was capable of interpreting.

Although the comment was not directed at my client or me, I felt that what had happened was wrong. I did not know exactly what to do; I did not want to react in a way that would anger the judge and potentially hurt my client's case. The main target of my outrage was the judge. While I believed the opposing attorney acted in an inappropriate, offensive manner, I was particularly troubled that the judge essentially condoned her behavior. I thought that the judge, at a minimum, should have stopped the attorney's repeated efforts to prevent my client from having an interpreter and should have been more sensitive to the difficulties that many who speak English as a second language have in testifying in open court. I also thought he should have admonished the attorney not to use unsubstantiated allegations based on race in his courtroom. I was not sure, however, that there were grounds to file a formal complaint.

I spoke to several colleagues about the matter and they advised me to try to find a less risky way of addressing the situation than filing a formal complaint. I eventually decided to take an informal route. My boss happened to be conducting a judicial training on cultural sensitivity that all trial court judges were required to attend. I described the incident and she used it as a hypothetical during the training exercises. The judge in question was sitting front and center at the training. Other judges reacted with harsh criticism to the response of the "hypothetical" judge. [S.L.B.]

Exercise 16.8 Record your reactions to my situation in your journal. What do you think about the judge's behavior? Should I have made a formal complaint? What do you think of my decision to use the scene as a hypothetical case at the training session? How do you think the judge reacted to the surrogate condemnation of his behavior? Do you think the comments of the other judges influenced his future behavior or his attitudes?

As a law student, what can you do ahead of time to prepare for dealing with issues of bias that will arise during your legal career? The following exercises are designed to help develop techniques for coping with biased behavior.

Exercise 16.9 Reactions to Bias in a Legal Setting Break into groups of no more than five. Each group should spend approximately ten minutes creating a role play to enact in front of the class based on one of the situations described below. Each group will spend another ten minutes generating a list of possible responses to each act of bias and then, next to each potential response, list the likelihood of taking such action. Outline why you would or would not be likely to take such action. Each group should pick one individual from the group to report back to the class on the list generated by each group.

You are one of four legal externs working at a government agency. One of the externs is African-American. You and your colleagues are sitting around the lunchroom table discussing your assignments when it becomes apparent that the African-American extern is receiving much less challenging work than the others. Indeed, a couple of the projects seem more administrative or secretarial than legal.

You are a female attorney appearing before a middle-aged, male judge who comments on your physical appearance in open court, immediately prior to the start of a hearing on your motion for summary judgment.

You are a junior associate in a small law firm and you are negotiating a settlement for a client. The opposing counsel is approximately twenty years older than you. Opposing counsel refers to you as "young lady" or "young man," interrupts you, asks when you got out of law school, and refers to your inexperience: "When you have tried as many cases as I have, you will understand . . . ."

You are one of two recent law graduates clerking for a trial judge. You have become good friends with your co-clerk. During the course of your conversations, he discloses to you that he is gay, but you know that he has not discussed his sexual orientation with the other law clerks in the court. You and your co-clerk are in the court cafeteria eating lunch with a few other clerks when someone at the table tells a joke that disparages gay men. A few people laugh, some look embarrassed. No one says anything.

You are a partner in a medium-sized law firm who is currently helping one of the firm's most important clients negotiate a commercial lease. You have selected a talented associate in the firm to assist in the negotiations. When the client meets the associate and learns that she is blind, he calls you and expresses concern that the associate is "not right for the project" because she might be viewed as vulnerable rather than as a tough negotiator.

Exercise 16.10 Using the same scenarios, reflect on the following questions. Do you have an ethical obligation to respond to any of these actions? Suppose you wanted to object to the judge's comments, but were afraid that the judge would take it out on your client by ruling against you. Do you have an ethical obligation not to object? You are the senior partner of the law firm where the associate works. The associate has just complained to you about opposing counsel's behavior. What do you do? As an observer to the acts of bias, how do you determine when to intervene?

Informal Strategies

As you have discussed in the role plays, there are many ways to address an incident reflecting bias. How one responds often will depend upon the forum in which the conduct takes place and one's role in the system. For example, in the courtroom an attorney can choose to confront directly the offending party (whether it be judge, attorney, clerk); ignore the behavior; seek a sidebar with the judge and ask to address the issue; or communicate with the offending party by letter following the hearing or trial (ensuring that as an attorney you do not engage in *ex parte* communications with the judge).

Much of the biased interpersonal conduct that takes place during the course of litigation or transactional matters occurs outside of the courtroom, in depositions or negotiations. Members of the legal profession can address this conduct in a variety of ways. In a deposition an attorney might decide initially to ignore offensive behavior or use humor in response to a comment intended to intimidate. In cases of more egregious behavior, however, a lawyer can preserve offensive comments as part of the transcript of a deposition. The lawyer also can note inappropriate behavior on the record and, if necessary, halt the proceeding and bring the conduct to the attention of the judge or bar. Lawyers often point out that one of the most effective ways to fight biased or offensive tactics is to be extremely well prepared on the substantive issues at hand. See for example, J. Stratton Shartel, *Litigators Describe Depositions as Hotbed of Gender Bias*, Inside Litigation, Jul. 1994, at 13.

Bias also may manifest itself among colleagues or peers in the office, outside a law school classroom, or in the hallways of a court. One might choose to discuss the issue directly with the offending party or to seek out a supervisor, a professor, or a trusted colleague who can intervene. Others may try to use humor to alert the person to the offensive nature of his or her behavior. In some situations, one might ignore the conduct if it appears that a reaction is exactly what the offending party intended to elicit. Rather than directly confronting someone about the issue, one can adopt a more indirect approach such as organizing or participating in an office training on multicultural competence and using real life examples that put the offending party on notice that certain behavior is unacceptable.

Another powerful way to address bias is to support a co-worker who has been treated inappropriately. Rather than idly standing by as you witness an incident, let the offending party know that you do not approve of the attitude or behavior. If, for example, you are a male and you witness a male co-worker making sexist remarks to a female colleague, you may be able to influence your male co-worker's future conduct by demonstrating your disapproval of his behavior. Take opportunities to let colleagues know that terminology they are using in their writing or oral advocacy is inappropriate or could be considered offensive. Most colleagues would rather have this information, even if the exchange is a bit awkward, than risk harming their case or tarnishing their reputation.

The manner in which someone confronts offensive conduct and the timing of such response depends upon a number of factors including one's own personal style (for example, do you feel comfortable using humor or do you prefer a more serious, straightforward approach) and your analysis of whether raising the issue or failing to raise the issue will negatively impact your client, your credibility, or your case.

Lee Gardenswartz and Anita Rowe, diversity consultants and trainers who have written extensively in the area, recommend the following ways for managers to cope with inappropriate conduct in the workplace. Their recommendations may be adapted to deal with inappropriate conduct in other settings as well.

Lee Gardenswartz and Anita Rowe, *Dealing with Prejudice and Stereotypes on the Job*, Managing Diversity, Mar. 1994.

Incidents of prejudicial treatment, stereotypical comments, and racial, ethnic, or gender slurs, while not common, are nevertheless troublesome to managers when they happen. We're often asked how to deal with this demeaning and divisive behavior in work groups. Here are ten ways you as a manager can prevent such occurrences and deal with them once they've happened.

1. Model the behavior you expect.

Your position as a manager makes you a role model for your staff, and your behavior broadcasts a very clear message. When John Sculley, the former CEO of Apple Computer, was asked why he marched in the Gay Rights parade, he responded that it was a human rights issue. That behavior left no doubts in the minds of Apple employees about where he stood on the topic of diversity.

If you refrain from telling jokes that could be hurtful to others or confront racist comments, you will set a tone of tolerance in your work group.

2. Let staff know clearly what is off limits.

In one organization an incident of racist graffiti had sparked anger and a search for an appropriate response. Leaders went to the minority support group whose members were the targets of the slur. The group advised the CEO to write a response in the next company-wide newsletter. His response was clear and direct in stating that such behavior would not be tolerated and that any future incident would be thoroughly investigated and those responsible punished. There were no more incidents.

3. Challenge stereotypical assumptions.

One manager we work with deals with stereotyping on a one-on-one basis. Whenever she hears a comment such as, "Those immigrants are just lazy and they deplete our social services," she stops and asks questions. "Do you know anyone like that?" "How many immigrants have you come across who abuse the system?" She may also point out some examples of individuals who refute the stereotype. "Do you think this is true of Juan and Luisa?" Generally her questions at least get people to stop and think about their knee-jerk generalizations.

4. Increase understanding about cultural differences.

Many stereotypes arise from misunderstood cultural differences. Someone who does not make eye contact is not sneaky or unassertive, but may be showing respect. Someone who doesn't adhere to rigid time frames is not necessarily lazy or unreliable, but may have a different sense of time. Someone who stands close and makes direct eye contact may not be aggressive and challenging, but may have different rules about communication.

When employees come to understand some of the cultural differences underlying behaviors, they may find them less difficult and less irritating.

5. Use each incident as a teaching opportunity.

Often employees don't know why their behavior is hurtful or upsetting to others. "Hey, what's the big deal? I was just kidding," they respond. These situations give you a chance to teach. Have employees who are the objects of comments or jokes talk about how it feels or what a particular term means to them. For example, explaining why some women balk at being called "ladies," why a person of Mexican descent may prefer to be called Chicano rather than Hispanic, or why an African-American mail clerk doesn't want to be called an "errand boy," can be instructive.

6. Structure opportunities for cross-group sharing.

When employees of different groups have a chance to share, on a more personal level, information about their lives, their families, and their values, they are often surprised to find they have more similarities than differences. Bonds built in this kind of mutual self-disclosure enable people to see one another as unique individuals rather than stereotypical groups.

7. Use team meetings and training to develop understanding and empathy.

Activities that get people interacting with coworkers in a deeper way build relationship and team cohesiveness. It's not uncommon to see colleagues who may appear to be quite different in background and lifestyle find that they have much in common when they talk about dearly held values or significant milestones in their lives. Having employees talk with one another about how it feels to be an outsider or share an experience when they were the object of prejudice helps develop empathy.

8. Group employees across cultural, racial, and gender lines for tasks and projects.

Another way to break down walls between people is to give them a work-related reason to interact and a common goal. Having mixed groups on shifts, committees, or task forces tends to forge teams of diverse individuals. In the course of working on projects with one another, people develop relationships with others different from themselves.

9. Focus on common ground.

While staff may be different in many ways, there are also many common experiences and ways they are alike that can be emphasized. What team goals can everyone buy into? What activities such as sports or hobbies do people share? What common life experiences such as raising children, taking vacations, or preparing for the holidays can staff build on? What company activities are of interest to the group?

10. Remember we are all perpetrators and victims of stereotypes.

None of us is free of the effects of stereotypes. We are all on the sending and the receiving end, and the behavior hurts us all. Focusing on the damage this kind of thinking does and on how it feels to be on the receiving end of such views can change the tone of the discussion about stereotypes from one of wrist slapping to one of empathy and sharing.

Exercise 16.11 Prepare your answers to these discussion questions by reflecting on the preceding discussion of informal strategies and on your experiences. Whose responsibility is it to remedy a situation of bias or to improve cultural sensitivity in a legal setting? How can diversity strengthen an organization? Can diversity weaken an organization? Do diversity training and educational programs work? What can employers or professional associations do to change biased attitudes among members of the legal profession? How would you describe the work environment at the office or organization where you are doing your externship? Are you aware of educational programs or other approaches used by the organization to address the issue of multicultural sensitivity? What are the informal policies or practices for dealing with issues of bias at your externship?

Formal Strategies

The discriminatory behavior may be so egregious that informal responses are inadequate and more serious action must be taken. One avenue may be to register a complaint against a co-worker or supervisor with an internal or external grievance committee set up by the organization, agency, firm, or court in which you work.

If the conduct takes place during litigation, one can seek sanctions against an attorney who has engaged in improper conduct. State and federal rules of civil procedure authorize the imposition of sanctions against attorneys, law firms, or parties who engage in improper conduct designed to harass another party during the course of litigation. Using biased statements in pleadings or engaging in biased behavior during depositions or in court can constitute conduct designed to harass and result in a sanction. For example, in *Mullaney v. Aude*, 730 A.2d 759 (Md. Ct. Spec. App. 1999), the Maryland Court of Special Appeals upheld a lower court's decision to issue a protective order against an attorney and require him to pay attorney's fees to opposing counsel for having made gender-based derogatory comments during a deposition. In New York, a trial court judge sanctioned an attorney for repeatedly referring to opposing counsel as "little girl." The court then commended the attorney who sought sanctions for taking action and refusing to allow the conduct to remain "another hidden, 'dirty little secret' which, while undoubtedly occurring on a daily basis, no one speaks about in public." *Principe v. Assay Partners*, 586 N.Y.S.2d. 182, 185 (N.Y. 1992).

Another option may be filing a complaint with the local board that licenses and regulates attorney conduct. Rule 8.4 of the ABA Model Rules of Professional Conduct prohibits lawyers from engaging in conduct that is "prejudicial to the administration of justice." The comment to this rule clarifies that

> A lawyer who, in the course of representing a client, knowingly manifests by words or conduct, bias or prejudice based upon race, sex, religion, national origin, disability, age, sexual orientation or socioeconomic status, violates paragraph (d) when such actions are prejudicial to the administration of justice. Legitimate advocacy respecting the foregoing factors does not violate paragraph (d). A trial judge's finding that peremptory challenges were exercised on a discriminatory basis does not alone establish a violation of this rule.

At least twenty-nine states have adopted a version of Model Rule 8.4 and its comments or have adopted language in their rules of professional conduct, disciplinary rules, or local trial rules which restrict biased or discriminatory conduct. For example, according to Rule 8.4 of the Washington Rules of Professional Conduct, it is professional misconduct for a lawyer to

(g) Commit a discriminatory act prohibited by state law on the basis of sex, race, age, creed, religion, color, national origin, disability, sexual orientation, or marital status, where the act of discrimination is committed in connection with the lawyer's professional activities. In addition, it is professional misconduct to commit a discriminatory act on the basis of sexual orientation if such an act would violate this rule when committed on the basis of sex, race, age, creed, religion, color, national origin, disability, or marital status. This rule shall not limit the ability of a lawyer to accept, decline, or withdraw from the representation of a client in accordance with RPC 1.15;

(h) In representing a client, engage in conduct that is prejudicial to the administration of justice toward judges, other parties and/or their counsel, witnesses and/or their counsel, jurors, or court personnel or officers, that a reasonable person would interpret as manifesting prejudice or bias on the basis of sex, race, age, creed, religion, color, national origin, disability, sexual orientation, or marital status. This rule does not restrict a lawyer from representing a client by advancing material factual or legal issues or arguments.

State rules differ in scope. Some prohibit lawyers from engaging in biased behavior generally, while others proscribe employment discrimination or other biased conduct by a lawyer while the lawyer is engaged in professional activities or during the course of representation of a client.

Courts have disciplined lawyers for violating these rules. See *In re Thomsen*, 837 N.E. 2d 1011 (Ind. 2005) (attorney reprimanded for making racially derogatory comments during a divorce trial in violation of Rule 8.4(g) prohibiting biased or prejudicial conduct based on race); *Florida Bar v. Martocci*, 791 So.2d 1074, 1077 (Fla. 2001) (attorney received a public reprimand and two years probation for making inappropriate gestures as well as sexist, racial, and ethnic insults to opposing counsel).

In addition to specific rules prohibiting biased conduct, many jurisdictions have more general ethical rules requiring attorneys to conduct themselves in a professional manner and prohibiting attorneys from engaging in behavior designed to harass or denigrate witnesses or parties to an action. Attorneys who are found to violate ethical rules may face sanctions ranging from warnings to disbarment.

While many states have adopted such rules over the last decade, critics argue that these rules can have a detrimental effect on an attorney's ability to zealously represent clients and may infringe upon a lawyer's ability to engage in free speech in professional or non-professional contexts. Others worry that attorneys will use these rules as tactical weapons to delay or otherwise secure advantage in litigation.

During your legal career you may find it necessary to report biased behavior of an attorney to a disciplinary board. In some cases you may decide, after reading the rules of your particular jurisdiction and consulting with colleagues or local bar counsel, that you have an obligation to report. In other circumstances, you may believe you have a moral responsibility to do so even if you are not legally obligated to report.

If the problem you are having involves a judge, then you will need to refer to the standards of professional conduct imposed upon judges as well as to the rules of civil or criminal procedure and determine whether you have a basis for filing a complaint or seeking other remedial action. The American Bar Association adopted a Model Code of Judicial Conduct in 1990 that addresses bias. Canon 3(B)(5) provides

> A judge shall perform judicial duties without bias or prejudice. A judge shall not, in the performance of judicial duties, by words or conduct manifest bias or prejudice, including but not limited to bias or prejudice based upon race, sex, religion, national origin, disability, age, sexual orientation or socioeconomic status, and shall not permit staff, court officials and others subject to the judge's direction and control to do so.

Under the Model Code, judges are prohibited from engaging in biased or prejudiced behavior, and they also are required to ensure that lawyers refrain from such conduct when appearing in legal proceedings. According to Canon 3B(6),

> A judge shall require lawyers in proceedings before the judge to refrain from manifesting, by words or conduct, bias or prejudice based upon race, sex, religion, national origin, disability, age, sexual orientation, or socioeconomic status, against parties, witnesses, counsel or others. This Section 3B(6) does not preclude legitimate advocacy when race, sex, religion, national origin, disability, age, sexual orientation or socioeconomic status, or other similar factors, are issues in the proceeding.

At least forty-three states have adopted a version of Canon 3(B)(5) and (6) or have adopted other rules prohibiting judicial conduct based on bias or prejudice. In addition, many federal trial courts, bankruptcy courts, administrative tribunals and local courts have promulgated rules prohibiting judges from engaging in biased conduct based on race, ethnicity, gender, sexual orientation, or other personal characteristics or background factors. For example, Rule 1000-1 of the Local Rules governing the United States Bankruptcy Court in Arizona and Rules of Practice of the U.S. District Court for the District of Arizona, LRCiv 83.5, state that "[l]itigation, inside and outside the courtroom, in the United States District Court for the District of Arizona, must be free from prejudice and bias in any form. Fair and equal treatment must be accorded all courtroom participants, whether judges, attorneys, witnesses, litigants, jurors, or court personnel. The duty to be respectful of others includes the responsibility to avoid comment or behavior that can reasonably be interpreted as manifesting prejudice or bias toward another on the basis of categories such as gender, race, ethnicity, religion, disability, age, or sexual orientation."

Judges have been overruled, removed from cases, censured, or removed from the bench as a consequence of engaging in biased behavior. See, for example, *In re Ellender*, 889 So.2d 225 (La. 2004) (a state district court judge found to have violated the judicial canon of ethics and suspended for a year without pay for having appeared at a party in a costume which was racist and derogatory of African-Americans); *In re Barr*, 13 S.W.3d 525 (Tex. Rev. Trib. 1998) (removal of judge upheld based, in part, on inappropriate comments made to female employees and litigants); *In re Mulroy*, 731 N.E.2d 120, 121-22 (N.Y. 2000) (decision of the State Commission on Judicial Conduct to remove a judge from office based, in part, on the fact that the judge had used derogatory racial epithets and ethnic slurs, upheld, with the court noting, "such language, whether provoked or in jest, manifested an impermissible bias that threatens public confidence in the judiciary"); *In re C.M.A.*, 715 N.E.2d 674, 679 (Ill. App. Ct. 1999) (upholding removal of trial court judge from hearing two adoption cases due to her "extreme and patent bias against the adoptive parents based upon their sexual orientation").

Every jurisdiction has a board or committee that reviews the conduct of judges. Members of the bar can submit complaints against judges who engage in biased behavior. Many courts and bar associations also routinely conduct surveys of the bar seeking information on judges currently sitting in local courts. These surveys provide opportunities to inform the bar and the judiciary about problems of bias in local courts. Similarly, whether judges are elected or appointed to the bench, individuals in the community often have an opportunity to comment on a particular individual's fitness to serve as a judge. One can report incidents in which the judicial candidate has previously engaged in biased behavior.

In addition to rules of professional conduct governing judicial behavior, there are codes of conduct for mediators and arbitrators. While these standards, unless adopted by a court or other regulatory body, do not have the force of law, they may be used to demonstrate or establish a standard of care. For example, the Model Standards of Conduct for Mediators, developed and approved by the American Bar Association, the American Arbitration Association, and the Association for Conflict Resolution, require mediators to conduct mediations in an impartial manner. Standard II.B.1 specifies that "[a] mediator should not act with partiality or prejudice based on any participant's personal characteristics, background, values and beliefs . . . . "

Depending on the offensive behavior, one also may choose to file a claim with the local Human Rights Commission, the Equal Employment Opportunity Commission or to file a discrimination lawsuit to remedy the situation. Filing an administrative claim is usually a prerequisite for filing lawsuits seeking a remedy for an employer's discriminatory conduct. Note that, depending on the circumstances of the case, the individual whose conduct is at issue and the employer of the individual both may be liable under discrimination statutes. In addition to civil rights statutes, tort law may provide a remedy if the behavior constitutes invasion of privacy, intentional infliction of emotional distress, assault, or battery.

The decision whether to utilize formal mechanisms to combat a situation of bias is a difficult decision to make. In many cases, you will not have an ethical obligation to report the conduct. Instead, you will have discretion about which course of action to take. You must weigh the likelihood of obtaining a favorable result through formal channels against the impact that taking formal action will have on your career. Each individual must fully consider the consequences of his or her actions and decide on an appropriate strategy. It is also important to think ahead to the time when you, as an attorney, may become an employer. As an employer, it is imperative that you establish policies and procedures designed to eliminate biased or discriminatory behavior in your firm or organization.

In this final excerpt, Nancy Lasater offers practical advice on how lawyers who are employers can minimize the likelihood of ethical complaints and lawsuits based on discrimination or harassment.

Nancy Lasater, *Discrimination Can Mean Disbarment*, The Washington Lawyer, Jan./Feb. 1996, at 25, 29.

How to Minimize Legal Exposure

1. Institute a written anti-discrimination and anti-harassment policy and procedure, which defines the concepts, emphasizes the firm's zero tolerance for such behavior, carefully outlines the firm's internal complaint procedure, and prohibits retaliation against anyone submitting a complaint.

2. The complaint procedure should (a) set out precisely how to lodge a charge and with whom; (b) detail how investigations will be conducted and to whom the results will be reported; (c) describe the decision-making process, including the identity of the persons or entity involved (i.e. will the managing partner find the facts and impose proper punishment, or will it be the management committee or full partnership?); and (d) emphasize the importance of confidentiality. The procedure must also include a paragraph describing the backup process to be followed in the event anyone in the decision-making chain of command is the alleged discriminator or harasser, which specifies also that he or she will play no role in finding the facts or deciding what discipline should be imposed.

3. Distribute the new policy and procedure to everyone at the firm, possibly in conjunction with an in-house seminar. Often the audience is divided into two and sometimes even three groups: owners and all others or owners, other attorneys, and all staff. The groups are segregated in this way because the message to each audience necessarily varies, with the owners receiving the most detail about potential firm and individual liability.

4. Consistently and uniformly apply the new policy to everyone, regardless of rank, with no exceptions. If the firm community understands that even the most powerful senior partners face severe discipline for egregious misconduct, the new policy will be taken as seriously as it should be.

5. Investigate promptly and thoroughly, and treat everyone involved with respect. The employee whose internal complaint is dismissed with the back of the corporate hand is much more likely to sue than the one who is sincerely heard.

6. If the facts confirm that misconduct has occurred, swiftly impose punishment that fits the crime. For firm attorneys, appropriate discipline may include reduction in pay, disqualification for that year's bonuses or partner distributions, dismissal from firm committees, public censure, apologies, reprimands, suspension, and, in egregious or repeated cases, termination.

7. Announce to the firm as much detail as possible about the discipline imposed (particularly if the whole firm already knows about what happened).

8. The firm's internal complaint procedure should clearly state that anyone making a groundless charge in bad faith is subject to discipline up to and including possible termination. If, though, the firm's investigation confirms that the allegations are correct, seriously consider offering to make the plaintiff whole. While dyed-in-the-wool litigators sometimes blanch at this suggestion, doing so should limit the plaintiff's compensatory damages and vastly reduce the firm's exposure to punitive damages . . . .

9. Most important, do not discriminate against or sexually harass anyone, and do not tolerate a biased or hostile firm culture. Promote an open and frank atmosphere, where those who are justifiably offended by prejudiced remarks or improper sexually oriented conduct can confront the perpetrator directly, without fear or reprisal or submit a complaint that the victim knows will be taken seriously and investigated promptly.

Exercise 16.12 Record your answers to these discussion questions in your journal. At your externship, are there formal office policies or grievance procedures in place to deal with bias and discriminatory behavior? Should lawyers, as officers of the judicial system, be held to a higher standard of conduct than other individuals when it comes to engaging in biased behavior? Can one readily distinguish when a lawyer is acting in his or her capacity as a lawyer as opposed to speaking or acting in an individual capacity? How would you counsel a friend who is considering formal action against a judge or another attorney? What are the pros and cons you would want your friend to consider?

Conclusion

An externship provides a unique opportunity to reflect upon your professional goals and to start developing strategies for addressing the challenges you will face as an attorney. One challenge you will encounter, either directly or indirectly, is the issue of bias. Will you recognize bias when you are confronted with it? How will you respond? What steps can you take to develop cultural awareness and improve your cross cultural communication skills? You will grapple with these difficult questions throughout your career. Let your externship be one vehicle through which to devise creative ways to address individual and institutional bias in the legal profession.

FURTHER READING

Commission Reports and Model Standards

DIVERSITY IN FIRMS, U.S. EQUAL EMPLOYMENT OPPORTUNITY COMMISSION REPORT (2003).

ABA COMMISSION ON RACIAL AND ETHNIC DIVERSITY IN THE LEGAL PROFESSION, MILES TO GO: PROGRESS OF MINORITIES IN THE LEGAL PROFESSION, (Elizabeth Chambliss 2004).

NATIONAL CENTER FOR STATE COURTS, PERCEPTIONS OF THE COURTS IN YOUR COMMUNITY: THE INFLUENCE OF EXPERIENCE, RACE, AND ETHNICITY (2003).

JUDICIAL COUNCIL OF CALIFORNIA, SEXUAL ORIENTATION FAIRNESS IN THE CALIFORNIA COURTS (2001) available at *http://www.courtinfo.ca.gov/programs/access/reports.htm.*

ABA, THE UNFINISHED AGENDA: WOMEN AND THE LEGAL PROFESSION (Deborah Rhode, 2001).

ABA COMMISSION ON WOMEN IN THE LEGAL PROFESSION, VISIBLE INVISIBILITY: WOMEN OF COLOR IN LAW FIRMS (2006).

ABA SECTION OF DISPUTE RESOLUTION, AMERICAN ARBITRATION ASSOCIATION & ASSOCIATION FOR CONFLICT RESOLUTION, THE MODEL STANDARDS OF CONDUCT FOR MEDIATORS (August 2005).

Articles and Books

ABA MULTICULTURAL WOMEN ATTORNEYS NETWORK, THE BURDENS OF BOTH, THE PRIVILEGES OF NEITHER (1994).

Susan Bryant, *The Five Habits: Building Cross-Cultural Competence in Lawyering*, 8 CLIN. L. REV. 33 (2001).

KENNETH CUSHNER & RICHARD W. BRESLIN, INTERCULTURAL INTERACTIONS (1995).

Kari M. Dahlin, *Actions Speak Louder than Thoughts: The Constitutionally Questionable Reach of the Minnesota CLE Elimination of Bias Requirement*, 84 MINN. L. REV. 1725 (2000).

FEDERAL JUDICIAL CENTER, DIVERSITY IN THE COURTS: A GUIDE FOR ASSESSMENT AND TRAINING (1995).

Michelle Jacobs, *People From the Footnotes: The Missing Element in Client-Centered Counseling*, 27 GOLDEN GATE U. L. REV. 345 (1997).

STEFAN H. KRIEGER & RICHARD K. NEUMANN, JR., ESSENTIAL LAWYERING Skills 130-132 (2d ed. 2003).

Daniel LANDIS, JANET M. BENNETT, & MILTON J. BENNETT, HANDBOOK OF INTERCULTURAL TRAINING (3d ed. 2003).

Molly McDonough, *Demanding Diversity: Corporate Pressure Is Changing the Racial Mix at Some Law Firms*, ABA J., Mar. 2005, at 52.

Laurence H. Silberman, *The D.C. Circuit Task Force on Gender, Race, and Ethnic Bias: Political Correctness Rebuffed*, 19 HARV. J. L. & PUB. POL. 759 (1996).

Paul R. Tremblay, *Interviewing and Counseling Across Cultures: Heuristics and Biases*, 9 CLIN. L. REV. 373 (2002).

Videos

Ginzberg Video Productions, 1136 Evelyn Ave., Albany, CA 94706; telephone: (510) 528-9116.

Summary Judgments (training for judges on overcoming racial and gender bias).

Obstacle Courts (training for judges and court personnel on overcoming bias against people with disabilities).

Inside/Out: A Portrait of Gay and Lesbian Lawyers.

All in a Day's Work (addresses gender bias in the legal profession).

A Firm Commitment (retention of minority lawyers).

All Things Being Equal (training for law firm recruiters about racial, sexual, and age-based stereotypes).

Breaking Down Barriers: Overcoming Discrimination Against Lawyers with Disabilities.

Chapter 17

Balancing Personal Life and Professional Life

Leah Wortham

Law Students' and Lawyers' Concerns

When asked "What worries or troubles you about becoming a lawyer?" my extern and professional responsibility students frequently respond with concerns about balance in personal life and professional life. Articles on law firm management trends predict that those of you born from 1961 to 1981 (often labeled Generation X) and those of you born after 1981 (sometimes called the Millennials) come to the legal workplace with a higher priority on work-life balance and a greater willingness to change jobs to seek that balance than the Boomers and Silent Generation who preceded you.

> **Exercise 17.1** Think about your life as a law student thus far. Have you felt stretched in too many directions? Jot down the list of things that have consumed your time and energy and note parts of your life that you think may have suffered from a lack of attention.
>
> Do you perceive a difference in the work-life balance you would like to have from that you think existed in the work lives of your parents and their contemporaries?

Concerns about the Legal Profession

This chapter focuses on balance in lawyers' personal and professional lives. That topic is entwined with four other issues.

The first is job satisfaction among lawyers and the way concern about balancing work life and personal life may relate to career dissatisfaction. The second concern is differences in the experience of men and women in the legal profession. The culture of legal workplaces and the ways in which management practices affect lawyers' ability to balance personal and professional lives comprise the third point. The fourth issue is stress in the legal profession and strategies that lawyers employ to cope with the pressures of the profession.

In this chapter we discuss each of these four topics in relation to balance in personal life and professional life. Then we propose a process, using exercises, questions for thought, and suggestions for actions to take, by which to plan for and work toward a personal life and professional life balance that you will find satisfying.

"It is said that a renowned physicist's answering-machine greets callers with:

This is not an answering machine; this is a questioning machine. Who are you and what do you want? Lest you think these are trivial questions, rest assured that most people leave this world without ever answering either one!"

Step one asks you to sort out priorities for what is most important to you in both spheres and the balance you think desirable. Earlier in this book, we challenged you to think about what you wanted out of your externship. Here we ask you to project ahead to what you want out of the professional and personal parts of your life. Step two lays out an approach to making a realistic assessment of a job setting's demands and paths to advancement in order to contemplate how to reconcile work demands with your personal goals. Step three suggests identification of options for resolving conflicts when there is a clash in the realistic assessment of what it would take to achieve both work priorities and personal priorities. Step four challenges you to consider positive and negative strategies for coping with stress.

Psychologists and legal educators have applied research from the field of positive psychology to legal education and the legal profession. Positive psychology focuses on human strengths and concentrates on studying what makes people happy and satisfied rather than on illness and pathology. The results of this research suggest that directing one's life toward intrinsic, rather than extrinsic, motivations is key in attaining satisfaction and happiness. Intrinsic motivations are those focusing on personal and interpersonal goals while extrinsic motivations are rewards such as power, money, or the opinions of others. Suggestions from this work align with the chapter's focus on determining your own priorities as a key starting point for a satisfying life.

In the final section of this chapter we report on recommendations for practicing lawyers to achieve a desirable balance in their personal and professional lives, suggest how these might apply to law students, and identify steps you might take now to better position yourself to achieve your goals after law school.

How Does This Material Relate to Your Legal Externship?

In your externship you have an opportunity for first-hand observation of a legal workplace. You also have access to lawyers doing their jobs and living their lives whom you can observe and with whom you can talk. Externships provide opportunities for reflection to enhance learning from experience. Just as reflection may help you to think about ethical issues or improve skills, reflective work may help you work toward satisfaction in your personal life and professional life.

Some of the ideas in this chapter can be put into practice during law school. You can consider how the way you spend your time as a law student relates to your life priorities. You can learn and practice positive ways of coping with stress now. You can think about how to balance your externship with other academic demands and with the requirements of your personal life. You can take steps suggested in this chapter to position yourself to find the personal and professional balance that you will seek in the future.

You may wonder if it is premature to begin now to think about reconciling conflict between personal life and professional life. It is not. Sheila Nielsen, who offers counseling and consulting services on alternative work schedules for attorneys, says

> I am always hoping to get a call from a law student which would sound like this: "Hello, I'm a law student, graduating in two years. I'd like to plan a career with you." That phone call has not yet come. People do not call until they are up to their necks in quicksand.
> Sheila Nielsen, *The Balancing Act: Practical Suggestions for Part-Time Attorneys*, 35 N.Y.L. Sch. L. Rev. 369, 375 (1990).

You might say, "Even if thinking about how I would resolve personal and professional conflicts is not premature, it is useless for me to think about how a workplace could change to support a better balance because I am not going to be in charge of any workplace for a long time." This may be true, but eventually some of you will be creating the workplace rules. It also is important to challenge the notion that the fault is in workers wanting to "have it all." It is useful to think about problems caused by excessive and inflexible institutional demands. This may help you to avoid blaming yourself for these conflicts when they arise. Framing personal life concerns as solely the employee's problem ignores the work productivity loss that often results from conflicts between the employee's personal life and professional life. Studies cited in this chapter have looked carefully at strategies that can both support a desirable professional and personal balance for employees *and* enhance the employing organization's performance.

Lawyers' Career Satisfaction

See, for example, the 1991 ABA Young Lawyers Division report cited in Further Reading.

Some excellent reports, cited in the Further Reading section of this chapter, include several by the Catalyst organization, Deborah Rhode's work for the ABA Commission on Women, Susan Saab Fortney's study for the National Association of Law Placement, the Project for Attorney Retention undertaken by Joan Williams and Cynthia Calvert, and Joan Williams's Corporate Counsel Work/Life Report.

In addition to the readings and exercises in this chapter, I highly recommend that you read two booklets by Lawrence Krieger, *The Hidden Sources of Law School Stress* and *A Deeper Understanding of Your Career Choices*, which are available at www.law.fsu.edu/academic_programs/humanizing_lawschool/booklet.html. These short well-researched works offer practical sugestions for how one can establish positive patterns in law school that can make one happier both now and in one's later career.

In the 1990s, the professional and popular press prominently reported some surveys showing widespread lawyer dissatisfaction. Studies with more rigorous social science methodology showed somewhat contrary findings with lawyer respondents reporting high levels of satisfaction with their jobs and choice of career. Researchers noted, however, that employees across occupations tend to report high levels of satisfaction and that a significant number of those reporting high satisfaction still indicated that they intended to change jobs in the near term. In some surveys, women's expressions of satisfaction parallel those of men. In others, women express greater dissatisfaction, and greater numbers say they are considering or likely to change jobs in the near future. Results for lawyers of color sometimes show satisfaction rates equal or higher to that of white lawyers but also often evidence a higher incidence of plans to seek different employment. While the evidence on the depth and breadth of lawyer dissatisfaction presents a mixed picture, evidence of the incidence of despondency, depression, and substance dependency, discussed later in this chapter, is consistently higher for lawyers than that of the general population. Lawyers also leave law firms at significant rates, and women and people of color of both genders leave large firms more often than white men.

The citations at the end of the chapter provide a gateway to the voluminous literature on the themes in this chapter, including many empirical studies. While referring to findings from some of those surveys and studies, the chapter's text concentrates on what you can do in your externship and as a law student to prepare for a legal career that you are most likely to find satisfying.

One focus is looking critically at workplace conditions that make it difficult to achieve a satisfactory balance between personal life and professional life. A number of studies provide carefully documented evidence and recommendations on how legal workplaces can provide a better quality of life to employees while achieving the client service and profitability goals of legal employers.

While stressing a critical look outward at employment practices that may frustrate balanced lives, the chapter also makes suggestions regarding a critical look inward to what is in your direct control—your attitudes, actions, and beliefs. You have been pressed to think about your goals for your externship. This chapter encourages thinking about what is most important to you in your work life and how that relates to the integration with the personal life that you desire.

Differences in the Professional Lives and Personal Lives of Men and Women Lawyers

Women comprised just over 30% of the 1,116,967 lawyers in the U.S. in 2006. The head of the National Association of Women Lawyers identifies what she calls the "50-15-15 problem." Women are about 50% of law students but only 15% of partners and 15% of chief legal officers in other organizations. While women often express overall satisfaction, in numbers similar to men, with their decision to become lawyers and with their careers, they more often say they intend to change jobs and they leave law firms in greater numbers. Women also report higher incidence of feelings of despondency and depression than men.

Prominent work and family researcher Joan Williams describes the barrier for women not as the glass ceiling but the maternal wall. For many women, the first years out of law school, in which one normally sets the track record on which to build career advancement, coincide with the prime child-bearing years. Higher numbers of women lawyers remain unmarried, are married without children, and have fewer children than their male counterparts. Desire for time with family, of course, also affects men who want time with their children and to shoulder their share of the work in maintaining a household, but it appears to impact women more directly.

Analysis of cognitive biases and stereotyping about parenthood shows that mothers are pressed into a role of "good mother" that assumes they now will take work less seriously, be less reliable, and so on. On the other hand, the role of a "good father" is often limited to being a good provider with the assumption that a male who becomes a parent is even more likely to throw himself into total devotion to the firm so he can advance and attain greater financial rewards. David Chambers' study of University of Michigan law alumni found many women had taken time off and worked reduced hours during their legal careers. Some male respondents, however, reported they felt constrained by gender role expectations to work full time in demanding schedules. They believed their expressions of concern for family needs were seen as weakness. They felt it was accepted that women could take extended family leaves but was not accepted for men to do so.

The legal workplace has assumed the "ideal worker" is one who can devote himself totally to work. This depends on the work of a supportive partner at home. Even though more and more male lawyers are likely to be in relationships with partners who also work, the number of women with a partner at home or working part time is still much smaller than the comparable number for male lawyers.

To discuss arrangements for reduced hours, Joan Williams favors the term "balanced hours" because she considers part time as implying a lesser commitment. In practice, of course, part time in a law firm may mean a 40-hour week as opposed to the 50, 60 or more hours that may be the norm. Many analyses have shown that management in legal workplaces often think the problem is solved because they have part-time policies in place, but interviews with employees show them reluctant to use the policies because they believe it will lead to less interesting work, a devaluation of their worth, and dead-end their careers. Balanced hours programs require visible support from top management and implementation follow-through to make such programs effective for employees and their workplaces. Even though people of both genders often desire balanced hours and flexible work arrangements, study after study documents that women are much more likely than men to avail themselves of these options when they are offered, even when they recognize that exercising the option may have a negative effect on their careers. Women also most often report the reason for reducing hours as child-rearing responsibilities.

Caring for children, of course, is not the only reason that lawyers care about time free from work demands. Experts making recommendations on balanced hours programs and flexible work arrangements in legal workplaces urge the importance of focusing on how the arrangement can work for clients, employers, and employees—not the reason the employee seeks balance. Flexibility directed only to parenting responsibilities may generate resentment in employees without this need but who may have other reasons for which additional time and flexibility is important to them. Commentators periodically lament the toll that excessive work hour demands place on lawyers' participation in civic life. Lawyers of both genders may want to care for an elderly parent, write a novel, work on a Ph.D., teach part time, work on a political campaign, serve in the military reserves, or a host of other examples of enriching their lives, helping others, or both.

The Legal Workplace

In the same period that women entered the legal profession in increasing numbers, the nature of the compensation structure in law firms was changing. By the 1970s, hourly billing was the norm in much of legal practice. In an hourly billing system, partners' profits are determined directly by the number of hours billed by lawyers in the firm. Many also speculate that expectations for the degree of affluence that partnership in a law firm will bring also has elevated in recent decades.

Hence it is not surprising that annual billing expectations have increased dramatically. An ABA Lawyer's Handbook published in 1962 said there were only about 1300 fee-earning hours in a year "unless the lawyer works overtime." Recent surveys of billing hour expectations show 1900-2000 hours to be the norm, with many firms expecting more and giving bonuses for exceeding the already considerable time that must be spent on firm work to reach those hour targets. In addition to the toll on balancing personal life, critics lament that billable hour pressure pushes firms' senior lawyers away from time spent mentoring new lawyers and all lawyers away from *pro bono* work, which would reap rewards in experience gained and in satisfaction in serving others.

In addition, firms shifted from what has been called a client service model to a client generation model with considerable emphasis on bringing in new business. Firms moved away from lock-step compensation to a compensation structure significantly giving "origination credit" for hours billed to the lawyer who brought a client to the firm, not just at the outset of the retention but throughout the relationship. This discouraged the past practice of passing on clients from senior to more junior lawyers and the notion of firm, rather than individual, clients. This is said to create a more competitive atmosphere among lawyers in a firm.

A stable world in which clients gave all or most of their business to a particular firm and stayed with that firm switched to a world in which large institutional clients divided business among many firms, kept more work in-house, and shopped aggressively for lower fees. That volatile client world was matched with a switch from a stable legal workforce in which lawyers grew up in a firm to one in which many individual lawyers and practice groups may switch firms several times in their career. The desire to increase overall profit fuels a firm quest for the maximum numbers of billable hours and lawyers who can bring in clients to sustain the demand for those hours. Some lawyers comment that one pressure against reduced hour programs is a perceived need to keep firm profitability figures high to attract "laterals," lawyers coming from other firms with their existing clients.

With the considerable emphasis on business generation, many law firms have abandoned former "up or out" policies for associates and have created income (as opposed to equity) partners, of counsel, or staff attorney positions, as alternative or intermediate statuses to equity partnership. Opinions differ on whether such alternative tracks are good or bad for women. Some say they offer a way to get a more balanced life while staying in a firm. Others say they relegate women to a dead-end track and perpetuate their scarcity in management of firms.

Some legal workplaces resist employees' requests to exchange reduced hours for reduced pay. The reasons for resistance vary, but a report by Williams and Calvert identifies seven common myths about balanced-hour programs:

1. Balanced-Hour Attorneys Cost Firms Too Much Money

2. Some Practice Areas Are Not Amenable to a Balanced Schedule

3. Balanced Hours Cannot Work in a High-Powered Law Firm

4. Lawyers Who Will Work Balanced Hours Are Not Committed to the Firm

5. Clients Will Not Accept Balanced Schedules

6. Fear of Floodgates: The Whole Firm Cannot Work Balanced Hours

7. It's Not Practical to Offer Balanced Hours to Support Staff

The report presents the empirical evidence why each is a myth but acknowledges that many managers of legal workplaces still subscribe to these beliefs. Thus, the myths can present obstacles for employees seeking balance in their lives. The centerpiece of the report is the importance of such policies to retention. Costs to large law firms of lost associates have been estimated at $200,000 to $500,000 per departing lawyer, not including "the hidden costs of client dissatisfaction due to turnover, lost business of clients who leave with departing attorneys, and damage to the firm's reputation and morale."

A number of national organizations focused on the legal profession, as well as state bar associations, have assessed various dimensions of these changes in the legal workplace and their effects on those who work in them. An Arizona bar project on quality of life termed a number of management practices found in many firms to be unsound ones resulting in a negative firm culture and damaging to motivation, as well as deleterious to other aspects of quality of life. Such deleterious practices include

encouraging lawyers to sacrifice themselves to their firms by working ever increasing billable hours;

failure to share information regarding firm management with all lawyers in the firm;

failure to communicate practice and time expectations to lawyers, and failure to measure performance against those communicated expectations;

failure to provide adequate training, mentoring, and feedback;

compensating lawyers solely on the basis of hours worked, rather than on the value of the services they provide and contribution to the firm;

failure to provide equal opportunities for women and minorities, including failure to provide an environment free of actions that demean, embarrass, or harass;

failure to delegate client work properly;

failure to encourage lawyers to communicate openly their professional and personal needs and problems, and to develop collegiality, mutual support, and institutional loyalty.

While it is sensible to consider what individual lawyers can do toward balancing personal and professional life, the policies and practices of the places in which they work can support or block such efforts. Looking at long-term firm health and profitability by taking into account factors like the costs of poor management and turnover reveals more compatibility with policies supporting balancing personal life and professional life for employees than legal employers may perceive by focusing only on the short term alone.

Stress, Mental Health Problems, and Substance Abuse Among Lawyers

A 1996 article in the *Journal of Law and Health* reviews evidence on mental health and alcohol-related problems among a survey of Washington state lawyers. The Washington survey showed that almost 21% of the men and 16% of women exceeded the psychological distress measures for depression. Only 2.27% of the general population show depression symptoms at this level. More than 20% of the male Washington lawyers scored above the cut-off for probable alcohol-related problems. The rate for the general population is estimated to be only 9%. The ABA's Commission on Impaired Attorneys estimates 18%-20% of American lawyers have alcohol or drug problems. Chemical dependency and mental illness are estimated to be involved in 40%-75% of disciplinary actions taken against lawyers. Studies show that lawyers exhibit more depression than any other occupational group. A recent analysis of data comparing men and women lawyers finds that women more often express feelings of depression and despondency, even when they respond positively to questions about job satisfaction. The authors speculate that women may be more likely to turn feelings of frustration inward rather than pressing against work structures that create specific problems in the workplace that the survey identifies.

A Kansas physician and medical director of an addiction medicine practice reports that he finds physicians, lawyers, and airline pilots the most resistant to admitting their addiction problems. He cites a study from another addiction professional who identified the primary obstacle identified for lawyers in seeking treatment the belief they could handle their problems on their own. Fear of loss of professional reputation among peers was a second obstacle to lawyers seeking treatment.

During my more than two and a half decades of teaching, I found that students who had incurred significant academic problems often had serious personal difficulties that impeded their ability to concentrate on their studies. When asked why they did not seek help from the law school earlier, the answer almost invariably was, "I thought I could handle it." Law students and lawyers need relationships with others to whom they can turn when the going gets rough. They also need to realize that each of us has emotional and physical limits, and it is critical to realize when one needs to cut back or otherwise find a different way to manage demands when one approaches those limits.

A previous boss once said to me, "If the toothpaste splats on the mirror and you explode or melt down in response—remember— it's not about the toothpaste; something else is bothering you." I've tried to use the "toothpaste test" as a measure of when I am approaching the edge of my emotional and physical resilience.

> **Exercise 17.2** Did the chapter's overview of these topics square with your experience? What questions did the discussion raise for you? Would you relate the topics in different ways than those suggested? Your answers are possibilities for journal entries or class discussion.

Taking Steps Toward Balancing Personal Life and Professional Life

Here are some suggestions for how to optimize your chances of finding a workable balance in personal life and professional life.

- Sort out your priorities in each sphere and consider options to achieve balance between them.

- Make a realistic assessment of what it will take to be successful in professional situations.

- Consider options if your assessment of professional demands conflicts with your personal goals.

- Adopt positive strategies for coping with pressure.

Sort Out Your Priorities in Each Sphere and Consider Options to Achieve Balance

> **Exercise 17.3** Write down some ideas on the following. Approach this as a brainstorming exercise. Do not self censor. Write whatever comes into your mind. Let your thoughts percolate. See if new or different ideas occur to you. Important insights are likely to pop into your head when you are doing something else, once you have started focusing on the questions. Make a list of your values or write one or more paragraphs about the things you consider most important in your life. What things are important to you in a job? What do you want to happen in the rest of your life outside your job?

Make a second list by approaching the questions in reverse. What values do you reject or find unimportant? What things do you not want to happen in your professional life and in your personal life?

Defining what one *really* wants is difficult. It is easy to become confused by conflicting desires and diverted by what others think one should want. One easily can become absorbed in immediate demands and avoid thinking about bigger and longer term questions.

To provide effective client representation, a lawyer must know what the client wants to accomplish and how an array of possibilities square with the client's hierarchy of values. In the dissolution of a marriage, the client's values will affect what the client will accept with regard to custody, support, property division, future relationship between the spouses and children, and so on. A lawyer cannot know when to settle, when to litigate, or the desired terms in a settlement or contract without knowing what the client really wants. Like the law student anxious about her future, the client also may need help in sorting through what is *really* important. A lawyer's practice in sorting out his own goals may help in working out those questions when they are important to representation of the client.

Exercise 17.4 Think about some people you admire. Think of some who are famous and some others you know personally and fairly well. Define what you admire about them. Do not limit yourself to people whose careers you would like to emulate. Think more broadly regarding those you admire generally.

As to each person you identify, do you admire one characteristic or accomplishment of the person or the totality of his or her life? If you admire the person in total, what balance has the person established between attention to work and to other pursuits? Have you listed some people whose professional lives you admire but whose personal lives you find wanting? And vice versa?

> **Exercise 17.5** Think of someone of whom you can ask questions about his or her life. Interview the person about choices he or she has made, particularly about the choices of time and energy devoted to career. Ask what balance has been achieved and what compromises the person has made. Ask about ways that each sphere may have supported or enriched the other. Are there skills, insights, or relationships that have developed in one sphere and carried over to the other?

> **Exercise 17.6** Read a biography or memoir of someone you think you admire. Write in your journal your reactions to the life choices described.

In reading a draft of this chapter, my husband commented that, while a law student, he probably would have given much more emphasis to conventional definitions of professional success and less consideration to personal goals than is his view today. As a law student, I already recognized how important having a family would be to me, but I do not think I fully appreciated how important my career would be.

Your view of what you want from your personal life and professional life and how you reconcile the two likely will change over time. As with other parts of the book, our hope is to accustom you to asking questions of yourself periodically. Today's answers may not hold for all time, but many of the questions should remain the same throughout your life, as will the need to make time to examine those questions.

Make a Realistic Assessment of What It Will Take to Be Successful in Professional Situations

> **Exercise 17.7** Define what professional success means to you—not the student next to you, not the editors of *American Lawyer* magazine, not television show lawyers—to you. Your thoughts about values should give guidance on your definition of job success, for example, the relative importance of money, recognition, influence, providing help to others, and so on.

Exercise 17.8 What would it take to get that kind of success in a job of interest to you? Suppose you aspire to obtain the financial rewards and recognition of being a partner in a well-respected, large law firm. Suppose you are an associate in such a firm. How would you find out what it would take to become a partner in this firm? What information would you need to answer that question? You might wish to learn something about each of the following questions: Who selects new partners? What evaluations occur along the way? What counts toward attaining the goal: hours billed, client development, a senior lawyer as one's advocate? What accomplishments are important? How will the people who will evaluate you know you attained those accomplishments?

Think about the implications of the answers to those questions for the allocation of your time. What are the choices in how you could spend your working hours? Will some activities be valued more than others? Consider where business development (and learning how to do it), mentoring and being mentored, obtaining or improving skills, and becoming generally known in the firm fit in the calculus.

For some lawyers, a realistic assessment of the answers leads to a conclusion that becoming a partner, and the life thereafter, is not consistent with their personal goals. For some individuals and some firms, however, an extremely high number of hours is not the key to success. The effectiveness of hours spent and targeted publicity about one's value to the firm may be more crucial.

Law students have many different aspirations. The law firm scenario is but one example. The point is to consider one's goals, what it would take to attain them, the probability of success, and whether the attainment of those goals would be worth the likely price. If it is, you can use the product of your research to plot a course toward the goal.

Many lawyers are surprised when they are passed over for partnership, laid off, or compensated at lower levels than they thought they deserved. Many such people never learned what was important for success or did not figure out how to do what was necessary. Far too many people put in a vast number of hours without examining whether the number of hours and how they are spent are crucial to the goal sought. Sometimes the time *required* by a lawyer's professional goals can impede personal goals such that something has to give. In this chapter, we urge you to gather information to make a realistic assessment of time required. Do not put in hours

Sheila Nielsen is quoted elsewhere in this chapter. The Columns section of her website includes some useful articles on effective strategies for associates in navigating the shoals of law firm survival and advancement. www.nielsencareer consulting.com

reflexively as a substitute for thinking about what is really necessary to succeed. More is not always better.

Exercise 17.9 Interview a lawyer you know about the keys to advancement in the lawyer's organization. If possible, talk to your supervisor and one or two other lawyers in your placement about those questions. If you interview multiple people in your organization, consider whether their ideas match. If not, whose perceptions are most realistic? How would you get information to test differing perceptions?

Exercise 17.10 From your own experience, observations, or discussions, describe a situation in which a supervisor made a request or demand that created a problem for an employee. Do you think the assignment was reasonable from the employer's point of view? What were the employee's alternatives in responding to the request? Develop the situation into a role play on how an employee might set limits on an employer's demands while attempting to minimize the career cost to the employee.

A Personal Reflection

In an earlier draft of this chapter, I developed competing metaphors for the reconciliation of personal life and professional life. Much of the discussion I heard seemed to be about the need for a dam against work to protect one's personal life from being engulfed. To me, that no longer seemed the issue as I saw the two spheres of my life as more like two parallel streams that sometimes flowed separately and sometimes together. The comments of a younger colleague, with fresh memories of her time at a New York law firm, suggested I had not given the dam its due. I realized that my own first years of practice involved a struggle to preserve some personal time against the flood of work. I was a poverty lawyer so the pressure was not the firm's billing expectations, but rather inexperience, my sense of obligation, and the overwhelming needs of my clients.

A friend who funds research in work and family pointed out that many working in the field have switched from talking about balance to integration. This seemed to me to track the difference in my dam and par-

allel stream metaphors. Today, my personal and work selves generally seem integrated. I draw on strengths, experiences, and skills learned in one to face challenges in the other, but I did not change the name of the chapter because integration seemed much too far from where many lawyers and legal work places are today.

What If Your Professional Demands Conflict with Your Personal Goals?

Faced with such a clash between professional demands and personal goals, a worker has four options:

- Conform to the workplace's requirements for success and compromise personal goals;

- Find a different job that is more compatible with personal goals or leave the job market altogether;

- Find a more accommodating track in the present workplace;

- Try to change the workplace to reduce personal/professional conflicts.

The first three options theoretically are in the worker's control, but one can debate how freely they are made. The middle two may provide more time and energy for personal life but also raise the question of how freely women make these choices and how free men are to make them. This section discusses the possibility of phasing—becoming the nearly ideal worker in the early years of one's career to position oneself to negotiate the best option in a different job or a more accommodating arrangement in the current workplace.

Conform to the Workplace's Requirements for Success and Compromise Personal Goals

A 2000 study of ABA Young Lawyers Division members asked them to rate on a scale of 1 (strongly agree) to 5 (strongly disagree) whether they (a) spent too much time on work-related activities, (b) did not allocate sufficient time to personal life, (c) spent more time than necessary on work-related activities. More than 47% responded with a 1 or 2 indicating strong to moderately strong agreement that they spent too much time on work and almost as many responded the same on allocation of insufficient time to personal life. Thirty-one percent strongly or moderately agreed that they spent more time than necessary on work-related activities. Such results suggest that lawyers themselves may question whether their time allocation relates to employment success.

Sheila Nielsen consults with law firms and lawyers on alternative work schedules. She suggests how to position oneself to ask for a reduced time schedule. The end of this chapter includes a list of suggestions for achieving balance between personal life and professional life. Both lists suggest that working full time for a few years and performing exceptionally may increase the employer's receptivity to a lawyer's request for an alternative work schedule. This could be seen as a compromise of personal goals as a short-term strategy to position oneself for the longer term. For some, this "life staging" may work, but for others, like those who delayed entry to law school for a few years, the first five to eight years of law practice may coincide with the years in which child bearing is optimum or may coincide with the time when the demands of other personal responsibilities are acute.

Many two career families cope with competing time demands by alternating preference for one spouse's career and then the other's or by contracting out many family and personal maintenance tasks. Restaurants and takeout food services across the country report increased revenues. Contractors can be hired to clean houses, pick up dry cleaning, and so on, albeit for a price. The most difficult issues arise around maintenance of relationships with spouse, family, and friends, care of children, and care for elderly or ill adults and friends.

Find a Different Job That Is More Compatible with Personal Goals or Leave the Job Market Altogether

Studies of women's career tracks find many opting for jobs in government, other public organizations, or in-house counsel offices because they find them more compatible with the work life-personal life balance they seek, and many men make those choices as well. A recent study of work-life issues in corporate counsel offices suggested, however, that practices vary widely among corporations, with some much more balance friendly than others. Many more women than men leave the legal job market altogether, and it is hard to know how many of them would have considered continuing employment if jobs offering a more desirable work-life balance, along with interesting work and adequate compensation, were available.

Find a More Accommodating Track in the Present Workplace

A "more accommodating track" is used to include reduced hours and that is flexible as to place and time of performance, like telecommuting. Sheila Nielsen, who was quoted earlier on the wisdom of law students thinking ahead to engage in career planning, suggests the following as steps to "line up your options before reduced hours are needed." For more explanation of these recommendations, consult her excellent article cited in the Further Reading section below.

• Locate a good workplace.

• Work full time for a few years before seeking reduced hours options.

• Pick a specialty carefully.

• Develop a track record for excellence and professionalism.

• Develop true mentors.

• Develop a marketable specialty.

• Become valuable to your firm.

• Prepare your workplace before you need the reduced hours option.

Try to Change the Workplace to Reduce Personal/Professional Conflicts

As previously described, bar associations and other prestigious national and state organizations have focused considerable attention on what legal workplaces need to do to be more accommodating to the need of workers for balanced lives. An important aspect is the workplace culture's definition of good work and commitment to the employer. The Ford Foundation supported collaborative work with major corporations in their study *Relinking Life and Work: Toward a Better Future.* This included a reanalysis of some worklife culture issues. Here is one example from the Ford Foundation report that may sound like some legal workplace cultures.

> In one sales environment . . . we found that a sales team habitually worked around the clock to complete proposals for prospective customers. In the morning, the workers were rewarded with cheers from managers and co-workers, complimenting them on their commitment and willingness to get the job done. In response to [the consultants'] interventions, one manager recognized that this behavior reflected poor work habits and made it tough on these people's family lives. Not only were their families suffering, but it took several days for these workers to recover, during which time they were less productive.
>
> The manager told his team that he was disappointed in their behavior, that it demonstrated an inability to plan. He also began to share his perceptions with other managers. As a result, the sales team began to recognize and reward new work habits such as planning ahead and anticipating problems rather than waiting until they were crises. Rhona Rapoport *et al.*, *Relinking Life and Work: Toward a Better Future* 21 (1996).

The consultants, working with corporations, challenged ideas about a work culture that rewarded long hours on the job, measured employees' commitment by their continuous willingness to give work their highest priority, and prized high visibility problem solving drop everything and get it done over less visible everyday problem prevention plan ahead and avoid the crisis.

Law firm profitability is directly linked to hours billed but ultimately is determined by client satisfaction with the quality of service provided. Client representation sometimes involves genuine emergencies for which no advance planning can prepare, but some crises are generated by poor planning by the lawyers rather than by the unpredictability of a client's situation. Several analysts have seen a key to improvement of quality of life in private practice in breaking the link to hourly billing and movement to client service and lawyer evaluation linked more to quality and value of the services rendered. Resistance to change, however, is significant.

The Ford Foundation consultants sometimes recommended encouraging employees to work better as teams so they could assist and cover for each other when individuals were attending to personal situations. This not only assisted the workers by promoting better coordination of work among employees but also often aided customers by ensuring there was always someone familiar with their situation available to help them. They looked at how well employees were able to control their work time to get the job done most efficiently. They considered whether the management measures of success ultimately contributed to a better bottom line; for example, were people rewarded for their productivity rather than "face time" at the work site?

Exercise 17.11 Envision an organization in which you would like to work. This may be a real employer with which you are familiar, or it might be the type of firm, public interest group, government office, or other setting in which you think you would like to be employed after law school. What kind of policies by that employer would support the type of personal life that you would like to have? Consider the organization's goals. Are the policies you have articulated inconsistent with the organization's goals? If they seem so at first, think further. Are they inconsistent in the long run? If you see conflicts, are there modifications in your proposed policies that reconcile the needs of the organization with the needs of employees like you? Reread the description of the Ford Foundation report. What kind of restructuring of the workplace might lead to greater collective productivity while also supporting a healthy personal life for employees?

Exercise 17.12 Interview a lawyer in private practice. What are the billing expectations in the person's law firm? How are they communicated, for example, a formal policy, an informal understanding? Do they include minimum monthly or annual hourly billings? To what extent are these billing expectations linked to retention, pay, and promotion? How many hours do lawyers spend at work in order to meet the hourly billing expectations? How many hours billed are written off rather than billed to clients? Does evaluation of an associate's work relate only to hours recorded or also to hours billed to clients? Does the firm offer billing arrangements other than hourly? What percentage of the practice is not based on hourly billing? How is the productivity of lawyers working under non-hourly arrangements evaluated?

Student presentation topic. Assume you have worked in the organization you envisioned in Exercise 17.11 for several years and are now part of the management team. Prepare a presentation to other senior managers to convince them to accept the policies you advocate. Role play your presentation with class members. Encourage them to raise the types of questions that they think other lawyers in such an organization would raise.

Exercise 17.13 Through interviews or review of written material, identify the policies of your externship that support or inhibit efforts to maintain a balance in personal and professional life that you would find desirable. Through observation and interviews, articulate some conclusions on how these policies work in practice. Is the workplace assisting employees in maintaining a desirable balance in personal and professional life and meeting the demands of both? If yes, is this because of the policies or other factors? If no, what types of changes do you think would help? Drawing on this analysis, what kinds of things would you look for in a job after law school? How would you find out if these factors are present?

Exercise 17.14 Assume you are a management consultant who has been retained by your externship to reduce overhead. What aspects of the placement's work require physical presence at the work place? Could more work be done at home? Would this reduce the need for office space?

Sometimes employers make demands that are unreasonable or incompatible with the needs of their employees' personal lives. If the excessive work demands are real, not self-generated, and are repeated over time, you may have to consider moving on to another job. As an interim step, however, you may need to set limits on what an employer can expect. Look back to Exercise 17.10 on strategies for declining work.

When requirements for your definition of personal success clash with personal goals, your choice of options may be influenced by your income requirements. For the definition of professional success, we asked you to include ideas about income level. If need for income is driving your choices, reexamine how solid the need is.

Exercise 17.15 Get from your financial aid office (FAO) the information on your current indebtedness. Project how much you expect to borrow for the remainder of law school. Your FAO or lender should be able to tell you the monthly payments that will be required for these debts. There may be options for different lengths of the loan that will affect the payment levels. Is there any flexibility in your expenses for the remaining time in law school that might cut your final indebtedness? What choices about long-term financial commitments will you face after law school, for example, renting an apartment, purchasing a car, buying a home? Consider whether you want to structure commitments to allow a switch to lower compensation if that becomes necessary to achieve the personal life and professional life balance you desire.

Adopt Positive Strategies for Coping with Pressure

The 1990 American Bar Association study on the state of the legal profession asked lawyers whether a number of statements taken from psychological literature about negative and positive skills for coping with stress were descriptive of their situation. The following table shows that more than half of lawyers reported getting anxious and becoming more critical of themselves when they were under stress. The other bad coping responses were reported by less than half of the lawyers responding but still by some significant numbers.

Table 17.1 Lawyers' Descriptions of Reactions to Stress

Negative Coping Skills	If Descriptive= Bad Coping
Get anxious	79%
Become more critical of myself	52%
Eat more	39%
Become depressed	37%
Watch more TV/read	35%
Take time off	25%
Drink more	17%
Smoke more	13%
Become disoriented/confused	9%
Take prescribed medication	6%
Positive Coping Skills	If Not Descriptive = Bad Coping
Try to deal with underlying problem	15%
Think about life/priorities	39%
Don't let it bother me and forge on	49%
Look at it humorously	59%
Talk with close friends/family	60%
Exercise	65%
Get involved in other groups	86%
Practice mediation/relaxation	88%
Talk with a counselor/therapist	93%

Source: The State of the Legal Profession: 1990 at 73.

On the positive coping side, 85% of the lawyers reported that they tried to deal with the underlying problem. This is not surprising among a group with the analytical bent of lawyers. Sixty-one percent reported they were coping by thinking about life and priorities. That group seems already attuned to a central message of this chapter. Slightly more than half report not letting the stressor bother them and forging on. Fewer than half of the lawyers responding said the other positive coping skills were descriptive of them. For example, 7% reported talking with a counselor/therapist as a coping skill, 35% reported employing exercise to fight stress. Lawyers also were asked directly how much they exercised. Fifty-three percent reported exercising several times a week; the remaining 47% percent reported exercising once a week or less.

> **Exercise 17.16** Which of the coping skills above are descriptive of the way you are coping with stress in law school or have coped with stress at other points in your life? Which of the positive coping skills have you tried? What ways of coping with stress have been most successful for you?

see Chapter 10
on Problem Solving

In his book on stress management for lawyers, Amiram Elwork describes his approach to stress management in terms of the classic options of humans and animals in the face of threat: surrender, flee, or fight. He describes surrender in the lawyer stress context as succumbing to the emotions of fear and helplessness that can result in anxiety disorders and clinical depression. Flight is relieving stress by removing yourself from its sources temporarily or more permanently. Flight strategies range from quick breaks for relaxation exercises, longer breaks for vacations, cutting back on hours or responsibilities, and the more dramatic flight of changing jobs. Under fight, Elwork suggests improving the work environment, reducing stress physically through nutrition and exercise, and controlling stress psychologically through learning to challenge destructive thoughts and emotions. His book, cited in the Further Reading section, includes suggestions on undertaking these techniques, references to additional materials on them, and suggestions on how to find others to help you with these efforts.

An earlier note in the margin to this chapter gave you the web citation for Professor Lawrence Krieger's booklet called *The Hidden Sources if Law School Stress*, which provides an excellent analysis of sources of negative stress and positive strategies for reducing it.

Recommendations for Lawyers and Law Students for Enhancing Job Satisfaction

The following are suggestions to practicing lawyers for enhancing job satisfaction and achieving a desirable balance between the personal life and professional life. These were developed by San Francisco lawyer Monica Bay and quoted in *Life, Law, and the Pursuit of Balance*, a book published jointly by the Maricopa County Bar Association, Arizona Young Lawyers Division, and the ABA Young Lawyers Division. Consider which suggestions resonate with you. Could some apply to your life now, or are there things that you could do now to position yourself for a better quality of life in the future? Ms. Bay's suggestions appear in bold, and the accompanying text suggests how these might apply to law students.

If you are in a large firm, redefine your responsibilities within the firm or change your outlook and attitude. Cultivate the habit of thinking about what you want and how you can work within a situation to meet your needs. Setting a Learning Agenda for your externship, looking for opportunities to do what you want in the externship, and negotiating with the supervisor are practice for doing what is suggested here.

Find a practice in which other people share your values. Use the externship to observe what factors in a workplace demonstrate its values and affect the personal lives of employees. How could you get information in the interview process for a new job to determine the values of the workplace and policies that effectuate these values?

Schedule blocks of time when your staff intercepts your telephone calls and does not knock on your door. As a student, do you manage your time so you can work most effectively and so you are able to feel some periods of calm?

Set aside one day a month where your calendar is absolutely blank. Are you keeping some breathing space in your current class and work schedules?

Incorporate nutrition and exercise into your life. Establish healthy patterns now. The pressures on your time that you feel in school are likely very similar to the ones you will feel with demands of work and personal life.

Organize your life in a way that lets you do your work, enjoy your family, and have fun. Does your current life reflect your priorities for your personal life? Are you reserving some time to maintain relationships with family and friends? Are you setting aside some time to relax?

Accept that it is difficult, if not impossible, to achieve balance in your first five years of practice at a big firm and it is unrealistic to expect to do so. Is phasing a realistic option for you? Do plans for your life overall suggest that you could tip the balance to work for the first years after law school, or will that require too great a compromise of personal goals? If you think this phasing will work, look at the Nielsen article cited in the Further Reading section for suggestions on how best to lay the groundwork for later accommodations to personal life if you expect those to be important to you.

As a new lawyer, concentrate on becoming a bankable commodity by building a strong area of expertise and a strong client base. This also is one of Nielsen's suggestions on how to position oneself to negotiate an alternative work schedule. Start researching now what are likely to be sought-after practice areas in the future. Consider whether particular practice areas may be more or less amenable to accommodations that are important to the personal and professional integration that you seek, like those types of practice that might be easier to carry out through telecommuting or those requiring less extended stays out of town. Even today as a law student, start learning about client development and building strong client relations.

Be open to changing practice areas within a law firm as a way to increase your career satisfaction. Practice remaining flexible and open to learning about new possibilities.

Set realistic goals in billable hours, making sure that you are above average but not going for the top of the chart. Practice now establishing reasonable allocations of time "billed" to study, extra-curricular activities, part-time work, and so on. Force yourself to think about how much time is necessary to do well at your school obligations, but consider what time allocations would be so high as to start to compromise other life goals and push you toward unproductive exhaustion.

Develop a diverse circle of friends. If you have friends who are not lawyers, you cannot always talk shop and have to be a normal person. Hold onto important relationships from prior to law school. Spend some time with people who are not law students.

To keep perspective, develop an avocation or hobby. Think about what activities excite, relax, and clear your head. Find time for such activities now, and start a list of things you would like to try if additional time or money is required.

Get advice from colleagues, both inside and outside your firm, if you are seeking a career change. Form the habit of seeking advice from friends or from a professional counselor if it seems helpful. Do not be afraid to ask help from others.

Equip your home with a computer, fax, modem and separate phone line so that you have the option from time to time of staying home and avoiding the com-

mute, without losing billable hours. Think now about the work conditions in which you are most productive. If working at home or telecommuting is an option you want to consider in the future, think about what types of legal work and employers are more likely to permit it. Develop facility with technology and upgrade your skills as technology changes.

As a solo, avoid unhappiness by learning to say no to cases that are more than you can handle or that you do not want to handle. If you are thinking of solo practice, get as much supervised practice experience as possible so you can begin to assess what types of cases are feasible and desirable. Practice learning to say no in your life as a law student to those who want you to take on obligations that you know you do not have time to handle or do not want to do.

If you are facing dissatisfaction issues, consider counseling to explore your options and strategies. When you are troubled, think about seeking help. You may start with friends and colleagues but often a professional counselor can be an important help in sorting out what is troubling you and in developing options to address them.

The challenges in balancing personal life and professional life vary among law students and lawyers. Almost all legal jobs are demanding and have some inherent stresses. The types of pressure and options available to cope will differ, in some ways, among a large law firm, a solo practice, an urban prosecutor's office, staff to a legislative committee, and so on. Chapter 18 gives a framework for considering what type of job you want in the future and provides some additional dimensions that may go into the calculus. Job pressures may differ not only by type of work but also with the particular employer or region of the country.

see Chapter 18
on Career Planning

Your goals may change, perhaps dramatically, as you grow older and have more life experiences from which to learn and as your circumstances change. Assess and reassess what you want from your personal life and professional life. Compare the results with how you are living your life. Probe what it will take to achieve the goals you seek. Consider the options when personal and professional goals seem to clash. Do not give up on the notion that the legal profession can support a healthy balance in personal lives and professional lives for its members. You will be the generation in charge sooner than you think. Be ready!

FURTHER READING

Balance Between Personal Life and Professional Life

American Bar Association Young Lawyers Division, *The Report of At the Breaking Point: A National Conference on the Emerging Crisis in the Quality of Lawyers' Health and Lives, and Its Impact On Law Firms and Client Services* (1991).

Monica Bay, *Life, Law, and the Pursuit of Balance*, BARRISTER MAGAZINE, Winter 1994, At 4.

Susan Saab Fortney, IN PURSUIT OF ATTORNEY WORK-LIFE BALANCE: BEST PRACTICES IN MANAGEMENT, The NALP Foundation (2005).

LIFE, LAW AND THE PURSUIT OF BALANCE: A LAWYER'S GUIDE TO QUALITY OF LIFE, (Jeffrey R. Simmons ed., Maricopa County Bar Ass'n in Partnership with the State Bar of Arizona Young Lawyers Division and the ABA Young Lawyers Division 1996).

Deborah Rhode, *Balanced Lives for Lawyers*, 70 FORDHAM L REV. 2207 (2002).

Jean E. Wallace, *Juggling It All: A Study of Lawyers' Work, Home, and Family Demands and Coping Strategies, Report of Stage Two Findings*, LSAC RESEARCH REPORT 01-03, November 2004.

Joan C. Williams, *Better On Balance? The Corporate Counsel Work/life Report*, 10 WM. & MARY WOMEN & L. 367 (2004).

Differing Experiences Of Men and Women: Gender Expectations

American Bar Association Commission on Women in the Profession, *A Current Glance at Women in the Law* 2006.

American Bar Association Commission on Women in the Profession (Deborah Rhode, principal author), *The Unfinished Agenda: Women and the Legal Profession* (2001).

Stacy Caplow & Shira A. Scheindlin, *"Portrait of A Lady": The Woman Lawyer in the 1980s*, 35 N.Y.L. SCH. L. REV. 391 (1990).

David L. Chambers, *Accommodation and Satisfaction: Women and Men Lawyers and the Balance of Work and Family*, 14 L. & SOC. INQUIRY 251 (1989).

Nancy E. Dowd, *Resisting Essentialism and Hierarchy: A Critique of Work/Family Strategies for Women Lawyers*, 16 HARV. BLACKLETTER L.J. 185 (2000).

Cynthia Fuchs Epstein, Robert Saute, Bonnie Oglensky, Martha Geyer, *Advancement in the Legal Profession*, 64 FORDHAM L. REV. 291 (1995).

Mona Harrington & Helen Hsi (Sponsored By the Equality Commission supported by the Women's Bar Association of Massachusetts, the Boston Bar Association, & the Massachusetts Bar Association), *Women Lawyers and Obstacles to Leadership: A Report of MIT Workplace Center Surveys on Comparative Career Decisions and Attrition Rates of Women and Men in Massachusetts Law Firms* (2007).

Rebecca Korzec, *Working On the "Mommy-track": Motherhood and Women Lawyers*, 8 HASTINGS WOMEN'S L.J. 117 (1997).

Paula A. Patton, *Women Lawyers, Their Status, Influence, and Retention in the Legal Profession*, 11 WM. & MARY J. WOMEN & L. 173 (2005).

Nicole Buonocore Porter, *Re-defining Superwoman: An Essay on Overcoming the "Maternal Wall" in the Legal Workplace*, 13 DUKE J. GENDER L. & POL'Y 55 (2006).

Joan C. Williams, *Beyond the Glass Ceiling: the Maternal Wall as a Barrier to Gender Equality*, 26 T. JEFFERSON L. REV. 1 (2003).

Joan C. Williams, Stephanie Bornstein, Diana Reddy & Betsy A. Williams, *Law Firms as Defendants: Family Responsibilities Discrimination in Legal Workplaces,* 34 PEPP. L. REV. 393 (2007).

Generational Differences

Institute of Management and Administration Inc., Law Office Management and Administration Report, *Managing the Generational Divide in Your Law Firm,* 05-7 COMPENSATION & BENEFITS FOR L. OFF. 1 (2005).

Tracy L. McGaugh, *Generation X in Law School: The Dying of the Light or the Dawn of A New Day?* 9 LEGAL WRITING: J. LEGAL WRITING INST. 119 (2003).

Job Satisfaction

American Bar Association Young Lawyers Division, *Survey Career Satisfaction* (2000), Available at http://www.abanet.org/yld/satisfaction_800.doc.

Rosalind Chait Barnett & Janet Shibley Hyde, *Women, Men, Work, and Family: An Expansionist Theory,* 56 AM. PSYCHOLOGIST 781 (2001).

Susan Daicoff, *Asking Leopards to Change Their Spots: Should Lawyers Change? A Critique of Solutions to Problems with Professionalism by Reference to Empirically-derived Attorney Personality Attributes,* 11 GEO. J. OF LEGAL ETHICS 547 (1998).

Ronit Dinovtizer & Bryant G. Garth, *Lawyer Satisfaction in the Process of Structuring Legal Careers,* 41 LAW & SOC. REV. 1 (2007).

Kathleen E. Hull, *Cross-examining the Myth of Lawyers' Misery,* 52 VAND. L. REV. 1 (1999).

Lawrence S. Krieger, *What We're Not Telling Law Students—and Lawyers—That They Really Need to Know: Some Thoughts-in-action Toward Revitalizing the Profession From Its Roots,* 13 J. L. & HEALTH 1 (1998-99).

Lawrence S. Krieger, *The Inseparability of Professionalism and Personal Satisfaction: Perspectives On Values, Integrity and Happiness,* 11 CLIN. L. REV. 425 (2005).

NALP Foundation & American Bar Foundation, *After the JD: First Results of a National Study of Legal Careers,* 2004.

Patrick J. Schiltz, *On Being a Happy, Healthy, and Ethical Member of an Unhappy, Unhealthy, and Unethical Profession,* 52 VAND. L. REV. 871 (1999).

Positive Psychology

Catherine Gage O'Grady, *Cognitive Optimism and Professional Pessimism in the Large-firm Practice of Law: the Optimistic Associate,* 30 LAW & PSYCHOL. REV. 23 (2006).

Martin E.P. Seligman & Mihaly Csikszentmihalyi, *Positive Psychology: An Introduction,* 55 AM. PSYCHOLOGIST 5 (2000).

Martin E.P. Seligman, Paul R. Verkuil & Terry H. Kang, *Why Lawyers Are Unhappy,* 23 CARDOZO L. REV. 33 (2001).

Kennon M. Sheldon & Tim Kasser, *Goals, Congruence, and Positive Well-being: New Empirical Support for Humanistic Theories,* 41 J. OF HUMANISTIC PSYCHOL. 30 (2001).

Psychological Distress and Substance Dependency

Connie J.A. Beck, Bruce D. Sales & G. Andrew H. Benjamin, *Lawyer Distress: Alcohol-related Problems and Other Psychological Concerns Among a Sample of Practicing Lawyers,* 10 J.L. & HEALTH 1 (1995-96).

G. Andrew H. Benjamin, Elaine J. Darling & Bruce D. Sales, *The Prevalence of Depression, Alcohol Abuse, and Cocaine Abuse Among United States Lawyers,* 13 INT'L. J.L. & PSYCHIATRY 223 (1990).

Eric Drogin, *Alcoholism in the Legal Profession: Psychological and Legal Perspectives and Interventions,* 15 LAW & PSYCHOL. REV. 117 (1991).

Amiram Elwork & G. Andrew H. Benjamin, *Lawyers in Distress,* 23 J. PSYCHIATRY & L. 205 (1995).

Amiram Elwork, *Stress Management For Lawyers: How to Increase Personal & Professional Satisfaction in the Law,* 3d. ed. (2007).

John Hagan & Fiona Kay, *Even Lawyers Get the Blues: Gender, Depression, and Job Satisfaction in Legal Practice,* 41 LAW & SOCIETY REV. 51 (2007).

Timothy Scanlan, M.D., *Lawyers' Alcohol or Drug Problems—Twice the Rate of General Population,* 74 J. KAN. B.A. 23 (Sept. 2005).

Timothy J. Sweeney, *Statistical Demographics and Outcome Study of Chemically Dependent Attorneys,* 65 ALA. L. 494 (2004).

Restructuring the Workplace

American Bar Association Commission on Billable Hours Report 2001-2002.

American Bar Association Commission on Women in the Profession (Deborah Rhode, principal author), *Balanced Lives Changing the Culture of Legal Practice* (2001).

Steven K. Berenson, *Creating Workplace Solutions for Women Attorneys: Report of the Lawyers Club of San Diego Balance Campaign*, 28 T. JEFFERSON L. REV. 449 (2006).

Catalyst, *Beyond a Reasonable Doubt: Lawyers State Their Case on Job Flexibility* (2006); *Beyond a Reasonable Doubt: Creating Opportunities for Better Balance* (2005); *Beyond a Reasonable Doubt: Building the Business Case for Flexibility* (2005); *Women in Law: Making the Case* (2001).

Institute of Management and Administration Inc., Law Office Management and Administration Report, *Building a New Business Case for Work/Life Balance*, 05-6 COMPENSATION & BENEFITS FOR L. OFF. 1 (2005).

Susan Saab Fortney, *The Billable Hours Derby: Empirical Data on the Problems and Pressure Points*, 33 FORDHAM URBAN L.J. 171 (2005).

Sheila Nielsen, *The Balancing Act: Practical Suggestions for Part-Time Attorneys*, 35 N.Y.L. SCH. L. REV. 369 (1990).

Rhona Rapoport et al., *Relinking Life and Work: Toward a Better Future*, Ford Foundation 1996.

Joan Williams & Cynthia Thomas Calvert, *Balanced Hours: Effective Part-Time Policies for Washington Law Firms: The Project for Attorney Retention*, 8 WM. & MARY J. WOMEN & L. 357 (2001 - 02).

Chapter 18

Externships and Career Planning

Avis L. Sanders

The Role of Externships in Creating a Career Plan

Many students begin law school assuming it will help them focus their career goals. Instead, they find themselves with a panoply of options they had never even imagined. Courageously, some enroll in externships, challenging themselves and their career assumptions and assuming responsibility for their own happiness and career satisfaction. It takes courage to apply to field placements and risk rejection. It takes courage to take on responsibilities for which one does not feel prepared. Students who take these risks reap the rewards. Almost any lawyer who participated in an externship while in law school will tell of the sometimes subtle and often profound influence the experience had on developing the attorney's career path. Generally, career plans evolve over time. The externship is a crucial part of the learning process through which experience and skills are gained and decisions are made.

With reflection and honest self-assessment, the externship becomes a laboratory in which you can test a wide variety of hypotheses regarding your career. This reflective process begins with the drafting of your cover letter and résumé, which will provide you with a road map to connect your prior experiences with your current interests and ultimate goals. As you begin work, you will gain a clearer idea of your preferences regarding areas of practice, types of legal work, styles of supervision and management, and other factors that blend together to create a work environment that you find pleasant and fulfilling. You will learn what aspects of law practice you find most enjoyable, intriguing, and exciting and those you find boring or enervating. You will get a sense of the parts of legal practice for which you have a natural affinity and the areas in which you will need to work harder to develop your skills in order to practice successfully. These are very much individual preferences and proclivities, learned only through actual experience.

You also can use your externship to further your career plans. You will gain skills and knowledge that employers seek. You will have the opportunity to create or enlarge the network of attorneys who can provide you with advice and assistance as you plan your career. You may find that the connections you have made lead directly to job opportunities—sometimes in the field to which you were planning to focus but in many cases to jobs in other practice areas to which you never imagined you would be drawn.

Some of the lessons will be negative. You may discover, over the course of the externship, that you have no interest in pursuing a career in that legal field, or with that placement. You may have difficulties getting along with your supervisor or with colleagues. You may struggle with certain aspects of the assigned work. While these can be painful lessons, they are likely to provide useful insights for your career plans.

Perhaps the most valuable insight to be gained is that there is no straight line trajectory that will lead you from your field placement to your "dream job." Your externship is not a line item that you check off as you move forward. Through your experience, your goals will shift, your skills will grow, and your attitude will change. You may end your externship with a completely different set of personal and professional goals than when you started. Your path may take you far astray of your original goals and may even take you back again. None of this is unfortunate; it means you are doing your job. You are using the tools of reflection and self-assessment discussed in this and the other chapters of this book to ensure that you gain as much as you can from the externship experience.

True Stories: ALS

My own legal career has been anything but a straight path. I went to law school with the sole purpose of becoming a civil rights lawyer and was thrilled to be selected for an externship in my second year to do prisoners' rights work at the Legal Aid Society. Prisoners would call and write with their complaints, and I would take the appropriate steps to provide them with relief—access to medical care one day, a food strike averted the next. I learned that providing legal assistance to those who would otherwise have no ability to protect themselves was as satisfying as I had imagined it would be, and I became resolute in my decision to practice public interest law.

When I graduated from law school and moved, I didn't know anyone in my new city and was unable to find work in a public interest setting. Although a cousin gave me the name of one organization in particular for which she thought I would be a perfect fit, neither that organization nor the other civil rights firms to which I applied were hiring. I decided that if I could not find a job in the public interest field, I would not practice law.

Instead, I worked as a contractor for the Library of Congress, taught civics to high school students, and worked as a consultant, first on prison issues (based on my law school externship) and then on marketing research. Eventually, I decided I wanted to pursue my legal career and applied to a number of organizations including a civil rights firm that was looking for someone to evaluate employment discrimination complaints. My experience interviewing prisoners at the Legal Aid Society was exactly on point but so was my teaching experience, since I was to conduct training for attorneys. Likewise, my consulting work provided me with the administrative and technical expertise I needed to run a large program. I was hired and loved what I could only call my "dream job."

One day, looking through some old papers, I found my notes from the conversation with my cousin years earlier. The name of the organization to which she had suggested I apply was the same organization for which I now worked. The individuals she had told me to contact were my supervisors. There was no straight line trajectory, but somehow I had managed to reach the goal.

Career Planning Begins With the Application Process

Self-Assessment

Learning more about yourself, including your values, interests, skills, communication style, and personal preferences is an essential part of using your externship experience to further your long-term goals. Standardized tests that purport to tell you the career for which you are best suited can be helpful but are only an adjunct to the primary question: what do you want to do? The point of self-assessment is to focus on your interests so that you can locate opportunities that match those interests. Neither your interests nor the opportunities available to you are static and you will want to learn the skills of self-assessment so that you can meet those changes as they occur.

This is the perfect opportunity for you to spend some time and imagination on your vision of your career. What is the perfect job for *you*? This may seem like a moot point given the competitiveness of the job market. It is true that your first job may not be perfect. It only may be part of what you want or may offer only a portion of the experience you need, but if you stay unaware of the elements of the job that you would ultimately find most satisfying, it will be almost impossible to meet those needs. Many of the exercises in this chapter are designed to help you highlight important aspects of yourself, to use that information to seek an externship or define the externship activities, to evaluate the externship, and to refine subsequent career goals. They will create benchmarks against which you can evaluate your externship experience.

403

The process of self-assessment in the context of externships begins with the process of selecting and applying for your field placement. This includes researching and choosing the field placements to which you will apply, drafting a résumé and cover letter, interviewing,` and then deciding whether to accept or reject an offer. This will help you clarify your goals and expectations and can prepare you to design a job search strategy for your first job after graduation from law school. While some schools provide students with a pre-selected list of placements and do not require direct applications, those students too can benefit from the exercises described below. If you already have obtained your field placement, it is still worthwhile to review the application process to consider the steps you took and how you might prepare differently for the next externship or other position for which you apply.

Some students approach the process of searching for externships with trepidation. You do not need to dread the application process; it is part of the externship learning process through which you will gain tremendous perspective on your legal career. You will find yourself open to a world of possibilities that you had not even considered, meet some experienced and knowledgeable attorneys whom you would never have met otherwise, and begin to develop clarity about your vision for a career in the law.

Selecting a Field Placement

Some students have a clear sense of their ultimate career goals and need to select a field placement that will best serve these interests. Other students feel they have no sense of their ultimate career goals but seek legal experience to help them advance their legal skills, to learn more about the legal community and the practice of law, and to sharpen their career focus. Most students fall somewhere between these two. They may have some general ideas about what they want to do but have not come to any firm conclusions. Regardless of whether you have no idea what you might like to do, or think you know with certainty, there are certain steps to take before selecting the field placements to which you will apply.

The first step is to engage in a thorough assessment of your own strengths, interests, and goals; the skills and substantive areas in which you excel already; and those in which you need improvement. Each of us brings something different to the table. Some of us are born negotiators, applying salve to difficult situations and figuring out solutions. Others of us are advocates, anxious to fight for our clients who will consider the challenge of the courtroom fun and exciting. What if you feel you are not very good at the tasks you most enjoy? What if you do not enjoy the research and writing you have encountered in law school but know it is necessary for you to gain these skills? Law school gives you the opportunity to target the skills you want to develop. Lawyers are constantly improving their skills and acquiring new ones. You can look at your strengths, interests, skills, and values to consider how you might create careers that are invigorating, challenging, and enjoyable. At the same time, you should honestly appraise the skills you are lacking and work to develop them.

Exercise 18.1 What do you consider your personal strengths? This can include elements of your personality, your knowledge, your skills, etc. Be specific. For example, are you a good listener? Are you detail oriented? Do you have a good sense of humor? Do you have a background in engineering?

For each of the strengths listed above, describe a way in which you have used that strength to succeed in your academic, career, or outside activities. Examples might be "my writing skills helped me to edit my school's paper" or "my gregarious nature helped me make new students feel welcome when I was a resident advisor in college."

Did you come to these strengths naturally, or did you improve through some experiences?

In what ways do you feel most secure about your ability to practice law? Which of the strengths listed above do you think will be of the most use to you in your legal career?

What are the personal traits that you feel might impede your ability to practice law? Do you think these are permanent or do you think they are susceptible to change? What would you need to do to improve?

Related to self-assessment of your skills and knowledge is an assessment of the work environment you would prefer and the types of work you might enjoy. This can include the areas of law in which you are interested but also includes the environment in which you would like to practice. The exercise below is designed to assist you in clarifying some of the aspirations you have for your career and for your life, or expanding your objectives if you already have some clear direction. Review the chapter Setting Goals for the Externship as you complete this exercise and consider the field placements to which you might apply. Many students find it useful to use instruments such as the Myers-Briggs Type Inventory (MBTI) to gain additional insights into how their personality traits might influence their career plans. At the conclusion of the exercise below, brainstorm with your partner to create a list of practice areas and working environments that might meet your goals. Review the lists of practice areas and institutional choices at the end of this chapter to broaden the list of jobs you consider.

see Chapter 2 *on Setting Goals*

Exercise 18.2 Devise a list of questions regarding your long-term career goals. After you have created the list, sit down with a partner and have the person ask you each question and take notes on your answers. Here are some of the questions you may want to include. Create additional questions or revise the ones listed, as necessary.

- Why do I want to be a lawyer?

- What do I want my day-to-day life to look like?

- How do I want to feel when I wake up and face going to work?

- How many hours do I want to spend at work each day, week, year?

- Do I have or want a family, and what does that mean about what kind of job I want?

- What type of office environment am I looking for? (Do I want to wear flats or high heels? Lace up black shoes or sneakers?)

- What stress level am I looking for? Do I want to be motivated, pushed, and feel important, or do I want to be laid back, taking a day off when it suits me?

- Where do I want to live—a city, a town, the country? Another country?

- How much interaction do I want to have with my colleagues? Do I prefer working alone or in collaboration?

- How much supervision do I want? Would I prefer regular contact with my supervisor or would I prefer to work alone with minimal supervision?

- What kind of work do I want to do? Something in the courtroom? Criminal prosecution or defense? Civil litigation? Would I prefer transactional work? Do I want to have direct contact with clients?

- With what populations do I want to work? Who do I want my clients to be? Poor people? Businesses?

- What kinds of interactions am I looking for? Do I want to work on policy, or do I want to work directly with people who need my help?

- How much money do I want to make (or how little am I willing to make)?

Some students find it difficult to narrow their externship search because they are unclear as to their ultimate goals. If you are starting out with only a vague idea of what you might like to do but know that you want to gain some sort of legal experience somewhere, welcome to the club. This can be an ideal place to be. Everything is open to you, and your opportunities are limited only by your imagination. Still, when it seems as though there are a thousand directions in which you could go and no way to know which path to take, it can be quite daunting. It is important to remember that part of the reason for doing an externship, and the reflective exercises described in this chapter, is to help you figure out what career you might like to pursue and how.

Some people know exactly what type of law they want to practice almost from the time they start law school. Perhaps they have a family member who practices tax law and know this interests them, or they have worked in the health field for a number of years and are sure they want to continue in this field, or they have a passion for international human rights law. If you fall into this category, you still have many decisions to make as to which path to take in terms of your coursework and field placements.

The first question for students who have selected a field in which to practice is whether it is better to focus entirely on the area of law that is their ultimate career goal or whether to use the time in law school to gain experience and knowledge they might otherwise never learn. If you know that you will be doing tax work immediately upon graduation, do you want to take this opportunity to try working for a litigation firm or doing public interest work? Do you believe that this is necessary to a well-rounded legal education?

Some students decide to spend their fieldwork time in law school pursuing experience and expertise that is directly related to their goals in order to obtain credentials for the full-time positions they eventually will pursue. Other students decide to spend some time in law school pursuing experiences that are unrelated to their primary goals but that will provide them with a broader legal education.

A related question is whether you should apply to an externship where you feel you are more likely to succeed or whether you should apply to an externship that will be more of a challenge but might allow you to take risks that you would not want to take in a job after graduation. For example, if you believe your legal writing is weak but your interpersonal communication skills are strong, you may want to work in a field placement that will require you to write extensively, such as drafting appellate briefs or "clerking" for a judge, even if you may initially have some difficulty performing satisfactorily.

Regardless of whether you feel certain you know the area of law in which you might like to practice or are in the process of considering many possibilities, there are a number of resources of which you can take advantage in order to find the placement that will meet your needs. Even if your school provides students with a limited number of field placements from which to choose, you should research your choices to the fullest extent possible. Here are some suggestions.

Review the field placements that are recommended by your law school. Many law schools provide a list of placements interested in accepting applications from law students. These organizations are generally most likely to accept externs and will be a better bet than making "cold calls" to organizations that have never used law students as externs before.

Read evaluations/talk to former externs. This will enable you to get a general description of the work environment as well as specific information such as whether the externs drafted documents that could be used as writing samples or were given research projects that provided them with substantive legal skills. Before relying on the evaluations of previous externs, make sure that the supervisor is the same one with whom you will be working. This is particularly important for judges' chambers where many students are supervised primarily by clerks who turn over every year or two.

Talk to lawyers, professors, and others in the field. You can start with full-time and adjunct faculty at the law school who teach courses related to your interests. They may be able to recommend attorneys with whom you might speak and suggest field placements that would meet your goals. In addition, attend bar association meetings and conferences in the fields you find of interest. When you interview attorneys, particularly those in legal fields in which you think you might want to practice, ask them about their own career paths. Find out what courses they took and what legal work they did during law school. Ask whether they would advise you to do the same. Ask whether they think there are some fieldwork experiences that are essential in order to be qualified for a job in the field. If you interview lawyers who have hiring responsibilities, ask whether they prefer applicants who have certain substantive knowledge and have worked in the field or whether they are more interested in applicants who have a broad range of experience. If they are seeking specific knowledge, find out whether it is something better gained through coursework or through experiential learning.

Review websites. An organization's website will provide you with general information about the field placement such as the issues and cases on which they focus and how much of its efforts center on policy, litigation, or direct services. A careful reading also may highlight more comprehensive information such as whether the field placement has a particular political agenda. Often there is background information available on the attorneys with whom you would be working.

True Stories: E. C.

E.C. decided early on during law school that he wanted to work for the Department of Justice, where, as he explains, "I could pursue my passion for civil rights work and still draw a decent salary." During his first year, he met with professors and law school alumni who had worked at DOJ to find out what their own career paths had been and what they thought the Department would find the most appealing in an applicant. Since one recommendation he received was to obtain some experience working for the government, he chose to spend his first summer externing with the Governor's Office. The following summer, he worked at a large law firm that had a public interest program that allowed him to work part of the summer at a civil rights firm, which he was sure the Civil Rights Division would like to see. After he graduated, he clerked for a judge, focusing on the job experience that he had been told was valued by DOJ.

E.C. notes, "At this point, I had created the perfect résumé for a job with DOJ, except for one problem. I applied to the DOJ Honors Program and was not accepted. I realized I had made a tactical mistake in my career plan by putting all my hopes and dreams into the one job. I had to switch gears and start applying for other jobs." E.C. applied to civil rights organizations but had no luck. Big firms were more receptive but he was reluctant to give up on the DOJ. "I was beginning to get concerned when I learned that DOJ was taking lateral transfers with one to three years experience. I wrote to them, arguing that my clerkship should count as one year of experience. To my delight, I was hired, which was a good thing because I had really not counted on having a Plan B."

Drafting Your Résumé

Drafting your résumé is a crucial stage in planning your career. The process allows you to reflect on the experiences you had in the past and how they might be organized to showcase the skills and knowledge relevant to the employer to whom you are applying.

Many students do not focus on their résumés when applying for externships, believing such positions do not require the same degree of attention and sophistication as the résumé they would provide to employers offering paid positions. This is a mistake. First, many externships are extremely competitive, and the student who has spent the time to execute a thoughtful and well-presented résumé is more likely to be offered the position. Second, the writing of your résumé will help you reflect on the ways in which your career path is built on your past experience and interests and will help you tie together what may seem like disparate parts of your life. Third, as with all things, practice makes better, if not perfect. The more time you spend on your résumé now, the better it will be for your future applications.

For many students, this résumé will be the first one intended for an audience of attorneys. It should be an accurate reflection of who you were, who you are, and who you want to become. You will need to frame your experience in a different way than you have in the past, reinterpreting your previous experience in language that attorneys will find helpful in evaluating you for a legal position. Your résumé is an advocacy piece intended to convince a very specific audience that you have the skills, experience, and potential to provide it with the assistance it seeks. If you have a résumé that you have used for other purposes, it can serve as a starting point, but there are some important changes that you may need to make as you apply for a legal externship. Consider the following suggestions.

Move education to the top of the page. Now that you are in law school, your educational status and anticipated graduation date gain new significance. You are applying for jobs for which you would not be considered if you were not in law school. You are defining yourself as an attorney.

Change the focus of each job description to the skill sets relevant to the practice of law. No one expects you to have legal experience. The challenge is to take the experience you do have and frame it in such a way that it focuses on the skills that are relevant to the legal work for which you are applying. Generally, attorneys hiring legal externs want to know that you can write quickly, clearly, and accurately; that you can read legal text closely and carefully; that you can analyze and synthesize material that you read; and that you are detail oriented. In addition, employers hiring for positions involving client contact will be interested to know whether you have any background that would prepare you to provide direct services such as experience in interviewing or counseling. Review each job listed on your current résumé (and perhaps some you left off) to see how you can emphasize your writing and analytical skills. Many parts of your previous job descriptions that would be relevant in other circumstances are less relevant here.

A student who, prior to law school, had been applying for positions as a fundraiser changed her résumé as follows [all company names have been changed] :

Original Résumé	**Environmental Solutions, Program Assistant.** Organized fundraiser supporting pro-environment candidates for Senate and House seats. Assisted and raised funds for state and local candidates with pro-environment voting records. Researched legal issues relating to environmental law.

New Résumé	**Environmental Solutions, Program Assistant.** Researched and summarized regulations relating to Clean Water Act. Drafted summaries of pending environmental legislation for congressional candidates. Organized fundraiser for candidates for Senate and House seats.

Explain your experience for an uninformed reader. It is very common for students who have worked in one field of employment to write in a shorthand that is easily understood by their former colleagues but incomprehensible to anyone else. As you apply for your externship, even if it is related to the work you used to do, review your résumé for acronyms, jargon, and technical language. If the lawyers reviewing your résumé do not understand the job description you have provided to them, you have wasted the space.

A student with a marketing background drafted a job description that was fairly unintelligible. The second description also accurately describes her experience in the position but in accessible language that focuses on her accomplishments.

Technics, Inc., Platform Specialist. Drafted channel strategy and created programs that addressed goals of the division. Created and launched CORteam. Program included education and training deliverables, reseller recruitment tools, demand generation programs, and electronic lead distribution program.

Original Résumé

Technics, Inc. Platform Specialist. Drafted extensive market strategy report and developed and executed multimillion dollar international marketing program for new software product.

New Résumé

Be specific when describing your legal experience. Your prospective employers will be most interested in your recent law-related work experience; this is not the place to be stingy to try to save space. They will want to know your specific assignments and the context in which you worked. "Assisted attorneys in preparing discovery" provides very little information to the reader regarding the actual scope of your responsibilities. It might mean that you provided administrative support with document production, cite-checking, collating of documents, etc. On the other hand, it might mean that you researched legal issues relating to a specific area of law, drafted documents such as interrogatories or production requests, and interviewed potential witnesses to determine whether they should be deposed. A more helpful entry might be "Drafted interrogatories and reviewed and summarized responses for large medical malpractice case."

Do not understate or overstate your experience. Jobs that seem unrelated to the practice of law such as working as a lifeguard or a waitress may be of interest to the externship employer. Dealing with anxious customers can be excellent training for providing direct legal services. A summer as a lifeguard can indicate a willingness to take on responsibility and an ability to stay focused and attentive. Students who have worked as secretaries will understand the importance of attention to detail. Do not feel you need to ignore these jobs. On the other hand, do not overstate your experience, which will give a much worse impression than simply forthrightly stating your job duties.

411

Exercise 18.3 Select one non-law-related job on your résumé. Following the example below, list 10 transferable skills you learned as a result of that job.

Job: Administrative Assistant

Transferable skills: attention to detail, meeting deadlines, anticipating needs, ensuring schedule is met, getting along with others, good work habits (showing up on time, calling in when sick, etc.), data processing, editing, organizational ability, typing skills.

Exercise 18.4 Review your résumé with a partner. Ask the partner to read each job description and explain what you did that might be relevant to a legal employer. Was your partner able to identify correctly what you did and its relevance to the practice of law? If not, discuss your job with your partner to determine how you might clarify the description you provided.

Get Help. As a general rule, you should not try to draft a résumé without help, particularly as you shift to one that you will use for a legal externship. Almost everyone has a tendency to underestimate his or her own contributions. In addition, it can be quite difficult to re-work your résumé while facing the stress and esteem issues sometimes brought on by the first year of law school. It may take an outsider to remind you of how much you have to offer and to help you see how your past experiences can benefit your future employers. There are many excellent resources for you to use in drafting and editing your résumé. Most law schools offer assistance through the Office of Career Services. You should take advantage of this assistance and, if possible, meet with a counselor, not just once but again after you have re-drafted your résumé in accordance with the career counselor's suggestions. Your school's Career Services Office is likely to have many excellent books and helpful articles on writing effective résumés.

Drafting a Cover Letter

Drafting cover letters to apply to externships will assist you in reflecting on your academic and career goals and on the path you have travelled so far. A cover letter is not a recitation of what you have done; it is a guide to help the reader understand how your past work, life, and academic experiences have prepared you to be of service to the organization to which you are applying. A well-drafted cover letter picks out selected details from the résumé and weaves them together in a coherent whole. Whereas your résumé may be more inclusive, your cover letter should be focused on the particular field placement to which you are applying. It should answer the question in the interviewer's mind: What can she do for me?

Writing a cover letter is a skill to be learned and improved like any other. You need to guide the reader through the relevant portions of your résumé in a couple of brief paragraphs. Like the résumé itself, it is an advocacy piece. The more cover letters you draft, the more adept you will become. It is not necessary to write an entirely different cover letter for each organization to which you are applying, but you should be sure each letter adequately explains your interest in *that* employer and highlights the relevance of your qualifications in light of *that* organization's needs. Your cover letter can provide additional fodder for your interviews, at which you will want to expand on the ways in which your background provides you with the experience the employer is seeking.

The single most important task in drafting the cover letter is making it free of typographical errors and mistakes in grammar, punctuation, and spelling. Your cover letter is your first writing sample. If it is well written, it may be the only writing sample that is read. Ask someone else to do the final proofread, since it is hard for the author of the letter to spot mistakes—especially the typical one of failing to remove references to another organization to which you previously applied using the same letter.

Overcoming Application Block

Many students find the process of applying for externships sufficiently daunting that they procrastinate, eventually contacting only a few employers at random. To avoid this, do not become emotionally attached to any particular job to which you are applying. Simply apply, and move on. If you are selected for an interview, be enthusiastic in your response, but hold back a little of yourself until you receive an offer. One way to help yourself stay detached is to apply to a variety of field placements, rather than limiting yourself to one or two "dream jobs."

Do not get caught up in the fear that you are not sufficiently qualified. The attorneys who are reviewing applications for externships do not expect you to be a lawyer. They realize someone who has completed one or two years of law school is likely to have limited legal experience and will have taken only basic courses. They expect a well-written résumé that presents your experience clearly and concisely, without grammatical or typographical errors. While they may have some substantive requirements, generally they are looking for individuals who are motivated and have good work habits. Keep in mind that there is a role for serendipity in the application process. A candidate may be offered an interview not because of law review membership but because she has a black belt in karate or because he is from the interviewer's home state.

Interviewing

The application interview is one of the important learning experiences of an externship. This is a great opportunity to hone your communication skills, to prepare for the types of questions that your particular background generates, and to practice the answers you will give. Regardless of the outcome, it is a great way to meet attorneys and learn more about the practice of law, and, if you can relax, it even can be fun.

The most important aspect of an interview is to remember that there are two interviews taking place. The potential employer is assessing whether you meet its qualifications and if it would enjoy working with you. Equally important, you are interviewing the employer to see if it meets your needs, and, likewise, whether you will enjoy working there. Keep in mind the distinction between an externship and other forms of employment. The employer must be willing to accept that the central purpose of an externship is to provide educational opportunities for the extern. If you do not take advantage of the interview to probe whether the employer actually accepts this fundamental premise, you may end up in an externship that does not meet your academic or career goals.

Preparing for Your Interview

- **Know your résumé.** Just as your cover letter assists employers in focusing on certain elements of your résumé, so the résumé assists the employers in focusing the interview. Be prepared to answer questions about information you have presented. If you say that you wrote a thesis on a particular topic, be prepared to summarize what you wrote and the conclusions that you drew. If your résumé lists a job in which you assisted an attorney in drafting a motion for summary judgment, be prepared to discuss the case and the type of work you did. (Keep in mind your obligation to preserve the confidences of the client.)

- **Know your goals.** Either employers will ask you questions about your goals outright, for example, "Where do you see yourself five years out of law school?" or they will be listening to your responses to see whether you have a sense of direction. Most employers respond favorably to a student who presents herself as having selected the field placement after careful consideration of how the organization fits into the student's academic and career goals. Moreover, you need to have an understanding of your own goals if you want to use the interview to determine if a particular field placement will provide you with the type of experience and legal skills you are hoping to acquire. It is up to you to know what you are looking for and to use the interview process to help you in getting a better understanding of the work in which you will be engaged.

- **Know the employer.** Although you did some preliminary research on the organization with which you are interviewing before you decided to apply, update it. Review the organization's website carefully and find out whatever other background information you can. An employer will be impressed with someone who has done his homework. Your preparation will show that you are interested in this organization and its work. It will enable you to ask detailed questions and will assist you in framing your own experience in relation to the work of the organization.

- **Relax.** One of the most important factors determining whether or not someone is hired is whether the employer feels comfortable during the interview. The externship interview is a great place to practice presenting yourself as relaxed and pleasant. If you find it difficult to relax, focus on the needs of the employer and how you might be able to assist with those needs, rather than on how you are presenting yourself. Force yourself to ask questions, even though it may not be comfortable for you. This is, after all, just another part of the externship learning process, and you are not expected to perform with perfect poise or confidence. You are practicing for what is to come. You will not improve unless you try.

After the Interview

After you have interviewed, you should write a follow-up letter thanking those with whom you interviewed and affirming your interest. The period while you wait for a decision can be an awkward and sometimes stressful. During this time, you should continue to interview for other positions. Until you accept an offer, there is no problem with applying to other placements. Remember not to focus too much emotional energy on any one field placement. You may find that a second or third choice turns out to be a transformative experience.

Accepting or Rejecting Offers

One of the most difficult aspects of any job search is deciding whether to accept an offer, especially if you are still waiting to hear from other prospective placements. Should you risk losing the offer you have in favor of another you may or may not get? It is not uncommon to ask the employer, "May I take some time to get back to you? I am waiting to hear from another organization, and I would like to be able to consider both options." Most employers will be willing to comply with this request, although there is a tradition of accepting immediately when offered a position from a judge.

Similarly, if you receive an offer, there is nothing wrong with contacting the employers from whom you are still waiting to hear. Say simply, "I have received an offer from another employer, and I was wondering when I might hear from you regarding this position." You should not ask for a rapid response unless you would accept the second offer over the first one. Placements are rightly frustrated by speeding up the process for an applicant only to have the person turn down the offer.

If you have any confusion about the offer, get your questions answered before you accept the offer. Make sure that you and the employer understand how many hours you will be working and for how many weeks. Also, be certain you know what your job duties and responsibilities will be, who will be supervising you, etc. If you receive two offers and are deciding between them, take the opportunity to check with each of them about those things that were uppermost on your goals list. Will you have responsibility for drafting a document that can be used as a writing sample? Will you be working directly with someone who has the subject matter expertise in which you are most interested? Will you have a chance to attend hearings and meetings relating to the work of the office?

What if I get my dream job after accepting an offer from my second choice? Can I tell the employer I have changed my mind?

see ▷ Chapter 2
on Setting Goals

This issue is dealt with in Chapter 2. Once you accept an offer, the employer usually informs the other candidates that the position has been filled and discontinues the selection process. If you accept an offer and then change your mind, you will inconvenience a busy professional. As a matter of personal ethics and of good career strategy, given that most legal communities are actually quite small, it is a bad idea to decline an offer after accepting it. Like all other professional decisions, however, you should use your judgment and deal honestly with others. For example, if you believe the employer may not be inconvenienced by a change in your status because interviews are still taking place, you may inquire of the employer whether there would be a problem if you revoked your acceptance.

What if I do not hear back or do not get the offer I was hoping for?

Persevere. Attorneys often are overworked and may neglect to contact applicants simply because they do not have a spare moment to focus on the situation. For example, one of the extern coordinators for the Department of Justice said that she was often too swamped to contact students. She noted of students who sent follow-up communication regarding the status of their applications, "It doesn't make me think they're pests; it makes me think they really want the job." Others tell stories of organizations losing the selected candidate at the last minute and hiring the next person who called.

Be flexible. Remember that most work skills and legal skills are transferable and all field placements enhance your ability to negotiate your way through the legal work world. It is very common to look back over one's career and realize that each experience added a crucial building block, even when that was not apparent at the time. Sometimes the best experiences come when you least expect them. Even when you do get the position you thought was the perfect fit, you may find that it is not what you anticipated. Staying flexible and doing your best in the situation is as important as any skill.

Should I consider an externship in another part of the country?

If you know that you want to practice law in another state, it can be very helpful to spend a summer or semester (if permitted by your law school) working there. Because many people get jobs through the network of contacts they have made in law school, you may find yourself adrift if you move to a new state without having made such connections. Finding an out-of-state externship, however, can be challenging. Use the Internet's search engines to look for field placements in the city or state in which you think you are going to practice law. If there are a limited number of law firms or legal organizations in that area, you may want to consider state or local government agencies. You can check with your school's alumni office or attorney directories to determine whether there are graduates of your college or law school practicing law in that state. Call such potential contacts to find out whether they can recommend field placements to which you might apply. Also, ask them what legal issues are of unusual importance in the state—this may provide you with some guidance as you consider which field placements would be best for your long-term career goals.

On the Job: Using On-the-Job Reflection and Self-Assessment to Guide Your Career Plans

Reflection on the Field Placement

> **Exercise 18.5** Before your first day on the job, make a list of assumptions you have about the field placement and how it might fit into your long-term career goals. Describe what you believe is a typical day for the attorneys. After reviewing the topics below, create a list of your expectations. After a few weeks on the job, compare what you are observing in the workplace to the list you created.

It is vital to long-term career planning for you to be mindful at each stage of your law school education of those things that you find most energizing and absorbing. Many students, with their eyes on some ultimate career progression, view each academic and work experience on the way as a "ticket to get punched." They neglect to ask themselves crucial questions: Am I enjoying myself? Is this satisfying? If so, why? If not, why not? What could I do to make this experience more enjoyable? What do I want to learn? What I am learning? They get so caught up in where they are going that they neglect to make observations about where they are.

Your field placement offers an excellent "classroom" in which to observe the workplace as you consider your own job and career priorities. Consider the issues raised in the previous chapters of this book within the realities of your field placement. This includes the substantive knowledge you might acquire, but it also includes everything you might want to know in order to determine whether this is the area in which you would like to specialize and any additional insights you can gather regarding your long-term career plans. You will have to look outside of your own work assignments to a larger understanding of how the firm or organization works and whether the attorneys who work there are thriving or, perhaps, merely surviving. Take care not to confuse your experience as an extern with the experience of the full-time attorneys. While your memoranda may be scrutinized carefully, the attorney for whom you work may not be receiving the same degree of supervision. While you may be leaving by 6:00 p.m., others may be staying late. While you may be leaving for home from the courthouse, your supervisor may be returning to the office to prepare for tomorrow's hearing. If you cannot tell from observation, you may want to consider asking your supervisor some of these questions so that you get the fullest possible picture of the actual work environment. Consider the following questions.

How do the attorneys balance their work with their personal lives?

The externship is an excellent opportunity to observe how the attorneys with whom you are working balance work with the rest of their lives and to consider whether this career path would offer you the balance you seek.

Exercise 18.6 If you worked full-time at your field placement, would you be able to maintain a balanced life? How does the workload that the attorneys have compare to the one you have now in law school? Would you find it very difficult to work the hours that the attorneys put in regularly? Do you want to start your day as early or stay as late? How important is it to you to find a balance between your professional life and your personal life? Would you be energized by the work or would you burn out without more vacation or relaxation time?

Consider these questions:

What time do attorneys arrive in the morning? What time do they leave? How often does each attorney work beyond eight hours in a day? Beyond 10? Beyond 12? Do they work on the weekends? Do they eat lunch at their desks while they continue to work, or do they take a break to relax? How much vacation time do they get? While they are on vacation, do they continue to stay in contact with the office and involved in their cases, or do they leave the office behind? Do they take their full allotment of vacation time? What is the pay scale? What are the benefits? Does the workplace accommodate the needs of employees with families? Are there opportunities for civic involvement, for bar service, for *pro bono* work?

 Chapter 17
on Work-Life Balance

How do the attorneys in your field placement interact?

Through the exercises on self-assessment, you might find that you prefer certain work conditions and ways of interacting with colleagues and supervisors. Some of you prefer to work alone while others have a strong need for collaboration. Some prefer close supervision while others bristle at "micro-management." After surveying your own preferences, observe the interactions you see in the field placement.

see Chapter 15
*on Management
Skills*

Exercise 18.7 Often a legal institution will have a certain type of culture that permeates it. This can affect how attorneys are supervised, the extent to which they work together, how they interact with each other, and how connected the attorneys feel to the institution and clients. Given your own predilections, would this field placement be a match for you as a permanent position?

Consider the following questions:

To what extent is there a collegial atmosphere among the attorneys? Do they work collaboratively? Are the attorneys generally autonomous or do they work under some degree of close supervision? Who decides which attorney will work on which issue or case? Does the attorney have any say in the matter? How much control does the attorney have over the final product? Are attorneys given positive feedback? Are there clear lines of supervision? Is there effective delegation of responsibilities? Can you tell who is supervising whom and whether or not they are being provided with guidance? Are attorneys provided with sufficient administrative assistance? Is the office well-organized? Are important dates tracked to ensure that deadlines will not be missed? Do the attorneys appear to be happy and enjoying themselves at work? Do the attorneys appear to be stressed? Are there ever outbursts of anger from any of the attorneys? If so, what is the reaction of colleagues and supervisors?

What is the mission of the organization or firm? Do the attorneys seem to be connected to and concerned with that mission? Are they effective at carrying it out? If the attorneys work directly with clients, do they seem genuinely concerned about their clients' welfare? Do they care about the quality of their work? Do they communicate effectively with clients?

How are the attorneys trained?

Attorneys do not begin their legal careers as experts; they become experts. How you receive your training can influence the extent to which you feel comfortable practicing law and can influence the career decisions you make. It may not be obvious how the attorneys in your field placement gain their knowledge and expertise, but it is worthwhile to find out.

> **Exercise 18.8** Consider how important is it to you to receive specific training before taking on new responsibilities and compare that to the training provided to the attorneys in your field placement. Is this important enough to you to influence your career choices?

How much training are you receiving as an extern? Do your supervisors make themselves available to respond to questions? Are attorneys at your field placement given special training, or are they thrown into the work and expected to pick it up as they go along? If training is provided, what topics are covered and how extensive is it? If attorneys litigate, are they given any special training in litigation? Are there opportunities outside the office for the lawyers to develop their lawyering skills and to stay abreast of changes in the law? Does the employer subscribe to newsletters, etc. in relevant fields? Do lawyers take on new responsibilities after they have been working for a few years?

Reflection and Self-Assessment On the Job

After you have observed and reflected on characteristics of the attorneys' work and interactions, the next step is to observe and reflect on your own attitudes and behavior. You engaged in self-assessment as you considered the field placements to which you might apply. After you have spent some time in your externship, return to the list of questions in Exercises 18.1 and 18.2. Have your responses changed over the course of the semester?

Are there any areas in which you have been surprised to find you are having some difficulties? Issues that come up in one job can appear to be caused by particular circumstances or individuals. If those same issues surface in the next job, a clear-eyed appraisal may lead you to conclude that the common denominator is you. Unless you elect to make some changes, you can expect the same issues to recur throughout your career. For both the positive and the negative circumstances, consider the extent to which you are a participant in and not a victim or benefactor of the circumstances in which you find yourself.

> **Exercise 18.9** Make a list of two of your previous jobs and rate your satisfaction with those jobs on a scale of 1-10. List those parts of the job that provided you with the most satisfaction and those that caused you the greatest consternation. Do the same for your current externship. List each

situation that you thought was particularly challenging or difficult (a boss who seemed never to be around or who imposed unrealistic deadlines, for example).

For the areas that you found most difficult, write down what happened and, putting aside the ways in which others may have been at fault, describe how you might have contributed to the situation. Make a separate list for each job and then compare them to see whether you have exhibited the same behavior more than once.

Do the same thing for situations that you felt were particularly positive. Describe your own contributions, and compare your current externship to your last few jobs to see whether any patterns emerge.

If you are enrolled in an externship seminar, take advantage of the resources it provides. Ask the other students pointed questions about the concerns you have at your job. One of my seminar students commented, "It seems as though all I do is sit at a computer all day every day. I read, and I write, and I write some more. I rarely talk to anyone, except for the occasional discussion with my supervisor. Is this the same for all of you?" To everyone's surprise, the response was a resounding "yes." It turned out that almost everyone in the class was having a similar experience, and all of them were anxious about the prospect of doing this for the rest of their lives. After returning to their field placements and carefully watching what the full-time attorneys were doing, the students discovered that many of the attorneys had a far broader range of activities than those given to the externs. In addition to research and writing, they met with clients, talked with co-counsel and opposing counsel, and met with other attorneys in the office. With this information, the students were able to ask whether they might be included in some of these other activities, if only as observers. Other students found that the full-time attorneys also were primarily engaged in research and writing, spending most of the day working at the computer. This information was useful as the students decided whether or not to pursue a career in the same type of employment. The externship seminar can provide a very useful forum for discussing such issues.

Time set aside for reflection and self-assessment will have as much or greater effect on your long-term career goals as any legal skills you may acquire. In our busy lives, it is difficult to find the time to stop and consider whether we are choosing a career path that will allow us to use our strengths to the greatest extent possible and that will bring a sense of fulfillment to our lives.

Exercise 18.10 List three aspects of your externship you most enjoy, and explain why.

List three aspects of your externship you least enjoy, and explain why.

In what ways does your reaction to your field placement inform your long-term career goals?

Developing Skills for Career Development

It is important to have a clear notion of the legal skills you want to acquire or develop more fully through your externship. Create a list of these skills and periodically check your progress. If there are areas in which your development is lagging, consider whether there are ways of correcting your tack. You may find that you are developing skills in your field placement that you did not even have on your list. Every few weeks, make a note of these, as you will soon take them for granted. Keeping a list of "things I learned this week" will help you to develop your future résumés and cover letters and to prepare for interviews. Include skills that are not necessarily legal in nature but that will enhance your ability to practice law, including technical proficiency and communication skills.

In addition to listing the skills you learned, reflect on the issues they raise for you. For example, if you were asked to assist in creating a trial notebook, you might realize that you are not particularly well-organized and that this is more of a challenge than you had expected. You might ask for some advice from attorneys, paralegals, and secretaries in your field placement. In this way, you gain not just the particularized skill of creating the notebook, but develop the more general skill of developing organizational systems for all of your legal work.

There will be times in your externship when you will have a choice as to whether or not to take on a task with which you have little prior experience and for which you feel unprepared. Your supervisor may say, "We need to file a complaint." Offer to draft it. Those who undertake such assignments will increase their skills, improve their confidence, and gain a reputation for being helpful. Focusing your own concern that you lack competence makes you less likely to provide the support

There is an adage that an expert is someone who has done something once, when no one else has done it at all.

needed by those with whom you are working. To gain the courage to volunteer for assignments, think first of the needs of the organization and how you might be able to assist them. If you keep "How can I be of maximum service to this organization?" in the forefront of your mind, your fears will largely dissipate.

Exercise 18.11 List every new skill you have developed over the course of your externship and every skill you have improved over the course of your externship.

Are these skills related to possible career options?

What skills were you hoping to acquire but have not yet had the opportunity?

Is there any way to ask for assignments that would provide you with the opportunity to learn these skills?

On the Job: Creating a Network

Once you have begun your field placement, the opportunities for shaping your legal career go far beyond improving your legal skills. You will develop your network of attorneys, obtain invaluable mentoring, and to create the good impression you will use to parlay your work experience into a career path.

There is no better time than while you are working in a field placement to take concrete steps toward your career plans by interacting and networking with attorneys. Some students think networking means using people to help you get a job. A better way to think of it is that you are working to build a community, a network of mutually interdependent individuals who are available to help one another as the need arises. It is not a one-way street; those who help you also may need help in the future. Lawyers understand that there is no way for them to succeed without this inter-connectedness. Whether it is in work, activities, or professional growth, we all need one another.

Why should you put your time and energy into creating relationships with your colleagues?

The obvious reason is that it will increase your chances of finding a legal job in the field in which you are interested in practicing. Most legal communities are small.

Even in very large cities, attorneys who work in the same field will tend to know, or know of, one another. Attorneys working in different fields will be acquainted through mutual friends, relatives, classmates, and former places of employment. Socially, attorneys have friends who are attorneys. Some positions are not well-advertised and knowing attorneys in the field can improve your chances of finding out that a position has become available. Also, many attorneys prefer hiring a known entity.

The benefit of creating legal networks is far greater than just job search assistance. It can help you feel a part of a larger community and give meaning to your work. It can help you become a more effective attorney as you give and receive assistance. It can build your social network to give you a fuller life outside of work and, perhaps most important, it can make your work more enjoyable.

Some people take naturally to networking; they seem to have been born to it. How do the rest of us create our networks?

Everyone with whom you interact in your externship can become part of your network. It is one of the main benefits of an externship. When you sit alone in a library, you do not have an opportunity to interact with other attorneys. Working jointly on a task can foster mutual respect. Since a good way to get to know someone is to work with them, you should look for opportunities to work with a variety of attorneys. If you are working with just one person and have the chance to work on a project with a second lawyer, take it. Your network has doubled. Your legal network can include anyone you have met who is involved in the legal field. This includes colleagues, friends, supervisors, and even opposing counsel.

At some point everyone needs assistance—with finding a job, helping a client, researching a legal issue. Along the way, people become friends and create a community. If the sole reason for your interest in another person is to advance your career, do not bother. You will come across as insincere. If you are actually interested in furthering your relationship and learning from the person, take the time to build a solid relationship.

How to network with the attorneys in your field placement.

> Make a good impression. Be on time. Work hard. Show enthusiasm. Volunteer for projects. Often it will be up to you to set the number of hours you plan to work during the semester. If you agree to work 15 hours a week, and work 18, you will make a good impression; work the same 18 hours when you have promised 20 hours and the impression will be the opposite.

> Do not focus exclusively on what your externship can do for you. Employers and colleagues respond very favorably to employees who make

it clear that their main concern is to be of assistance to the organization and to the supervisor to whom they are assigned. While it is important to lay out your goals and expectations, it is equally important to recognize the organization's needs and meet them, regardless of whether they fit into your job description. This does not mean you should take on an inordinate number of administrative tasks; after all this is a legal externship and is intended as a learning experience for you. Still, when the attorneys are working to meet a deadline, an offer to assist with putting together a trial binder, or summarizing witness interviews, or other law-related work that is time consuming and adding to the attorneys' overall burden, will be much appreciated. Every overworked lawyer longs to hear someone say, "How can I help?" Later, when you are seeking assistance in your job search, your willingness to provide assistance will be recalled with appreciation.

Get to know your colleagues as human beings not just co-workers. Do not be afraid to occasionally "schmooze" with your colleagues, talking about non-work-related matters with them. Obviously, you do not want to do this when you should be working and, worst of all, you do not want to interrupt someone who is in the middle of conducting serious business with an extended non-work discussion. Informal conversation while waiting for a meeting to start or riding down in the elevator at the end of the day, for example, is often the way in which relationships are formed.

Ask attorneys for advice on the legal field. The "informational interview" is a discussion that takes place with the stated purpose of obtaining information from a more experienced attorney. Everyone understands that this is one of the ways law students learn about practice areas. Most attorneys like to talk about themselves and their practice. As long as they feel that you honestly are interested in them as people, and not simply as a means to an end, many lawyers will be pleased to speak with you. You may want to ask for such an interview with an attorney at your placement with whom you do not regularly work. Information interviews are obviously for the benefit of the student, and, therefore, you need to be attentive to the attorney's schedule. Prepare for the meeting in advance, and do not take up too much of the attorney's time.

Engage in activities with attorneys outside of work. Take advantage of walking with a co-worker to the Metro, lunch events, and other social activities. Take any opportunity you can find to get to know your colleagues.

Include the support staff. All of the networking techniques that you have learned are appropriate for staff as well as attorneys. Everyone understands that a good relationship with administrative staff helps get the work done. It is also a way of demonstrating respect and appreciation for all colleagues—not just those with law degrees. Networking is not about using people; it is about creating relationships.

Exercise 18.12 Make a list of everyone you can think of who could be in your legal network. These would be individuals whom you know well enough that you might ask them for some form of assistance. Include colleagues from your current field placement and previous jobs, friends, family, and classmates.

True Stories: L. K.

L.K. grew up in Washington, D.C. with what she calls "the policy bug." Initially, she thought she might like to be a reporter, but, during a college internship for a Senator, she decided she wanted to have an impact on the law, shaping policy decisions, not just reporting on them.

Although she was fairly confident that her interests would lead to a career in policy, she decided to use her time in law school to explore different areas of law. She says "I felt like I would not be a well-rounded lawyer without exposing myself to a variety of practice areas." With this in mind, she spent her first summer externing for a federal district court judge. "Although I felt the experience was invaluable, I realized I would not want to clerk after graduation because I preferred more interaction with people." L.K.'s next externship was with the U.S. Attorney's Office. While she enjoyed the insights into that world, it confirmed for her that she did not want to be a prosecutor. To round out her background, and get experience in the implementation of the law, she externed with a government agency to learn more about regulatory enforcement.

Throughout law school, L.K. stayed in touch with some of the people she met in her various externships, including the chief of staff in the Senator's office where she had worked while she was in college. After graduation and several years of practice, she let the Senator's office know she was looking to return to D.C. and do policy work. It turned out that they were hiring, and, while she had to compete with others for the position, she was offered the job.

According to L.K., "I always developed a plan for how to pursue my field placements and each of my career goals. I created an outline for *myself. Here is what I have done; here is why I want to work in D.C.; here is my two minute pitch on how I can sell myself. As I applied to field placements, I made a list of everyone I knew and each time I spoke to someone, I would ask them to provide me with at least one more contact. Still, I have tried to be open and flexible and 'tack' the way sailors do, rather than worrying about taking the direct route to some particular job or career. My most important goal has been to enjoy each externship and job I have had and not to do anything because I 'should.'"*

Mentoring/Supervision

One of the most helpful things you can do for yourself is to find a mentor (or mentors) in your field placement. This may or may not include your direct supervisor. It could be an attorney who indicates an interest in supporting you in your career. The role of a mentor is different from the role of a supervisor, although you may establish a mentor relationship with your immediate supervisor. A supervisor reviews and critiques your legal work. A mentor provides guidance on career advancement and job performance and can help you see your legal career in a broader context.

A mentor may do some or all of the following:

Advise you on how to maneuver through the field placement in order to get the most from your experience.

Provide suggestions as to how to make a good impression on other attorneys.

Describe and evaluate the various organizations and firms that work in the same practice area and advise you on how you might break into the field.

Review your résumé and provide suggestions on how to reframe your description of your experience to make it more appealing to attorneys in the field.

Discuss your career plans with you and provide you with advice on how you might best reach these goals.

While many field placements encourage attorneys to act as mentors, the mentoring relationship tends to be a personal one and not all supervisors and attorneys will be interested in taking on this role. Field placements provide an excellent opportunity to build mentoring relationships, and you should keep your eyes open for such prospects. To find a mentor, you can try asking for assistance from your supervisor or from another attorney in the office with whom you feel you have some rapport. Ask if you might meet for a few minutes, and come prepared with some specific questions. For example, "I am signing up for my fall courses and I wondered if you might have some suggestions on the ones that would help me the most if I am interested in this field of law." Another conversation might be to ask for a few minutes to discuss some of the career options for someone interested in the field. Do not feel you need to ask someone to take on the role of "mentor." It is generally a relationship that builds over time, as you seek and are provided with assistance. Be specific with requests for information and open to whatever advice is offered.

Leaving Your Externship

As your externship comes to its conclusion, there are a number of things you can do to ensure that you will be remembered favorably and that your supervisor will provide good references to future employers. Employers are always impressed with students who leave their position in a professional manner. Keep these steps in mind.

see Chapter 20 on Looking Back and Forward

Remind your employer of your end date a few weeks in advance. Find out how you should focus your efforts before you leave.

Finish your assignments to the extent possible. Write closing memoranda on each project that you are leaving open, including a summary of the work you have completed. This will ensure that your supervisor will not be frustrated wondering where to find something you worked on, and that your successor will not have to replicate your work. Provide your contact information on the closing memoranda and offer to be available to answer any questions.

Get names and numbers. Do not assume you will remember all of the attorneys and staff with whom you worked. Make sure you have names and contact information for them. If you have reason to think that someone with whom you worked might leave the organization, ask if there is another way to contact them. Do not ask directly for home or other personal contact information. It may be offered to you, but you should not ask for it.

Make sure that your supervisor gives you an honest appraisal of your work. A few weeks before your end date, schedule a date for an exit interview. It may be wise to set this date when you still expect to be at the placement for at least another week or two in case something comes up that can be corrected in your final days. Be prepared to ask specific questions. Many employers are reluctant to provide negative comments directly to a student, but if you make clear that you would like to hear constructive criticism, you are more likely to receive it. Ask about specific projects you worked on and how you might have improved. If you are interested in pursuing a career in the field, ask what additional skills would be helpful for you to obtain. Do not be defensive about anything that you are told. Thank them for the feedback they give, even if it is negative. Make sure you tell your employer how much you enjoyed yourself, and show enthusiasm for the experience.

Ask your supervisor to write a letter of recommendation for you before you leave your externship even if you do not need it yet. The letter might be addressed "to whom it may concern," which would allow you to distribute copies to any prospective employers. By the time you need a recommendation, your supervisor will have had many more student externs and may no longer remember the details of the projects to which you were assigned and the quality of your work. Worse yet, your supervisor may leave the organization and may be impossible to track down. To reduce the burden on your supervisor in writing this letter, you might provide her with a detailed list of the projects you worked on and what work you did on each.

After you leave your placement, stay in touch with your supervisor and with your colleagues. If you developed friendly relationships, occasionally call or write to the people with whom you worked to say hello, ask them how they are doing, and let them know what is going on with you. If you see a decision you think would help on a case or one that further develops the law in an area they work in, send it to them. Send a thank you note. Call for advice. If you are struggling with some career issues, use this as an excuse to contact them. This keeps your network strong and ensures they will remember you after you have gone. Develop and maintain a list of people for whom you have worked and send an update to each person on that list each time you start a new job.

Keep Expectations Realistic

Do not assume that you will be offered a permanent job from your placement. While an externship can be tremendously beneficial to your career, it is not likely to lead to an immediate offer of a full-time paid position after graduation. In fact, this is relatively uncommon, given how most organizations do their hiring and the reality of the labor market.

Relax. There Is No One Right Track

True Stories: R.D.

R.D. never expected to become a litigator in a large firm. Prior to law school, She had a background in community and economic development. She spent her first law school summer working in a public interest organization that relied heavily on the resources and expertise of attorneys working in law firms to accomplish its goal of systemic reform. While she was committed to the goals of the organization and felt that it was extremely well-run, ironically the job convinced her that she should work for a firm. "I felt I would be in a better position to offer effective assistance if I had the resources and the expertise I could only acquire at a firm," she explains. R.D. was already enrolled in her school's joint JD/MBA program and began focusing her studies on transactional law. She spent a summer working for a large law firm and was offered a job there in the area of corporate venture capital. As it turned out, the economy changed suddenly and just as she arrived firms throughout the city were downsizing that practice area. The firm offered her a chance to work instead in its securities litigation section, so she switched practice areas. Unfortunately, because she had never planned to litigate, she had never taken the courses that would best prepare her to be a trial attorney. R.D. notes, "I had not taken evidence, moot court, or trial practice — nothing remotely related to litigation. The big surprise was that I liked being in the courtroom far more than I expected." After about six months the firm offered to switch her back into a transactional practice but by then she was enjoying her work and her colleagues, and she decided to stay where she was. After about five years, she was ready to leave the large firm and to specialize in the areas she liked most, so when she was offered a job in a smaller firm starting up their securities litigation and enforcement practice, she took it. "My biggest surprise in all of this is that I would end up a litigator and love it. That was never in my plan."

There is not just one satisfying career. There are many careers in which you can be happy. While staying completely focused on one particular career goal may increase your chances of practicing in that field of law, it may be limiting and may keep you from finding out what brings you the most satisfaction.

Does that mean that there is no connection between your externship and your career? Of course not. The entire externship process is helpful to you in planning your legal career, but not necessarily in the ways you think it might be. Some lawyers will tell you that if you look at their current jobs and work backwards, it will appear as if they had well-structured career plans, moving steadily and confidently from step to step. Each undergraduate internship, legal externship, and early career experience looks like a purposeful step in an inexorable progression toward some specific career goal. In fact, most lawyers' career paths are filled with unplanned twists and turns. Sometimes their original goals remained unchanged. Sometimes there were giant shifts. You do not need to be concerned about the long-term implications of your field placement. It will provide a hands-on workshop for learning about your interests and, perhaps, your passions. You will not know until much later how it will affect your career and your life. You can relax in knowing that you will not control all aspects of your externship. All you can control are your own reactions—the extent to which you will face the challenges with good humor, a willingness to learn, and a desire to be helpful to those who need your assistance.

FURTHER READING

KATE WENDLETON, TARGETING THE JOB YOU WANT (3d ed. 2000). This book has an extensive series of exercises intended to assist law students and attorneys in identifying their strengths and interests to find satisfying career choices.

KIMM ALAYNE WALTON, GUERRILLA TACTICS FOR GETTING THE LEGAL JOB OF YOUR DREAMS (1999). This resource extensively covers the job application process, offering many useful suggestions.

MARK BYERS, DON SAMUELSON & GORDON WILLIAMS, LAWYERS IN TRANSITION (1988). Although written primarily for lawyers considering a job or career change, the ideas and materials are as useful for a lawyer-to-be.

■ Appendix 18.1

Substantive Practice Areas

Administrative Law & Regulatory Practice

Air, Sea and Space Law

Animal Law

Antitrust Law

Aviation Law

Banking Law

Bankruptcy Law: Business

Bankruptcy Law: Consumer

Biotechnology Law

Child Advocacy

Children's Law

Civil Rights Law

Civil Service Law

Commercial Law/Contract Law

Communication Law/Telecommunication Law

Consumer Law

Corporate Law (agency and partnership, business planning, corporate finance, merger and acquisitions)

Criminal Defense

Criminal Justice Administration

Criminal Prosecution

Cyberspace Law

Discrimination Law: employment, housing, disability, education, public accommodations

Domestic Relations Law

Drug Law

Elder Law

e-Commerce

Election Law

Employee Benefits Law

Employment Discrimination Law

Energy Law

Entertainment and Sports Law

Environmental Law (natural resources, toxic waste, water rights, pollution)

Disability Law

Domestic Relations Law

Gaming Law

Health Law

Homeland Security Law

Housing Law

Immigration Law

Insurance Law

Intellectual Property Law (copyright, trademark, patent)

International Law (trade, development, human rights, comparative, business transactions, arms control)

Legal Ethics

Malpractice Law (medical, products, legal)

Matrimonial Law

Mediation

Military Law

National Security Law

Nonprofit Law

Ombudsman

Personal Injury Law (plaintiffs)

Personal Injury Law (defense)

Privacy Law

Probate

Products Liability

Property Law

Public Utilities

Real Estate Law: commercial

Real Estate Law: residential

Real Estate Law: land use, zoning, condemnation

Securities

Social Security/Benefits Law

Sports and Entertainment Law

Tax Law

Transportation Law

Institutional Choices

Private Law Firms

    Large Firms, Mid-Size Firms, Small Law Firms, and Solo Practice

Government Agencies

    State and Local Government

    Federal Government

    Judicial Branch

    Executive Branch

    Legislative Branch

Corporations

    In-house Counsel

Non-profit Organizations

    Policy, Direct Services, Impact Litigation, Advocacy

    Educational Institutions

    Bar Associations

    Lobbying organizations/Consulting Firms

    Unions

Non-legal Alternative Careers

Practice Activities

Adjudication

Administrative Practices

Arbitration and Mediation

Community Organizing

Counseling and Advisory Work

Drafting (contracts, legislation, regulations)

Legal Journalism

Legislative Advocacy

Litigation

    Civil/Criminal

    Trial Appellate

Policy Analysis and Advocacy

Teaching

Transactional Work (negotiating contracts)

Chapter 19

Presentations

Leah Wortham

Know what you want to accomplish;
know your audience; be prepared; have fun.

— Anonymous

Student class presentations provide a number of learning opportunities for both presenters and their audiences. I have learned many things from my students' presentations and gained new insights into effective presentation methods.

Presentations allow students to see beyond their own externships into other types of legal workplaces with which their classmates are engaged. Students can compare their field experience with the experience and observations of others. This cross-fertilization expands each student's information about the legal profession. Students also can compare what they have learned and their learning strategies with those of other students in the class. As stressed in Chapter 2, externships encourage students to consider their individual learning goals, offer an additional avenue to pursue those goals, and allow the fruits of that work to be shared with other students.

Law school courses generally focus on oral presentation skills related to trial and appellate advocacy, interviewing and counseling clients, and negotiation. While many lawyers never will conduct a trial or make an appellate argument, virtually all lawyers are involved in other kinds of face-to-face communication, for example, oral briefings of colleagues or supervisors, presentations to interest potential clients in retaining the lawyer, meetings to bring people in an organization to a decision, in-service training of law firm or clients' employees, teaching continuing legal education courses. Law students and lawyers sometimes have trouble switching out of "moot court mode" and analyzing the type and manner of presentations that will be effective in other situations. They may forget to consider the audience and often fail to make legal information accessible and useful to people without legal training. Class presentations require students to think about oral communication situations other than appellate arguments or trial advocacy, focus on goals to accomplish with a particular audience, and consider methods effective to accomplish those goals.

Presentations permit students to share responsibility for the externship course and thus learn in several ways generally preferred by adult learners, for example, to be self-directed and active participants in the educational process and to relate past experiences to current learning. Presentations allow the focus of the course to shift from semester to semester to reflect the interests of students in the particular class. Presentations allow class members to benefit from the backgrounds, experiences, and talents of other law students. Faculty members can move out of the traditional active teacher/passive student model and coach students as they plan their presentations.

see Chapter 3
on Getting Supervision

Some externship teachers assign class members to critique the presentations. This allows students to practice giving feedback and critiques, important skills that are seldom a central focus in law school courses but are important in getting the best work from those whom students will supervise in later lawyering jobs.

Getting Started

Review the guidance that your faculty supervisor has provided on the presentations and ask questions if anything is unclear. Your faculty supervisor may tell you

> how much time you will have and whether there are any guidelines on how the time should be used;

> whether and how far in advance you should meet in advance with your teacher and how you must prepare for that meeting;

> whether audiovisual or computer equipment is available, when and how to reserve such equipment, and whether there are law school resources (staff, materials, training videos) to train you on using such resources;

> whether you can assign homework to other students and deadlines for distribution of assignments and materials;

> guidelines on topics;

> expectations on the depth of the presentation, for example, whether library research in literature on the topic is expected;

> any particular goals that students are expected to pursue in the presentations.

Choose a topic of significant interest to you. Review your initial learning agenda or goals statement for the externship. Is there a topic that could further one of the goals you listed?

Suppose you are externing at a prosecutor's office and one of your goals is "Explore a possible career path in criminal prosecution." You might prepare a presentation on career paths in prosecution covering such topics as useful credentials in securing a position, thoughts of prosecutors as to what law school preparation would be helpful, and common career paths after the entry level job. Researching this topic would push you to look in law review and bar journal literature and give you a reason to talk with lawyers about these questions.

Suppose one of your goals is "Learning about practice management in solo practice." You might envision a presentation on the top ten things to consider when going out on your own. To prepare, you could review articles on this topic in bar journals and legal newspapers and interview some solo practitioners.

Do not seize upon your first idea. Make notes on several possibilities. Start sufficiently in advance of the deadline for choosing a topic so ideas can percolate.

Consider selecting a topic that will allow you to practice an unfamiliar skill. You could plan a simulation, lead a discussion, or develop some diagrams or other visual aids to illustrate your ideas. If you are interested in learning more about technology, you could explore what equipment and resources your law school has available. Can someone assist you with the editing of a video recording regarding your presentation or help you learn how to use presentation software more effectively?

Consider the effect you want your presentation to have on the audience. The ultimate measure of a class is not what is *taught* but what is *learned*. When lawyers communicate with others in the situations described above, the lawyer usually seeks to give the lawyer's audience the skills or knowledge to do something or to motivate the audience to behave in a particular way, which may require persuasion to change a pre-existing attitude. Ask yourself what your audience should be able to do or be motivated to do after your presentation. In what way would you like them to be different as a result of your presentation? This book generally urges that each step you take as a lawyer and your overall approach to your career should be guided by "What am I trying to accomplish?" One dimension of the class presentation is what you want to accomplish in your own learning, but a principal measure of success of presentations to others in your lawyering career will be the effect on the audience. Acquire the habit of making an explicit statement to yourself of what you seek to achieve with your audience and use this in planning for communications with others.

As you read through the topic examples below, think about the differences among them in the behavior that the presenter would want to elicit from the audience. If your presentation involves circulating a piece of writing for critique, you presumably want to generate a dialog on what is effective writing for that type of piece. You also might have a secondary teaching objective of stimulating discussion on how a supervisor is most effective in giving critique.

If you chose the topic suggested below of making a client development or funding application presentation, you would be asking the audience to play the role of prospective clients or funders. You are not expecting your classmates to hire or fund you, but they can give opinions on whether a real audience would have been persuaded by your presentation and how it could have been strengthened. This could lead to a group discussion on what makes such a presentation effective.

If you choose to simulate the briefing of a supervisor on research you have done, the class again would be in role. Class members would be asked to put themselves in the shoes of busy attorneys and give feedback on whether the presenter was clear and gave sufficient information. A presenter also might take on the role of a lawyer briefing a non-lawyer client or manager about law relevant to a decision to be made, and the audience then would be challenged to try and think what the effect would be on people without legal training and with concerns different from their own.

Link the goals for your externship, the fieldwork, and the presentation. Do not make this a research exercise that is unrelated to the fieldwork. Use this as a chance to enhance the learning from your fieldwork and share some benefits with other students.

Possible Topics

The following is a list that was developed by faculty supervisors at my law school. It includes examples of some student presentations from my classes that were particularly interesting and effective. Your teacher may have class guidelines for presentations that would exclude some of these topics or may have an additional or different list of suggestions. This list is presented as a stimulus to your creativity rather than a menu from which you should make a choice. Additional topic possibilities can be generated from exercises in other chapters of this book.

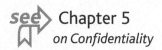

see Chapter 5
on Confidentiality

While you are urged to link the presentation to your fieldwork, be mindful of confidentiality considerations. You, of course, must be careful not to disclose client confidences. Merely deleting client names often is not enough for adequate protection. Consider also office confidence regarding the people with whom you work. You may want to take an idea from something at work but change the personalities and details enough so that it is not recounted as what happened at your externship. Concerns about an externship that would be appropriate to discuss with your teacher might require adaptation before a presentation to the full class. Questions in this regard should be worked out with your teacher.

- Identify a serious problem that can arise in the workplace. Plan a presentation on how it could be addressed and resolved. For example, a presentation might focus on possible steps if one faces a colleague with a substance abuse problem, a supervisor engaging in sexual harassment, or an office director with poor management skills. You might get the class started with an illustrative incident or situation presented in a scripted video, a scripted live role play, or a written description. The situation may not have come up in your externship, but you can use your externship experience to envision how the situation might be handled there and the difficulties it would present.

- Consider some of the methods mentioned in the previous paragraph for presenting a situation specific to the externship/supervisor relationship, such as a supervisor who seems threatened by the extern in some way, a supervisor who is always too busy to talk, or a supervisor who does not give useful feedback.

- Interview some lawyers or other employees in your office about a topic of interest and report the results to the class. One of my students, externing at the General Counsel's office of a government agency, made an excellent presentation based on interviews with lawyers there about whether they had ever had to do things or take positions on issues that differed from their personal political or moral views and how they handled it. You might talk with employees of your judge's chambers and some of your neighboring chambers about common mistakes made by novice litigators. You could interview lawyers in your office about their career decisions, job satisfaction, or concerns about balancing personal life and professional life. You also might interview lawyers on the criteria for making partner in a law firm or comparable advancement in another type of workplace. Some library work would turn up bar journal and legal press articles on all the previous topics to help shape the questions to ask and give a basis for comparison with the answers.

- Practice a presentation related to the funding of the type of organization in which you are externing or wish to work in the future.

- Invent a law firm or other legal services organization and market its services. Law firms sometimes refer to presentations to prospective clients as "beauty contests." Plan the agenda for such a presentation, which might be in the form of a lunch with a prospective client or a written advertising piece. Ask your classmates to critique your effectiveness and consider the propriety of your approach in light of bar ethics rules. Two students who externed at a recording industry trade association simulated a presentation for agents to explain how the recording artists they represented would benefit from the association's service that would collect royalties gathered by a central fund and return the royalties to them. This required explaining provisions of the copyright law and offering a quick and persuasive explanation why the artists would be better off using the association's services rather than trying to collect the royalties on their own

• Write a draft grant proposal or fund-raising letter for a public interest group or legal services organization. For a grant proposal, gather criteria from government or foundation funding sources on how such proposals are evaluated and ask your classmates to evaluate your draft against the criteria. This exercise might lead to a discussion of funding sources and strategies for a particular type of organization.

• Circulate copies of a piece of writing that you did for the externship. Ask the class to edit and critique it. This exercise could be used to discuss standards against which this type of writing should be judged. Be sure the writing sample does not include any confidential information.

• Re-enact a situation in which you had to give an oral briefing to a supervisor on research results or create a scenario in which research you have done would be presented in this fashion. Have your classmates critique whether the presentation was clear, easy to follow, contained an appropriate amount of detail, and would have given the supervisor sufficient information to take the next step. Discussion then could follow on questions like how a presentation might vary based on the supervisor's knowledge and personality and how to seek clarification from a supervisor on what the supervisor wants in the research and the report.

• Use your observations and interviews to gather material on a topic to present to the class and elicit discussion from class members on how their organizations compare on various dimensions such as the following.

Mission: What is the purpose or mission of the legal organization where you are doing your fieldwork? What is it trying to accomplish? Who decides the mission? Do the people who work there have a shared vision and sense of purpose? What characteristics of the organization make the work go better or worse? What, if any, lawmaking function is performed by the institution, and how does that occur?

Chapter 17
on Work-Life Balance

Opportunity to balance personal and professional life: What policies are in place to assist employees in balancing personal life and professional life? Are employees availing themselves of them? If not, why not? What changes in workplace policy, structure, or culture might be useful to employees?

Planning: How is a project planned in your externship? Who if anyone does the planning and how is it done? What is the role of collaboration?

Chapter 16
on Bias

Diversity: Share observations about the impact of sex, race, age, political beliefs, or other differences on the working relationships of the people in the externship with one another or with you.

Development of lawyering skills or ethical decision making: Re-enact part of a hearing or a deposition, using a transcript if available, as a take-off point for a discussion on lawyering skills or an ethical issue.

Career planning: Discuss the impact the fieldwork is having on your career goals or on how you plan to carry them out and stimulate comparisons with the experience of your classmates.

see> Chapter 18
on Career Planning

- Create a simulation that would place all or some of the students in the class in a situation in which you participated, that you observed, or that you could imagine occurring. For example, put the class members in role as lawyers in a firm or public interest group and ask them to make a decision of the type that could arise in such an organization. This might relate to strategy on a particular case or to a policy, business, or ethical decision facing the entity. A former student, working for a high-technology company, assigned each class member a company management position with instructions about the concerns a person with that type of job would have. He then assumed the role of in-house counsel briefing company top management about changes in export control laws with a goal of securing their cooperation in compliance. The presenting student had to consider how much information about the new law was sufficient, how to make it intelligible to this sophisticated but not legally trained group, and how to motivate managers to be interested in compliance.

- Was there a situation in the externship in which you had to teach yourself something new, for example, use of particular software, a scientific topic, background on an area of law in which you had not taken a course? Consider a presentation on how you went about this on-the-job learning. What worked well and what did not? What other ways might you have gone about it? Classmates might suggest other options, and the class members might consider how they would differ among themselves on effective ways to learn new things.

- What is your previous academic training or work experience? If you studied business management, give your classmates a quick course in some management theory and discuss its application in your various externships. If you studied communication, give some examples of effective and ineffective communication that you have noted in the externship and link it to material from your earlier studies. Someone with a grounding in math or science may have noted an instance in the externship in which use of statistics or a scientific concept was a problem for the lawyers. Recreate the situation and fill in what people needed to know. A student with a previous career in social work might talk about lessons that lawyers in the current externship could take from the other discipline.

- Is there a novel, short story, movie, or television show that stimulated your thinking about the externship or lawyering generally? Show your classmates an excerpt and share reactions. An excerpt from a law review article also could be a takeoff point for discussion of its relevance or irrelevance to the fieldwork experience.

Planning Your Presentation

Too often, people spend the bulk of their time on the content of a presentation and too little time on how to present it. An important part of the presentation assignment is to push your thinking on what captures and holds people's attention and will achieve the desired behavioral outcome with audience members.

Do not wait until you have finished your background research or interviews before you start to rough out the presentation. At the start, write down some initial ideas on how your presentation might look. Keep refining these notes as your research progresses. Thinking through the steps of what you will present and how you will present it exposes holes and gaps in what you need to know and for which you need to plan.

Sources for Background Research

Readings: Computerized research tools offer a quick way to check most topics in the law review literature, legal press articles (for example, *National Law Journal, American Lawyer, Legal Times*), bar journal articles (for example, state bar journals, national bar associations and their section publications), and popular press. Your presentation may take off from something in literature or from a nonfiction book on a controversial topic. The topic you contemplate may involve some additional research in cases or statutes.

Things to view: Check the audiovisual resources available from your law school library. Many have training videos made specifically for lawyers. Some will have a library of mass market films or television shows on topics related to legal practice.

Material available online: Are there resources on the Internet that might be pertinent to your topic? Would you be able to use live, online materials in the room where you will give your presentation?

see > Chapter 12 *on Observation*

Observation: Chapter 12 talks about learning from observation. Could you undertake some structured observation related to your topic? Do you have past observations that are relevant to your topic?

Interviews: A number of the topic examples suggest interviewing lawyers in your externship or elsewhere. The interviewee's responses can be compared to ideas found in your background reading. Interviewing co-workers for a presentation can provide an opportunity for more personal contact with them, which may be useful if networking was one of your goals.

Structuring the Class

Lecture

When we need to present something, we often instinctively think of lecturing. Lectures offer some advantages. A lecture can provide material not available in writing and a synthesis of diverse sources. Some listeners prefer to receive information orally. A dynamic lecturer can add visual and other physical cues to focus attention. A live lecturer can observe the audience, ask and answer questions, and otherwise adapt to visual cues about what interests the listeners and how they are grasping the material. The credentials, position, and personal presence of the lecturer may enhance the lecturer's credibility and the interest of the audience in the lecture.

see ▷ Chapter 1 *on adult learning preferences*

Lecturing, however, has its pitfalls and should not be presumed to be the best method. As a listener, have you ever thought, "Why couldn't the speaker just give me the material to read so I don't have to sit here?" Adults can read at an average speed of 700 to 800 words per minute. Average oral communication is 100 to 125 words per minute, with a rapid speaker only reaching 150 to 175. Thus, it takes an hour to say something that probably could be read in ten to fifteen minutes.

Lecturing allows listeners to be passive, and their thoughts easily can wander. The lecturer can get some visual cues, but this may not provide reliable information on whether the listeners are learning, being informed, being persuaded, or whatever other objective the lecturer may have. Lecturing puts the burden on the speaker to perform without challenging the listener to think about what he may want to learn or need to know.

A lecture may be a useful component of your presentation. It may set up the exercise that you want the class to do. It may introduce a discussion. It may report on some interviews. It may synthesize some theory from another discipline to be applied to the learning situation. Given the comparison to the relative efficiency of reading, you should consider whether any of these purposes might better be served by written material, but lecture may be a good choice for some part of the presentation. Be wary, however, of lecture as the major focus.

Consider the following alternatives (and complements) to lecture:

Simulations and Role Plays

A number of the topic examples suggest putting class members in role. People often gain insights and reach different conclusions about a topic when they confront what they would do and how they would react in a situation.

You may plan a large single role play in which everyone in the class participates, for example, where all the class takes on the role of the supervisor being briefed. You might script a situation and ask small groups of students to take the roles involved, such as having all students form pairs as a supervisor and supervisee to act out a situation. For such a role play, you may want to script instructions for each participant on differing things they know, assumptions they have about proper behavior, and personal characteristics they are to exhibit.

You might script a role play and have it recorded or performed live for the class. It can be useful to freeze frame a video or a live role play by stopping the action and interspersing discussion.

Video Recordings

The previous paragraph suggested use of a video recording of a role play. The background research section suggests additional sources of filmed material that might be useful in a presentation. If you are going to show a video recording, you may want to let participants know in advance of seeing the video what you will ask them to do with it afterward. For example, you might direct the participants to watch for certain types of behavior, to pay particular attention to body language, or to think about what they would have done if they were the student in the role play. Unless you plan to freeze frame frequently, it may be useful to direct viewers to take notes consistent with the purposes for which you are asking them to view the video recording.

Discussion

Discussion usually will be more fruitful if people have a common example or experience as a starting point—a case study, a video, a role play, or a reading. Think about effective and tactful ways to involve the whole class in the discussion and to avoid monopolization by one or two students. Watch the professors in your classes for a few days. What techniques do they use in this regard?

Brainstorming can be an effective technique for getting a discussion started. Record responses to a question on a board or flip chart page. As leader, you might ask follow-up questions to clarify a comment or make affirming comments like "interesting," but in the original idea-gathering stage, you should seek to avoid discussion or argument about the ideas being put up as well as evaluative comments that could restrain the free flow of ideas that brainstorming is meant to promote. This technique is meant to stimulate creativity by urging people to think broadly and not self-censor initial ideas. Brainstorming can free people to offer a number of possible points of view without a need to own the ideas offered as necessarily their own or good ones. Putting ideas on the board can encourage more honest and free-wheeling discussion because disagreement is directed to the board rather than toward the person who offered it. Flip charts allow one to tear off the initial page and mount it on a wall while then grouping ideas or homing in on particular points for further discussion. Asking each person in turn for an idea can assure that shyer participants also are part of the discussion.

Once brainstorming is complete and you move to a discussion phase, watch the group dynamics. Are people submerging disagreements that would stimulate discussion? Was a student's interesting point passed over by the group such that you should restate it? "Carmen said a moment ago _____. What about that?" (or some other more pointed question).

You could assign particular points of view to class members and ask them to reflect these perspectives in the discussion. It may be more comfortable for people to represent another's viewpoint than their own.

Consider breaking people into pairs or small groups for some preliminary discussion before opening the floor to the full class. This gives everyone a chance to verbalize their thoughts. Some people are more confident about sharing their thoughts with the class if they have a chance first to refine their ideas in a less public setting. Each group can be asked for a report on a question. This can give a more accurate sense of the views of the full group than hearing from only a few volunteers.

Much of good communication is asking good questions. Anticipate the way discussion might go and prepare a list of possible follow-up questions. Listen carefully to the discussion to consider when insertion of a new question would move things along.

Do not be afraid of silence. Ask a question and force yourself to wait for an answer. Time and again, I have seen student discussion leaders, uncomfortable after even five or ten seconds of silence, jump in and answer their own questions. Silence is powerful. Eventually someone will break it—and it should not be the discussion leader.

Carefully listen to answers. Ask follow-up questions to probe more deeply if seems that more commentary or explanation would stimulate the thoughts of others. If one student has commented about how something works in the placement in which the student has externed, ask another student whose placement might raise the similar issues if things there are the same or different.

Leading a discussion is an active role—framing provocative questions, careful listening to responses, managing silence. Too much talking by the discussion leader becomes a lecture rather than a discussion.

Self-tests and Games

A quick written or oral self-test of the audience can shift the audience from "What are you going to teach me?" to "What do I need to learn?" The device requires some engagement from the audience and presses them from a passive role to a more engaged one. A self-test about the audience's current knowledge, attitudes, or past experience also gives the presenter a baseline to gauge what it will take to achieve the presenter's goals with regard to increasing the audience's knowledge or changing attitudes.

A contest or competition can be motivating. Two former students' joint presentation sought to interest classmates in the relevance of public international law to day-to-day domestic law practice and to their lives. Class members divided into teams and competed on knowledge of some public international law concepts, which were presented as they arose in situations in current events.

Some effective presentations have used various board game or quiz show formats to engage participants actively in the substance.

Guests

You might bring an expert to talk about the topic or react to a presentation. Many fieldwork supervisors are pleased to be asked to come to the law school and meet with a seminar group. You may know a lawyer who would be a good resource on your topic. Your teacher may have suggestions. We have found our alumni and other lawyers enjoy opportunities to interact with students in the externship class.

Logistics and Rehearsal

Consider how *much time* you have for the presentation. Decide how long to spend on each part. Class presentations often go more slowly than one expects. Time a trial run. Plan for contingencies if the presentation goes more slowly or more quickly.

Consider the *physical layout* of the room where the presentation will be conducted. Where will you position yourself within the room so all students can see you and so you will not have your back to any audience members? If you will divide students into groups or involve them in some exercise, how will that be accommodated in the space?

Eye contact with the audience is important to establish rapport and maintain attention. Looking at your audience also will allow you to read the audience's reaction and respond to them. If you will be using something visual, where will you stand so the audience can all see the screen or the board and allow you to maintain eye contact?

People vary in their preferences for auditory, visual, and kinesthetic learning. Consider whether it is possible to incorporate elements of each. Consider some kind of *visual reinforcement* of points being made orally or whether there is some *experience* they might have or *thing they might do* as part of the presentation.

If you are using PowerPoint or other *presentation software*, think about things like how much text to put on a screen, whether the text size and color are readable with the size of the room, and whether the slides are visually appealing. Rehearse with a partner so you can get feedback on whether the pace and coordination of your speaking with the slide allows the audience to comprehend what you are communicating. In my observation, it becomes boring if the speaker merely reads everything on every slide. Slides are helpful to emphasize key points or to display data about which the speaker will talk. On the other hand, I find it difficult to read a quotation while a speaker is talking. If a quote is important, I want the speaker to read it to me so I can focus upon it for a moment. Think about whether audience members might want hard copies of some or all of your slides.

Consider information that will be too complicated to follow if explained orally, for example, a case study for discussion, simulation instructions. Prepare *written materials* in advance and think about those for which it would be easiest for audience members to have their own copies rather than reading from a slide or board.

Be conscious of the *intelligibility* of your voice: pitch, volume, speed, projection, diction, articulation, and grammar. Ask your practice partner to comment on intelligibility and on *mannerisms*. Do you fiddle with your hair or repeat certain phrases, for example, "if memory serves" or "like," in a way that is distracting or annoying?

I complete a feedback form for each student presentation, and each student receives a critique from two class members as well. I often find myself writing these critiques several days after the presentation and find that I remember a presentation better if I received some *take-away* from it. When I pick up a written handout from a presentation such as a summary of important points, a document copy used in an exercise, or some discussion question, I find that the substance of the presentation comes back to me, while I find it much more difficult to remember a presentation for which I have nothing in writing that came away with me.

If you will be *distributing written materials*, think carefully about when and how to do it. If there are several pieces, generally it is best to collate them and distribute at the outset or have them waiting for students at their places. If there is a piece people should look at later, you can ask them to put it aside. Photocopying multiple handouts on different colored paper can make it easier for people to keep track of what they are supposed to work with at a particular time, *i.e.,* "Please look at the problem on the yellow sheet of paper." In watching many student presentations, I have noticed how distracting it can be when multiple handouts come around separately and how much of the speaker's time can be wasted on assuring everyone in the audience has the right materials and understands with which one the group is working now.

Review your presentation for *unity*, selecting only that which is necessary; *coherence*, connecting and relating each part to each other; and *emphasis*, giving the correct degree of *prominence* to each part.

Rehearse what you plan and try to have at least one run-through with someone observing. As previously mentioned, your practice partner can provide you with feedback on intelligibility of your voice, distracting mannerisms, and effectiveness of visual aids. Practice also will free you from notes to maintain eye contact, expose gaps in logic or clarity to be filled in, and allows you to explore with your test audience whether your goals for the presentation were met. Be sure you have *rehearsed use of any technology* in the room where the presentation will be and with the equipment that will be used. Have a *back-up plan* for what you will do if technology fails.

Enjoy yourself. Presentations are a good learning opportunity for you and your fellow students.

Chapter 20

Looking Back
Looking Forward

J.P. Ogilvy

> To look backward for a while is to refresh the eye, to restore it and to render it fit for its prime function of looking forward.
>
> — Margaret Fairless Barber

Looking Back

Now that your externship is over or coming to a close, it is time to review your experience and to plan how you might consolidate what you have learned from your experience and build on it for the future. Although it is very important to review your externship, it is less important how you do it. There are several techniques you can use to review your externship. Each technique has advantages and disadvantages. You should choose the method that best suits your learning preferences and best serves your goals for the review. After considering the following six approaches, we suggest that you select one or two and write out your responses.

Review of Goals and Objectives

One approach to reviewing your externship involves reexamining the goals and objectives you set for yourself when you began your externship. If you committed your goals to writing, retrieve the document. If you did not prepare a written Learning Agenda or Goals Memo, try to recall the goals you set for yourself and write them down. Take a look at what you have written.

 Chapter 2
on Setting Goals

Did you meet the goals and objectives you set for yourself? As we suggested in Chapter 2, goals are targets set far enough beyond your reach or present abilities to make you stretch, but close enough to be attainable. Were they too ambitious to attain within the few months you had to devote to your externship? Even if you set realistic goals, it is likely that you have not met them fully. Goals typically are reached in steps that may be expressed in terms of objectives. Although you may not have achieved any of your goals within a time period as short as a semester or even an academic year, you probably did achieve many of your objectives for the externship.

Consider each objective under each of your goals. Describe each objective you met and how you met it. If you failed to meet an objective, say why. What factors inhibited you from meeting the objective? Was the objective unrealistic given the nature of the externship? Did you come to realize the objective was not worth pursuing and abandon it before the end of the externship? Were you unable to devote sufficient time to working on the objective because the tasks you were assigned did not lend themselves to your pursuit of the objective? Did you fail to achieve the objective because you did not work hard enough on it? With respect to objectives that you partially fulfilled, describe how you met them and why they were not fully met.

This exercise should tell you about your ability to set goals and objectives. Do you set realistic goals in light of available information? Could your goal-setting process be improved by gathering more information about the situation before you draft your goals? Did you review your goals and objectives periodically to check your progress? Did you make a list your of goals and then never look at it again? Did the goal-setting exercise guide your behavior during the externship, or was it just a task to accomplish for the class, unconnected to your externship experience? Did you jettison goals that were no longer realistic and draft new ones to reflect changes in circumstances and interests?

The exercise also allows you to analyze your success in achieving goals and objectives you set for yourself. The information you gain through review and reflection on your goals allows you to devise better strategies for more successfully achieving your goals in the future. For example, you may discover you failed to achieve several objectives because you lacked sufficient opportunities to work on tasks that would help you to achieve the objectives. You need to analyze whether this was due to factors within your control, such as your failure to seek out relevant tasks or your failure to recognize alternative ways to work on the objectives. On the other hand, you might attribute your inability to attain certain objectives to institutional factors over which you had no control. What changes would you make in your process for setting goals? How will you do it differently for your next externship, a summer job, or first job after graduation?

Review of Time Records

A second technique to consider for reviewing your externship is analyzing your time records. Time records can be a valuable source of information if you maintained accurate and detailed records. Create a summary of your time. Which tasks occupied most of your time? Is this summary consistent or inconsistent with your goals and objectives for the externship? If inconsistent, consider what you might have done differently to spend more time on tasks related to your goals. Did you manage your time well? Did you create blocks of time for tasks that were likely to take longer to complete? Did you use small blocks of time efficiently? If you identify some inefficiencies, what can you do in the future to improve? In retrospect, did you spend too much time on any types of tasks? For example, did you spend too much time researching a question to which there was no clear answer? If so, consider why you might have spent so much time on the assignment. Was it because you did not receive clear instructions from your fieldwork supervisor? How might you have obtained better guidance? Did you perform background research before tackling the question because you were researching in an area of law unfamiliar to you? This should not be characterized as spending too much time, unless there was a more efficient and effective method for gathering the background information. Did you ask someone familiar with the field for a recommendation for a primer?

Review of your time records permits you to ask other types of questions as well. Did you keep detailed and accurate records? If you had been required to bill a client for your time, could you produce a detailed summary of the work you did on behalf of the client? Do your time records capture all of the time that you devoted to a task? Did the lapse of time between completing a task and recording it in your time record cause you to under count or over count your time? What other information about your work skills can you derive from analyzing your time records?

Review of Journal Entries

If you maintained a journal during your externship, reviewing your journal entries can be a valuable technique for reflecting on your experience. Simply by rereading your journal, you can gain new insights from your experiences. By reflecting on your original journal entries from the perspective of hindsight, you are in a position to discover themes and to perform a deeper and richer analysis of the experiences captured in your journal. Where you merely described an event from your externship, the passage of time and the accumulation of additional experiences provides a platform from which to create a more sophisticated analysis of the event you described. In terms of Bloom's taxonomy of thinking skills, you can move from superficial comprehension of the event you recorded to an

opportunity to make evaluative judgments about what you observed and recorded. Reread your journal, draft a title for each entry, and then identify two or three
themes that are recurrent throughout the journal. What topics were important to
you during the externship? Why? In retrospect, do these topics continue to be
important? Why or why not? Write a short summary of one or more themes
reflected in your journal.

Review of Skill Development

see▷ Chapters
14&15 *on*
*Skill Development
and Management
Skills*

Create a list of the skills that you learned or improved during the externship.
As a starting place, review Chapters 14 and 15 that discuss a variety of skills that
can be pursued in most externships. Consider also the list of lawyering skills from
the MacCrate Report at pages 459-463. You may find that your descriptions of
skills fit into more than one category. That should not be surprising. Many skills
you learn in law school are the domain-specific application of skills you already
employ in other contexts. Brainstorm as many variations of the skill as possible.
For example, assume that you are listing skills associated with becoming proficient
at conducting negotiations. What you learned in negotiating with the secretary
assigned to you concerning when she will work on your projects in light of her
other duties may be just as important as what you learned in the negotiations you
conducted with a legislative staff member about whether your client can testify at
a hearing.

For each item on your list, identify your strengths and weaknesses. In which
areas are you confident of your skills? In which areas are you aware of continuing
deficiencies or weaknesses? How did your assessment compare to your supervisor's?
How do you plan to work on your perceived weaknesses in the future? This question
brings full circle the process that you began when you initiated your externship—the
identification of goals for yourself.

Review Your Approach to Learning from Experience

Create a list describing what you have learned about learning from experience.
Do you approach learning from experience differently from the way you did before
your externship? Are you more attentive to your surroundings now that you have
observed attorneys in court or elsewhere? Do you make more of an effort to record
your reactions to events? If you believe that you learn best by doing, describe what
you mean by that. Are there any things that you learn best by seeing someone else do
it first? What are the limits of learning by doing?

Review Your Career Goals

Consider whether and to what extent the externship moved you closer to your career goals. Take some time to reflect in writing on what you liked about your externship and the work you did. Reflect as well on what you disliked about your externship and the work you did. As we suggested above, if you maintained a reflective journal throughout your externship, review your journal for recurring themes or patterns. Your discussion of likes and dislikes should provide you with some guidance as you continue to engage in career planning and assess for yourself the types of jobs for which you will apply. How do you plan to use your externship experiences to enhance your employment prospects both immediately and in the longer term?

see Chapter 18
on Career Planning

Looking Forward

Creating a Sound Bite

If you are like most law students, you probably are currently engaged in a job search. Perhaps you are seeking a way to pay your rent during the academic year, looking for a summer job to help pay for next year's tuition, or hunting for a position to begin after graduation. Whatever your situation, you undoubtedly will participate in a number of interviews. Most initial job interviews are short, lasting no longer than twenty minutes. To use your time effectively, you must plan for each interview and prepare for the unexpected. Although an interviewer probably will know about your externship from your résumé, the short entry will not convey much about your experience there. You should be prepared to describe your externship experience to an interviewer in a five-minute sound bite.

Imagine that you are being interviewed for a job that you really want. The interviewer asks you to describe what you did at your externship. What would you say? What information do you want to give the interviewer about the experience that may help convince the employer to hire you? Five minutes is not much time within which to convey all that you might wish to say about a semester- or year-long experience, but it is probably about as much time as you will want to spend on such a question within the scope of the entire interview.

Begin constructing your sound bite by reflecting, in writing, on what you did in your externship and what you learned from it. First make a list of the discrete tasks that you performed during your externship. Try to be concrete and specific. Do not just say "legal research," say "Review of Maryland Pattern Jury Instructions, Maryland statutes, and Maryland and other Atlantic jurisdiction cases on effect of settlement proceeds on amount of judgment against a non-settling joint tortfeasor." Do not say "fact investigation," say "reviewed police report and newspaper articles for names of witnesses; contacted witnesses; interviewed witnesses re: sequence of events leading to accident." Do not say "attended meeting with client," say "conference with client to report on results of legal research, obtain additional information, and recommend settlement." If you maintained detailed time records, you can refer back to them to assist you in capturing all that you did during the externship.

After gathering the data from the various lists you constructed, draft a five-minute sound bite. Revise and rewrite the draft until you are satisfied with the result. Aim for a sound bite that can be used to respond to a variety of questions in an interview. You want to be able to use some variation of your sound bite to tell the interviewer what you want the person to know about you, regardless of the question asked. For instance, if the interviewer asks, "What sort of projects did you work on at your externship?" You can quickly relate the nature of the projects, your participation in them, and how having done them makes you a good candidate for the job for which you are interviewing. If the interviewer asks, "Why do you want to work here?" You can respond, "I knew I wanted to work here when during my last externship I was able to work on . . . ." If the interviewer asks, "Is Professor Jones still making people stand up when they recite?" You might say, "Yes, Professor Jones is as formal as ever, and, although I enjoyed the class, I was much more comfortable at my externship where I was able to . . . ."

After you write your sound bite, try to use variations of it to answer typical questions such as: What do you see yourself doing in ten years? Why are you interested in real estate/public interest law/tax planning? Why did you go to law school? How is the new building/renovation? Where is Northwestern School of Law, anyway? What did you enjoy most about your externship? What would you do differently the next time you began a research project? What division/department/group did you work with? Why did you decide to clerk for a judge/work in a small firm/go with a government agency? What can I tell you about this firm/agency/position?

Saying Good-bye, Staying in Touch

Thinking about how to use your externship experiences to enhance your employment prospects should include thinking about how you will terminate your relationship with your externship placement. Will you walk out the door on the day that you finish your required hours with a simple good-bye? Or do you plan to spend some time with each person with whom you have had some meaningful contact during your externship in bringing your experience to closure? Will you send a written acknowledgment of the termination of your externship? Do you plan to maintain some form of contact with the people at your externship? If so, what type of contact do you plan? These are important questions to which you should have answers.

Your answers may depend on the overall quality of the experience or your evaluation of this work as part of your immediate future. Lawyers are often a close community. They know one another. Even if this organization is not an exact fit for the career of your dreams, there may be lawyers in the organization who could help you take the next step. They may be interested in your progress, so it makes sense to maintain contact.

There are several other things that you may want to do at the very end of your externship. Create a portfolio of your written work. Writing you did in the externship that can be retained, consistent with the applicable norms of privacy and confidentiality, should be placed in a folder. You may have occasion to use one or more of these writings as samples of your work for prospective employers. You may want to place a cover sheet on any sample you intend to circulate that states clearly you have obtained permission to use the document as a writing sample. This eliminates potential issues of confidentiality and demonstrates your professionalism to the reader.

Talk to supervisors about being a reference for you in the future. In some instances you may want to request a general letter of reference, addressed "To whom it may concern." Usually, however, you simply want some assurance that the supervisor is willing, sometime in the future, to write a targeted letter of reference for you when you request it.

Ask a supervisor for a detailed letter of evaluation. There are at least three purposes to which a letter may be put. First, since you may share the letter with prospective employers, the evaluation can serve as an unsolicited letter of reference from your fieldwork supervisor. Second, the letter can be useful should you decide sometime in the future to request a formal letter of reference from your fieldwork supervisor to a specific potential employer. The letter of evaluation created at the end of your externship can provide details of your work and performance that might otherwise become lost to the supervisor's memory after the passage of time. Many fieldwork supervisors work with multiple externs or with different externs each semester. It becomes increasingly difficult for supervisors to remember each extern distinctly without a written record. Third, the evaluation can provide useful information about your performance in the externship. You can measure your self-evaluation against that of your fieldwork supervisor.

Conclusion

With the conclusion of an externship you contemporaneously begin the next cycle of experiential learning. Your final reviews and reflection on one experience prepares you to establish new goals and objectives. Those new goals and objectives will guide you through your next experience. We hope that this book has contributed to your learning how to realize more from your experiences through all phases of the experiential learning cycle. We know that you will use that knowledge throughout your career because one of the hallmarks of belonging to a profession is learning how to learn from experience.

■ Appendix: MacCrate Report

The following form is adapted from the MacCrate Report, Overview of Skills and Values [American Bar Association Section of Legal Education and Admissions to the Bar, Legal Education and Professional Development (Report of the Task Force on Law Schools and the Profession: Narrowing the Gap), pp. 138-141, July 1992]

We use the form in several ways. Some of us ask students to rate their own proficiency on each skill on a scale of 0-5. Five indicates the level of proficiency on the skill that the rater believes would be desirable for a new law graduate. Zero indicates no proficiency in that skill as yet. Students may be asked to rate themselves at the beginning and end of the externship experience to assess the impact of the externship. Chapter 2 suggests that this inventory be completed for assistance in developing the Learning Agenda or Goals Memo.

We usually ask students to note for each skill the experience(s) that the student believes provided the skill level, *e.g.*, a classroom course, a summer legal job, the first year research and writing program.

Fundamental Lawyering Skills

Skill § 1: Problem Solving

In order to develop and evaluate strategies for solving a problem or accomplishing an objective, a lawyer should be familiar with the skills and concepts involved in:

___ 1.1 Identifying and Diagnosing the Problem;

___ 1.2 Generating Alternative Solutions and Strategies;

___ 1.3 Developing a Plan of Action;

___ 1.4 Implementing the Plan;

___ 1.5 Keeping the Planning Process Open to New Information and New Ideas.

Skill § 2: Legal Analysis and Reasoning

In order to analyze and apply legal rules and principles, a lawyer should be familiar with the skills and concepts involved in:

____   2.1   Identifying and Formulating Legal Issues;

____   2.2   Formulating Relevant Legal Theories;

____   2.3   Elaborating Legal Theory;

____   2.4   Evaluating Legal Theory;

____   2.5   Criticizing and Synthesizing Legal Argumentation.

Skill § 3: Legal Research

In order to identify legal issues and to research them thoroughly and efficiently, a lawyer should have:

____   3.1   Knowledge of the Nature of Legal Rules and Institutions;

____   3.2   Knowledge of and Ability to Use the Most Fundamental Tools of Legal Research;

____   3.3   Understanding of the Process of Devising and Implementing a Coherent and Effective Research Design.

Skill § 4: Factual Investigation

In order to plan, direct, and (where applicable) participate in factual investigation, a lawyer should be familiar with the skills and concepts involved in:

____   4.1   Determining the Need for Factual Investigation;

____   4.2   Planning a Factual Investigation;

____   4.3   Implementing the Investigative Strategy;

____   4.4   Memorializing and Organizing Information in an Accessible Form;

____   4.5   Deciding Whether to Conclude the Process of Fact-Gathering;

____   4.6   Evaluating the Information That Has Been Gathered.

Skill § 5: Communication

In order to communicate effectively, whether orally or in writing, a lawyer should be familiar with the skills and concepts involved in:

___   5.1   Assessing the Perspective of the Recipient of the Communication;

___   5.2   Using Effective Methods Of Communication.

Skill § 6: Counseling

In order to counsel clients about decisions or courses of action, a lawyer should be familiar with the skills and concepts involved in:

___   6.1   Establishing a Counseling Relationship That Respects the Nature and Bounds of a Lawyer's Role;

___   6.2   Gathering Information Relevant to the Decision to Be Made;

___   6.3   Analyzing the Decision to Be Made;

___   6.4   Counseling the Client About the Decision to Be Made;

___   6.5   Ascertaining and Implementing the Client's Decision.

Skill § 7: Negotiation

In order to negotiate in either a dispute-resolution or transactional context, a lawyer should be familiar with the skills and concepts involved in:

___   7.1   Preparing for Negotiation;

___   7.2   Conducting a Negotiation Session;

___   7.3   Counseling the Client About the Terms Obtained From the Other Side in the Negotiation and Implementing the Client's Decision.

Skill § 8: Litigation and Alternative Dispute-Resolution Procedures

In order to employ—or to advise a client about—the options of litigation and alternative dispute resolution, a lawyer should understand the potential functions and consequences of these processes and should have a working knowledge of the fundamentals of:

___   8.1   Litigation at the Trial-Court Level;

___   8.2   Litigation at the Appellate Level;

___   8.3   Advocacy in Administrative and Executive Forums;

___   8.4   Proceedings in Other Dispute-Resolution Forums.

Skill § 9: Organization and Management of Legal Work

In order to practice effectively, a lawyer should be familiar with the skills and concepts required for efficient management, including:

_____ 9.1 Formulating Goals and Principles for Effective Practice Management;

_____ 9.2 Developing Systems and Procedures to Ensure that Time, Effort, and Resources Are Allocated Efficiently;

_____ 9.3 Developing Systems and Procedures to Ensure that Work is Performed and Completed at the Appropriate Time;

_____ 9.4 Developing Systems and Procedures for Effectively Working with Other People;

_____ 9.5 Developing Systems and Procedures for Efficiently Administering a Law Office.

Skill § 10: Recognizing and Resolving Ethical Dilemmas

In order to represent a client consistently with applicable ethical standards, a lawyer should be familiar with:

_____ 10.1 The Nature and Sources of Ethical Standards;

_____ 10.2 The Means by Which Ethical Standards are Enforced;

_____ 10.3 The Processes for Recognizing and Resolving Ethical Dilemmas.

Fundamental Values of the Profession

Value § 1: Provision of Competent Representation

As a member of a profession dedicated to the service of clients, a lawyer should be committed to the values of:

_____ 1.1 Attaining a Level of Competence in One's Own Field of Practice;

_____ 1.2 Maintaining a Level of Competence in One's Own Field of Practice;

_____ 1.3 Representing Clients in a Competent Manner.

Value § 2: Striving to Promote Justice, Fairness, and Morality

As a member of a profession that bears special responsibilities for the quality of justice, a lawyer should be committed to the values of:

___ 2.1 Promoting Justice, Fairness, and Morality in One's Own Daily Practice;

___ 2.2 Contributing to the Profession's Fulfillment of its Responsibility to Ensure that Adequate Legal Services Are Provided to Those Who Cannot Afford to Pay for Them;

___ 2.3 Contributing to the Profession's Fulfillment of its Responsibility to Enhance the Capacity of Law and Legal Institutions to Do Justice.

Value § 3: Striving to Improve the Profession

As a member of a self-governing profession, a lawyer should be committed to the values of:

___ 3.1 Participating in Activities Designed to Improve the Profession;

___ 3.2 Assisting in the Training and Preparation of New Lawyers;

___ 3.3 Striving to Rid the Profession of Bias Based on Race, Religion, Ethnic Origin, Gender, Sexual Orientation, or Disability, and to Rectify the Effects of These Biases.

Value § 4: Professional Self-Development

As a member of a learned profession, a lawyer should be committed to the values of:

___ 4.1 Seeking Out and Taking Advantage of Opportunities to Increase His or Her Knowledge and Improve His or Her Skills;

___ 4.2 Selecting and Maintaining Employment That Will Allow the Lawyer to Develop As a Professional and to Pursue His or Her Professional and Personal Goals.

Index

A note on indexing: Some chapters include quotes at the introduction of sections. The people quoted are included in the index with the notation (quote). Authors of excerpted material are included in the index with the notation (excerpt). Other people named in the text of book chapters are also included in the index with the exception of those mentioned only with a citation in text, a bibliography or a footnote. The names chosen for fictional characters in problems or used as pseudonyms for students are not included in the index.